Lecture Notes in Computer Science 7681

Commenced Publication in 1973
Founding and Former Series Editors:
Gerhard Goos, Juris Hartmanis, and Jan van Leeuwen

Burkhart Wolff
Marie-Claude Gaudel
Abderrahmane Feliachi (Eds.)

Unifying Theories of Programming

4th International Symposium, UTP 2012
Paris, France, August 27-28, 2012
Revised Selected Papers

Springer

Volume Editors

Burkhart Wolff
Université Paris-Sud
Laboratoire de Recherche en Informatique (LRI)
Gif-sur-Yvette, France
E-mail: burkhart.wolff@lri.fr

Marie-Claude Gaudel
Université Paris-Sud
Laboratoire de Recherche en Informatique (LRI)
Gif-sur-Yvette, France
E-mail: mcg@lri.fr

Abderrahmane Feliachi
Université Paris-Sud
Laboratoire de Recherche en Informatique (LRI)
Gif-sur-Yvette, France
E-mail: abderrahmane.feliachi@lri.fr

ISSN 0302-9743 e-ISSN 1611-3349
ISBN 978-3-642-35704-6 e-ISBN 978-3-642-35705-3
DOI 10.1007/978-3-642-35705-3
Springer Heidelberg Dordrecht London New York

Library of Congress Control Number: 2012954013

CR Subject Classification (1998): F.3, D.3, D.2, F.1, F.4

LNCS Sublibrary: SL 1 – Theoretical Computer Science and General Issues

Typesetting: Camera-ready by author, data conversion by Scientific Publishing Services, Chennai, India

Printed on acid-free paper

Springer is part of Springer Science+Business Media (www.springer.com)

Preface

These proceedings contain the papers presented at UTP 2012, the 4th International Symposium on Unifying Theories of Programming, held during August 27–28, 2012, in Paris. It was co-located with the 18th International Symposium on Formal Methods, FM 2012.

UTP 2012 was the fourth in a series of symposia that have been successful in bringing together innovators and practitioners working on unifying theories of programming. Previous editions of the Symposium on Unifying Theories of Programming include UTP 2006 (County Durham, UK), UTP 2008 (Dublin, Ireland), and UTP 2010 (Shanghai, China).

The UTP 2012 symposium was organized by the ForTesSE research group of the LRI and Paris-Sud XI University. There were 13 submissions. Each submission was reviewed by at least 3, and on average 3.3, Program Committee members. The committee decided to accept eight papers. The program also included two invited speakers and one invited lecture. We gratefully thank the council of the Région Île de France, the Digiteo Research Cluster, the Conservatoire National des Arts et Métiers (CNAM), of course our Laboratoire de Recherche en Informatique (LRI), and last but not least Microsoft Research for their generous support in the organization of this scientific event. We also appreciated EasyChair in managing the scientific evaluation process and generating this conference volume; over the years it has become a powerful and extremely valuable tool helping in the organization of various scientific events.

October 2012

Burkhart Wolff
Marie-Claude Gaudel
Abderrahmane Feliachi

Organization

Program Committee

Bernhard K. Aichernig	TU Graz, Austria
Hugh Anderson	National University of Singapore, Singapore
Andrew Butterfield	Trinity College Dublin, Ireland
Ana Cavalcanti	University of York, UK
Yifeng Chen	Peking University, China
Steve Dunne	University of Teesside, UK
Abderrahmane Feliachi	LRI, University of Paris-Sud and CNRS, France
Colin Fidge	Queensland University of Technology, Australia
Marie-Claude Gaudel	LRI, University of Paris-Sud and CNRS, France
Lindsay Groves	Victoria University of Wellington, New Zealand
Will Harwood	University of York, UK
Jeremy Jacob	University of York, UK
Bernhard Möller	Universität Augsburg, Germany
David Naumann	Stevens Institute of Technology, USA
Geguang Pu	East China Normal University, China
Shengchao Qin	Teesside University, UK
Zongyan Qiu	Peking University, China
Georg Struth	University of Sheffield, UK
Jun Sun	Singapore University of Technology and Design, Singapore
Meng Sun	Peking University, China
Burkhart Wolff	LRI, University of Paris-Sud and CNRS, France
Jim Woodcock	University of York, UK
Naijun Zhan	Chinese Academy of Sciences, China
Huibiao Zhu	East China Normal University, China

Additional Reviewers

He, Guanhua
Huang, Yanhong
Shi, Ling
Wang, Shuling

Table of Contents

Unifying Theories of Undefinedness in UTP

Jim Woodcock and Victor Bandur

The University of York

Abstract. In previous work, based on an original idea due to Saaltink, we proposed a unifying theory of undefined expressions in logics used for formally specifying software systems. In our current paper, we instantiate these ideas in Hoare and He's Unifying Theories of Programming, with each different treatment of undefinedness formalized as a UTP theory. In this setting, we show how to use classical logic to prove facts in a monotonic partial logic with guards, and we describe the guards for several different UTP theories. We show how classical logic can be used to prove semi-classical facts. We apply these ideas to the COMPASS Modelling Language (*CML*), which is an integration of VDM and CSP in the *Circus* tradition. We link *CML*, which uses McCarthy's left-to-right expression evaluation, and to VDM, which uses Jones's three-valued Logic of Partial Functions.

1 Introduction

We consider the problem of potentially undefined expressions, which arise from two language constructs: partial function application and definite description.

A simple example of the problem is in the expression $(y = 1/0)$. Here, the division operator is a partial function that is not defined for a zero divisor: it is being applied outside its domain of definition. So what should we make of the expression $(1/0)$? Does it denote a value? If so, then which value? If not, then what do we make of the containing predicate $(y = 1/0)$? Is this defined? Does it denote a truth value or not?

More generally, if we choose a specific treatment of undefined expressions, then is it possible to use verification tools that employ different treatments? For example, there are two different treatments of undefined expressions for VDM: Jones's VDM uses the Logic of Partial Functions (LPF), which has been implemented in Isabelle [1], whilst Larsen's VDM in Overture uses left-to-right evaluation [8]. What is the relationship between these? Formal verification in the increasingly popular setting of heterogeneous systems of systems demands an answer to this question. In our own context of the COMPASS Modelling Language (*CML*), the nature of the language suggests the use of several verification tools, where the treatment of undefinedness must be taken into account. For example, in the FDR implementation of CSPM [5], undefinedness is handled by a combination of arithmetic overflow and boolean short-circuit expressions. In the *Circus* tools, undefinedness is handled through the use of classical logic and arbitrary undefined values. Furthermore, if *CML* is used for a system of systems

B. Wolff, M.-C. Gaudel, A. Feliachi (Eds.): UTP 2012, LNCS 7681, pp. 1–22, 2013.

with heterogeneous constituents using different formalisms with different solutions to the undefined problem, this combination of tools must be able to cope with these differences, for the sake of correctness as well as efficiency.

One possible solution to all these problems is to adopt a single treatment of undefinedness, such as the one used in UTP [7], where the basic relational calculus is classical: there is no undefinedness and every expression denotes a value. There is an outline of a more specific treatment of undefined expressions in UTP, but this is explored only briefly in the book by Hoare & He [7, Sect. 9.3]. There are several other possible treatments, and in this section we describe some of them. In doing so we develop a unifying theory for monotonic partial logics (we explain this term fully below).

This work is based on original ideas due to Mark Saaltink in his underpinnings for the Z/Eves theorem prover [10]. Together we have published joint papers at Marktoberdorf [11] and ICECCS 2007 [12].

In Sect. 2, we augment UTP's alphabetised relational calculus with a basic treatment of three-valued logic with possibly undefined expressions and predicates. In Sect. 3, we give a treatment of first-order theories for monotonic partial logics and prove a theorem about construct monotonicity (Theorem 1). In Sect. 4, we formalise three theories of undefinedness: strict logic, McCarthy's left-to-right logic, and Kleene's three-valued logic. In Sect. 5, we describe a theory of guard systems for generating verification conditions for the definedness of expressions and predicates. We present our main theorem that allows us to trade theorems between different logics by proving facts about the guard in a stronger system and guaranteeing that the construct is defined in a weaker logic (Theorem 2). We also present a guard system for the definite McCarthy logic and state its soundness (Theorem 3). Finally in Sect. 6, we draw some conclusions and plan future work.

2 Three-Valued Logic in UTP

In this section we illustrate our approach to undefinedness by describing a restricted semi-classical three-valued logic in UTP. The logic has a distinguished semantic value for undefined expressions and predicates. Operators of the predicate calculus are Bochvar's strict internal operators [4], but equality is classical (Bochvar's external $\equiv$ operator), allowing a fine control of undefinedness.

2.1 Basic Sets and Constructors

The set of boolean values is $\mathbb{B} = \{\mathit{true}, \mathit{false}\}$. The universe of values, disjoint from $\mathbb{B}$, is $\mathbb{U}$. We introduce a specific semantic undefined value: $\bot$. Any set not already equipped with an undefined value can be lifted to include it: $X^{\bot} = X \cup \{\bot\}$. Notice that $\bot$ is neither a tuple, nor a function, nor is it a designated value from $\mathbb{B}$ or $\mathbb{U}$.

For k, a natural number, X^k is the set of k-tuples over X, with X^0 having the single element: the 0-tuple $()$. X^* is the union of all X^ks.

As usual, we have two kinds of function space: $X \rightarrow Y$, the set of total functions, and $X \nrightarrow Y$, the set of partial functions.

We take inspiration from Rose's standard encoding of three-valued logic [9], which is reminiscent of Hoare & He's UTP designs [7, Chap. 3], in modelling three logical values using just a pair of predicates: (P, Q). The intuitive meaning is that P describes the region where the predicate (P, Q) is true and Q describes the region where (P, Q) is defined. Just like Hoare & He designs, we can combine the pair of predicates into a single predicate by introducing an observational variable, in this case *def*: the observation that the predicate is defined. This gives us a model for the pair.

Definition 1 (TVL predicate pair). *The observation def is true exactly when the pair is defined (Q) and, providing it is defined, then P determines whether it is true or not.*

$$(P, Q) \mathrel{\widehat{=}} (def \Rightarrow P) \wedge (Q = def)$$

□

The next example demonstrates that this definition accounts for all three logical values.

Example 1 (TVL extreme points). Consider the four extreme points for the pair:

$$\begin{array}{lcccc} R = true & = & (true, true) & = & def \\ R = false & = & (false, true) & = & false \\ R = \bot & = & \left\{ \begin{array}{c} (true, false) \\ (false, false) \end{array} \right\} & = & \neg\, def \end{array}$$

□

It is noteworthy that if *def* and Q do not agree then the entire TVL predicate is false, as expected.

Two lemmas follow immediately from Definition 1. The first shows how we can make use of the definedness condition in the pair.

Lemma 1 (Definedness trading). *The definedness condition can be traded back and forth in a TVL predicate pair:*

$$(P \wedge Q, Q) = (P, Q)$$

Proof

$$\begin{aligned} & (P \wedge Q, Q) \\ & = (def \Rightarrow P \wedge Q) \wedge (Q = def) \\ & = (def \Rightarrow P) \wedge (Q = def) \\ & = (P, Q) \end{aligned}$$

□

The second lemma shows that every three-valued predicate can be expressed as a TVL pair.

Lemma 2 (Canonical form of TVL predicates). *Every three-valued predicate has a canonical form:*

$$R = (R^t, \neg\, R^f), \text{ where } R^b = R[b/def], \text{ and } t \text{ and } f \text{ abbreviate } true \text{ and } false, \text{ respectively.}$$

Proof

$$\begin{aligned}
&((P,Q)^t, \neg\,(P,Q)^f)\\
&= (((def \Rightarrow P) \wedge (Q = def))^t, \neg\,((def \Rightarrow P) \wedge (Q = def))^f)\\
&= ((true \Rightarrow P) \wedge (Q = true), \neg\,((false \Rightarrow P) \wedge (Q = false)))\\
&= (P \wedge Q, \neg\,(true \wedge \neg\, Q))\\
&= (P \wedge Q, Q)
\end{aligned}$$

□

Example 2 (Definedness of partial expressions). Consider the predicate $(z = x/y)$ interpreted as a three-valued predicate. It is defined exactly when $(y \neq 0)$, and when it is defined, it is true when $(x = y * z)$, where $(\_ * \_)$ is the total multiplication operator. So the three-valued predicate $(z = x/y)$ is modelled by the pair:

$$((x = y * z), (y \neq 0))$$

We can consider three examples with specific values for x, y, and z.

$$\begin{aligned}
&(3 = 6/2)\\
&= ((6 = 2 * 3), (2 \neq 0))\\
&= (true, true)\\
&= def
\end{aligned}
\qquad
\begin{aligned}
&(2 = 6/2)\\
&= ((6 = 2 * 2), (2 \neq 0))\\
&= (false, true)\\
&= false
\end{aligned}
\qquad
\begin{aligned}
&(2 = 6/0)\\
&= ((6 = 0 * 2), (0 \neq 0))\\
&= (false, false)\\
&= \neg\, def
\end{aligned}$$

□

The model that we have chosen for three-valued predicates is not closed under any of the propositional operators, so we must choose particular definitions for them. There are plenty of choices: for two operands of three values, there are nine possible results, each of three values, making a total of: $3^9 \simeq 20,000$ combinations, although as Bergstra *et al.* point out, only a very small number of these are desirable [3]. In this section we choose strict interpretations of each operator.

2.2 Conjunction

The strict conjunction of two three-valued predicates is defined as follows.

Definition 2 (TVL conjunction). *$T \wedge_3 U$ is defined exactly when both T and U are defined; it is true exactly when both T and U are true.*

$$(P, Q) \wedge_3 (R, S) \mathrel{\widehat{=}} (P \wedge R, Q \wedge S)$$

It is useful to see the truth table for conjunction:

$\wedge_3$	*def*	$\neg$ *def*	*false*
def	*def*	$\neg$ *def*	*false*
$\neg$ *def*	$\neg$ *def*	$\neg$ *def*	$\neg$ *def*
false	*false*	$\neg$ *def*	*false*

This truth table looks a little better if we replace the values in the model by the three truth values themselves:

$\wedge_3$	$true_3$	$\bot$	$false_3$
$true_3$	$true_3$	$\bot$	$false_3$
$\bot$	$\bot$	$\bot$	$\bot$
$false_3$	$false_3$	$\bot$	$false_3$

□

An example of the conjunction of the two three-valued predicates $(y = 3)$ and $(z = x/y)$ helps clarify the separation between a predicate's truth and definedness conditions.

Example 3 (Partial conjunction).

$$\begin{aligned}
&(y = 3) \wedge_3 (z = x/y)\\
&= ((y = 3), true) \wedge_3 ((x = y * z), (y \neq 0))\\
&= ((y = 3) \wedge (x = y * z), true \wedge (y \neq 0))\\
&= ((y = 3) \wedge (x = 3 * z), (y \neq 0))
\end{aligned}$$

□

2.3 Negation

The strict negation of a three-valued predicate is defined as follows.

Definition 3 (TVL negation). *The negation of a three-valued predicate R is defined exactly when R is defined, and is true exactly when R is false:*

$$\neg_3 (P, Q) = (\neg P, Q)$$

The truth table is:

$\neg_3$	
def	*false*
$\neg$ *def*	$\neg$ *def*
false	*def*

$\neg_3$	
$true_3$	$false_3$
$\bot$	$\bot$
$false_3$	$true_3$

□

An example illustrates how the negation of a three-valued predicate can be simply pushed into the underlying representation.

Example 4 (Partial negation).

$$\begin{aligned}
&\neg_3 (z = x/y) \\
&= \neg_3 ((x = y * z), (y \neq 0)) \\
&= ((x \neq y * z), (y \neq 0))
\end{aligned}$$

□

2.4 Disjunction

The strict disjunction of two three-valued predicates is defined as follows.

Definition 4 (TVL disjunction). *The disjunction of two three-valued predicates $T \vee_3 U$ is defined exactly when both T and U are defined; it is true when either of them is true.*

$$(P, Q) \vee_3 (R, S) \mathrel{\widehat{=}} (P \vee R, Q \wedge S)$$

The truth tables are:

$\vee_3$	*def*	$\neg$ *def*	*false*
def	*def*	$\neg$ *def*	*def*
$\neg$ *def*	$\neg$ *def*	$\neg$ *def*	$\neg$ *def*
false	*def*	$\neg$ *def*	*false*

$\vee_3$	$true_3$	$\perp$	$false_3$
$true_3$	$true_3$	$\perp$	$true_3$
$\perp$	$\perp$	$\perp$	$\perp$
$false_3$	$true_3$	$\perp$	$false_3$

□

Example 5 (Partial disjunction). Define $P \Rightarrow_3 Q$ as $\neg_3 (P \vee_3 Q)$. Now suppose that f is a partial function symbol, such that

$$(y = f(x)) = ((y = f(x)), x \in \operatorname{dom} f)$$

Now consider the predicate $(x \in \operatorname{dom} f \Rightarrow_3 (y = f(x)))$, which is reminiscent of a precondition guarding the application of the partial function f. When interpreted as a three-valued predicate we have,

$$\begin{aligned}
&x \in \operatorname{dom} f \Rightarrow_3 (y = f(x)) \\
&= \neg_3 (x \in \operatorname{dom} f) \vee_3 (y = f(x)) \\
&= \neg_3 (x \in \operatorname{dom} f, \mathit{true}) \vee_3 (y = f(x)) \\
&= (x \notin \operatorname{dom} f, \mathit{true}) \vee_3 (y = f(x)) \\
&= (x \notin \operatorname{dom} f, \mathit{true}) \vee_3 ((y = f(x)), x \in \operatorname{dom} f) \\
&= (x \notin \operatorname{dom} f \vee (y = f(x)), \mathit{true} \wedge x \in \operatorname{dom} f) \\
&= (x \in \operatorname{dom} f \Rightarrow (y = f(x)), x \in \operatorname{dom} f) \\
&= ((y = f(x)), x \in \operatorname{dom} f)
\end{aligned}$$

It is defined exactly when $(x \in \operatorname{dom} f)$, and when it is defined, it is true exactly when $(y = f(x))$. □

2.5 Equality

There is nothing special about equality in our treatment of undefined values: it is just the existing classical equality in UTP. So, two three-valued predicates are equal exactly when their representation as pairs are equal. This is the symmetric closure of the following rules:

$$\begin{array}{rr} (def =_3 \neg\, def) = false & (true_3 =_3 \bot) = false \\ (def =_3 false) = false & (true_3 =_3 false_3) = false \\ (\neg\, def =_3 false) = false & (\bot =_3 false_3) = false \end{array}$$

Equality over the lifted domain $\mathbb{U}^\bot$ behaves similarly.

Example 6 (Partial equality). One of the definitions that we use later is a conditional containing five equations between three-valued predicates and expressions:

$$(f(x,y) =_3 \bot) \lhd (x = \bot) \vee (y = \bot) \rhd (f(x,y) =_3 (x = y))$$

Each equation is by definition either true or false: it cannot be undefined. In this way, UTP equality contains the use of three-valued logic. We also restrict our use of quantifiers to avoid undefinedness. □

A very simple lemma is a consequence of these definitions.

Lemma 3 (Normality of TVL operators). *When they are defined, the TVL propositional operators behave exactly like their classical counterparts (sometimes called "normality" [2]).*

1. $Q \Rightarrow (\neg_3\, (P, Q) = \neg\, P)$
2. $Q \wedge S \Rightarrow ((P, Q) \wedge_3 (R, S) = P \wedge R)$
3. $Q \wedge S \Rightarrow ((P, Q) \vee_3 (R, S) = P \vee R)$

□

This justifies UTP with three-valued logic, and allows the definition of theories in which definedness is elegantly available as a predicate, rather than appealing to obtrusive comparison with an explicitly designated undefined value. What is more, we will not introduce definite description or partial functions as fundamental concepts, so that it remains impossible to manufacture undefined values at the level of the logical calculus of the UTP. But we can build logics that do have these features, as we show later.

3 First-Order Theories

With the groundwork laid for a three-valued logical landscape in UTP, in this section we develop theories for various types of three-valued logics encountered in the literature and in the field. These theories depart from the classical world of UTP by making use of the lifted domain $\mathbb{U}^\bot$ and the lifted set of boolean values $\mathbb{B}^\bot$, soundly admitting the undefined value $\bot$ through the approach presented above.

3.1 Contexts for First-Order Theories

We introduce a context theory ***CXT*** for our first-order theories, which will all be subtheories of it. The alphabet of ***CXT*** contains two observational variables:

$$\begin{aligned} PShape &: \mathbb{P}((\mathbb{U}^{\perp})^{*} \twoheadrightarrow \mathbb{B}^{\perp}) \\ FShape &: \mathbb{P}((\mathbb{U}^{\perp})^{*} \twoheadrightarrow \mathbb{U}^{\perp}) \end{aligned}$$

and its signature is:

$$\begin{aligned} =_3 &: \mathbb{U}^{\perp} \times \mathbb{U}^{\perp} \rightarrow \mathbb{B}^{\perp} \\ \neg_3 &: \mathbb{B}^{\perp} \rightarrow \mathbb{B}^{\perp} \\ \vee_3 &: \mathbb{B}^{\perp} \times \mathbb{B}^{\perp} \rightarrow \mathbb{B}^{\perp} \\ \forall_3 &: (\mathbb{U} \twoheadrightarrow \mathbb{B}^{\perp}) \rightarrow \mathbb{B}^{\perp} \\ \iota_3 &: (\mathbb{U} \twoheadrightarrow \mathbb{B}^{\perp}) \rightarrow \mathbb{U}^{\perp} \end{aligned}$$

PShape describes all the possible denotations for the predicate symbols of this theory. Every denotation is a partial function from some number of parameters, each of which could be drawn from $\mathbb{U}$ or could be undefined, to a boolean result, which could also be undefined. The purpose of *PShape* is to constrain all the theory's predicate symbols in a uniform way. *FShape* does the same job as *PShape*, except that it describes the possible denotations of function symbols. The operators $=_3$, $\neg_3$, and $\vee_3$ give the syntax for equality, negation, and disjunction, respectively. Since they operate over lifted domains, they allow the construction of TVL predicates.

The $\forall_3$ function takes as its argument a function $\mathbb{U} \twoheadrightarrow \mathbb{B}^{\perp}$ that describes a binding for the universal quantifier that characterises the predicate that must be universally true. The function considers each element of its domain in turn and assigns to it one of the three logical values. The $\forall_3$ function takes this binding function and decides whether the universally quantified predicate is true, false, or undefined. Notice that the binding function ranges only over defined values. This means that we are excluding logics where bound variables may be undefined, as is the case in LCF [6].

The ι_3 function also takes a binding function as its argument. It decides whether this binding is a definite description of a value in $\mathbb{U}$ or is undefined. Once more, the bound variable must be everywhere defined.

We add a single healthiness condition to constrain the definite description function:

$$\textbf{\textit{CXT}}(P) = P \wedge (\forall f : \mathbb{U} \twoheadrightarrow \mathbb{B}^{\perp} \bullet f \neq \emptyset \Rightarrow \iota_3(f) \in \operatorname{dom} f^{\perp})$$

This requires that the definite description of a non-empty binding function returns either an undefined value or an element from the domain of the binding. We require this result in Lemma 6, where we prove that theories are closed under constructs over their signature.

Example 7 (Context). Consider a context with no predicate symbols and only monadic and dyadic function symbols.

$$\textbf{\textit{X1}}(P) = P \wedge (PShape = \emptyset) \wedge (FShape = (\mathbb{U}^{\perp} \cup (\mathbb{U}^{\perp})^2 \twoheadrightarrow \mathbb{U}^{\perp}))$$

PShape and *FShape* are used to add type information: we use them to restrict how predicate and function symbols behave, particularly, as we shall see later, with respect to undefinedness. □

3.2 First-Order Theories

A first-order theory (FOT) is an enrichment of a particular context and acts as its model. We add to the context six more alphabetical variables and three healthiness conditions. The set of names A is partitioned into three sets: variables, predicate symbols, and function symbols.

$$\langle \mathit{Var}, \mathit{Pred}, \mathit{Fun} \rangle \text{ partition } A$$

The set $\mathit{Dom} : \mathbb{P}\mathbb{U}$ describes the domain of values for the first-order theory. Finally, the rank function $\rho : \mathit{Pred} \cup \mathit{Fun} \to \mathbb{N}$ describes the number of parameters that each predicate and function symbol can take.

The first healthiness condition requires that every variable is defined and has a value drawn from Dom:

$$\mathbf{DV}(P) = P \wedge (\forall v : \mathit{Var} \bullet v \in \mathit{Dom})$$

The second and third healthiness conditions require that every predicate and function symbol ranges over arguments taken from $\mathit{Dom}^{\perp}$ and produces results in $\mathbb{B}^{\perp}$ and $\mathbb{U}^{\perp}$, respectively:

$$\mathbf{DP}(P) = P \wedge (\forall p : \mathit{Pred} \bullet p \in ((\mathit{Dom}^{\perp})^{\rho(p)} \to \mathbb{B}^{\perp}) \cap \mathit{PShape})$$
$$\mathbf{DF}(P) = P \wedge (\forall f : \mathit{Fun} \bullet f \in ((\mathit{Dom}^{\perp})^{\rho(f)} \to \mathbb{U}^{\perp}) \cap \mathit{FShape})$$

Example 8 (First-order theory). Consider a theory ***T1*** with context ***X1*** that has just a single function symbol for integer division:

$$\begin{aligned} &\mathbf{T1}(P) = \\ &\quad \mathbf{X1}(P) \\ &\quad \wedge \mathit{Var} = \emptyset \\ &\quad \wedge \mathit{Pred} = \emptyset \\ &\quad \wedge \mathit{Fun} = \{\_/\_\} \\ &\quad \wedge \mathit{Dom} = \mathbb{N} \\ &\quad \wedge \rho = \{\_/\_ \mapsto 2\} \\ &\quad \wedge \_/\_ \in (\mathbb{N}^{\perp} \times \mathbb{N}^{\perp} \to \mathbb{N}^{\perp}) \cap \mathit{FShape} \end{aligned}$$

□

3.3 Information-Theoretic Ordering

Our whole approach to unifying the treatment of undefinedness in different logics is built on a rather flat information-theoretic ordering. The goal is to allow for the comparison of logics that are more or less discriminant in the presence of undefinedness. This means that the undefined value is considered to be worse than every other value; these other values are themselves incomparable with each other in this sense. The notion is captured below.

Definition 5 (Information-theoretic ordering). *The information-theoretic ordering* $\sqsubseteq$ *is defined as follows.*
Elements: for any set X *with* $a, b \in X$

$$a \sqsubseteq b \mathrel{\widehat{=}} (a \neq \bot) \Rightarrow (a = b)$$

Pointwise extension to tuples: for $x, y \in X^k$

$$x \sqsubseteq y \mathrel{\widehat{=}} \forall i : 1 \mathinner{..} k \bullet x_i \sqsubseteq y_i$$

Pointwise extension to functions: for $f, g \in X \rightarrow Y$

$$f \sqsubseteq g \mathrel{\widehat{=}} (\operatorname{dom} f = \operatorname{dom} g) \wedge (\forall x : \operatorname{dom} f \bullet f(x) \sqsubseteq g(x))$$

Comparing sets of functions: for $A, B : \mathbb{P}\, X$*, the Hoare preorder is defined:*

$$A \sqsubseteq_H B \mathrel{\widehat{=}} \forall a : A \bullet \exists b : B \bullet a \sqsubseteq b$$

□

These definitions are illustrated in the following set of examples.

Example 9 (Ordering).

1. On elements:

$$\begin{aligned} \bot &\sqsubseteq 1 \\ 1 &\sqsubseteq 1 \\ \neg\,(1 &\sqsubseteq 2) \end{aligned}$$

2. On tuples:

$$\begin{aligned} (0, \bot, 2) &\sqsubseteq (0, 1, 2) \\ () &\sqsubseteq () \\ (1, 2) &\sqsubseteq (1, 2) \\ \neg\,((1, 2) &\sqsubseteq (2, 2)) \end{aligned}$$

3. On functions:

$$(\lambda\, x, y : \mathbb{N} \bullet \bot \lhd (y = 0) \rhd x/y) \sqsubseteq (\lambda\, x, y : \mathbb{N} \bullet 0 \lhd (y = 0) \rhd x/y)$$
$$(\lambda\, n : \mathbb{N} \bullet \bot \lhd (n \bmod 2 = 0) \rhd n) \sqsubseteq (\lambda\, n : \mathbb{N} \bullet n)$$

4. On sets of functions:

$$\begin{aligned} &\{(\lambda\, x, y : \mathbb{N} \bullet \bot \lhd (y = 0) \rhd x/y), \\ &\;(\lambda\, n : \mathbb{N} \bullet \bot \lhd (n \bmod 2 = 0) \rhd n), \\ &\;(\lambda\, n : \mathbb{N} \bullet n)\} \\ &\sqsubseteq_H \\ &\{(\lambda\, x, y : \mathbb{N} \bullet 0 \lhd (y = 0) \rhd x/y), \\ &\;(\lambda\, n : \mathbb{N} \bullet n)\} \end{aligned}$$

□

We further generalise the ordering by lifting it to contexts.

Definition 6 (Ordering on contexts).

$$\boldsymbol{S} \sqsubseteq_H \boldsymbol{T} = \forall P : \boldsymbol{S};\ Q : \boldsymbol{T} \bullet P \sqsubseteq_H Q$$

where

$$
\begin{aligned}
P \sqsubseteq_H Q = \; & \\
& PShape_{\boldsymbol{S}} \sqsubseteq_H PShape_{\boldsymbol{T}} \\
& \wedge FShape_{\boldsymbol{S}} \sqsubseteq_H FShape_{\boldsymbol{T}} \\
& \wedge (=_{\boldsymbol{S}}) \sqsubseteq (=_{\boldsymbol{T}}) \\
& \wedge (\neg_{\boldsymbol{S}}) \sqsubseteq (\neg_{\boldsymbol{T}}) \\
& \wedge (\vee_{\boldsymbol{S}}) \sqsubseteq (\vee_{\boldsymbol{T}}) \\
& \wedge (\forall_{\boldsymbol{S}}) \sqsubseteq (\forall_{\boldsymbol{T}}) \\
& \wedge (\iota_{\boldsymbol{S}}) \sqsubseteq (\iota_{\boldsymbol{T}})
\end{aligned}
$$

□

Intuitively it can be seen that all functions and predicates admissible in $\boldsymbol{S}$ are less discriminant of the undefined value than those admissible in $\boldsymbol{T}$. We say that undefinedness is more *contagious* in $\boldsymbol{S}$.

Example 10 (Subtheory). Consider $\boldsymbol{X2}$, a subtheory of $\boldsymbol{X1}$, where the following holds:

$$\forall f : FShape_{\boldsymbol{X1}} \bullet zero \circ f \in FShape_{\boldsymbol{X2}}$$

and where the total function *zero* is defined:

$$zero(x) \mathrel{\widehat{=}} (0 \lhd (x = \bot) \rhd x)$$

All other components remain unchanged. Then $P_{\boldsymbol{X1}} \sqsubseteq_H P_{\boldsymbol{X2}}$, since

$$
\begin{aligned}
& f \sqsubseteq zero \circ f \\
& = (\operatorname{dom} f = \operatorname{dom}(zero \circ f)) \wedge \forall x : \operatorname{dom} f \bullet f(x) \sqsubseteq zero \circ f(x)
\end{aligned}
$$

and so we have $FShape_{X1} \sqsubseteq_H FShape_{X2}$.

□

In the following sections, we introduce the three important notions of strictness, definiteness, and monotonicity.

3.4 Strictness

The notion of strictness is a familiar one from the definition of programming languages. A function f is strict if $f(\bot) = \bot$, and it is usually used to denote that a function loops forever or performs an illegal operation, such as division by zero. Generally no distinction is made if the function in fact delivers a useable result before this happens. We can interpret a strict function operationally as one that always evaluates all of its arguments. A restricted notion considers functions that are strict in one or more arguments.

Definition 7 (Strict). *Function $f : (X^{\perp})^{\rho(f)} \to Y^{\perp}$ is strict if, whenever at least one of its arguments is undefined, then the result is undefined:*

$$\textbf{strict}(f) = \forall x : (X^{\perp})^{\rho(f)} \bullet (\exists i : 1 \mathrel{..} \rho(f) \bullet (x_i = \perp)) \Rightarrow (f(x) = \perp)$$

□

Example 11 (Strict function). Suppose that $\_ * \_$ is the standard multiplication operator on natural numbers: $\_ * \_ : \mathbb{N} \times \mathbb{N} \to \mathbb{N}$. We can define a strict version of the operator:

$$\_ *_3 \_ : \mathbb{N}^{\perp} \times \mathbb{N}^{\perp} \to \mathbb{N}^{\perp}$$
$$x *_3 y = \perp \lhd (x = \perp) \vee (y = \perp) \rhd x * y$$

□

We can extend the notion of strictness to a context, where every predicate has only strict denotations for its predicate and function symbols. We find it useful to define a healthiness function **strict**() that is applied to a context (which of course is a set of predicates).

Definition 8 (Strict contexts). *We make a context $\boldsymbol{T}$ strict:*

$$\begin{aligned}
&\textbf{strict}(\boldsymbol{T}) = \{ P : \boldsymbol{T} \bullet \textbf{strict}(P) \} \\
&\textbf{where strict}(P) = \exists\, PShape_0, FShape_0 \bullet \\
&\qquad PShape = \{ p : PShape_0 \mid \textbf{strict}(p) \} \\
&\qquad \wedge FShape = \{ f : FShape_0 \mid \textbf{strict}(f) \} \\
&\qquad \wedge P[PShape_0, FShape_0 / PShape, FShape]
\end{aligned}$$

□

3.5 Definiteness

Definiteness is, in a sense, a dual notion to strictness. If a function is definite, then it cannot manufacture undefinedness. That is, if the function produces an undefined result, then it must have had an undefined argument.

Definition 9 (Definite). *Function $f : (X^{\perp})^{\rho(f)} \to Y^{\perp}$ is definite:*

$$\textbf{definite}(f) = \forall x : (X^{\perp})^{\rho(f)} \bullet (f(x) = \perp) \Rightarrow (\exists i : 1 \mathrel{..} \rho(f) \bullet (x_i = \perp))$$

□

Example 12 (Definite function). The function $\_ *_3 \_$ above is definite. □

As for strictness, we define a healthiness function for contexts.

Definition 10 (Definite contexts). *Making a context definite:*

$$\begin{aligned}
&\textbf{definite}(\boldsymbol{T}) = \{ P : \boldsymbol{T} \bullet \textbf{definite}(P) \} \\
&\textbf{where definite}(P) = \\
&\qquad \exists\, PShape_0, FShape_0 \bullet \\
&\qquad\qquad PShape = \{ p : PShape_0 \mid \textbf{definite}(p) \} \\
&\qquad\qquad \wedge FShape = \{ f : FShape_0 \mid \textbf{definite}(f) \} \\
&\qquad\qquad \wedge P[PShape_0, FShape_0 / PShape, FShape]
\end{aligned}$$

□

3.6 Monotonicity

A monotonic function on ordered sets is one that preserves that order. In our unifying theory, we are interested in defined-monotonic functions, that is, ones that preserve the definedness ordering.

Definition 11 (Monotonic). *Function* $f : (X^{\perp})^{\rho(f)} \rightarrow Y^{\perp}$ *is monotonic:*

$$\textsf{monotonic}(f) = \forall x_1, x_2 : (X^{\perp})^{\rho(f)} \bullet x_1 \sqsubseteq x_2 \Rightarrow f(x_1) \sqsubseteq f(x_2)$$

□

Example 13 (Monotonic operator). The TVL negation operator $\neg_3$ from Sect. 3 is monotonic:

$\neg_3$	
$true_3$	$false_3$
$\perp$	$\perp$
$false_3$	$true_3$

□

Here also it is convenient to define a predicate that is true if a context is monotonic.

Definition 12 (Monotonic contexts). $\boldsymbol{T}$ *is a monotonic context:*

$$\begin{aligned}
&\textsf{monotonic}(\boldsymbol{T}) = \forall P : \boldsymbol{T} \bullet \textsf{monotonic}(P)\\
&\textsf{where monotonic}(P) =\\
&\qquad (\forall p : Pred_{T} \bullet \textsf{monotonic}(p))\\
&\qquad \wedge (\forall f : Fun_{T} \bullet \textsf{monotonic}(f))\\
&\qquad \wedge \textsf{monotonic}(=_{T})\\
&\qquad \wedge \textsf{monotonic}(\neg_{T})\\
&\qquad \wedge \textsf{monotonic}(\vee_{T})\\
&\qquad \wedge \textsf{monotonic}(\forall_{T})\\
&\qquad \wedge \textsf{monotonic}(\iota_{T})
\end{aligned}$$

□

The following simple lemma is useful.

Lemma 4 (Strict monotonic). *Every strict function is monotonic.* □

3.7 Comparing First-Order Theories

In Definition 6, we lifted our information-theoretic ordering up to contexts; now we lift it to first-order theories. This makes sense only if the two FOTs in question have the same domain of values.

Definition 13 (Comparing FOTs). *Comparing FOTs* $\boldsymbol{U}$ *and* $\boldsymbol{V}$*: for* $P : \boldsymbol{U}$ *and* $Q : \boldsymbol{V}$

$$P \sqsubseteq_H Q = Dom_U = Dom_V \wedge Pred_U \sqsubseteq_H Pred_V \wedge Fun_U \sqsubseteq_H Fun_V$$

□

Using this definition, we can state an important lemma. If $\boldsymbol{S}$ and $\boldsymbol{T}$ are two contexts, such that $\boldsymbol{S}$ is less defined than (or equal to) $\boldsymbol{T}$, and we have a FOT that models $\boldsymbol{S}$, then there will also be a FOT that models $\boldsymbol{T}$.

Lemma 5 (Models). *Suppose that we have two CXTs $\boldsymbol{S}$ and $\boldsymbol{T}$, where $\boldsymbol{S} \sqsubseteq_H \boldsymbol{T}$. Suppose further that $\boldsymbol{U}$ is a FOT extending $\boldsymbol{S}$. Then there is a FOT $\boldsymbol{V}$ extending $\boldsymbol{T}$ such that $\boldsymbol{U} \sqsubseteq \boldsymbol{V}$.* □

The proof of this lemma is quite straightforward. The relationship between $\boldsymbol{S}$ and $\boldsymbol{T}$ shows where undefined values in the former have been replaced by defined values in the latter. This is used as a guide to construct an appropriate model.

Example 14 (Application of Models lemma). Suppose that we have two contexts $\boldsymbol{S}$ and $\boldsymbol{T}$. Suppose further that $\boldsymbol{S}$ has only a single monadic function symbol $inc : \mathbb{U}^{\perp} \nrightarrow \mathbb{U}^{\perp}$. Define a simple model $\boldsymbol{U}$ for $\boldsymbol{S}$ that instantiates inc as a rather trivial increment operation on binary digits. This operation is easy to define on the argument 0, it returns the result 1. It is undefined otherwise. The context $\boldsymbol{T}$, on the other hand produces only defined results $inc : \mathbb{U}^{\perp} \nrightarrow \mathbb{U}$. There must be a model $\boldsymbol{V}$ for $\boldsymbol{T}$, such that $\boldsymbol{U} \sqsubseteq \boldsymbol{V}$. This is easy to construct. The domain of values has to be the same as for $\boldsymbol{U}$. The inc can return an arbitrary value for any argument that returns $\perp$. Note that this makes it non-strict: it must produce a defined value for the argument $\perp$. All this is summarised in the following table:

	$\boldsymbol{S}$	$\boldsymbol{T}$
PShape	$\emptyset$	$\emptyset$
FShape	$\textbf{strict}(\mathbb{U}^{\perp} \nrightarrow \mathbb{U}^{\perp})$	$\mathbb{U}^{\perp} \nrightarrow \mathbb{U}$
	$\boldsymbol{U}$	$\boldsymbol{V}$
Dom	$\{0, 1\}$	$\{0, 1\}$
ρ	$\{inc \mapsto 1\}$	$\{inc \mapsto 1\}$
A	$inc(\perp) = \perp$	$inc(\perp) = 0$
	$inc(0) = 1$	$inc(0) = 1$
	$inc(1) = \perp$	$inc(1) = 1$

□

We state another important lemma about the closure of a FOT under the syntax of expressions.

Lemma 6 (Expression consistency). *Suppose that e is an expression over a FOT $\boldsymbol{U}$, then every $\boldsymbol{U}$-healthy predicate P ensures:*

$$P \Rightarrow e \in Dom_{U}^{\perp}$$

□

This lemma is proved by syntactic induction.

A third important result is the following theorem that states that constructs (expressions or predicates) are monotonic.

Theorem 1 (Construct monotonicity). *Suppose* $\mathbf{S} \sqsubseteq_H \mathbf{T}$*, that* $\mathbf{U}$ *extends* $\mathbf{S}$*,* $\mathbf{V}$ *extends* $\mathbf{T}$*, and that either* $\mathbf{S}$ *or* $\mathbf{T}$ *is monotonic. Then, for any construct* c*, we have*

$$c_U \sqsubseteq c_V$$

Proof (Construct monotonicity). The proof of the theorem is by induction on the syntax of the construct c. To illustrate the proof, we consider only the second induction case: application of a function symbol to actual parameters. This is enough to demonstrate the role of monotonicity in one of the two contexts.

The induction hypothesis is that $x_S \sqsubseteq x_T$*.*

Case 2.1: $\mathbf{S}$ *is monotonic*

$$\begin{aligned}
& (f(x))_U && \{\ \text{interpretation}\ \} \\
&= f_U(x_U) && \{\ \text{hypothesis } x_U \sqsubseteq x_V + \mathbf{S} \text{ monotonic, and so } f_U \text{ is monotonic}\ \} \\
&\sqsubseteq f_U(x_V) && \{\ \text{assumption: } P_U \sqsubseteq Q_V\text{, and so } Fun_U \sqsubseteq Fun_V \text{ and so } f_U \sqsubseteq f_V\ \} \\
&\sqsubseteq f_V(x_V) && \{\ \text{interpretation}\ \} \\
&= (f(x))_V
\end{aligned}$$

Case 2.2: $\mathbf{T}$ *is monotonic*

$$\begin{aligned}
& (f(x))_U && \{\ \text{interpretation}\ \} \\
&= f_U(x_U) && \{\ \text{assumption: } P_S \sqsubseteq P_T\ \} \\
&\sqsubseteq f_V(x_U) && \{\ \text{hypothesis} + \mathbf{V} \text{ monotonic}\ \} \\
&\sqsubseteq f_V(x_V) && \{\ \text{interpretation}\ \} \\
&= (f(x))_V
\end{aligned}$$

□

4 Specific First-Order Theories

In this section we consider three different theories of logic with undefinedness: strict logic, McCarthy's logic and Kleene's logic. In our definitions, we demonstrate the differences between these three; in our theorems, we demonstrate the similarities.

4.1 Strict Logic

Strict logic treats undefinedness as extremely contagious: whenever an undefined value appears in an expression or predicate, the overall construct collapses to become undefined. As we saw in Definition 7, this is strictness. First of all, every predicate in this theory is strict (see Definition 8). This means that *PShape* and *FShape* both contain only strict denotations.

$$\mathbf{S1}(P) = \mathbf{strict}(P)$$

Next, equality is strict:

$$(=_s(x,y) =_3 \bot) \lhd (x = \bot) \vee (y = \bot) \rhd (=_s(x,y) =_3 (x = y))$$

Recall Example 6 for an explanation of the definedness of this definition. If either argument is undefined, then the equality is undefined: otherwise, strict equality depends on the underlying UTP equality.

Definite description is strict:

$$(\iota_s(f) = x) \lhd \bot \notin \operatorname{ran} f \wedge (\operatorname{dom}(f \rhd \{true\}) = \{x\}) \rhd (\iota_s(f) = \bot)$$

The argument to ι_s is a function f that binds elements of its domain to one of three truth values. If this binding is everywhere defined and there is only one element of f's domain that satisfies f's characteristic predicate, then the definite description is exactly this element. Otherwise, it is undefined.

The universal quantifier is strict. Once more, the argument to $\forall_s$ is a binding. If this binding is anywhere undefined, then the universal quantifier is itself undefined. Otherwise, it depends on whether every element evaluates to true or not.

$$(\forall_s(f) =_3 \bot) \lhd \bot \in \operatorname{ran} f \rhd (\forall_s(f) = (\operatorname{ran} f =_3 \{true\}))$$

Negation is strict and is modelled by the underlying strict UTP operator:

$$\neg_s(P) = \neg_3 P$$

Similarly, disjunction is strict and is modelled by the underlying UTP strict operator:

$$\vee_s (P, Q) = P \vee_3 Q$$

These are the two operators introduced in Sect. 2. Their definitions are perhaps more appealing as truth tables.

$\neg_s$	
$true_3$	$false_3$
$\bot$	$\bot$
$false_3$	$true_3$

$\vee_s$	$true_3$	$\bot$	$false_3$
$true_3$	$true_3$	$\bot$	$true_3$
$\bot$	$\bot$	$\bot$	$\bot$
$false_3$	$true_3$	$\bot$	$false_3$

4.2 Kleene System

Kleene's system makes the logical connectives as defined as possible, whilst still being monotonic. So, every function is monotonic:

$$\mathbf{K1}(P) = P \wedge (\forall f : PShape_k \cup FShape_k \bullet \mathbf{monotonic}(f))$$

Equality and definite description are both strict:

$$(=_k) = (=_s)$$
$$(\iota_k) = (\iota_s)$$

If the binding function f for the universal quantifier evaluates anywhere to *false*, then this is enough information to constitute a counterexample, and so $\forall_k(f)$ is also *false*. Otherwise, if it evaluates everywhere to *true*, then clearly it is universally satisfied. Otherwise, it is undefined.

$$
\begin{array}{l}
((\forall_k(f) =_3 false_3) \lhd false \in \operatorname{ran} f \rhd \\
\quad ((\forall_k(f) =_3 true_3) \lhd (\operatorname{ran} f = \{true\}) \rhd (\forall_k(f) =_3 \bot)))
\end{array}
$$

Negation is strict:

$$\neg_k = \neg_s$$

If either operand of a disjunction is *true*, then the disjunction is also *true*, regardless of whether the other operand is defined or not. If both are false, then so is the disjunction. Otherwise the disjunction is undefined. We end up with the following refinement to the initial definition of strict disjunction.

$$
\begin{array}{l}
((\vee_k(P, Q) =_3 true_3) \lhd (P =_3 true_3) \vee (Q =_3 true_3) \rhd \\
\quad ((\vee_k(P, Q) =_3 false_3) \lhd (P =_3 false_3) \wedge (Q =_3 false_3) \rhd \\
\quad\quad (\vee_k(P, Q) =_3 \bot)))
\end{array}
$$

As usual, the truth table paints a clearer picture:

$\vee_k$	$true_3$	$\bot$	$false_3$
$true_3$	$true_3$	$true_3$	$true_3$
$\bot$	$true_3$	$\bot$	$\bot$
$false_3$	$true_3$	$\bot$	$false_3$

4.3 McCarthy System

McCarthy's system is very operational in flavour: it is assumed that there is an interpreter working through the text of logical constructs from left to right. The left-hand operand is evaluated first. The right-hand operand is evaluated only if it is needed. Function and predicate symbols are monotonic, just like in Kleene's system.

$$\mathit{M1} = \mathit{K1}$$

Equality and definite description are both strict.

$$
\begin{array}{l}
(=_m) = (=_k) \\
\iota_m = \iota_k
\end{array}
$$

In general, universal quantification in McCarthy's system is just the same as in Kleene's system. However, Overture [8] uses a variant of McCarthy logic where the binding function itself is executed from left to right, which distinguishes it from Kleene logic.

$$\forall_m = \forall_k$$

Negation is the same as Kleene's.

$$\neg_m = \neg_k$$

Finally, disjunction has a short-circuit semantics which induces the distinguishing left-to-right evaluation order:

$$((\vee_m (P, Q) =_3 true_3) \lhd (P =_3 true_3) \vee ((P =_3 false_3) \wedge (Q =_3 true_3)) \rhd ((\vee_m (P, Q) =_3 \bot) \lhd (P =_3 \bot) \vee (Q =_3 \bot) \rhd (\vee_m (P, Q) =_3 false_3)))$$

The truth table has the following structure:

$\vee_m$	$true_3$	$\bot$	$false_3$
$true_3$	$true_3$	$true_3$	$true_3$
$\bot$	$\bot$	$\bot$	$\bot$
$false_3$	$true_3$	$\bot$	$false_3$

All three systems are monotonic.

Lemma 7 (Strict-Kleene-McCarthy monotonicity).

1. *The strict system is monotonic*
2. *The Kleene system is monotonic*
3. *The McCarthy system is monotonic*

□

There exists an interesting definedness order between the three systems. It shows the relative resilience of the three logics to undefinedness:

Lemma 8 (Strict-McCarthy-Kleene ordering). *For* $\rho_s = \rho_m = \rho_k$ *and* $Dom_s = Dom_m = Dom_k$ *we have*

$$FOT_s \sqsubseteq FOT_m \sqsubseteq FOT_k$$

□

This lemma allows us to relate theorems proved in the different systems. Suppose that P is a theorem in the strict system; then it would also be true in the McCarthy and Kleene systems. More concretely, if we prove a theorem in VDM in Overture, then it would still be a theorem if we interpreted it in LPF, since the former is a McCarthy system and the latter is a Kleene system.

5 Guard Systems

We turn our attention now to the proof obligations that different systems can use to demonstrate the definedness of constructs.

5.1 Validity

Suppose $\boldsymbol{T}$ is a $\boldsymbol{CXT}$ and P is a predicate. Then define P is *valid* in $\boldsymbol{T}$:

$$\boldsymbol{T} \models P \mathrel{\widehat{=}} \text{for all } \boldsymbol{U}, \boldsymbol{T} \sqsubseteq_H \boldsymbol{U} \text{ implies } P_{\boldsymbol{U}} = \mathit{true}$$

That is, any construct that is valid in a given logical system will also be valid in a logical system that refines it in the definedness order.

5.2 Guards

Suppose that c is a construct. Then predicate G is a *guard* for c in $\boldsymbol{CXT}_T$ (denoted by $G \leadsto_T c$) iff for every $\boldsymbol{FOT}_V$ that extends $\boldsymbol{CXT}_T$ we have

1. $(G_V \neq \bot)$
2. $(G_V = \mathit{true}) \Rightarrow (c_V \neq \bot)$

G is a *tight guard* if we also have

3. $(G_V = \mathit{false}) \Rightarrow (c_V = \bot)$

Now we are ready to state and prove our main result, which is due originally to Saaltink.

Theorem 2 (Main theorem (Saaltink)). *Suppose that $\boldsymbol{CXT}_S \sqsubseteq \boldsymbol{CXT}_T$, that either one is monotonic, and that G is a guard for P in $\boldsymbol{CXT}_S$. Then, if $(\boldsymbol{T} \models G)$ and $(\boldsymbol{T} \models P)$, we have that $(\boldsymbol{S} \models P)$.* □

The significance of this result is in trading theorems between provers, as shown in the next example.

Example 15 (Trading theorems). Suppose that we want a proof of P in Larsen's VDM, as implemented in the Overture toolset [8], but the only theorem prover we have is for Jones's VDM. Overture uses a form of McCarthy's logic, whilst Jones's VDM uses LPF, a form of Kleene's logic. By Lemma 8, we have Overture $\sqsubseteq$ LPF. We could find a guard G for P in Overture (McCarthy logic), and then can carry out the proof of both G and P in Jones's logic (Kleene). Our Main Theorem then tells us that P is a theorem in Overture. All proofs are carried out in the stronger logic, but hold in weaker one. Perhaps more interestingly, a similar theorem holds for using classical logic instead of Kleene's logic. In this way, classical logic could be used to prove results in Overture. □

Proof (Main theorem).

1. From the Models Lemma 5, since $\boldsymbol{CXT}_S \sqsubseteq \boldsymbol{CXT}_T$ and $\boldsymbol{FOT}_U$ extends $\boldsymbol{CXT}_S$, then there exists $\boldsymbol{FOT}_V$ that extends $\boldsymbol{CXT}_T$ and for which we have $\boldsymbol{FOT}_U \sqsubseteq \boldsymbol{FOT}_V$.
2. Since $G \leadsto_S P$, know that $(G_U \neq \bot) \wedge ((G_U = \mathit{true}) \Rightarrow (P_U \neq \bot))$ from the definition of a guard.

3. Now, from construct monotonicity (since $\mathbf{S}$ is monotonic) we have that $G_U \sqsubseteq G_V$. But because $(G_U \neq \bot)$, it must be that $(G_U = G_V)$. We are assuming that G is valid in T ($\mathbf{T} \models G$), so we have that $(G_V = true)$ and so $(G_U = true)$. Now, from the definition of a guard, we must have that $(P_U \neq \bot)$
4. We now repeat this argument for P. By construct monotonicity, ($\mathbf{S}$ monotonic), we have $P_U \sqsubseteq P_V$, therefore $(P_U = P_V)$. But $\mathbf{T} \models P$, so $(P_V = true)$ and therefore $(P_U = true)$.

□

5.3 Definedness Guards

Suppose that e is an expression. We use the notation $\mathcal{D}e$ to define the circumstances under which e is defined.

Example 16 (Definedness guard)

$$\mathcal{D}((x+y)/z) = z \neq 0$$

□

The definedness guards that we are interested in are all first order; that is, the guards themselves are always defined.

Definition 14 (First-order definedness). *The definedness function is first order:*

$$\mathbf{D1}(\mathcal{D}\Phi) \mathrel{\widehat=} \mathcal{D}\Phi \wedge \mathcal{D}(\mathcal{D}\Phi)$$

□

If we define a system of guards for every construct in our language, then we can use this system inductively to generate verification conditions for the definedness of all constructs. In the next section we demonstrate this for the case of the definite McCarthy system.

5.4 Guards for Definite McCarthy System

Assuming we have a theory $\mathbf{T}$ of McCarthy logic, we can develop the following recursive definedness conditions for constructs c of that theory.

$$\begin{aligned}
\mathcal{D}_m x &= true \\
\mathcal{D}_m(p(e)) &= \forall i : 1 \,..\, \rho(P) \bullet \mathcal{D}_m e_i \\
\mathcal{D}_m(f(e)) &= \forall i : 1 \,..\, \rho(f) \bullet \mathcal{D}_m e_i \\
\mathcal{D}_m(e_1 = e_2) &= \mathcal{D}_m e_1 \wedge \mathcal{D}_m e_2 \\
\mathcal{D}_m(\neg P) &= \mathcal{D}_m P \\
\mathcal{D}_m(P \vee Q) &= \mathcal{D}_m P \wedge (P \vee \mathcal{D}_m Q) \\
\mathcal{D}_m(\forall x \bullet P) &= \forall x \bullet \mathcal{D}_m P \\
\mathcal{D}_m(\iota x \bullet P) &= (\forall x \bullet \mathcal{D}_m P) \wedge (\exists_1 x \bullet P)
\end{aligned}$$

A theorem follows immediately, which has a Kleene analogue and (trivially) a strict analogue as well.

Theorem 3 (McCarthy guards). *If c is a construct, then $\mathcal{D}_m(c)$ is a guard for c in* **definite**(**T**)*, and a tight guard for c in* **strict**(**definite**(**T**)). □

No analogue of this theorem exists for indefinite systems, but the partitioning of predicates into TVL pairs (P, Q) allows us to extract the guard condition immediately from Q. The advantage is that Q may be tailored to be either a plain or a tight guard, depending on the application.

6 Conclusions

The notion of undefinedness has played a prominent role in the study of logic, and continues to be a relevant research problem. With tools emerging that employ more than simple classical logic, and their use being adopted for verification in the heterogeneous landscape of systems of systems, a treatment of the relationships among different logics becomes necessary. In this section we summarize our specific contributions and prospects in this direction.

6.1 Contributions

We have presented a unifying theory for monotonic partial logics with undefined expressions, as a foundation for exploring the formal basis for migrating theorems between tools and methods that employ different types of logic and treatments of undefinedness. The aim is to support the forthcoming COMPASS Modelling Language. Based closely on Saaltink's original work, but cast in Hoare & He's Unifying Theories of Programming, we have demonstrated an information-theoretic unification for three logical systems: strict, McCarthy, and Kleene. Other approaches are possible and are under investigation.

6.2 Future Work

In this paper we have told only part of the story, since *CML* is not restricted to definite constructs: precondition predicates are needed for handling indefinite expressions and predicates. Our next step will be to extend our work in this way, thus developing a comprehensive treatment of undefined expressions for *CML*.

Fortunately we see many avenues of research starting here. Can our unifying theory cope with every treatment of undefinedness, such as (i) the Alloy paradigm, where there is no function application; (ii) the logic of LCF, where quantifiers also range over undefined values; (iii) second-order undefinedness; (iv) logics with more than three values. These are all important contemporary logical treatments of undefinedness that can not be excluded from such an unification effort.

References

1. Agerholm, S., Frost, J.: An Isabelle-based Theorem Prover for VDM-SL. In: Gunter, E.L., Felty, A.P. (eds.) TPHOLs 1997. LNCS, vol. 1275, pp. 1–16. Springer, Heidelberg (1997)

2. Bergmann, M.: An Introduction to Many-Valued and Fuzzy Logic: Semantics, Algebras and Derivation Systems. Cambridge University Press (2008)
3. Bergstra, J.A., Bethke, I., Rodenburg, P.: A propositional logic with 4 values: true, false, divergent and meaningless. Journal of Applied NonClassical Logics 5, 199–217 (1995)
4. Bochvar, D.A., Bergmann, M.: On a three-valued logical calculus and its application to the analysis of the paradoxes of the classical extended functional calculus. History and Philosophy of Logic 2(1), 87–112 (1981)
5. Goldsmith, M.: FDR2 user's manual. Technical Report Version 2.82. Formal Systems (Europe) Ltd. (2005)
6. Gordon, M., Wadsworth, C.P., Milner, R.: Edinburgh LCF. LNCS, vol. 78. Springer, Heidelberg (1979)
7. Hoare, C.A.R., He, J.: Unifying Theories of Programming. Series in Computer Science. Prentice Hall (1998)
8. Larsen, P.G., Battle, N., Ferreira, M.A., Fitzgerald, J.S., Lausdahl, K., Verhoef, M.: The Overture initiative: integrating tools for VDM. ACM SIGSOFT Software Engineering Notes 35, 1–6 (2010)
9. Rose, A.: A lattice-theoretic characterisation of three-valued logic. Journal of the London Mathematical Society 25, 255–259 (1950)
10. Saaltink, M.: The Z/EVES System. In: Bowen, J.P., Hinchey, M.G., Till, D. (eds.) ZUM 1997. LNCS, vol. 1212, pp. 72–85. Springer, Heidelberg (1997)
11. Woodcock, J., Saaltink, M., Freitas, L.: Unifying theories of undefinedness. In: Summer School Marktoberdorf 2008: Engineering Methods and Tools for Software Safety and Security. NATO ASI Series F. IOS Press, Amsterdam (2009)
12. Woodcock, J., Freitas, L.: Linking VDM and Z. In: Hinchey, M. (ed.) ICECCS, pp. 143–152. IEEE Computer Society (2008)

Unifying Theories of Programming with Monads

Jeremy Gibbons

Oxford University Department of Computer Science
Wolfson Building, Parks Road, Oxford OX1 3QD, UK
`jeremy.gibbons@cs.ox.ac.uk`

Abstract. The combination of probabilistic and nondeterministic choice in program calculi is a notoriously tricky problem, and one with a long history. We present a simple functional programming approach to this challenge, based on algebraic theories of computational effects. We make use of the powerful abstraction facilities of modern functional languages, to introduce the choice operations as a little embedded domain-specific language rather than having to define a language extension; we rely on referential transparency, to justify straightforward equational reasoning about program behaviour.

1 Introduction

Hoare and He's *Unifying Theories of Programming* [17] presents a coherent model of a number of programming idioms—imperative, nondeterministic, concurrent, reactive, higher-order, and so on. The approach follows Hoare's own earlier "programs are predicates" [16] slogan: rather than separate domains of syntax and semantics, and a translation from one to the other, there is just one domain of discourse; programming notations like sequencing and choice are *defined* as operations on predicates like composition and disjunction, rather than being *interpreted* as such. The result is a simple and streamlined framework for reasoning about programs, without the clumsiness and noise imposed by ubiquitous semantic brackets.

Another streamlined vehicle for reasoning about programs is provided by pure functional programming. This too allows one to elide the distinction between syntax and semantics, on account of referential transparency: familiar *equational reasoning* works as well for expressions denoting programs as it does for expressions denoting numbers. Again, we do not need two distinct domains of discourse—a programming notation in which to express computations, and a logic in which to reason about them—because the same language works for both.

Functional programming also conveniently allows one to discuss a variety of programming idioms within the same unifying framework. Moggi [36] showed how "notions of computation" such as mutable state, exceptions, nondeterminism, and probability can be elegantly encapsulated as *monads*, and safely embedded within an otherwise pure functional language. It may seem that purity rules out interesting computational effects, such as update, exception handling,

B. Wolff, M.-C. Gaudel, A. Feliachi (Eds.): UTP 2012, LNCS 7681, pp. 23–67, 2013.

and choice; after all, if *coin* denotes the computation modelling a fair coin toss—a 50–50 choice between heads and tails—then do not two occurrences of *coin* denote possibly different outcomes, thereby destroying referential transparency? The apparent problem is eliminated by distinguishing between types that represent *values*, such as 'true' or 'heads', and those that represent *computations*, such as *coin*. Two occurrences of *coin* denote the same computation, and it is the executions of these computations that may yield different outcomes. Each class of effects, such as probabilistic choice, determines a notion of computation, in this case of probability distributions; *coin* denotes not a single outcome, but a distribution of outcomes. The operations and axioms of a notion of computation can be precisely and elegantly abstracted via the categorical notion of a monad. Equivalently, the operations and axioms can be captured as an *algebraic theory*, and equational reasoning can be safely conducted within such a theory.

One advantage that functional programming offers over the "programs are predicates" approach is the facilities it provides for defining new abstractions 'within the language', rather than requiring one to step out into the meta-language in order to define a new feature. Our chosen language Haskell does not itself provide constructs for specific notions of computation such as probabilistic choice, but that is no obstacle: instead, it provides the necessary *abstraction mechanisms* that allow us to define those constructs ourselves. Rather than a new language 'probabilistic Haskell', we can define probabilistic choice within standard Haskell; one might characterize the result as an embedded domain-specific language for probabilistic programming.

We believe that the UTP and FP communities have much in common, and perhaps much to learn from each other. In this paper, we make a step towards bringing the two communities closer together, by way of unifying theories of nondeterminism and probability expressed in a functional style. The paper is intended as a tutorial and a manifesto, rather than presenting any new results. We start with a brief introduction to pure functional programming and to the use of monads to capture computational effects (Section 2)—readers familiar with functional programming in general, and Haskell in particular, may wish to skip this section. We then introduce theories of nondeterministic choice (Section 3) and probabilistic choice (Section 4) separately, and in combination (Section 5). Section 6 presents an extended example based on the infamous Monty Hall problem. In Section 7 we consider the possibility of failure and the effect of exceptions, which gives rise to conditionally probabilistic computations; and in Section 8 we look at recursive definitions. Section 9 concludes with a discussion of related work and some thoughts about future developments.

2 Effectful Functional Programming

Pure functional programming languages constitute a very appealing model of computation: *simple*, due to abstraction from the details of computer architecture, yet still *expressive*, allowing concise specification of complex constructions. These strengths derive from *referentially transparency*: as far as the semantics is concerned, the only relevant aspect of any expression is the value it denotes. In particular, expressions have no side-effects; so any subexpression can be replaced by any other having the same value, without affecting the surrounding context. Expressions therefore behave like ordinary high-school algebra, and reasoning about programs can be conducted using ordinary high-school *equational reasoning*, substituting one subexpression for another with equal value. Consequently, one's language for programming is simultaneously one's language for reasoning about those programs—there is no need to step outside the programming notation to a different logical domain such as predicate calculus.

2.1 Functional Programming

The essence of functional programming is that *programs are equations* and *functions are values*. For example, the squaring function on integers might be defined:

$$\begin{array}{l} \mathit{square} :: \mathit{Int} \rightarrow \mathit{Int} \\ \mathit{square}\ x = x \times x \end{array}$$

or equivalently

$$\begin{array}{l} \mathit{square} :: \mathit{Int} \rightarrow \mathit{Int} \\ \mathit{square} = \lambda x \rightarrow x \times x \end{array}$$

As well as specifying an action, namely how to compute squares, this program also serves as an equation: for any x, the expression $\mathit{square}\ x$ is equivalent to the expression $x \times x$, and either may be replaced anywhere by the other (taking due care over bound variables); similarly, the identifier *square* itself may be replaced by the lambda expression $\lambda x \rightarrow x \times x$ denoting the squaring function. Likewise, function composition $(\circ)$ is a value, just like any other, albeit a higher-order one:

$$\begin{array}{l} (\circ) :: (b \rightarrow c) \rightarrow (a \rightarrow b) \rightarrow a \rightarrow c \\ (f \circ g)\ x = f\ (g\ x) \end{array}$$

Functional programmers restrict themselves to manipulating *expressions*, rather than statements. So in order to regain the expressivity provided by statements in imperative languages, functional programming must provide an enriched expression language. Higher-order operators like functional composition go some way towards this. Another powerful tool is to allow complex data structures to be denotable as expressions; for example, the datatype $[a]$ of lists of elements each of type a might be defined as follows:

$$\mathbf{data}\ [a] = [\,]\ \mid\ a : [a]$$

With this device, a data structure such as the list of three elements $1 : (2 : (3 : [\,]))$ can be denoted as an expression; in contrast, in conventional imperative languages, complex data structures such as lists and trees can generally be constructed only via a sequence of side-effecting assignment statements acting on a mutable heap.

Functions over such data structures can conveniently be defined by pattern matching. For example, here is the standard function *foldr* to fold a list to a value:

$$\begin{aligned}
&\mathit{foldr} :: (a \to b \to b) \to b \to [a] \to b \\
&\mathit{foldr}\ f\ e\ [\,] \qquad\quad = e \\
&\mathit{foldr}\ f\ e\ (x : xs) = f\ x\ (\mathit{foldr}\ f\ e\ xs)
\end{aligned}$$

This is another higher-order function, since it takes a function as its first argument. One instance of *foldr* is the function *sum* that sums a list of integers:

$$\begin{aligned}
&\mathit{sum} :: [\mathit{Int}] \to \mathit{Int} \\
&\mathit{sum} = \mathit{foldr}\ (+)\ 0
\end{aligned}$$

Another is the higher-order function *map* that applies an argument f to each element of a list:

$$\begin{aligned}
&\mathit{map} :: (a \to b) \to ([a] \to [b]) \\
&\mathit{map}\ g = \mathit{foldr}\ (\lambda x\ ys \to g\ x : ys)\ [\,]
\end{aligned}$$

Lists are a *polymorphic datatype*; the polymorphism is expressed precisely by *map*. *Polymorphic functions* such as $\mathit{reverse} :: [a] \to [a]$ are those that depend only on the structure of a datatype, oblivious to the elements; their polymorphism is expressed precisely by a corresponding *naturality property* [52], stating that they commute with the appropriate *map* function—for example,

$$\mathit{reverse} \circ \mathit{map}\ f = \mathit{map}\ f \circ \mathit{reverse}$$

2.2 Equational Reasoning

Referential transparency means that plain ordinary equational reasoning suffices for proving properties of programs. For example, one very important property of the *foldr* function is the *fusion law*:

$$h \circ \mathit{foldr}\ f\ e = \mathit{foldr}\ f'\ e' \Longleftarrow h\ (f\ x\ y) = f'\ x\ (h\ y) \wedge h\ e = e'$$

One way of proving this law is by induction over lists (which we assume here to be finite). For the base case, we have:

$$\begin{aligned}
&\ \ h\ (\mathit{foldr}\ f\ e\ [\,]) \\
= &\quad [\![\text{ definition of } \mathit{foldr} \ ]\!] \\
&\ \ h\ e \\
= &\quad [\![\text{ assumption }]\!] \\
&\ \ e' \\
= &\quad [\![\text{ definition of } \mathit{foldr} \ ]\!] \\
&\ \ \mathit{foldr}\ f'\ e'\ [\,]
\end{aligned}$$

For the inductive step, we assume that the result holds on xs, and calculate for $x : xs$ as follows:

$$
\begin{array}{ll}
& h\ (\mathit{foldr}\ f\ e\ (x : xs)) \\
= & [\![\ \text{definition of } \mathit{foldr}\ ]\!] \\
& h\ (f\ x\ (\mathit{foldr}\ f\ e\ xs)) \\
= & [\![\ \text{assumption}\ ]\!] \\
& f'\ x\ (h\ (\mathit{foldr}\ f\ e\ xs)) \\
= & [\![\ \text{inductive hypothesis}\ ]\!] \\
& f'\ x\ (\mathit{foldr}\ f'\ e'\ xs) \\
= & [\![\ \text{definition of } \mathit{foldr}\ ]\!] \\
& \mathit{foldr}\ f'\ e'\ (x : xs)
\end{array}
$$

A simple consequence of the fusion law is the *fold–map fusion law*, when h is itself an instance of *foldr*, and follows a *map* over lists, which is another instance of *foldr*. In this case, the fusion result

$$\mathit{foldr}\ f\ e \circ \mathit{map}\ g = \mathit{foldr}\ f'\ e'$$

follows from the fusion conditions

$$\mathit{foldr}\ f\ e\ (g\ x : ys) = f'\ x\ (\mathit{foldr}\ f\ e\ ys) \wedge \mathit{foldr}\ f\ e\ [\,] = e'$$

These in turn are satisfied if $e' = e$ and $f' = \lambda x\ z \to f\ (g\ x)\ z = f \circ g$; that is,

$$\mathit{foldr}\ f\ e \circ \mathit{map}\ g = \mathit{foldr}\ (f \circ g)\ e$$

For most of the paper we will work within SET—that is, with total functions between sets. In this setting, arbitrary recursive definitions do not in general admit canonical solutions; we restrict attention to well-founded recursions such as that in *foldr*, and correspondingly to finite data structures. We only have to relax this restriction in Section 8, moving to CPO—continuous functions between complete partial orders.

2.3 Effects in Pure Functional Languages

Equational reasoning about pure computations is all very well, but to be useful, computations must have some observable effects. It may seem at first that equational reasoning must then be abandoned. After all, as soon as one allows state-mutating statements such as $x := x + 1$ in a programming language, the high-school algebra approach to reasoning no longer works; and similarly for other classes of effect, such as input/output, nondeterminism, probabilistic choice, exceptions, and so on.

Moggi [36] famously showed how the well-understood concept of a *monad* from category theory provides exactly the right interface to an abstraction of computational effects such as mutable state, allowing the development of an elegant yet expressive *computational lambda calculus* for modelling programming languages with effects. Wadler [54] popularized this approach within functional programming, and it quickly became the technology of choice for integrating effects into lazy functional programming languages such as Haskell.

With the monadic approach to computational effects, purely functional expressions are classifed into two kinds: those that denote values like integers and strings, and those that denote computations with possible effects. However, both are represented as pure data—the computations are represented as pure *terms* in a certain abstract syntax, rather than some kind of impure action. When the run-time system of a language encounters the first kind of expression, it evaluates it and prints it out; when it encounters the second kind, it evaluates it, interprets the term as the effectful computation it encodes, and executes that computation. Consequently, evaluation remains pure, and any impurities are quarantined within the run-time system.

The abstract syntax needed to capture effectful computations is very simple. There is a general framework consisting of just two operators, which in a sense model the compositional structure of computations; then for each class of effect, there is an extension to the general framework to model the primitives specific to that class. (In fact, the general framework and a specific extension together represent the free term algebra for the signature corresponding to the primitives for a particular class of effects. It is no coincidence that monads turn out to be useful for modelling such term algebras, because they were developed precisely as a categorical expression of universal algebra [30]. We return to this point in Section 9.3.)

The general framework can be expressed as a type class in Haskell:

$$
\begin{array}{l}
\mathbf{class}\ \mathit{Monad}\ m\ \mathbf{where} \\
\quad \begin{array}{ll}
\mathit{return} & :: a \rightarrow m\ a \\
(\gg\!=) & :: m\ a \rightarrow (a \rightarrow m\ b) \rightarrow m\ b \\
\mathit{fmap} & :: (a \rightarrow b) \rightarrow (m\ a \rightarrow m\ b) \\
\mathit{join} & :: m\ (m\ a) \rightarrow m\ a
\end{array} \\
\quad \begin{array}{l}
p \gg\!= k \;\;\;\;\; = \mathit{join}\ (\mathit{fmap}\ k\ p) \\
\mathit{join}\ pp \;\;\; = pp \gg\!= \mathit{id} \\
\mathit{fmap}\ f\ p = p \gg\!= (\mathit{return} \circ f)
\end{array}
\end{array}
$$

This declaration states that the type constructor (that is, operation on types) m is in the type class *Monad* if we can provide suitable definitions of the four methods *return*, $(\gg\!=)$, *fmap*, and *join*, with the given types. In fact, the methods are interdefinable, and some have default definitions in terms of others; it is necessary to define *return*, but it suffices to define either $(\gg\!=)$ or both *fmap* and *join*. (We have chosen this presentation allowing alternative definitions for flexibility; it is different from but equivalent to the *Monad* class in the Haskell standard libraries.)

Technically, the methods should also satisfy some laws, although these cannot be stated in the Haskell type class declaration:

$$
\begin{array}{lll}
\mathit{return}\ x \gg\!= k & = k\ x & \text{-- left unit} \\
p \gg\!= \mathit{return} & = p & \text{-- right unit}
\end{array}
$$

$$
\begin{array}{lll}
(p \gg\!= h) \gg\!= k & = p \gg\!= (\lambda x \to h\ x \gg\!= k) & \text{-- associativity} \\
\mathit{fmap}\ \mathit{id} & = \mathit{id} & \text{-- map–identity} \\
\mathit{fmap}\ (f \circ g) & = \mathit{fmap}\ f \circ \mathit{fmap}\ g & \text{-- map–composition} \\
\mathit{join} \circ \mathit{return} & = \mathit{id} & \text{-- left unit} \\
\mathit{join} \circ \mathit{fmap}\ \mathit{return} & = \mathit{id} & \text{-- right unit} \\
\mathit{join} \circ \mathit{fmap}\ \mathit{join} & = \mathit{join} \circ \mathit{join} & \text{-- associativity}
\end{array}
$$

(Throughout the paper, we make the following naming conventions: p, q, r denote monadic terms or 'programs', h, k denote functions yielding monadic terms, x, y, z denote polymorphic variables, a, b, c denote booleans, l, m, n denote integers, and u, v, w denote probabilities.) Informally, the type $m\ a$ denotes computations that may have some effect, and that yield results of type a. The function *return* lifts plain values into pure computations. The operator $\gg\!=$, pronounced 'bind', acts as a kind of sequential composition; the second computation may depend on the result returned by the first, and the overall result is the result of the second. The first three laws can be seen as unit and associativity properties of this form of sequential composition. The function *join* flattens a computation that yields computations that yield results into a computation that yields results directly, and the function *fmap* modifies each of the results of a computation; together with *return*, these two give an alternative (equivalent) perspective on sequential composition.

Two shorthands turn out to be quite convenient. We write *skip* for the pure computation that returns the sole element () of the unit type, also written ():

$$
\begin{array}{l}
\mathit{skip} :: \mathit{Monad}\ m \Rightarrow m\ () \\
\mathit{skip} = \mathit{return}\ ()
\end{array}
$$

and $\gg$ for the special case of $\gg\!=$ in which the second computation is independent of the result returned by the first:

$$
\begin{array}{l}
(\gg) \quad :: \mathit{Monad}\ m \Rightarrow m\ a \to m\ b \to m\ b \\
p \gg q = p \gg\!= (\lambda\_ \to q)
\end{array}
$$

These two shorthands more obviously form analogues of the 'skip' and 'sequential composition' operators of imperative programming languages. For example, with these we can form the sequential composition of a sequence of unit-returning computations, discarding all the unit results and returning unit overall. (This is actually a type specialization of the corresponding function in the Haskell standard library, but it is sufficient for our purposes.)

$$
\begin{array}{l}
\mathit{sequence}\_ :: \mathit{Monad}\ m \Rightarrow [m\ ()] \to m\ () \\
\mathit{sequence}\_ = \mathit{foldr}\ (\gg)\ \mathit{skip}
\end{array}
$$

This function reveals one of the beauties of pure and lazy functional programming: if a useful control construct is missing from the language, it is usually possible to define it as an ordinary value rather than having to extend the syntax and the compiler. Another famous example is the conditional; if Haskell didn't already provide the **if** ... **then** ... **else**... construct, something entirely equivalent (except for the concrete syntax) could be defined—the same cannot be said of a language providing only eager evaluation. And because conditional would be an ordinary value, the ordinary principles of reasoning would apply; for example, function application distributes leftwards and rightwards over conditional:

$$
\begin{aligned}
f\ (\mathbf{if}\ b\ \mathbf{then}\ x\ \mathbf{else}\ y) &= \mathbf{if}\ b\ \mathbf{then}\ f\ x\ \mathbf{else}\ f\ y \\
(\mathbf{if}\ b\ \mathbf{then}\ f\ \mathbf{else}\ g)\ x &= \mathbf{if}\ b\ \mathbf{then}\ f\ x\ \mathbf{else}\ g\ x
\end{aligned}
$$

These laws can easily be verified by considering the two cases $b = \mathit{True}$ and $b = \mathit{False}$. (In fact, the first law as stated only holds in SET. Once one moves to CPO, one also needs to consider the case that b is undefined; then the first law only holds when f is strict. The second law is still unconditional, provided that $\lambda x \to \bot = \bot$; this is the case with flat function spaces, the usual presentation in CPO, but not in fact in Haskell with the *seq* operator, which distinguishes between $\bot$ and $\lambda x \to \bot$.) In particular, letting f be $(\ggg\!= k)$ and $(p \ggg\!=)$ in turn, we deduce from the first law that composition distributes respectively leftwards and rightwards over conditional:

$$
\begin{aligned}
(\mathbf{if}\ b\ \mathbf{then}\ p\ \mathbf{else}\ q) \ggg\!= k &= \mathbf{if}\ b\ \mathbf{then}\ p \ggg\!= k\ \mathbf{else}\ q \ggg\!= k \\
p \ggg\!= (\mathbf{if}\ b\ \mathbf{then}\ k\ \mathbf{else}\ k') &= \mathbf{if}\ b\ \mathbf{then}\ p \ggg\!= k\ \mathbf{else}\ p \ggg\!= k'
\end{aligned}
$$

(Again, these laws hold unconditionally in SET; in CPO, they require $\ggg\!=$ to be strict in its left and right argument, respectively.)

2.4 State

So much for the general framework; here is an extension to capture mutable state—for simplicity, a single mutable value—as a class of effects. Just two additional operations are required: *get*, to read the state, and *put*, to update it. We declare a subclass *MonadState* of *Monad*; type constructor m is a member of the class *MonadState* if it is a member of *Monad* and it supports the two additional methods *get* and *put*. (To be precise, the subclass is *MonadState* s for some fixed state type s, and it encompasses type constructors m that support mutable state of type s; the vertical bar precedes a 'functional dependency', indicating that m determines s.)

$$
\begin{aligned}
&\mathbf{class}\ \mathit{Monad}\ m \Rightarrow \mathit{MonadState}\ s\ m \mid m \to s\ \mathbf{where} \\
&\quad \mathit{get} :: m\ s \\
&\quad \mathit{put} :: s \to m\ ()
\end{aligned}
$$

As with the two methods of the *Monad* interface, it is not sufficient simply to provide implementations of *get* and *put* that have the right types—they should also satisfy some laws:

$$
\begin{aligned}
\mathit{get} \ggg\!= \lambda s \to \mathit{get} \ggg\!= \lambda s' \to k\ s\ s' &= \mathit{get} \ggg\!= \lambda s \to k\ s\ s && \text{-- get–get} \\
\mathit{get} \ggg\!= \mathit{put} &= \mathit{skip} && \text{-- get–put}
\end{aligned}
$$

$$put\ s \gg put\ s' = put\ s' \quad \text{-- put–put}$$
$$put\ s \gg get \gg\!= \lambda s' \rightarrow k\ s' = put\ s \gg k\ s \quad \text{-- put–get}$$

Informally: two consecutive *get*s will read the same value twice; *get*ting a value then *put*ting it back is has no effect; two consecutive *put*s are equivalent to just the second one; and a *get* immediately after *put*ting a value will yield that value.

For example, here is a simple expression denoting a computation on a mutable integer state, which reads the current state, increments it, writes the new value back, and then returns the parity of the original value.

$$incrodd :: MonadState\ Int\ m \Rightarrow m\ Bool$$
$$incrodd = get \gg\!= (\lambda n \rightarrow put\ (n+1) \gg\!= (\lambda() \rightarrow return\ (odd\ n)))$$

There is an obvious simulation of mutable state in terms of state-transforming functions. A computation that acts on a state of type s, and yields a result of type a, can be represented as a function of type $s \rightarrow (a, s)$:

$$\mathbf{type}\ State\ s\ a = s \rightarrow (a, s)$$

Now, *State s* forms a type of computations, and so we should be able to make it an instance of the type class *Monad*. To do so, for *return a* we use the state-transforming function that yields x and leaves the state unchanged; *fmap f* applies f to the output value without touching the output state; and *join* collapses a state-transformer that yields a state-transformer by applying the output state-transformer to the output state:

$$\mathbf{instance}\ Monad\ (State\ s)\ \mathbf{where}$$
$$\quad return\ x \ = \lambda s \rightarrow (x, s)$$
$$\quad fmap\ f\ p = \lambda s \rightarrow \mathbf{let}\ (x, s') = p\ s\ \mathbf{in}\ (f\ x, s')$$
$$\quad join\ p \ = \lambda s \rightarrow \mathbf{let}\ (p', s') = p\ s\ \mathbf{in}\ p'\ s'$$

The reader may enjoy deriving from this the corresponding definition

$$p \gg\!= k = \lambda s \rightarrow \mathbf{let}\ (x, s') = p\ s\ \mathbf{in}\ k\ x\ s'$$

of bind, which chains state transformations together. (For technical reasons, this instance declaration is not quite in Haskell syntax: rather than a type synonym, *State* ought to be a **newtype** or **data**type, with a constructor and deconstructor. But what is shown is morally correct.)

Of course, by design, *State s* supports the features of mutable state—*get* yields a copy of the state, and *put* overwrites it:

$$\mathbf{instance}\ MonadState\ s\ (State\ s)\ \mathbf{where}$$
$$\quad get \ = \lambda s \rightarrow (s, s)$$
$$\quad put\ s' = \lambda s \rightarrow ((), s')$$

As it happens, the datatype *State s* is (isomorphic to) the free term algebra on the *MonadState s* signature, modulo the four laws of *get* and *put* [42].

2.5 Imperative Functional Programming

Wadler also observed [53] that the methods of the *Monad* interface are sufficient to implement a notation based on the set comprehensions of Zermelo–Fraenkel set theory. This too has found its way into Haskell, as the '**do** notation' [25], which is defined by translation into *Monad* methods as follows:

$$\begin{array}{ll}\mathbf{do}\,\{p\} & = p \\ \mathbf{do}\,\{x \leftarrow p\,;\,qs\} & = p \ggg\!= \lambda x \rightarrow \mathbf{do}\,\{qs\} \\ \mathbf{do}\,\{p\,;\,qs\} & = p \gg \mathbf{do}\,\{qs\} \\ \mathbf{do}\,\{\mathbf{let}\ decls\,;\,qs\} & = \mathbf{let}\ decls\ \mathbf{in}\ \mathbf{do}\,\{qs\}\end{array}$$

In particular, instead of having to write functions (typically lambda expressions) as the second argument of $\ggg\!=$, with the **do** notation we can write a generator $x \leftarrow p$ to bind a new variable x that is in scope in all subsequent qualifiers. Using this notation, we can rewrite the *incrodd* program above more elegantly as follows:

$$\begin{array}{l}incrodd :: MonadState\ Int\ m \Rightarrow m\ Bool \\ incrodd = \mathbf{do}\,\{n \leftarrow get\,;\,put\,(n+1)\,;\,return\,(odd\ n)\}\end{array}$$

The three monad laws appear in the **do** notation as follows:

$$\begin{array}{ll}\mathbf{do}\,\{x \leftarrow return\ e\,;\,k\ x\} & = \mathbf{do}\,\{k\ e\} \\ \mathbf{do}\,\{x \leftarrow p\,;\,return\ x\} & = \mathbf{do}\,\{p\} \\ \mathbf{do}\,\{y \leftarrow \mathbf{do}\,\{x \leftarrow p\,;\,h\ x\}\,;\,k\ y\} & = \mathbf{do}\,\{x \leftarrow p\,;\,y \leftarrow h\ x\,;\,k\ y\}\end{array}$$

(where, implicitly in the third law, x is not free in k). The operators *fmap* and *join* can be expressed in **do** notation like this:

$$\begin{array}{ll}fmap\ f\ p & = \mathbf{do}\,\{x \leftarrow p\,;\,return\,(f\ x)\} \\ join\ pp & = \mathbf{do}\,\{p \leftarrow pp\,;\,x \leftarrow p\,;\,return\ x\}\end{array}$$

Distribution of composition leftwards and rightwards over conditional looks like this:

$$\begin{array}{ll}\mathbf{do}\,\{x \leftarrow \mathbf{if}\ b\ \mathbf{then}\ p\ \mathbf{else}\ q\,;\,k\ x\} & = \mathbf{if}\ b\ \mathbf{then}\ \mathbf{do}\,\{x \leftarrow p\,;\,k\ x\} \\ & \phantom{= \mathbf{if}\ b\ }\mathbf{else}\ \ \mathbf{do}\,\{x \leftarrow q\,;\,k\ x\} \\ \mathbf{do}\,\{x \leftarrow p\,;\,\mathbf{if}\ b\ \mathbf{then}\ h\ x\ \mathbf{else}\ k\ x\} & = \mathbf{if}\ b\ \mathbf{then}\ \mathbf{do}\,\{x \leftarrow p\,;\,h\ x\} \\ & \phantom{= \mathbf{if}\ b\ }\mathbf{else}\ \ \mathbf{do}\,\{x \leftarrow p\,;\,k\ x\}\end{array}$$

(where, implicitly in the second law, x is not free in b). The four laws of state become:

$$\begin{array}{lll}\mathbf{do}\,\{s \leftarrow get\,;\,s' \leftarrow get\,;\,k\ s\ s'\} & = \mathbf{do}\,\{s \leftarrow get\,;\,k\ s\ s\} & \text{-- get–get} \\ \mathbf{do}\,\{s \leftarrow get\,;\,put\ s\} & = \mathbf{do}\,\{skip\} & \text{-- get–put} \\ \mathbf{do}\,\{put\ s\,;\,put\ s'\} & = \mathbf{do}\,\{put\ s'\} & \text{-- put–put} \\ \mathbf{do}\,\{put\ s\,;\,s' \leftarrow get\,;\,k\ s'\} & = \mathbf{do}\,\{put\ s\,;\,k\ s\} & \text{-- put–get}\end{array}$$

The **do** notation yields a natural imperative programming style, as we hope the rest of this paper demonstrates; indeed, it has been said that "Haskell is the world's finest imperative programming language" [40].

2.6 An Example of Simple Monadic Equational Reasoning

To summarize: the *Monad* class provides an interface for sequencing computations; one should program to that interface where appropriate, making subclasses of *Monad* for each specific class of effects; and the interface ought to specify laws as well as signatures for its methods. We have recently argued [10] that this perspective on monads is precisely the right one for equational reasoning about effectful programs—contrary to popular opinion, the impurities of computational effects offer no insurmountable obstacles to program calculation, at least when they are properly encapsulated. To illustrate this claim, we present a simple example of reasoning with stateful computations.

Here is a simple stateful computation to add an integer argument to an integer state:

$$
\begin{aligned}
&\mathit{add} :: \mathit{MonadState\ Int\ m} \Rightarrow \mathit{Int} \rightarrow m\ ()\\
&\mathit{add}\ n = \mathbf{do}\ \{m \leftarrow \mathit{get}\ ; \mathit{put}\ (m+n)\}
\end{aligned}
$$

We claim that adding each element of a list in turn to an integer state is the same as adding their sum all at once:

$$\mathit{addAll} = \mathit{add} \circ \mathit{sum}$$

where *addAll* turns each integer in a list into an integer-adding computation, then sequences this list of computations:

$$
\begin{aligned}
&\mathit{addAll} :: \mathit{MonadState\ Int\ m} \Rightarrow [\mathit{Int}] \rightarrow m\ ()\\
&\mathit{addAll} = \mathit{sequence\_} \circ \mathit{map\ add}
\end{aligned}
$$

Because *sequence_* is an instance of *foldr*, we can combine the two phases of *addAll* into one, using the fold–map fusion law:

$$\mathit{addAll} = \mathit{foldr}\ (\lambda n\ p \rightarrow \mathbf{do}\ \{\mathit{add}\ n\ ; p\})\ \mathit{skip}$$

Now, since *sum* and *addAll* are both instances of *foldr*, the claim is an instance of the standard fusion law, and follows from two simple fusion properties:

$$
\begin{aligned}
&\mathit{add}\ 0 &&= \mathit{skip}\\
&\mathit{add}\ (n+n') &&= \mathbf{do}\ \{\mathit{add}\ n\ ; \mathit{add}\ n'\}
\end{aligned}
$$

For the first of these, we have:

$$
\begin{aligned}
&\quad \mathit{add}\ 0\\
&= \quad [\![\ \mathit{add}\ ]\!]\\
&\quad \mathbf{do}\ \{l \leftarrow \mathit{get}\ ; \mathit{put}\ (l+0)\}\\
&= \quad [\![\ \mathit{arithmetic}\ ]\!]\\
&\quad \mathbf{do}\ \{l \leftarrow \mathit{get}\ ; \mathit{put}\ l\}\\
&= \quad [\![\ \text{get–put}\ ]\!]\\
&\quad \mathit{skip}
\end{aligned}
$$

And for the second, starting from the more complicated right-hand side, we have:

$$
\begin{array}{ll}
& \mathbf{do}\,\{\mathit{add}\ n\,;\,\mathit{add}\ n'\} \\
= & [\![\ \mathit{add}\ ]\!] \\
& \mathbf{do}\,\{\mathbf{do}\,\{m \leftarrow \mathit{get}\,;\,\mathit{put}\ (m+n)\}\,;\,\mathbf{do}\,\{l \leftarrow \mathit{get}\,;\,\mathit{put}\ (l+n')\}\} \\
= & [\![\ \text{associativity}\ ]\!] \\
& \mathbf{do}\,\{m \leftarrow \mathit{get}\,;\,\mathit{put}\ (m+n)\,;\,l \leftarrow \mathit{get}\,;\,\mathit{put}\ (l+n')\} \\
= & [\![\ \text{put–get}\ ]\!] \\
& \mathbf{do}\,\{m \leftarrow \mathit{get}\,;\,\mathit{put}\ (m+n)\,;\,\mathit{put}\ ((m+n)+n')\} \\
= & [\![\ \text{associativity of addition}\ ]\!] \\
& \mathbf{do}\,\{m \leftarrow \mathit{get}\,;\,\mathit{put}\ (m+n)\,;\,\mathit{put}\ (m+(n+n'))\} \\
= & [\![\ \text{put–put}\ ]\!] \\
& \mathbf{do}\,\{m \leftarrow \mathit{get}\,;\,\mathit{put}\ (m+(n+n'))\} \\
= & [\![\ \mathit{add}\ ]\!] \\
& \mathit{add}\ (n+n')
\end{array}
$$

which completes the proof.

Of course, *sum* and *addAll* are two rather special functions, both being instances of the easily manipulated *foldr* pattern. However, that is incidental to our point: if we had picked an example involving a more complicated pattern of computation, then the reasoning would certainly have been more complicated too, but it would still have been plain ordinary equational reasoning—reasoning about the computational effects would pose no more of a problem.

3 An Algebraic Theory of Nondeterministic Choice

Let us now turn to a different class of effects. Nondeterministic programs are characterized by the ability to choose between multiple results. We model this as a subclass of *Monad*.

$$
\begin{array}{l}
\mathbf{class}\ \mathit{Monad}\ m \Rightarrow \mathit{MonadAlt}\ m\ \mathbf{where} \\
\quad (\Box) :: m\ a \rightarrow m\ a \rightarrow m\ a
\end{array}
$$

We stipulate that $\Box$ is associative, commutative, and idempotent:

$$
\begin{array}{ll}
(p \Box q) \Box r & = p \Box (q \Box r) \\
p \Box q & = q \Box p \\
p \Box p & = p
\end{array}
$$

and that composition distributes leftwards over it:

$$\mathbf{do}\,\{x \leftarrow (p \Box q)\,;\,k\ x\} = \mathbf{do}\,\{x \leftarrow p\,;\,k\ x\} \Box \mathbf{do}\,\{x \leftarrow q\,;\,k\ x\}$$

However, we do not insist that composition distributes *rightwards* over choice: in general,

$$\mathbf{do}\,\{x \leftarrow p\,;\,(h\ x \Box k\ x)\} \neq \mathbf{do}\,\{x \leftarrow p\,;\,h\ x\} \Box \mathbf{do}\,\{x \leftarrow p\,;\,k\ x\}$$

This is in order to accommodate both angelic and demonic interpretations of nondeterminism. One distinction between the two is in terms of the number of branches of a choice that an implementation might choose to follow: angelic choice will explore both branches, whereas demonic choice is free to pick either branch but will not follow both. In particular, consider the case that computation p has some non-idempotent effects in addition to nondeterminism, such as writing output. If $\Box$ is angelic, then these effects happen once on the left-hand side of the equation, and twice on the right; whereas if $\Box$ is demonic, just one branch of each choice will be picked, and the two sides of the equation are indeed equal.

On account of the associativity, commutativity, and idempotence of choice, the essential—indeed, the initial, in the categorical sense—semantics of a nondeterministic computation amounts to a finite nonempty set of alternative results. In other words, we can simulate a computation that exploits just the effect of choice as a function that returns a finite nonempty set of results. A pure computation amounts to returning a singleton set, *fmap f* applies f to each element of a set, and a computation of computations can be flattened by taking the union of the resulting set of sets. (The operational behaviour of an implementation will differ, depending on the interpretation of choice: an angelic implementation will deliver the whole set of results; a demonic implementation will pick one arbitrarily. But either way, the semantics is represented as a set-valued function.)

A convenient approximate implementation of finite nonempty sets is in terms of nonempty lists—'approximate' in the sense that we consider two lists to represent the same set of results if they are equal up to reordering and duplication of elements.

$$
\begin{aligned}
&\textbf{instance}\ \mathit{Monad}\ [\,]\ \textbf{where} \\
&\quad \mathit{return}\ a\ \ = [a] \\
&\quad \mathit{fmap}\ f\ p = [f\ x \mid x \leftarrow p] \\
&\quad \mathit{join}\qquad = \mathit{concat}
\end{aligned}
$$

Naturally, we implement the nondeterministic choice as concatenation:

$$
\begin{aligned}
&\textbf{instance}\ \mathit{MonadAlt}\ [\,]\ \textbf{where} \\
&\quad (\Box) = (+\!\!+)
\end{aligned}
$$

In some other contexts, we might not want such a strong collection of laws for nondeterministic choice. For example, if we are modelling search strategies [14], we might want to treat as significant the order in which results are found, and so we might want to drop the commutativity axiom; and to keep track of nesting depth in search trees [47], we might want to drop associativity.

3.1 Example: Subsequences of a List

As an example of reasoning with nondeterministic programs, here is a rendition in terms of choice of the function *subs* that nondeterministically chooses a subsequence of a list. Of course, interpreted in the nonempty-list implementation of nondeterminism, *subs* returns the usual nonempty list of lists; but this definition supports other implementations of nondeterminism too, such as bags and sets.

$$
\begin{aligned}
&\mathit{subs} :: \mathit{MonadAlt}\ m \Rightarrow [\,a\,] \rightarrow m\ [\,a\,] \\
&\mathit{subs}\ [\,] \qquad\quad = \mathit{return}\ [\,] \\
&\mathit{subs}\ (x : xs) = \mathit{fmap}\ (x{:})\ \mathit{xss} \mathbin{\square} \mathit{xss}\ \textbf{where}\ \mathit{xss} = \mathit{subs}\ xs
\end{aligned}
$$

Informally, the empty list has a unique subsequence, the empty list itself; and a subsequence of a non-empty list $x : xs$ can be obtained by either prefixing x to or excluding it from a subsequence xss of xs.

Here is a simple property that we might wish to prove—that *subs* distributes over list concatenation:

$$\mathit{subs}\ (xs \mathbin{+\!\!+} ys) = \textbf{do}\ \{\, us \leftarrow \mathit{subs}\ xs\ ; vs \leftarrow \mathit{subs}\ ys\ ; \mathit{return}\ (us \mathbin{+\!\!+} vs)\,\}$$

Using the laws of nondeterminism, this property of an effectful program can be proved by induction over xs, using plain ordinary equational reasoning. For the base case $xs = [\,]$, we have:

$$
\begin{aligned}
&\quad \textbf{do}\ \{\, us \leftarrow \mathit{subs}\ [\,]\ ; vs \leftarrow \mathit{subs}\ ys\ ; \mathit{return}\ (us \mathbin{+\!\!+} vs)\,\} \\
&= \quad [\![\ \text{definition of } \mathit{subs}\ ]\!] \\
&\quad \textbf{do}\ \{\, us \leftarrow \mathit{return}\ [\,]\ ; vs \leftarrow \mathit{subs}\ ys\ ; \mathit{return}\ (us \mathbin{+\!\!+} vs)\,\} \\
&= \quad [\![\ \text{left unit}\ ]\!] \\
&\quad \textbf{do}\ \{\, vs \leftarrow \mathit{subs}\ ys\ ; \mathit{return}\ ([\,] \mathbin{+\!\!+} vs)\,\} \\
&= \quad [\![\ \text{definition of } \mathbin{+\!\!+}\ ]\!] \\
&\quad \textbf{do}\ \{\, vs \leftarrow \mathit{subs}\ ys\ ; \mathit{return}\ vs\,\} \\
&= \quad [\![\ \text{right unit}\ ]\!] \\
&\quad \mathit{subs}\ ys \\
&= \quad [\![\ \text{by assumption, } xs = [\,]\ ]\!] \\
&\quad \mathit{subs}\ (xs \mathbin{+\!\!+} ys)
\end{aligned}
$$

For the inductive step, we assume the result for xs, and calculate for $x : xs$ as follows:

$$
\begin{aligned}
&\quad \textbf{do}\ \{\, us \leftarrow \mathit{subs}\ (x : xs)\ ; vs \leftarrow \mathit{subs}\ ys\ ; \mathit{return}\ (us \mathbin{+\!\!+} vs)\,\} \\
&= \quad [\![\ \text{definition of } \mathit{subs}\text{; let } \mathit{xss} = \mathit{subs}\ xs\ ]\!] \\
&\quad \textbf{do}\ \{\, us \leftarrow (\mathit{fmap}\ (x{:})\ \mathit{xss} \mathbin{\square} \mathit{xss})\ ; vs \leftarrow \mathit{subs}\ ys\ ; \mathit{return}\ (us \mathbin{+\!\!+} vs)\,\} \\
&= \quad [\![\ \text{composition distributes leftwards over } \square\ ]\!] \\
&\quad \textbf{do}\ \{\, us \leftarrow \mathit{fmap}\ (x{:})\ \mathit{xss}\ ; vs \leftarrow \mathit{subs}\ ys\ ; \mathit{return}\ (us \mathbin{+\!\!+} vs)\,\} \mathbin{\square} \\
&\quad \textbf{do}\ \{\, us \leftarrow \mathit{xss}\ ; vs \leftarrow \mathit{subs}\ ys\ ; \mathit{return}\ (us \mathbin{+\!\!+} vs)\,\} \\
&= \quad [\![\ \mathit{fmap} \text{ and } \textbf{do} \text{ notation}\ ]\!] \\
&\quad \textbf{do}\ \{\, us' \leftarrow \mathit{xss}\ ; vs \leftarrow \mathit{subs}\ ys\ ; \mathit{return}\ ((x : us') \mathbin{+\!\!+} vs)\,\} \mathbin{\square} \\
&\quad \textbf{do}\ \{\, us \leftarrow \mathit{xss}\ ; vs \leftarrow \mathit{subs}\ ys\ ; \mathit{return}\ (us \mathbin{+\!\!+} vs)\,\} \\
&= \quad [\![\ \text{definition of } \mathbin{+\!\!+}\text{; } \textbf{do} \text{ notation}\ ]\!] \\
&\quad \mathit{fmap}\ (x{:})\ (\textbf{do}\ \{\, us' \leftarrow \mathit{xss}\ ; vs \leftarrow \mathit{subs}\ ys\ ; \mathit{return}\ (us' \mathbin{+\!\!+} vs)\,\}) \mathbin{\square} \\
&\quad \textbf{do}\ \{\, us \leftarrow \mathit{xss}\ ; vs \leftarrow \mathit{subs}\ ys\ ; \mathit{return}\ (us \mathbin{+\!\!+} vs)\,\} \\
&= \quad [\![\ \text{by assumption, } \mathit{xss} = \mathit{subs}\ xs\text{; inductive hypothesis, twice}\ ]\!]
\end{aligned}
$$

$$\begin{array}{l} \quad \mathit{fmap}\ (x{:})\ (\mathit{subs}\ (\mathit{xs} +\!\!+\ \mathit{ys}))\ \Box\ \mathit{subs}\ (\mathit{xs} +\!\!+\ \mathit{ys}) \\ = \quad [\![\ \text{definition of } \mathit{subs}\ ]\!] \\ \quad \mathit{subs}\ (x : (\mathit{xs} +\!\!+\ \mathit{ys})) \\ = \quad [\![\ \text{definition of } +\!\!+\ ]\!] \\ \quad \mathit{subs}\ ((x : \mathit{xs}) +\!\!+\ \mathit{ys}) \end{array}$$

Again, plain ordinary equational reasoning suffices, using programs as equations together with the axioms of nondeterminism.

4 An Algebraic Theory of Probabilistic Choice

Here is another class of effects. Probabilistic computations are characterized by the ability to make a probabilistic choice between alternatives. We suppose a type *Prob* of probabilities (say, the rationals in the closed unit interval), and define a *Monad* subclass for computations drawing from finitely supported probability distributions, that is, distributions in which only a finite number of elements have positive probabilities:

$$\begin{array}{l} \mathbf{class}\ \mathit{Monad}\ m \Rightarrow \mathit{MonadProb}\ m\ \mathbf{where} \\ \quad \mathit{choice} :: \mathit{Prob} \to m\ a \to m\ a \to m\ a \end{array}$$

The idea is that *choice* $w\ p\ q$ behaves as p with probability w and as q with probability $1-w$. From now on, we will write '$\overline{w}$' for $1-w$, and following Hoare's convention [15], write choice in infix notation, '$p \lhd w \rhd q$', because this makes the laws more legible. We have two identity laws:

$$\begin{array}{l} p \lhd 0 \rhd q = q \\ p \lhd 1 \rhd q = p \end{array}$$

a quasi-commutativity law:

$$p \lhd w \rhd q = q \lhd \overline{w} \rhd p$$

idempotence:

$$p \lhd w \rhd p = p$$

and quasi-associativity:

$$p \lhd u \rhd (q \lhd v \rhd r) = (p \lhd w \rhd q) \lhd x \rhd r \quad \Longleftarrow \quad u = w \times x \ \wedge\ \overline{x} = \overline{u} \times \overline{v}$$

As informal justification for quasi-associativity, observe that the likelihoods of p, q, r on the left are $u, \overline{u} \times v, \overline{u} \times \overline{v}$, and on the right are $w \times x, \overline{w} \times x, \overline{x}$, and a little algebra shows that these are pairwise equal, given the premise.

As a final pair of laws, we stipulate that bind distributes both leftwards and rightwards over choice:

$$\begin{array}{l} \mathbf{do}\ \{x \leftarrow (p \lhd w \rhd q)\,;\, k\ x\} \ = \mathbf{do}\ \{x \leftarrow p\,;\, k\ x\} \lhd w \rhd \mathbf{do}\ \{x \leftarrow q\,;\, k\ x\} \\ \mathbf{do}\ \{x \leftarrow p\,;\, (h\ x \lhd w \rhd k\ x)\} = \mathbf{do}\ \{x \leftarrow p\,;\, h\ x\} \lhd w \rhd \mathbf{do}\ \{x \leftarrow p\,;\, k\ x\} \end{array}$$

where, in the second law, x is assumed not to occur free in w. (In contrast to nondeterministic choice, we have both distributivities here. This means that, operationally, an implementation may take either branch of a probabilistic choice, but not both—like demonic choice, and unlike angelic.)

For example, a fair coin can be modelled as a 50–50 probabilistic choice between heads and tails (represented as booleans here):

$$\begin{array}{l} \mathit{coin} :: \mathit{MonadProb}\ m \Rightarrow m\ \mathit{Bool} \\ \mathit{coin} = \mathit{return}\ \mathit{True} \lhd {}^1\!/_2 \rhd \mathit{return}\ \mathit{False} \end{array}$$

One obvious representation to pick as an implementation of *MonadProb* uses probability-weighted lists of values; thus, *coin* might be represented as the list $[(\mathit{True}, {}^1\!/_2), (\mathit{False}, {}^1\!/_2)]$.

$$\mathbf{type}\ \mathit{Dist}\ a = [(a, \mathit{Prob})] \quad \text{-- weights sum to 1}$$

A pure computation is represented as a point distribution, mapping applies a function to each element, and a distribution of distributions can be flattened by taking a kind of weighted cartesian product:

$$\begin{array}{l} \mathbf{instance}\ \mathit{Monad}\ \mathit{Dist}\ \mathbf{where} \\ \quad \mathit{return}\ x \ = [(x, 1)] \\ \quad \mathit{fmap}\ f\ p = [(f\ x, w) \mid (x, w) \leftarrow p] \\ \quad \mathit{join}\ p \quad\ = \mathit{concat}\ [\mathit{scale}\ w\ x \mid (x, w) \leftarrow p] \end{array}$$

where

$$\begin{array}{l} \mathit{scale} :: \mathit{Prob} \to [(a, \mathit{Prob})] \to [(a, \mathit{Prob})] \\ \mathit{scale}\ v\ p = [(x, v \times w) \mid (x, w) \leftarrow p] \end{array}$$

On the other hand, $\lhd\rhd$ is a kind of weighted sum:

$$\begin{array}{l} \mathbf{instance}\ \mathit{MonadProb}\ \mathit{Dist}\ \mathbf{where} \\ \quad p \lhd w \rhd q = \mathit{scale}\ w\ p +\!\!+\ \mathit{scale}\ \overline{w}\ q \end{array}$$

Probability-weighted lists are not quite the initial model, because the identity, idempotence, quasi-commutativity, and quasi-associativity laws of $\lhd\rhd$ do not hold. In fact, the initial model of the specification consists of finite mappings from elements to probabilities, collected from these weighted lists in the obvious way—at least, for an element type in the type class *Eq*, supporting the equality operation == needed by finite maps, we can define:

$$\begin{array}{l} \mathit{collect} :: \mathit{Eq}\ a \Rightarrow \mathit{Dist}\ a \to (a \to \mathit{Prob}) \\ \mathit{collect}\ p\ y = \mathit{sum}\ [w \mid (x, w) \leftarrow p, x == y] \end{array}$$

That is, equivalences on *Dist* ought to be taken modulo permutations, zero-weighted elements, and repeated elements (whose weights should be added). Nevertheless, the datatype *Dist* itself provides a convenient approximation to the initial model.

Quasi-associativity can make the arithmetic of weights rather complicated, especially when choices are nested. Inspired by Morgan's *distribution comprehensions* [38], we sometimes make use of a flat notation for nested choices. For example, instead of $(p \lhd {}^{1}/_{2} \rhd q) \lhd {}^{1}/_{3} \rhd (r \lhd {}^{1}/_{4} \rhd s)$ we allow ourselves to write $\langle p@{}^{1}/_{6}, q@{}^{1}/_{6}, r@{}^{1}/_{6}, s@{}^{1}/_{2}\rangle$, multiplying out all the probabilities.

4.1 Example: Uniform Distributions

Extending the fair coin example, we might define uniform distributions

$$\begin{array}{l} \mathit{uniform} :: \mathit{MonadProb}\ m \Rightarrow [a] \to m\ a \quad \text{-- nonempty list} \\ \mathit{uniform}\ [x] \qquad = \mathit{return}\ x \\ \mathit{uniform}\ (x : xs) = \mathit{return}\ x \lhd {}^{1}/_{\mathit{length}\ (x:xs)} \rhd \mathit{uniform}\ xs \end{array}$$

so that $\mathit{coin} = \mathit{uniform}\ [\mathit{True}, \mathit{False}]$, and $\mathit{uniform}\ [1,2,3] = \mathit{return}\ 1 \lhd {}^{1}/_{3} \rhd (\mathit{return}\ 2 \lhd {}^{1}/_{2} \rhd \mathit{return}\ 3)$.

Choices drawn from uniform distributions but never used are free of side-effects, and so can be discarded: it is a straightforward proof by induction over xs that

$$\mathbf{do}\ \{x \leftarrow \mathit{uniform}\ xs\ ;\ p\} = p$$

when p does not depend on x. Similarly, *uniform* distributes over concatenation:

$$\mathit{uniform}\ (xs +\!\!+\ ys) = \mathit{uniform}\ xs \lhd {}^{m}/_{m+n} \rhd \mathit{uniform}\ ys$$

where $m = \mathit{length}\ xs$ and $n = \mathit{length}\ ys$. As a consequence of these properties of *uniform*, we can conclude that consecutive choices drawn from uniform distributions are independent; that is, choosing consecutively from two uniform distributions is equivalent to choosing in one step from their cartesian product:

$$\mathbf{do}\ \{x \leftarrow \mathit{uniform}\ xs\ ;\ y \leftarrow \mathit{uniform}\ ys\ ;\ \mathit{return}\ (x,y)\} = \mathit{uniform}\ (\mathit{cp}\ xs\ ys)$$

where

$$\begin{array}{l} \mathit{cp} :: [a] \to [b] \to [(a,b)] \\ \mathit{cp}\ xs\ ys = [(x,y) \mid x \leftarrow xs, y \leftarrow ys] \end{array}$$

We can prove this property by induction over xs, using equational reasoning with the laws of *MonadProb*. For the base case of singleton lists, we have:

$$\begin{array}{ll} & \mathit{uniform}\ (\mathit{cp}\ [x]\ ys) \\ = & [\![\ \text{definition of } \mathit{cp}\ ]\!] \\ & \mathit{uniform}\ [(z,y) \mid z \leftarrow [x], y \leftarrow ys] \\ = & [\![\ \text{comprehensions: } [f\ z \mid z \leftarrow [x], p] = [f\ x \mid p]\ ]\!] \\ & \mathit{uniform}\ [(x,y) \mid y \leftarrow ys] \\ = & [\![\ \text{comprehensions: } [f\ x \mid x \leftarrow xs] = \mathit{map}\ f\ xs\ ]\!] \\ & \mathit{uniform}\ (\mathit{map}\ (\lambda y \to (x,y))\ ys) \end{array}$$

$$
\begin{array}{ll}
= & [\![\text{ naturality: } \mathit{uniform} \circ \mathit{map}\ f = \mathit{fmap}\ f \circ \mathit{uniform}]\!] \\
& \mathbf{do}\ \{ y \leftarrow \mathit{uniform}\ ys\ ;\ \mathit{return}\ (x, y) \} \\
= & [\![\text{ left unit }]\!] \\
& \mathbf{do}\ \{ z \leftarrow \mathit{return}\ x\ ;\ y \leftarrow \mathit{uniform}\ ys\ ;\ \mathit{return}\ (z, y) \} \\
= & [\![\text{ definition of } \mathit{uniform}]\!] \\
& \mathbf{do}\ \{ z \leftarrow \mathit{uniform}\ [x]\ ;\ y \leftarrow \mathit{uniform}\ ys\ ;\ \mathit{return}\ (z, y) \}
\end{array}
$$

and for the inductive step, assuming the result for xs, we have:

$$
\begin{array}{ll}
& \mathit{uniform}\ (\mathit{cp}\ (x : xs)\ ys) \\
= & [\![\text{ definition of } \mathit{cp}]\!] \\
& \mathit{uniform}\ [(z, y) \mid z \leftarrow x : xs, y \leftarrow ys] \\
= & [\![\text{ comprehensions distribute over } +\!\!+]\!] \\
& \mathit{uniform}\ ([(z, y) \mid z \leftarrow [x], y \leftarrow ys] +\!\!+ [(z, y) \mid z \leftarrow xs, y \leftarrow ys]) \\
= & [\![\text{ as above; definition of } \mathit{cp}]\!] \\
& \mathit{uniform}\ (\mathit{map}\ (\lambda y \rightarrow (x, y))\ ys +\!\!+ \mathit{cp}\ xs\ ys) \\
= & [\![\mathit{uniform} \text{ distributes over } +\!\!+\text{; let } n = \mathit{length}\ ys,\ l = \mathit{length}\ (\mathit{cp}\ xs\ ys)]\!] \\
& \mathit{uniform}\ (\mathit{map}\ (\lambda y \rightarrow (x, y))\ ys) \lhd {}^{n}\!/_{n+l} \rhd \mathit{uniform}\ (\mathit{cp}\ xs\ ys) \\
= & [\![\text{ let } m = \mathit{length}\ xs \text{, so } l = m \times n]\!] \\
& \mathit{uniform}\ (\mathit{map}\ (\lambda y \rightarrow (x, y))\ ys) \lhd {}^{1}\!/_{1+m} \rhd \mathit{uniform}\ (\mathit{cp}\ xs\ ys) \\
= & [\![\text{ base case, inductive hypothesis }]\!] \\
& \mathbf{do}\ \{ z \leftarrow \mathit{uniform}\ [x]\ ;\ y \leftarrow \mathit{uniform}\ ys\ ;\ \mathit{return}\ (z, y) \} \lhd {}^{1}\!/_{1+m} \rhd \\
& \mathbf{do}\ \{ z \leftarrow \mathit{uniform}\ xs\ ;\ y \leftarrow \mathit{uniform}\ ys\ ;\ \mathit{return}\ (z, y) \} \\
= & [\![\text{ composition distributes leftwards over } \lhd\rhd]\!] \\
& \mathbf{do}\ \{ z \leftarrow \mathit{uniform}\ [x] \lhd {}^{1}\!/_{1+m} \rhd \mathit{uniform}\ xs\ ;\ y \leftarrow \mathit{uniform}\ ys\ ;\ \mathit{return}\ (z, y) \} \\
= & [\![\text{ definition of } \mathit{uniform}]\!] \\
& \mathbf{do}\ \{ z \leftarrow \mathit{uniform}\ (x : xs)\ ;\ y \leftarrow \mathit{uniform}\ ys\ ;\ \mathit{return}\ (z, y) \}
\end{array}
$$

The second step uses the property

$$[f\ z \mid z \leftarrow zs +\!\!+ zs', p] = [f\ z \mid z \leftarrow zs, p] +\!\!+ [f\ z \mid z \leftarrow zs', p]$$

Yet again, simple equational reasoning suffices.

5 Combining Algebraic Theories

We have seen algebraic theories separately characterizing nondeterministic and probabilistic choice. It is relatively straightforward to combine these two separate algebraic theories into one integrated theory incorporating both nondeterministic and probabilistic choice. No new operations are required; the operations of *MonadAlt* and *MonadProb* together suffice:

$$\mathbf{class}\ (\mathit{MonadAlt}\ m, \mathit{MonadProb}\ m) \Rightarrow \mathit{MonadAltProb}\ m$$

This Haskell type class declaration is complete; it has an empty collection of additional methods, beyond those inherited from the superclasses *MonadAlt* and

MonadProb. Implicitly, the laws of *MonadAlt* and *MonadProb* are also inherited; the only effort required is to consider the behaviour of interactions between the methods of the two superclasses. We stipulate that probabilistic choice distributes over nondeterministic:

$$p \lhd w \rhd (q \,\Box\, r) = (p \lhd w \rhd q) \,\Box\, (p \lhd w \rhd r)$$

(This is not an uncontentious decision—some authors [55,39] impose the opposite distributivity, of nondeterministic choice over probabilistic; we discuss this further in Sections 5.2 and 9.1.)

It turns out that there is a simple implementation of the combined interface, as finite non-empty sets of distributions. Again, we approximate finite sets by lists, for simplicity:

```
type Dists a = [Dist a]  -- nonempty lists
```

But the justification for this implementation is a little involved. The composition as functors $F\ G$ of two monads F, G does not necessarily yield a monad: it is straightforward to provide appropriate definitions of *return* and *fmap*, but not always possible to define *join* (or, equivalently, $\gg\!=$). However, it is a standard result [2] that the composite $F\ G$ does form a monad if there is a 'distributive law of G over F'—that is, a natural transformation $\mathit{swap} : G\ F \to F\ G$ satisfying certain coherence conditions. Given *swap*, it is also straightforward to define $\mathit{join} : F\ G\ F\ G \to F\ F\ G\ G \to F\ G$; that *join* satisfies the monad laws then follows from the coherence conditions on *swap*.

In programming terms, we have to provide a distributive law of distributions over lists

```
swap :: Dist [a] -> [Dist a]  -- nonempty lists
```

satisfying the following four coherence conditions:

$$\begin{aligned}
\mathit{swap} \circ \mathit{fmap}_D\ \mathit{return}_L &= \mathit{return}_L \\
\mathit{swap} \circ \mathit{return}_D &= \mathit{fmap}_L\ \mathit{return}_D \\
\mathit{swap} \circ \mathit{fmap}_D\ \mathit{join}_L &= \mathit{join}_L \circ \mathit{fmap}_L\ \mathit{swap} \circ \mathit{swap} \\
\mathit{swap} \circ \mathit{join}_D &= \mathit{fmap}_L\ \mathit{join}_D \circ \mathit{swap} \circ \mathit{fmap}_D\ \mathit{swap}
\end{aligned}$$

(where, to be explicit about typing, we have subscripted each use of *return*, *fmap*, and *join* with L or D to indicate the list and distribution instances, respectively). Then we can declare that the composite datatype *Dists* forms a monad, following the standard construction [2]:

```
instance Monad Dists where
  return x = return (return x)
  fmap f p = fmap (fmap f) p
  join pp  = fmap join (join (map swap pp))
```

A suitable definition of *swap* is as follows:

$$\begin{array}{l} \mathit{swap} = \mathit{foldr}_1\ \mathit{pick} \circ \mathit{map}\ \mathit{split}\ \textbf{where} \\ \quad \mathit{split}\ (\mathit{xs}, w) \ = [[(x, w)] \mid x \leftarrow \mathit{xs}] \\ \quad \mathit{pick}\ \mathit{xds}\ \mathit{yds} = [\mathit{xd} + \!\!\! + \ \mathit{yd} \mid \mathit{xd} \leftarrow \mathit{xds}, \mathit{yd} \leftarrow \mathit{yds}] \end{array}$$

(Here, foldr_1 is a variant of *foldr* for non-empty lists, taking only a binary operator and no starting value.) Informally, *swap* takes a distribution of nondeterministic choices to a nondeterministic choice of distributions, multiplying out all the possibilities; for example,

$$\begin{array}{l} \mathit{swap}\ ([([1,2], 1/3), ([3,4], 2/3)]) = [[(1, 1/3), (3, 2/3)], [(1, 1/3), (4, 2/3)], \\ \qquad\qquad\qquad\qquad\qquad\qquad\quad\ [(2, 1/3), (3, 2/3)], [(2, 1/3), (4, 2/3)]] \end{array}$$

The composite monad *Dists* inherits *MonadAlt* and *MonadProb* functionality straightforwardly from its two component parts:

$$\begin{array}{l} \textbf{instance}\ \mathit{MonadAlt}\ \mathit{Dists}\ \textbf{where} \\ \quad p \mathbin{\Box} q = p + \!\!\! + \ q \\ \textbf{instance}\ \mathit{MonadProb}\ \mathit{Dists}\ \textbf{where} \\ \quad p \triangleleft w \triangleright q = [\mathit{xd} \triangleleft w \triangleright \mathit{yd} \mid \mathit{xd} \leftarrow p, \mathit{yd} \leftarrow q] \end{array}$$

It is therefore an instance of the integrated theory of nondeterministic and probabilistic choice:

$$\textbf{instance}\ \mathit{MonadAltProb}\ \mathit{Dists}$$

Of course, we should check distributivity too; we return to this point in Section 5.2 below.

5.1 Example: Mixing Choices

Analogous to the fair coin, here is a biased coin:

$$\begin{array}{l} \mathit{bcoin} :: \mathit{MonadProb}\ m \Rightarrow \mathit{Prob} \rightarrow m\ \mathit{Bool} \\ \mathit{bcoin}_w \ = \mathit{return}\ \mathit{True} \triangleleft w \triangleright \mathit{return}\ \mathit{False} \end{array}$$

(we write the parameter w as a subscript) and an arbitrary nondeterministic choice between booleans:

$$\begin{array}{l} \mathit{arb} :: \mathit{MonadAlt}\ m \Rightarrow m\ \mathit{Bool} \\ \mathit{arb} = \mathit{return}\ \mathit{True} \mathbin{\Box} \mathit{return}\ \mathit{False} \end{array}$$

And here are two programs that each make an arbitrary choice and a probabilistic choice and compare them, but do so in different orders [12,31]:

$$\begin{array}{l} \mathit{arbcoin}, \mathit{coinarb} :: \mathit{MonadAltProb}\ m \Rightarrow \mathit{Prob} \rightarrow m\ \mathit{Bool} \\ \mathit{arbcoin}\ w = \textbf{do}\ \{a \leftarrow \mathit{arb}\ ; c \leftarrow \mathit{bcoin}_w\ ; \mathit{return}\ (a == c)\} \\ \mathit{coinarb}\ w = \textbf{do}\ \{c \leftarrow \mathit{bcoin}_w\ ; a \leftarrow \mathit{arb}\ ; \mathit{return}\ (a == c)\} \end{array}$$

Intuitively, because the probabilistic choice happens 'first' in *coinarb*, the nondeterministic choice can depend on it; whereas in *arbcoin*, the probabilistic choice happens 'last', so the nondeterministic choice cannot depend on it—and moreover, the probabilistic choice cannot be affected by the nondeterministic either, because it would not follow the distribution if it did so. We can justify this intuition calculationally, using the equational theory of the two kinds of choice. On the one hand, we have:

$$
\begin{aligned}
& \mathit{arbcoin}\ w \\
= \; & [\![\ \text{definition of } \mathit{arbcoin}\ ]\!] \\
& \mathbf{do}\ \{ a \leftarrow \mathit{arb} \ ;\ c \leftarrow \mathit{bcoin}_w \ ;\ \mathit{return}\ (a == c) \} \\
= \; & [\![\ \text{definition of } \mathit{arb}\ ]\!] \\
& \mathbf{do}\ \{ a \leftarrow (\mathit{return}\ \mathit{True} \ \square\ \mathit{return}\ \mathit{False}) \ ;\ c \leftarrow \mathit{bcoin}_w \ ;\ \mathit{return}\ (a == c) \} \\
= \; & [\![\ \text{composition distributes leftwards over } \square\ ]\!] \\
& \mathbf{do}\ \{ a \leftarrow \mathit{return}\ \mathit{True} \ ;\ c \leftarrow \mathit{bcoin}_w \ ;\ \mathit{return}\ (a == c) \} \ \square \\
& \mathbf{do}\ \{ a \leftarrow \mathit{return}\ \mathit{False} \ ;\ c \leftarrow \mathit{bcoin}_w \ ;\ \mathit{return}\ (a == c) \} \\
= \; & [\![\ \text{left unit, booleans}\ ]\!] \\
& \mathbf{do}\ \{ c \leftarrow \mathit{bcoin}_w \ ;\ \mathit{return}\ c \} \ \square\ \mathbf{do}\ \{ c \leftarrow \mathit{bcoin}_w \ ;\ \mathit{return}\ (\neg\ c) \} \\
= \; & [\![\ \text{right unit; definition of } \mathit{bcoin}_w\ ]\!] \\
& \mathit{bcoin}_w \ \square\ \mathit{bcoin}_{\overline{w}}
\end{aligned}
$$

On the other hand,

$$
\begin{aligned}
& \mathit{coinarb}\ w \\
= \; & [\![\ \text{definition of } \mathit{coinarb}\ ]\!] \\
& \mathbf{do}\ \{ c \leftarrow \mathit{bcoin}_w \ ;\ a \leftarrow \mathit{arb} \ ;\ \mathit{return}\ (a == c) \} \\
= \; & [\![\ \text{definition of } \mathit{bcoin}_w\ ]\!] \\
& \mathbf{do}\ \{ c \leftarrow (\mathit{return}\ \mathit{True} \lhd w \rhd \mathit{return}\ \mathit{False}) \ ;\ a \leftarrow \mathit{arb} \ ;\ \mathit{return}\ (a == c) \} \\
= \; & [\![\ \text{composition distributes leftwards over } \lhd\rhd\ ]\!] \\
& \mathbf{do}\ \{ c \leftarrow \mathit{return}\ \mathit{True} \ ;\ a \leftarrow \mathit{arb} \ ;\ \mathit{return}\ (a == c) \} \lhd w \rhd \\
& \mathbf{do}\ \{ c \leftarrow \mathit{return}\ \mathit{False} \ ;\ a \leftarrow \mathit{arb} \ ;\ \mathit{return}\ (a == c) \} \\
= \; & [\![\ \text{left unit, booleans}\ ]\!] \\
& \mathbf{do}\ \{ a \leftarrow \mathit{arb} \ ;\ \mathit{return}\ a \} \lhd w \rhd \mathbf{do}\ \{ a \leftarrow \mathit{arb} \ ;\ \mathit{return}\ (\neg\ a) \} \\
= \; & [\![\ \text{right unit; definition of } \mathit{arb}\ ]\!] \\
& (\mathit{return}\ \mathit{True} \ \square\ \mathit{return}\ \mathit{False}) \lhd w \rhd (\mathit{return}\ \mathit{False} \ \square\ \mathit{return}\ \mathit{True}) \\
= \; & [\![\ \text{commutativity of } \square\ ]\!] \\
& (\mathit{return}\ \mathit{True} \ \square\ \mathit{return}\ \mathit{False}) \lhd w \rhd (\mathit{return}\ \mathit{True} \ \square\ \mathit{return}\ \mathit{False}) \\
= \; & [\![\ \text{idempotence of } \lhd\rhd\ ]\!] \\
& \mathit{return}\ \mathit{True} \ \square\ \mathit{return}\ \mathit{False} \\
= \; & [\![\ \text{definition of } \mathit{arb}\ ]\!] \\
& \mathit{arb}
\end{aligned}
$$

That is, the nondeterminism in *arbcoin* can be resolved only by choosing the distribution provided by bcoin_w itself, or its opposite—the nondeterministic choice happens first, and depending on whether *True* or *False* is chosen, the probabilistic choice has chance either w or $\overline{w}$ of matching it. In particular, if $w = 1/2$, then the nondeterministic choice cannot influence the final outcome.

But in *coinarb*, the probabilistic choice happens first, and the subsequent nondeterministic choice has complete freedom to enforce any outcome.

5.2 Convex Closure

At the start of Section 5, we said that collections of distributions form a model of the combined theory *MonadAltProb*. In fact, this is not quite right: strictly speaking, there is no distributive law of distributions over sets [49], so the composition of the two monads is not a monad. Indeed, distribution of $\triangleleft\triangleright$ over $\Box$ and idempotence of $\triangleleft\triangleright$ together imply a convexity property:

$$
\begin{aligned}
& p \mathbin{\Box} q \\
= \; & [\![\text{ idempotence of } \triangleleft\triangleright\text{; arbitrary } w \;]\!] \\
& (p \mathbin{\Box} q) \triangleleft w \triangleright (p \mathbin{\Box} q) \\
= \; & [\![\text{ distributing } \triangleleft\triangleright \text{ over } \Box \;]\!] \\
& (p \triangleleft w \triangleright p) \mathbin{\Box} (q \triangleleft w \triangleright p) \mathbin{\Box} (p \triangleleft w \triangleright q) \mathbin{\Box} (q \triangleleft w \triangleright q)
\end{aligned}
$$

That is, if any two distributions p and q are possible outcomes, then so is any convex combination $p \triangleleft w \triangleright q$ of them. As a consequence, we should consider equivalence of collections of distributions *up to convex closure*. In particular, for *coinarb* we have:

$$
\begin{aligned}
& \mathit{coinarb}\ v \\
= \; & [\![\text{ calculation in previous section }]\!] \\
& \mathit{return\ True} \mathbin{\Box} \mathit{return\ False} \\
= \; & [\![\; \triangleleft\triangleright \text{ distributes over } \Box\text{, as above; arbitrary } w \;]\!] \\
& (\mathit{return\ True} \triangleleft w \triangleright \mathit{return\ False}) \mathbin{\Box} (\mathit{return\ False} \triangleleft w \triangleright \mathit{return\ False}) \mathbin{\Box} \\
& (\mathit{return\ True} \triangleleft w \triangleright \mathit{return\ True}) \mathbin{\Box} (\mathit{return\ False} \triangleleft w \triangleright \mathit{return\ True}) \\
= \; & [\![\text{ commutativity and idempotence of } \triangleleft\triangleright\text{; definition of } \mathit{bcoin}_w \;]\!] \\
& \mathit{bcoin}_w \mathbin{\Box} \mathit{return\ False} \mathbin{\Box} \mathit{return\ True} \mathbin{\Box} \mathit{bcoin}_{\overline{w}}
\end{aligned}
$$

and so the possible outcomes of *coinarb v* include all convex combinations bcoin_w of the two extreme distributions *return False* and *return True*, which as it happens encompasses all possible distributions of the booleans.

This convexity intuition is computationally reasonable, if one considers repeated executions of a computation such as $\mathit{bcoin}_{1/2} \mathbin{\Box} \mathit{bcoin}_{1/3}$. If the nondeterminism is always resolved in favour of the fair coin, the result will be heads half the time; if the nondeterminism is always resolved in favour of the biased coin, the result will be heads one third of the time. But if resolution of the nondeterminism alternates evenly between the two, the result will be heads five-twelfths of the time. Over repeated executions, any distribution between the two extremes can be obtained by some long-term strategy for resolving the nondeterminism; but no strategy will yield a distribution outside the two extremes.

One might wonder why one distributive law (of probabilistic choice over nondeterministic) should hold, while the other (of nondeterministic choice over probabilistic) need not. It turns out that the latter does not match intuitions about behaviour; for example, adopting the opposite distributive law, it is straightforward to calculate as follows:

$$
\begin{array}{ll}
& p \lhd w \rhd q \\
= & [\![\text{ idempotence of } \Box \text{ }]\!] \\
& (p \lhd w \rhd q) \Box (p \lhd w \rhd q) \\
= & [\![\text{ assuming that } \Box \text{ distributes over } \lhd\rhd \text{ }]\!] \\
& ((p \Box p) \lhd w \rhd (p \Box q)) \lhd w \rhd ((q \Box p) \lhd w \rhd (q \Box q)) \\
= & [\![\text{ idempotence and commutativity of } \Box \text{ }]\!] \\
& (p \lhd w \rhd (p \Box q)) \lhd w \rhd ((p \Box q) \lhd w \rhd q) \\
= & [\![\text{ flattened choices, as a distribution comprehension }]\!] \\
& \langle p @ w^2, (p \Box q) @ 2\, w\, \overline{w}, q @ \overline{w}^2 \rangle \\
= & [\![\text{ rearranging and renesting choices }]\!] \\
& (p \lhd {}^{w^2}/_{w^2+\overline{w}^2} \rhd q) \lhd w^2 + \overline{w}^2 \rhd (p \Box q)
\end{array}
$$

Informally, any straight probabilistic choice is inherently polluted with some taint of nondeterministic choice too. For example, letting $w = {}^1/_2$ and $w = {}^1/_3$ respectively, we can conclude that

$$
\begin{array}{l}
p \lhd {}^1/_2 \rhd q = (p \lhd {}^1/_2 \rhd q) \lhd {}^1/_2 \rhd (p \Box q) \\
p \lhd {}^1/_3 \rhd q = (p \lhd {}^1/_5 \rhd q) \lhd {}^5/_9 \rhd (p \Box q)
\end{array}
$$

This seems quite an unfortunate consequence, and so we do not require that nondeterministic choice distributes over probabilistic.

6 Monty Hall

As an extended example, we turn to the so-called Monty Hall Problem [45], which famously caused a controversy following its discussion in Marilyn vos Savant's column in *Parade* magazine in 1990 [50]. Vos Savant described the problem as follows, quoting a letter from a reader, Craig F. Whitaker:

> *Suppose you're on a game show, and you're given the choice of three doors: Behind one door is a car; behind the others, goats. You pick a door, say No. 1, and the host, who knows what's behind the doors, opens another door, say No. 3, which has a goat. He then says to you, "Do you want to pick door No. 2?" Is it to your advantage to switch your choice?*

Implicit in the above statement, the car is equally likely to be behind each of the three doors, the car is the prize and the goats are booby prizes, the host always opens a door, which always differs from the one you pick and always reveals a goat, and you always get the option to switch.

We might model this as follows. There are three doors:

data *Door* = *A* | *B* | *C*

doors :: [*Door*]
doors = [*A*, *B*, *C*]

First, Monty hides the car behind one of the doors, chosen uniformly at random:

$$\begin{array}{l} \mathit{hide} :: \mathit{MonadProb}\ m \Rightarrow m\ \mathit{Door} \\ \mathit{hide} = \mathit{uniform}\ \mathit{doors} \end{array}$$

Second, you pick one of the doors, also uniformly at random:

$$\begin{array}{l} \mathit{pick} :: \mathit{MonadProb}\ m \Rightarrow m\ \mathit{Door} \\ \mathit{pick} = \mathit{uniform}\ \mathit{doors} \end{array}$$

Third, Monty teases you by opening one of the doors—not the one that hides the car, nor the one you picked—to reveal a goat, choosing randomly among the one or two doors available to him:

$$\begin{array}{l} \mathit{tease} :: \mathit{MonadProb}\ m \Rightarrow \mathit{Door} \rightarrow \mathit{Door} \rightarrow m\ \mathit{Door} \\ \mathit{tease}\ h\ p = \mathit{uniform}\ (\mathit{doors} \setminus\setminus [h, p]) \end{array}$$

(Here, the expression $xs \setminus\setminus ys$ denotes the list of those elements of xs absent from ys.) Fourth, Monty offers you the choice between two strategies—either to switch to the door that is neither your original choice nor the opened one:

$$\begin{array}{l} \mathit{switch} :: \mathit{MonadProb}\ m \Rightarrow \mathit{Door} \rightarrow \mathit{Door} \rightarrow m\ \mathit{Door} \\ \mathit{switch}\ p\ t = \mathit{return}\ (\mathit{head}\ (\mathit{doors} \setminus\setminus [p, t])) \end{array}$$

or to stick with your original choice:

$$\begin{array}{l} \mathit{stick} :: \mathit{MonadProb}\ m \Rightarrow \mathit{Door} \rightarrow \mathit{Door} \rightarrow m\ \mathit{Door} \\ \mathit{stick}\ p\ t = \mathit{return}\ p \end{array}$$

In either case, you know p and t, but of course not h.

Here is the whole game, parametrized by your strategy, returning whether you win the car:

$$\begin{array}{lll} \multicolumn{3}{l}{\mathit{monty} :: \mathit{MonadProb}\ m \Rightarrow (\mathit{Door} \rightarrow \mathit{Door} \rightarrow m\ \mathit{Door}) \rightarrow m\ \mathit{Bool}} \\ \multicolumn{3}{l}{\mathit{monty}\ \mathit{strategy}} \\ \quad = \mathbf{do}\ \{ & h \leftarrow \mathit{hide}\ ; & \text{-- Monty hides the car behind door } h \\ & p \leftarrow \mathit{pick}\ ; & \text{-- you pick door } p \\ & t \leftarrow \mathit{tease}\ h\ p\ ; & \text{-- Monty teases you with door } t\ (\neq h, p) \\ & s \leftarrow \mathit{strategy}\ p\ t\ ; & \text{-- you choose, based on } p \text{ and } t \text{ but not } h \\ & \mathit{return}\ (s == h) & \text{-- you win iff your choice } s \text{ equals } h \\ & \} & \end{array}$$

We will show below that the switching strategy is twice as good as the sticking strategy:

$$\begin{array}{l} \mathit{monty}\ \mathit{switch} = \mathit{bcoin}_{2/3} \\ \mathit{monty}\ \mathit{stick}\ \ \ = \mathit{bcoin}_{1/3} \end{array}$$

The key is the fact that separate uniform choices are independent:

$$
\begin{array}{l}
\quad \mathbf{do}\ \{h \leftarrow hide\ ;\ p \leftarrow pick\ ;\ return\ (h,p)\} \\
= \quad [\![\ \text{definitions of } hide \text{ and } pick\ ]\!] \\
\quad \mathbf{do}\ \{h \leftarrow uniform\ doors\ ;\ p \leftarrow uniform\ doors\ ;\ return\ (h,p)\} \\
= \quad [\![\ \text{independent choices}\ ]\!] \\
\quad uniform\ (cp\ doors\ doors)
\end{array}
$$

and so we have

$$
\begin{array}{ll}
monty\ strategy = \mathbf{do}\ \{ & (h,p) \leftarrow uniform\ (cp\ doors\ doors)\ ; \\
& t \leftarrow tease\ h\ p\ ; \\
& s \leftarrow strategy\ p\ t\ ; \\
& return\ (s == h)\}
\end{array}
$$

Naturally, the doors h and p independently chosen at random will match one third of the time:

$$
\begin{array}{l}
\quad \mathbf{do}\ \{(h,p) \leftarrow uniform\ (cp\ doors\ doors)\ ;\ return\ (p == h)\} \\
= \quad [\![\ fmap \text{ and } \mathbf{do} \text{ notation}\ ]\!] \\
\quad \mathbf{do}\ \{b \leftarrow fmap\ (uncurry\ (==))\ (uniform\ (cp\ doors\ doors))\ ;\ return\ b\} \\
= \quad [\![\ \text{right unit}\ ]\!] \\
\quad fmap\ (uncurry\ (==))\ (uniform\ (cp\ doors\ doors)) \\
= \quad [\![\ \text{naturality of } uniform\ ]\!] \\
\quad uniform\ (map\ (uncurry\ (==))\ (cp\ doors\ doors)) \\
= \quad [\![\ \text{definitions of } doors,\ cp,\ ==\ ]\!] \\
\quad uniform\ [True, False, False, False, True, False, False, False, True] \\
= \quad [\![\ \text{simplifying: three } Trues \text{, six } Falses\ ]\!] \\
\quad uniform\ [True, False, False] \\
= \quad [\![\ \text{definitions of } uniform,\ bcoin_w\ ]\!] \\
\quad bcoin_{1/3}
\end{array}
$$

Therefore we calculate:

$$
\begin{array}{l}
\quad monty\ stick \\
= \quad [\![\ \text{definition of } monty \text{, independent uniform choices}\ ]\!] \\
\quad \mathbf{do}\ \{(h,p) \leftarrow uniform\ (cp\ doors\ doors)\ ; \\
\qquad t \leftarrow tease\ h\ p\ ;\ s \leftarrow stick\ p\ t\ ;\ return\ (s == h)\} \\
= \quad [\![\ \text{definition of } stick\ ]\!] \\
\quad \mathbf{do}\ \{(h,p) \leftarrow uniform\ (cp\ doors\ doors)\ ; \\
\qquad t \leftarrow tease\ h\ p\ ;\ s \leftarrow return\ p\ ;\ return\ (s == h)\} \\
= \quad [\![\ \text{left unit}\ ]\!] \\
\quad \mathbf{do}\ \{(h,p) \leftarrow uniform\ (cp\ doors\ doors)\ ;\ t \leftarrow tease\ h\ p\ ;\ return\ (p == h)\} \\
= \quad [\![\ t \text{ unused, and } uniform \text{ side-effect-free, so } tease \text{ can be eliminated}\ ]\!] \\
\quad \mathbf{do}\ \{(h,p) \leftarrow uniform\ (cp\ doors\ doors)\ ;\ return\ (p == h)\} \\
= \quad [\![\ \text{matching choices, as above}\ ]\!] \\
\quad bcoin_{1/3}
\end{array}
$$

and

$$
\begin{array}{ll}
& \mathit{monty}\ \mathit{switch} \\
= & [\![\text{ definition of } \mathit{monty}\text{, independent uniform choices }]\!] \\
& \mathbf{do}\ \{(h,p) \leftarrow \mathit{uniform}\ (\mathit{cp}\ \mathit{doors}\ \mathit{doors})\ ;\ t \leftarrow \mathit{tease}\ h\ p\ ; \\
& \quad s \leftarrow \mathit{switch}\ p\ t\ ;\ \mathit{return}\ (s == h)\} \\
= & [\![\text{ definition of } \mathit{switch}]\!] \\
& \mathbf{do}\ \{(h,p) \leftarrow \mathit{uniform}\ (\mathit{cp}\ \mathit{doors}\ \mathit{doors})\ ;\ t \leftarrow \mathit{tease}\ h\ p\ ; \\
& \quad s \leftarrow \mathit{return}\ (\mathit{head}\ (\mathit{doors} \setminus\!\setminus [p,t]))\ ;\ \mathit{return}\ (s == h)\} \\
= & [\![\text{ left unit }]\!] \\
& \mathbf{do}\ \{(h,p) \leftarrow \mathit{uniform}\ (\mathit{cp}\ \mathit{doors}\ \mathit{doors})\ ;\ t \leftarrow \mathit{tease}\ h\ p\ ; \\
& \quad \mathit{return}\ (h == \mathit{head}\ (\mathit{doors} \setminus\!\setminus [p,t]))\} \\
= & [\![\text{ case analysis on } h = p\text{---see below }]\!] \\
& \mathbf{do}\ \{(h,p) \leftarrow \mathit{uniform}\ (\mathit{cp}\ \mathit{doors}\ \mathit{doors})\ ; \\
& \quad \mathbf{if}\ h == p\ \mathbf{then}\ \mathit{return}\ \mathit{False}\ \mathbf{else}\ \mathit{return}\ \mathit{True}\} \\
= & [\![\text{ booleans }]\!] \\
& \mathbf{do}\ \{(h,p) \leftarrow \mathit{uniform}\ (\mathit{cp}\ \mathit{doors}\ \mathit{doors})\ ;\ \mathit{return}\ (h \neq p)\} \\
= & [\![\text{ analogously, mismatching choices }]\!] \\
& \mathit{bcoin}_{2/3}
\end{array}
$$

Now for the two branches of the case analysis. For the case $h = p$, we have:

$$
\begin{array}{ll}
& \mathbf{do}\ \{t \leftarrow \mathit{tease}\ h\ p\ ;\ \mathit{return}\ (h == \mathit{head}\ (\mathit{doors} \setminus\!\setminus [p,t]))\} \\
= & [\![\text{ using assumption } h == p]\!] \\
& \mathbf{do}\ \{t \leftarrow \mathit{tease}\ h\ p\ ;\ \mathit{return}\ (h == \mathit{head}\ (\mathit{doors} \setminus\!\setminus [h,t]))\} \\
= & [\![h \text{ is not in } \mathit{doors} \setminus\!\setminus [h,t]]\!] \\
& \mathbf{do}\ \{t \leftarrow \mathit{tease}\ h\ p\ ;\ \mathit{return}\ \mathit{False}\} \\
= & [\![t \text{ unused, and } \mathit{uniform} \text{ side-effect-free }]\!] \\
& \mathit{return}\ \mathit{False}
\end{array}
$$

And for the case $h \neq p$, we have:

$$
\begin{array}{ll}
& \mathbf{do}\ \{t \leftarrow \mathit{tease}\ h\ p\ ;\ \mathit{return}\ (h == \mathit{head}\ (\mathit{doors} \setminus\!\setminus [p,t]))\} \\
= & [\![\text{ definition of } \mathit{tease}]\!] \\
& \mathbf{do}\ \{t \leftarrow \mathit{uniform}\ (\mathit{doors} \setminus\!\setminus [h,p])\ ;\ \mathit{return}\ (h == \mathit{head}\ (\mathit{doors} \setminus\!\setminus [p,t]))\} \\
= & [\![h \neq p\text{, so } \mathit{doors} \setminus\!\setminus [h,p] \text{ is a singleton; } \mathit{uniform}\ [a] = \mathit{return}\ a]\!] \\
& \mathbf{do}\ \{t \leftarrow \mathit{return}\ (\mathit{head}\ (\mathit{doors} \setminus\!\setminus [h,p]))\ ;\ \mathit{return}\ (h == \mathit{head}\ (\mathit{doors} \setminus\!\setminus [p,t]))\} \\
= & [\![\text{ left unit }]\!] \\
& \mathbf{do}\ \{\mathbf{let}\ t = \mathit{head}\ (\mathit{doors} \setminus\!\setminus [h,p])\ ;\ \mathit{return}\ (h == \mathit{head}\ (\mathit{doors} \setminus\!\setminus [p,t]))\} \\
= & [\![h \neq p\text{, and } t \neq h,p\text{; so } t,h,p \text{ distinct }]\!] \\
& \mathbf{do}\ \{\mathbf{let}\ t = \mathit{head}\ (\mathit{doors} \setminus\!\setminus [h,p])\ ;\ \mathit{return}\ (h == h)\} \\
= & [\![t \text{ unused }]\!] \\
& \mathit{return}\ \mathit{True}
\end{array}
$$

So when you and Monty make uniform probabilistic choices according to the rules of the game, switching wins two thirds of the time and sticking only one third.

6.1 Nondeterministic Monty

Perhaps a more faithful model of the Monty Hall problem is to allow Monty to make nondeterministic rather than probabilistic choices [31]—nobody said that Monty has to play fair. That is, Monty's two moves in the game, hiding the car and teasing you, involve a nondeterministic rather than probabilistic choice among the available alternatives:

$$
\begin{aligned}
&\mathit{hide}_n :: \mathit{MonadAlt}\ m \Rightarrow m\ \mathit{Door}\\
&\mathit{hide}_n = \mathit{arbitrary}\ \mathit{doors}
\end{aligned}
$$

$$
\begin{aligned}
&\mathit{tease}_n :: \mathit{MonadAlt}\ m \Rightarrow \mathit{Door} \to \mathit{Door} \to m\ \mathit{Door}\\
&\mathit{tease}_n\ h\ p = \mathit{arbitrary}\ (\mathit{doors} \setminus\!\setminus [h, p])
\end{aligned}
$$

where

$$
\begin{aligned}
&\mathit{arbitrary} :: \mathit{MonadAlt}\ m \Rightarrow [a] \to m\ a\\
&\mathit{arbitrary} = \mathit{foldr}_1\ (\Box) \circ \mathit{map}\ \mathit{return}
\end{aligned}
$$

Then we define the game just as before, but with Monty behaving nondeterministically:

$$
\begin{aligned}
&\mathit{monty}_n :: \mathit{MonadAltProb}\ m \Rightarrow (\mathit{Door} \to \mathit{Door} \to m\ \mathit{Door}) \to m\ \mathit{Bool}\\
&\mathit{monty}_n\ \mathit{strategy} = \mathbf{do}\ \{h \leftarrow \mathit{hide}_n\ ;\\
&\qquad\qquad p \leftarrow \mathit{pick}\ ;\\
&\qquad\qquad t \leftarrow \mathit{tease}_n\ h\ p\ ;\\
&\qquad\qquad s \leftarrow \mathit{strategy}\ p\ t\ ;\\
&\qquad\qquad \mathit{return}\ (s == h)\}
\end{aligned}
$$

As it happens, making this change has no effect on the outcome. The first two choices—Monty's choice of where to hide the car, and your initial choice of door—can still be combined, because composition distributes leftwards over nondeterministic choice:

$$
\begin{aligned}
&\mathbf{do}\ \{h \leftarrow \mathit{hide}_n\ ; p \leftarrow \mathit{pick}\ ; \mathit{return}\ (h, p)\}\\
=\ &\ [\![\ \text{let } k\ h = \mathbf{do}\ \{p \leftarrow \mathit{pick}\ ; \mathit{return}\ (h,p)\}\ ]\!]\\
&\mathbf{do}\ \{h \leftarrow \mathit{hide}_n\ ; k\ h\}\\
=\ &\ [\![\ \text{definition of } \mathit{hide}_n, \mathit{arbitrary}\ ]\!]\\
&\mathbf{do}\ \{h \leftarrow (\mathit{return}\ A \Box \mathit{return}\ B \Box \mathit{return}\ C)\ ; k\ h\}\\
=\ &\ [\![\ \text{composition distributes leftwards over } \Box\ ]\!]\\
&\mathbf{do}\ \{h \leftarrow \mathit{return}\ A\ ; k\ h\} \Box \mathbf{do}\ \{h \leftarrow \mathit{return}\ B\ ; k\ h\} \Box\\
&\mathbf{do}\ \{h \leftarrow \mathit{return}\ C\ ; k\ h\}\\
=\ &\ [\![\ \text{left unit}\ ]\!]\\
&k\ A \Box k\ B \Box k\ C\\
=\ &\ [\![\ \text{definition of } k\ ]\!]\\
&\mathbf{do}\ \{p \leftarrow \mathit{pick}\ ; \mathit{return}\ (A,p)\} \Box \mathbf{do}\ \{p \leftarrow \mathit{pick}\ ; \mathit{return}\ (B,p)\} \Box\\
&\mathbf{do}\ \{p \leftarrow \mathit{pick}\ ; \mathit{return}\ (C,p)\}
\end{aligned}
$$

The remainder of the reasoning proceeds just as before. It is still the case that doors h and p will match one third of the time, even though h is now chosen nondeterministically rather than probabilistically. For brevity, let

$$try\ d = \mathbf{do}\ \{p \leftarrow pick\ ;\ return\ (d, p)\}$$

Then we have

$$\begin{array}{ll} & fmap\ (uncurry\ (==))\ (try\ d) \\ = & [\![\ \text{definition of } try\text{; } fmap \text{ and } \mathbf{do} \text{ notation}\ ]\!] \\ & \mathbf{do}\ \{p \leftarrow pick\ ;\ return\ (d == p)\} \\ = & [\![\ \text{definition of } pick\ ]\!] \\ & \mathbf{do}\ \{p \leftarrow \langle return\ A@^1/_3, return\ B@^1/_3, return\ C@^1/_3\rangle\ ;\ return\ (d == p)\} \\ = & [\![\ \text{composition distributes leftwards over } \lhd\rhd\text{; right unit}\ ]\!] \\ & \langle return\ (d == A)@^1/_3, return\ (d == B)@^1/_3, return\ (d == C)@^1/_3\rangle \\ = & [\![\ d :: Door\text{, and so } d \text{ is one of } A, B, C\ ]\!] \\ & \langle return\ True@^1/_3, return\ False@^1/_3, return\ False@^1/_3\rangle \\ = & [\![\ \text{definition of } bcoin_w\ ]\!] \\ & bcoin_{1/3} \end{array}$$

and therefore

$$\begin{array}{ll} & \mathbf{do}\ \{h \leftarrow hide_n\ ;\ p \leftarrow pick\ ;\ return\ (h == p)\} \\ = & [\![\ fmap \text{ and } \mathbf{do} \text{ notation}\ ]\!] \\ & fmap\ (uncurry\ (==))\ (\mathbf{do}\ \{h \leftarrow hide_n\ ;\ p \leftarrow pick\ ;\ return\ (h, p)\}) \\ = & [\![\ \text{combining first two choices, as above}\ ]\!] \\ & fmap\ (uncurry\ (==))\ (try\ A \Box try\ B \Box try\ C) \\ = & [\![\ \text{naturality: } fmap\ f\ (p \Box q) = fmap\ f\ p \Box fmap\ f\ q\ ]\!] \\ & fmap\ (uncurry\ (==))\ (try\ A) \Box fmap\ (uncurry\ (==))\ (try\ B) \Box \\ & fmap\ (uncurry\ (==))\ (try\ C) \\ = & [\![\ \text{matching choices, above}\ ]\!] \\ & bcoin_{1/3} \Box bcoin_{1/3} \Box bcoin_{1/3} \\ = & [\![\ \text{idempotence of } \Box\ ]\!] \\ & bcoin_{1/3} \end{array}$$

and the conclusion is still that

$$\begin{array}{ll} monty_n\ switch & = bcoin_{2/3} \\ monty_n\ stick & = bcoin_{1/3} \end{array}$$

Combining two classes of effect—here, probability and nondeterminism—did not make the reasoning any more difficult that in was with a single such class.

7 Failure Is an Option

Computations that may fail, and whose failures can be handled, are characterized by two operations for throwing and catching exceptions:

$$\textbf{class}\ \mathit{Monad}\ m \Rightarrow \mathit{MonadExcept}\ m\ \textbf{where}$$
$$\quad \mathit{throw} :: m\ a$$
$$\quad \mathit{catch} :: m\ a \rightarrow m\ a \rightarrow m\ a$$

For simplicity, we suppose that there is only a single exception, just as we assumed a single updatable location for stateful computations; the model is easily extended to cover multiple exceptions. The intuition is that *throw* is the computation that immediately fails, and that $p\,`\mathit{catch}`\,q$ represents the computation that behaves like p, except if this fails, in which case it continues as the exception handler q. (In Haskell, backquotes turn a prefix function into an infix operator; so $p\,`\mathit{catch}`\,q = \mathit{catch}\ p\ q$.) We stipulate that *throw* is a left zero of composition, so that a failure discards the subsequent part of a computation:

$$\textbf{do}\ \{x \leftarrow \mathit{throw}\ ;\ k\ x\} = \mathit{throw}$$

We do not stipulate that *throw* is a right zero of composition; that would require that a failure also discards the preceding part of the computation, and so that any effects of that part would have to be rolled back—quite a strong condition. Neither do we stipulate that composition distributes over *catch*; in general,

$$\textbf{do}\ \{x \leftarrow (p\,`\mathit{catch}`\,q)\ ;\ k\ x\} \neq \textbf{do}\ \{x \leftarrow p\ ;\ k\ x\}\,`\mathit{catch}`\,\textbf{do}\ \{x \leftarrow q\ ;\ k\ x\}$$

because the right-hand side brings exceptions raised by the first k under the influence of the handler q, whereas exceptions of k on the left are not handled. We do stipulate that *return* is a left zero of *catch*, so that pure computations never fail:

$$\mathit{return}\ x\,`\mathit{catch}`\,p = \mathit{return}\ x$$

Finally, *throw* and *catch* form a monoid:

$$p\,`\mathit{catch}`\,\mathit{throw} = p$$
$$\mathit{throw}\,`\mathit{catch}`\,p = p$$
$$p\,`\mathit{catch}`\,(q\,`\mathit{catch}`\,r) = (p\,`\mathit{catch}`\,q)\,`\mathit{catch}`\,r$$

That is: an exception handler that immediately propagates the exception has no effect; failures are indeed caught and handled; and exception handlers can be chained in sequence, with control passing along the chain as failures happen.

One obvious implementation of exceptions is via lifting:

$$\textbf{data}\ \mathit{Maybe}\ a = \mathit{Just}\ a \mid \mathit{Nothing}$$

Values are lifted into pure computations via *Just* and passed along by composition, whereas *Nothing* forms a left zero of composition:

$$\textbf{instance}\ \mathit{Monad}\ \mathit{Maybe}\ \textbf{where}$$
$$\quad \mathit{return}\ x = \mathit{Just}\ x$$
$$\quad \mathit{Just}\ x \gg\!= k = k\ x$$
$$\quad \mathit{Nothing} \gg\!= k = \mathit{Nothing}$$

Of course, *Nothing* represents failure; *Just* and *Nothing* partition computations into entirely pure ones and entirely failing ones, which form a left zero and a left unit of *catch*, respectively.

$$
\begin{aligned}
&\textbf{instance } \mathit{MonadExcept\ Maybe}\ \textbf{where}\\
&\quad \mathit{throw} \qquad\qquad = \mathit{Nothing}\\
&\quad \mathit{Just}\ x \ \text{`}\mathit{catch}\text{`}\ q \ \ = \mathit{Just}\ x\\
&\quad \mathit{Nothing}\ \text{`}\mathit{catch}\text{`}\ q = q
\end{aligned}
$$

The names *Maybe*, *Just*, and *Nothing* were coined by Spivey [46], and he gives a number of examples of equational reasoning about term rewriting operations that might fail. (In ML, the datatype analogous to *Maybe a* is written *'a option*.)

7.1 Combining Probability with Exceptions

Just as we did for nondeterministic and probabilistic choice, we can quite easily combine the theories of probability and exceptions. We simply combine the two interfaces, adding no new operations:

$$\textbf{class}\ (\mathit{MonadExcept}\ m, \mathit{MonadProb}\ m) \Rightarrow \mathit{MonadProbExcept}\ m$$

The laws of exceptions and of probability are inherited; the only effort required is to consider the interaction between the two theories. In this case, we have one additional distributivity law, which intuitively states that making a probabilistic choice cannot of itself cause a failure, so *catch* distributes over it:

$$(p \lhd w \rhd q)\ \text{`}\mathit{catch}\text{`}\ r = (p\ \text{`}\mathit{catch}\text{`}\ r) \lhd w \rhd (q\ \text{`}\mathit{catch}\text{`}\ r)$$

The same representation works as for plain probability distributions, but now we allow the weights to sum to less than one, and the list of weighted elements to be empty—these are sometimes called *subdistributions* [31] or *evaluations* [20]:

$$
\begin{aligned}
&\mathit{weight} :: \mathit{Dist}\ a \rightarrow \mathit{Prob}\\
&\mathit{weight}\ p = \mathit{sum}\ [w \mid (x, w) \leftarrow p]\\
&\textbf{instance } \mathit{MonadExcept\ Dist}\ \textbf{where}\\
&\quad \mathit{throw} \qquad = [\,]\\
&\quad p\ \text{`}\mathit{catch}\text{`}\ q = p +\!\!+\ \mathit{scale}\ (1 - \mathit{weight}\ p)\ (q)\\
&\textbf{instance } \mathit{MonadProbExcept\ Dist}
\end{aligned}
$$

Operationally, the exceptions are represented by the 'missing' bits of the distribution; for example, the subdistribution $[(\mathit{True}, 1/2), (\mathit{False}, 1/4)]$ has weight $3/4$, and represents a computation that fails the remaining $1/4$ of the time. The correctness of this implementation depends on the congruences we have imposed on distributions, specifically to ignore reordering and zero-weighted elements, and to coalesce duplicates.

For example, here is an attempt to simulate the biased $\mathit{bcoin}_{2/3}$ using two fair coin tosses, motivated by Knuth and Yao's trick [23] for simulating a fair die with three coins:

```
coins23 :: MonadProbExcept m ⇒ m Bool
coins23 = return True ◁ 1/2 ▷ (return False ◁ 1/2 ▷ throw)
```

We might illustrate the process as follows:

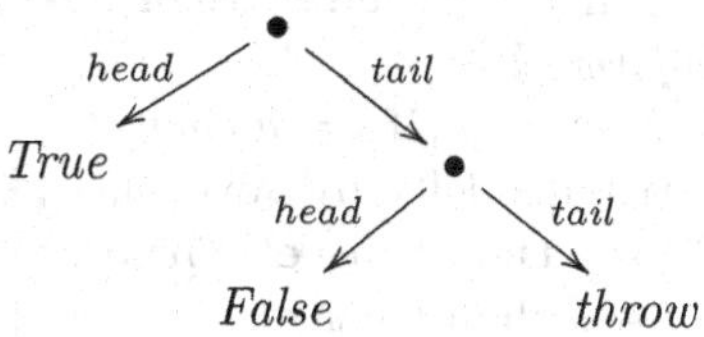

This does indeed yield *True* exactly twice as often as *False*. However, a quarter of the time it will fail to yield any result at all, and throw an exception instead; so the attempt was not entirely successful. We will pick up this example again in Section 8 below.

7.2 Forgetful Monty

Let us return to the purely probabilistic version of the Monty Hall game, but this time suppose that Monty is becoming increasingly forgetful in his old age—he can never remember where he has hidden the car [45, Chapter 3]. Therefore, when it comes to teasing you, he uniformly at random opens one of the two doors different from the door you picked. Of course he might accidentally reveal the car in doing so; we treat this as a failure in the protocol:

```
tease_f :: MonadProbExcept m ⇒ Door → Door → m Door
tease_f h p = do {t ← uniform (doors \\ [p]) ;
                  if t == h then throw else return t}

monty_f :: MonadProbExcept m ⇒ (Door → Door → m Door) → m Bool
monty_f strategy = do {h ← hide ;
                       p ← pick ;
                       t ← tease_f h p ;
                       s ← strategy p t ;
                       return (s == h)}
```

Investigating $tease_f$ in the case that $h = p$, we have:

```
  tease_f h p
=    [[ definition of tease_f ]]
  do {t ← uniform (doors \\ [p]) ; if t == h then throw else return t}
=    [[ h = p, so h is not in doors \\ [p] and hence t ≠ h ]]
  do {t ← uniform (doors \\ [p]) ; return t}
=    [[ right unit ]]
  uniform (doors \\ [p])
```

—so if you happen to pick the car initially, Monty cannot accidentally reveal it. In the case that $h \neq p$, let $d = head\ (doors \setminus\setminus [h, p])$, so that h, p, d are all distinct; then we have:

$$
\begin{array}{ll}
& \mathit{tease}_f\;h\;p \\
= & \llbracket \text{ definition of } \mathit{tease}_f \; \rrbracket \\
& \mathbf{do}\;\{t \leftarrow \mathit{uniform}\;(\mathit{doors} \mathbin{\backslash\backslash} [p])\;;\;\mathbf{if}\;t == h\;\mathbf{then}\;\mathit{throw}\;\mathbf{else}\;\mathit{return}\;t\} \\
= & \llbracket \text{ by assumption, } \mathit{doors} \mathbin{\backslash\backslash} [p] = [h,d] \; \rrbracket \\
& \mathbf{do}\;\{t \leftarrow \mathit{uniform}\;[h,d]\;;\;\mathbf{if}\;t == h\;\mathbf{then}\;\mathit{throw}\;\mathbf{else}\;\mathit{return}\;t\} \\
= & \llbracket \text{ definition of } \mathit{uniform} \; \rrbracket \\
& \mathbf{do}\;\{t \leftarrow \mathit{return}\;h \lhd {}^1\!/_2 \rhd \mathit{return}\;d\;;\;\mathbf{if}\;t == h\;\mathbf{then}\;\mathit{throw}\;\mathbf{else}\;\mathit{return}\;t\} \\
= & \llbracket \text{ composition distributes leftwards over } \lhd\rhd \; \rrbracket \\
& \mathbf{do}\;\{t \leftarrow \mathit{return}\;h\;;\;\mathbf{if}\;t == h\;\mathbf{then}\;\mathit{throw}\;\mathbf{else}\;\mathit{return}\;t\} \lhd {}^1\!/_2 \rhd \\
& \mathbf{do}\;\{t \leftarrow \mathit{return}\;d\;;\;\mathbf{if}\;t == h\;\mathbf{then}\;\mathit{throw}\;\mathbf{else}\;\mathit{return}\;t\} \\
= & \llbracket \text{ left unit } \rrbracket \\
& (\mathbf{if}\;h == h\;\mathbf{then}\;\mathit{throw}\;\mathbf{else}\;\mathit{return}\;h) \lhd {}^1\!/_2 \rhd (\mathbf{if}\;d == h\;\mathbf{then}\;\mathit{throw}\;\mathbf{else}\;\mathit{return}\;d) \\
= & \llbracket \text{ by assumption, } d \neq h\text{; conditionals } \rrbracket \\
& \mathit{throw} \lhd {}^1\!/_2 \rhd \mathit{return}\;d
\end{array}
$$

—that is, if you initially picked a goat, Monty has a 50–50 chance of accidentally revealing the car. Putting these together, we have:

$$
\begin{array}{l}
\mathit{tease}_f\;h\;p = \mathbf{if}\;h == p\;\mathbf{then}\;\mathit{uniform}\;(\mathit{doors} \mathbin{\backslash\backslash} [p]) \\
\qquad\qquad\qquad\qquad \mathbf{else}\;(\mathit{throw} \lhd {}^1\!/_2 \rhd \mathit{return}\;(\mathit{head}\;(\mathit{doors} \mathbin{\backslash\backslash} [h,p])))
\end{array}
$$

Clearly, in the 'else' case, tease_f is no longer necessarily side-effect-free—even if its result is not used, it cannot be discarded, because it might fail—and so the calculations for the purely probabilistic version of the game do not apply. Instead, we have:

$$
\begin{array}{ll}
& \mathit{monty}_f\;\mathit{stick} \\
= & \llbracket \text{ definition of } \mathit{monty}_f \; \rrbracket \\
& \mathbf{do}\;\{(h,p) \leftarrow \mathit{uniform}\;(\mathit{cp}\;\mathit{doors}\;\mathit{doors})\;; \\
& \qquad t \leftarrow \mathit{tease}_f\;h\;p\;;\;s \leftarrow \mathit{stick}\;p\;t\;;\;\mathit{return}\;(s == h)\} \\
= & \llbracket \text{ definition of } \mathit{stick}\text{; left unit } \rrbracket \\
& \mathbf{do}\;\{(h,p) \leftarrow \mathit{uniform}\;(\mathit{cp}\;\mathit{doors}\;\mathit{doors})\;;\;t \leftarrow \mathit{tease}_f\;h\;p\;;\;\mathit{return}\;(p == h)\} \\
= & \llbracket \text{ case analysis in } \mathit{tease}_f\text{, as above; let } d = \mathit{head}\;(\mathit{doors} \mathbin{\backslash\backslash} [h,p]) \; \rrbracket \\
& \mathbf{do}\;\{(h,p) \leftarrow \mathit{uniform}\;(\mathit{cp}\;\mathit{doors}\;\mathit{doors})\;; \\
& \qquad t \leftarrow \mathbf{if}\;h == p\;\mathbf{then}\;\mathit{uniform}\;(\mathit{doors} \mathbin{\backslash\backslash} [p])\;\mathbf{else}\;(\mathit{throw} \lhd {}^1\!/_2 \rhd \mathit{return}\;d)\;; \\
& \qquad \mathit{return}\;(p == h)\} \\
= & \llbracket \text{ conditionals } \rrbracket \\
& \mathbf{do}\;\{(h,p) \leftarrow \mathit{uniform}\;(\mathit{cp}\;\mathit{doors}\;\mathit{doors})\;; \\
& \qquad \mathbf{if}\;h == p\;\mathbf{then}\;\mathbf{do}\;\{t \leftarrow \mathit{uniform}\;(\mathit{doors} \mathbin{\backslash\backslash} [p])\;;\;\mathit{return}\;(p == h)\} \\
& \qquad\qquad\qquad \mathbf{else}\;\;\mathbf{do}\;\{t \leftarrow \mathit{throw} \lhd {}^1\!/_2 \rhd \mathit{return}\;d\;;\;\mathit{return}\;(p == h)\}\} \\
= & \llbracket \text{ first } t \text{ is unused and } \mathit{uniform} \text{ is side-effect-free; } p == h = \mathit{True} \; \rrbracket \\
& \mathbf{do}\;\{(h,p) \leftarrow \mathit{uniform}\;(\mathit{cp}\;\mathit{doors}\;\mathit{doors})\;; \\
& \qquad \mathbf{if}\;h == p\;\mathbf{then}\;\mathit{return}\;\mathit{True} \\
& \qquad\qquad\qquad \mathbf{else}\;\;\mathbf{do}\;\{t \leftarrow \mathit{throw} \lhd {}^1\!/_2 \rhd \mathit{return}\;d\;;\;\mathit{return}\;(p == h)\}\} \\
= & \llbracket \text{ composition distributes over } \lhd\rhd \; \rrbracket \\
& \mathbf{do}\;\{(h,p) \leftarrow \mathit{uniform}\;(\mathit{cp}\;\mathit{doors}\;\mathit{doors})\;; \\
& \qquad \mathbf{if}\;h == p\;\mathbf{then}\;\mathit{return}\;\mathit{True}
\end{array}
$$

$$\qquad\quad \mathbf{else}\ \ \mathbf{do}\ \{t \leftarrow \mathit{throw}\ ;\ \mathit{return}\ \mathit{False}\} \lhd {}^{1}\!/_{2} \rhd$$
$$\qquad\qquad\qquad \mathbf{do}\ \{t \leftarrow \mathit{return}\ d\ ;\ \mathit{return}\ \mathit{False}\}\}$$
$$= \quad [\![\ \mathit{throw}\ \text{is a left zero of composition, and}\ \mathit{return}\ \text{a left unit}\ ]\!]$$
$$\mathbf{do}\ \{(h,p) \leftarrow \mathit{uniform}\ (\mathit{cp}\ \mathit{doors}\ \mathit{doors})\ ;$$
$$\quad \mathbf{if}\ h == p\ \mathbf{then}\ \mathit{return}\ \mathit{True}\ \mathbf{else}\ \mathit{throw} \lhd {}^{1}\!/_{2} \rhd \mathit{return}\ \mathit{False}\}$$
$$= \quad [\![\ \text{matching choices, as in Section 6}\ ]\!]$$
$$\mathbf{do}\ \{b \leftarrow \mathit{bcoin}_{1/3}\ ;\ \mathbf{if}\ b\ \mathbf{then}\ \mathit{return}\ \mathit{True}\ \mathbf{else}\ \mathit{throw} \lhd {}^{1}\!/_{2} \rhd \mathit{return}\ \mathit{False}\}$$
$$= \quad [\![\ \text{composition distributes over}\ \lhd\rhd\ ]\!]$$
$$\mathbf{do}\ \{b \leftarrow \mathit{return}\ \mathit{True}\ ;$$
$$\quad \mathbf{if}\ b\ \mathbf{then}\ \mathit{return}\ \mathit{True}\ \mathbf{else}\ \mathit{throw} \lhd {}^{1}\!/_{2} \rhd \mathit{return}\ \mathit{False}\} \lhd {}^{1}\!/_{3} \rhd$$
$$\mathbf{do}\ \{b \leftarrow \mathit{return}\ \mathit{False}\ ;$$
$$\quad \mathbf{if}\ b\ \mathbf{then}\ \mathit{return}\ \mathit{True}\ \mathbf{else}\ \mathit{throw} \lhd {}^{1}\!/_{2} \rhd \mathit{return}\ \mathit{False}\}$$
$$= \quad [\![\ \text{left unit; conditionals}\ ]\!]$$
$$\mathit{return}\ \mathit{True} \lhd {}^{1}\!/_{3} \rhd (\mathit{throw} \lhd {}^{1}\!/_{2} \rhd \mathit{return}\ \mathit{False})$$
$$= \quad [\![\ \text{flattening choices}\ ]\!]$$
$$\langle \mathit{True}@{}^{1}\!/_{3}, \mathit{throw}@{}^{1}\!/_{3}, \mathit{False}@{}^{1}\!/_{3} \rangle$$

On the other hand:

$$\mathit{monty}_f\ \mathit{switch}$$
$$= \quad [\![\ \text{definition of}\ \mathit{monty}_f\ ]\!]$$
$$\mathbf{do}\ \{(h,p) \leftarrow \mathit{uniform}\ (\mathit{cp}\ \mathit{doors}\ \mathit{doors})\ ;\ t \leftarrow \mathit{tease}_f\ h\ p\ ;$$
$$\quad s \leftarrow \mathit{switch}\ p\ t\ ;\ \mathit{return}\ (s == h)\}$$
$$= \quad [\![\ \text{definition of}\ \mathit{switch}\ ]\!]$$
$$\mathbf{do}\ \{(h,p) \leftarrow \mathit{uniform}\ (\mathit{cp}\ \mathit{doors}\ \mathit{doors})\ ;\ t \leftarrow \mathit{tease}_f\ h\ p\ ;$$
$$\quad s \leftarrow \mathit{return}\ (\mathit{head}\ (\mathit{doors} \setminus\!\setminus [p,t]))\ ;\ \mathit{return}\ (s == h)\}$$
$$= \quad [\![\ \text{left unit}\ ]\!]$$
$$\mathbf{do}\ \{(h,p) \leftarrow \mathit{uniform}\ (\mathit{cp}\ \mathit{doors}\ \mathit{doors})\ ;\ t \leftarrow \mathit{tease}_f\ h\ p\ ;$$
$$\quad \mathit{return}\ (h == \mathit{head}\ (\mathit{doors} \setminus\!\setminus [p,t]))\}$$
$$= \quad [\![\ \text{case analysis in}\ \mathit{tease}_f\text{, as above; let}\ d = \mathit{head}\ (\mathit{doors} \setminus\!\setminus [h,p])\ ]\!]$$
$$\mathbf{do}\ \{(h,p) \leftarrow \mathit{uniform}\ (\mathit{cp}\ \mathit{doors}\ \mathit{doors})\ ;$$
$$\quad t \leftarrow \mathbf{if}\ h == p\ \mathbf{then}\ \mathit{uniform}\ (\mathit{doors} \setminus\!\setminus [p])\ \mathbf{else}\ \mathit{throw} \lhd {}^{1}\!/_{2} \rhd \mathit{return}\ d\ ;$$
$$\quad \mathit{return}\ (h == \mathit{head}\ (\mathit{doors} \setminus\!\setminus [p,t]))\}$$
$$= \quad [\![\ \text{composition distributes leftwards over conditional}\ ]\!]$$
$$\mathbf{do}\ \{(h,p) \leftarrow \mathit{uniform}\ (\mathit{cp}\ \mathit{doors}\ \mathit{doors})\ ;$$
$$\quad \mathbf{if}\ h == p\ \mathbf{then}\ \mathbf{do}\ \{t \leftarrow \mathit{uniform}\ (\mathit{doors} \setminus\!\setminus [p])\ ;$$
$$\qquad\qquad\qquad \mathit{return}\ (h == \mathit{head}\ (\mathit{doors} \setminus\!\setminus [p,t]))\}$$
$$\qquad\quad \mathbf{else}\ \ \mathbf{do}\ \{t \leftarrow \mathit{throw} \lhd {}^{1}\!/_{2} \rhd \mathit{return}\ d\ ;$$
$$\qquad\qquad\qquad \mathit{return}\ (h == \mathit{head}\ (\mathit{doors} \setminus\!\setminus [p,t]))\}\}$$
$$= \quad [\![\ \text{in}\ \mathbf{then}\ \text{branch,}\ h = p\text{, so}\ h\ \text{is not in}\ \mathit{doors} \setminus\!\setminus [p,t]\ ]\!]$$
$$\mathbf{do}\ \{(h,p) \leftarrow \mathit{uniform}\ (\mathit{cp}\ \mathit{doors}\ \mathit{doors})\ ;$$
$$\quad \mathbf{if}\ h == p\ \mathbf{then}\ \mathbf{do}\ \{t \leftarrow \mathit{uniform}\ (\mathit{doors} \setminus\!\setminus [p])\ ;\ \mathit{return}\ \mathit{False}\}$$
$$\qquad\quad \mathbf{else}\ \ \mathbf{do}\ \{t \leftarrow \mathit{throw} \lhd {}^{1}\!/_{2} \rhd \mathit{return}\ d\ ;$$
$$\qquad\qquad\qquad \mathit{return}\ (h == \mathit{head}\ (\mathit{doors} \setminus\!\setminus [p,t]))\}\}$$
$$= \quad [\![\ \text{composition distributes over}\ \lhd\rhd\ ]\!]$$
$$\mathbf{do}\ \{(h,p) \leftarrow \mathit{uniform}\ (\mathit{cp}\ \mathit{doors}\ \mathit{doors})\ ;$$

$$
\begin{array}{l}
\quad \mathbf{if}\ h == p\ \mathbf{then\ do}\ \{t \leftarrow \mathit{uniform}\ (\mathit{doors} \setminus\!\setminus [p])\ ;\ \mathit{return\ False}\} \\
\qquad\qquad \mathbf{else}\ \ \mathbf{do}\ \{t \leftarrow \mathit{throw}\ ;\ \mathit{return}\ (h == \mathit{head}\ (\mathit{doors} \setminus\!\setminus [p,t]))\} \lhd {}^{1}\!/_{2} \rhd \\
\qquad\qquad\qquad \mathbf{do}\ \{t \leftarrow \mathit{return}\ d\ ;\ \mathit{return}\ (h == \mathit{head}\ (\mathit{doors} \setminus\!\setminus [p,t]))\}\} \\
= \quad [\![\ \text{in } \mathbf{then} \text{ branch, } t \text{ is unused and } \mathit{uniform} \text{ is side-effect-free}\ ]\!] \\
\mathbf{do}\ \{(h,p) \leftarrow \mathit{uniform}\ (\mathit{cp\ doors\ doors})\ ; \\
\quad \mathbf{if}\ h == p\ \mathbf{then}\ \mathit{return\ False} \\
\qquad\qquad \mathbf{else}\ \ \mathbf{do}\ \{t \leftarrow \mathit{throw}\ ;\ \mathit{return}\ (h == \mathit{head}\ (\mathit{doors} \setminus\!\setminus [p,t]))\} \lhd {}^{1}\!/_{2} \rhd \\
\qquad\qquad\qquad \mathbf{do}\ \{t \leftarrow \mathit{return}\ d\ ;\ \mathit{return}\ (h == \mathit{head}\ (\mathit{doors} \setminus\!\setminus [p,t]))\}\} \\
= \quad [\![\ \mathit{throw} \text{ is left zero, } \mathit{return} \text{ is left unit}\ ]\!] \\
\mathbf{do}\ \{(h,p) \leftarrow \mathit{uniform}\ (\mathit{cp\ doors\ doors})\ ; \\
\quad \mathbf{if}\ h == p\ \mathbf{then}\ \mathit{return\ False} \\
\qquad\qquad \mathbf{else}\ \ \mathit{throw} \lhd {}^{1}\!/_{2} \rhd (\mathit{return}\ (h == \mathit{head}\ (\mathit{doors} \setminus\!\setminus [p,d])))\} \\
= \quad [\![\ h,p,d \text{ are distinct, so } \mathit{head}\ (\mathit{doors} \setminus\!\setminus [p,d]) = h\ ]\!] \\
\mathbf{do}\ \{(h,p) \leftarrow \mathit{uniform}\ (\mathit{cp\ doors\ doors})\ ; \\
\quad \mathbf{if}\ h == p\ \mathbf{then}\ \mathit{return\ False}\ \mathbf{else}\ \mathit{throw} \lhd {}^{1}\!/_{2} \rhd (\mathit{return\ True})\} \\
= \quad [\![\ \text{matching choices}\ ]\!] \\
\mathbf{do}\ \{b \leftarrow \mathit{bcoin}_{1/3}\ ;\ \mathbf{if}\ b\ \mathbf{then}\ \mathit{return\ False}\ \mathbf{else}\ \mathit{throw} \lhd {}^{1}\!/_{2} \rhd \mathit{return\ True}\} \\
= \quad [\![\ \text{composition distributes over } \lhd\rhd\ ]\!] \\
\mathbf{do}\ \{b \leftarrow \mathit{return\ True}\ ; \\
\quad \mathbf{if}\ b\ \mathbf{then}\ \mathit{return\ False}\ \mathbf{else}\ \mathit{throw} \lhd {}^{1}\!/_{2} \rhd \mathit{return\ True}\} \lhd {}^{1}\!/_{3} \rhd \\
\mathbf{do}\ \{b \leftarrow \mathit{return\ False}\ ; \\
\quad \mathbf{if}\ b\ \mathbf{then}\ \mathit{return\ False}\ \mathbf{else}\ \mathit{throw} \lhd {}^{1}\!/_{2} \rhd \mathit{return\ True}\} \\
= \quad [\![\ \text{left unit; conditionals}\ ]\!] \\
\mathit{return\ False} \lhd {}^{1}\!/_{3} \rhd (\mathit{throw} \lhd {}^{1}\!/_{2} \rhd \mathit{return\ True}) \\
= \quad [\![\ \text{flattening choices}\ ]\!] \\
\langle \mathit{False}@{}^{1}\!/_{3}, \mathit{throw}@{}^{1}\!/_{3}, \mathit{True}@{}^{1}\!/_{3} \rangle
\end{array}
$$

So, somewhat surprisingly, both the sticking and switching strategies are equivalent in the face of Monty's forgetfulness: with either one, you have equal chances of winning, losing, or of the game being aborted.

$$\mathit{monty}_f\ \mathit{stick} = \mathit{monty}_f\ \mathit{switch} = \langle \mathit{True}@{}^{1}\!/_{3}, \mathit{False}@{}^{1}\!/_{3}, \mathit{throw}@{}^{1}\!/_{3} \rangle$$

7.3 Conditional Probability

We have so far presented the combination of probability and exceptions as modelling computations that make probabilistic choices but that might fail. An alternative reading is in terms of *conditional probability*. In probability theory, the conditional probability $P(A \mid B)$ is the probability of event A occurring, given that event B is known to have occurred; it is defined to be the probability of both events A and B occurring, divided by the probability of B alone:

$$P(A \mid B) = \frac{P(A \wedge B)}{P(B)}$$

Operationally, a subdistribution p with weight $w > 0$ represents the distribution of outcomes drawn from the normalized distribution $\mathit{scale}\ ({}^{1}\!/_{w})\ p$, conditioned by the non-occurrence of the outcomes outside the support of p.

$$\mathit{normalize} :: \mathit{Dist}\ a \to \mathit{Dist}\ a$$
$$\mathit{normalize}\ p = \mathit{scale}\ ({}^{1}\!/_{\mathit{weight}\ p})\ p$$

For example, the subdistribution

$$\mathit{coins23} = [(\mathit{True}, {}^{1}\!/_{2}), (\mathit{False}, {}^{1}\!/_{4})]$$

from Section 7.1 has weight ${}^{3}\!/_{4}$, and so represents the distribution of outcomes

$$[(\mathit{True}, {}^{1}\!/_{2} \div {}^{3}\!/_{4} = {}^{2}\!/_{3}), (\mathit{False}, {}^{1}\!/_{4} \div {}^{3}\!/_{4} = {}^{1}\!/_{3})] = \mathit{bcoin}_{2/3}$$

given that one does not toss two tails—so the attempt to simulate the biased $\mathit{bcoin}_{2/3}$ using two fair coin tosses was not so far off after all. Similarly, one could say that playing against forgetful Monty using either the switching or the sticking strategy yields a 50–50 chance of winning, assuming that Monty successfully bluffs his way through his amnesia.

As a more extended example, consider the canonical 'wet grass' Bayesian reasoning problem [21]. Suppose that with probability ${}^{3}\!/_{10}$ it is raining; and when it rains, with probability ${}^{9}\!/_{10}$ it does so heavily enough to make the grass wet. Also, there is a lawn sprinker, operating with probability ${}^{1}\!/_{2}$; when this operates, with probability ${}^{8}\!/_{10}$ it has high enough water pressure to make the grass wet. Finally, with probability ${}^{1}\!/_{10}$ the grass is wet for some other unknown reason.

$$\mathit{rain} :: \mathit{MonadProb}\ m \Rightarrow m\ \mathit{Bool}$$
$$\mathit{rain} = \mathit{bcoin}_{3/10}$$

$$\mathit{sprinkler} :: \mathit{MonadProb}\ m \Rightarrow m\ \mathit{Bool}$$
$$\mathit{sprinkler} = \mathit{bcoin}_{1/2}$$

$$\mathit{grassWet} :: \mathit{MonadProb}\ m \Rightarrow \mathit{Bool} \to \mathit{Bool} \to m\ \mathit{Bool}$$
$$\mathit{grassWet}\ r\ s = \mathbf{do}\ \{x \leftarrow \mathit{bcoin}_{9/10}\ ;\ y \leftarrow \mathit{bcoin}_{8/10}\ ;\ z \leftarrow \mathit{bcoin}_{1/10}\ ;\ \mathit{return}\ ((x \wedge r) \vee (y \wedge s) \vee z)\}$$

What is the probability that it is raining, given that the grass is observed to be wet?

$$\mathit{experiment} :: \mathit{MonadProbExcept}\ m \Rightarrow m\ \mathit{Bool}$$
$$\mathit{experiment} = \mathbf{do}\ \{r \leftarrow \mathit{rain}\ ;\ s \leftarrow \mathit{sprinkler}\ ;\ g \leftarrow \mathit{grassWet}\ r\ s\ ;\ \mathbf{if}\ g\ \mathbf{then}\ \mathit{return}\ r\ \mathbf{else}\ \mathit{throw}\}$$

We simply return whether it is raining, conditioned on whether the grass is wet:

$$\mathit{normalize}\ \mathit{experiment} = [(\mathit{False}, {}^{1610}\!/_{3029}), (\mathit{True}, {}^{1419}\!/_{3029})]$$

—that is, it is raining with probability ${}^{1419}\!/_{3029} \simeq 0.47$.

8 Recursion

It is very tempting to write recursive programs in the style we have shown above. For example, here is a simple Markov model of the *coins23* attempt in Section 7.1:

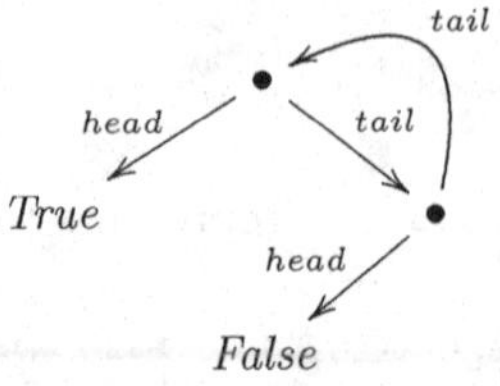

This depicts a process that recurses instead of failing. We can represent it symbolically with a recursive definition:

$$\begin{aligned}&\mathit{thirds} :: \mathit{MonadProbExcept}\ m \Rightarrow m\ \mathit{Bool}\\ &\mathit{thirds} = \mathit{coins23}\ \text{`}\mathit{catch}\text{`}\ \mathit{thirds}\end{aligned}$$

In fact, we can inline the exception and its handler, on account of the various laws of $\triangleleft\triangleright$: for any p,

$$\begin{aligned}&\mathit{coins23}\ \text{`}\mathit{catch}\text{`}\ p\\ =\quad&[\![\ \text{definition of } \mathit{coins23}\ ]\!]\\ &(\mathit{return}\ \mathit{True} \triangleleft {}^{1}\!/_{2} \triangleright (\mathit{return}\ \mathit{False} \triangleleft {}^{1}\!/_{2} \triangleright \mathit{throw}))\ \text{`}\mathit{catch}\text{`}\ p\\ =\quad&[\![\ \mathit{catch} \text{ distributes over } \triangleleft\triangleright\text{, twice}\ ]\!]\\ &(\mathit{return}\ \mathit{True}\ \text{`}\mathit{catch}\text{`}\ p) \triangleleft {}^{1}\!/_{2} \triangleright\\ &\quad((\mathit{return}\ \mathit{False}\ \text{`}\mathit{catch}\text{`}\ p) \triangleleft {}^{1}\!/_{2} \triangleright (\mathit{throw}\ \text{`}\mathit{catch}\text{`}\ p))\\ =\quad&[\![\ \mathit{return} \text{ is left zero of } \mathit{catch}\text{, and } \mathit{throw} \text{ is left unit}\ ]\!]\\ &\mathit{return}\ \mathit{True} \triangleleft {}^{1}\!/_{2} \triangleright (\mathit{return}\ \mathit{False} \triangleleft {}^{1}\!/_{2} \triangleright p)\end{aligned}$$

So we could have defined instead

$$\begin{aligned}&\mathit{thirds} :: \mathit{MonadProb}\ m \Rightarrow m\ \mathit{Bool}\\ &\mathit{thirds} = \mathit{return}\ \mathit{True} \triangleleft {}^{1}\!/_{2} \triangleright (\mathit{return}\ \mathit{False} \triangleleft {}^{1}\!/_{2} \triangleright \mathit{thirds})\end{aligned}$$

Note that this definition can be given a more specific type, because it no longer exploits the ability to fail.

8.1 Recursive Definitions

But what might the semantics of such a recursive definition be? Up until now, we have implicitly assumed a setting of sets and total functions, in which there is no guarantee that an arbitrary recursive definition has a canonical solution. And indeed, with the implementation of *MonadProb* in terms of finite probability-weighted lists from Section 4, the recursive equation defining *thirds* has no solution.

The usual response to this problem is to switch the setting from total functions between sets to continuous functions between complete partial orders; then all recursive definitions have a least solution. In this case, the least solution to the recursive definition of *thirds* above is the infinite probability-weighted list

$$[(\mathit{True}, 1/2), (\mathit{False}, 1/4), (\mathit{True}, 1/8), (\mathit{False}, 1/16), (\mathit{True}, 1/32), (\mathit{False}, 1/64), ...]$$

One might see this as a reasonable representation of $\mathit{bcoin}_{2/3}$: the weights of finite initial segments of the list converge to one; and two thirds of the weight is associated with *True*, one third with *False*. Moreover, if one samples from this distribution in the obvious way, with probability 1 one obtains an appropriate result—only in the measure-zero situation in which one tries to sample the distribution at precisely 1.0 does the computation not terminate. In fact, one can show that $\mathit{bcoin}_{2/3}$ is a solution to the same recursive equation as *thirds*:

$$\begin{array}{ll}
& \mathit{return}\ \mathit{True} \lhd 1/2 \rhd (\mathit{return}\ \mathit{False} \lhd 1/2 \rhd \mathit{bcoin}_{2/3}) \\
= & [\![\text{ definition of } \mathit{bcoin}_w \ ]\!] \\
& \mathit{return}\ \mathit{True} \lhd 1/2 \rhd (\mathit{return}\ \mathit{False} \lhd 1/2 \rhd (\mathit{return}\ \mathit{True} \lhd 2/3 \rhd \mathit{return}\ \mathit{False})) \\
= & [\![\text{ flattening choices }]\!] \\
& \langle \mathit{return}\ \mathit{True}@1/2, \mathit{return}\ \mathit{False}@1/4, \mathit{return}\ \mathit{True}@1/6, \mathit{return}\ \mathit{False}@1/12 \rangle \\
= & [\![\text{ combining collisions }]\!] \\
& \langle \mathit{return}\ \mathit{True}@2/3, \mathit{return}\ \mathit{False}@1/3 \rangle \\
= & [\![\text{ definition of } \mathit{bcoin}_w \ ]\!] \\
& \mathit{bcoin}_{2/3}
\end{array}$$

However, the nice behaviour in this case is a happy accident of the rather special form of the recursive definition. Had we written the ostensibly equivalent definition

$$\mathit{thirds} = (\mathit{thirds} \lhd 1/2 \rhd \mathit{return}\ \mathit{False}) \lhd 1/2 \rhd \mathit{return}\ \mathit{True}$$

instead, the least solution would be $\perp$, the least-defined element in the information ordering, because the definition of $\lhd\rhd$ on weighted lists is strict in its left argument. In fact, the codatatype of possibly-infinite, possibly-partial lists fails to satisfy all the necessary axioms: choice is not quasi-commutative when it involves undefined arguments, because lists are left-biased.

8.2 A Free Monad for Choice

As we have seen, one obvious implementation of *MonadProb* uses probability-weighted lists of values; thus, *coin* is represented as $[(\mathit{True}, 1/2), (\mathit{False}, 1/2)]$. However, an arguably more natural representation is in terms of the *free monad*—'more natural' in the sense that it arises directly from the signature of the $\lhd\rhd$ operation:

$$\mathbf{data}\ \mathit{DistT}\ a = \mathit{Return}\ a \mid \mathit{Choice}\ \mathit{Prob}\ (\mathit{DistT}\ a)\ (\mathit{DistT}\ a)$$

This being a free monad, *return* and bind have simple definitions arising from substitution:

$$
\begin{array}{l}
\textbf{instance } \mathit{Monad\ DistT} \textbf{ where} \\
\quad \mathit{return}\ x = \mathit{Return}\ x \\
\quad \mathit{Return}\ x \gg\!= k = k\ x \\
\quad \mathit{Choice}\ w\ p\ q \gg\!= k = \mathit{Choice}\ w\ (p \gg\!= k)\ (q \gg\!= k)
\end{array}
$$

and by design, $\lhd\rhd$ is trivial to implement:

$$
\begin{array}{l}
\textbf{instance } \mathit{MonadProb\ DistT} \textbf{ where} \\
\quad p \lhd w \rhd q = \mathit{Choice}\ w\ p\ q
\end{array}
$$

Again, because this is the free monad, the monad laws necessarily hold—the left unit law holds directly by construction, and the right unit and associativity laws are easily shown by induction over the structure of the left-hand argument. This is not quite the initial model of the *MonadProb* specification, though, because the remaining identity, idempotence, quasi-commutativity, and quasi-associativity laws of $\lhd\rhd$ do not hold. Indeed, as we have already argued, the initial model of the specification consists of finite mappings from elements to probabilities, collected from the choice tree in the obvious way:

$$
\begin{array}{l}
\mathit{collectT} :: \mathit{Eq}\ a \Rightarrow \mathit{DistT}\ a \to (a \to \mathit{Prob}) \\
\mathit{collectT}\ (\mathit{Return}\ x)\ y = \textbf{if } x == y \textbf{ then } 1 \textbf{ else } 0 \\
\mathit{collectT}\ (\mathit{Choice}\ w\ p\ q)\ y = w \times \mathit{collectT}\ p\ y + \overline{w} \times \mathit{collectT}\ q\ y
\end{array}
$$

and equivalences on *DistT* ought again to be taken modulo permutations, zero-weighted elements, and repeated elements (whose weights should be added). Nevertheless, the datatype *DistT* itself provides another convenient approximation to the initial model.

In order to guarantee solutions to arbitrary recursive definitions, we still have to accept the CPO setting rather than SET; so really, we mean to take the codatatype interpretation of *DistT*, including partial and infinite values as well as finite ones. (Which means that the inductive proofs of the monad laws need to be strengthened to cover these cases.)

The benefit we gain from this extra complication is that the representation is now symmetric, and so the laws of choice hold once more. Recursive definitions like those of *thirds* above give rise to *regular* choice trees—possibly infinite trees, but with only finitely many different subtrees. Moreover, $\lhd\rhd$ is non-strict in both arguments, so the semantics of a recursive definition is much less sensitive to the precise form of the recursion.

But of course, not all recursive equations give productive solutions. Clearly anything is a solution of the equation $p = p$, or, thanks to the monad laws, of $p = (p \gg\!= \mathit{return})$. Even some equations that completely determine proper choice trees do not define productive sampling behaviour; for example,

$$p = p \lhd 1 \rhd \mathit{return\ True}$$

does not, and even when restricting attention to weights strictly between 0 and 1, one can try

$p = p \triangleleft {}^1\!/_2 \triangleright p$

We believe that for a recursive definition to define a choice tree with a productive interpretation as a sampling function, it is sufficient for recursive occurrences of the variable being defined to be guarded by a $\triangleleft\triangleright$, and for each such $\triangleleft\triangleright$ to devote positive weight to a non-recursive subcomputation. But it seems rather unsatisfactory to have to consider specific implementations such as *DistT* of the *MonadProb* specification at all; in the rest of the paper, we have managed to conduct all our reasoning in terms of the algebraic theory rather than one of its models.

9 Conclusions

We have presented an approach to reasoning about effectful functional programs, based on algebraic theories. We have focussed in this paper on the effects of nondeterminism and probabilism and their combination, together with exceptions, but the approach works for any class of effects; our earlier paper [10] also discusses counting, generating fresh names, and mutable state. The problem of reasoning about effectful programs was an open one in the functional programming community before this point; for example, our work was inspired by a (not formally published) paper concerning a relabelling operation on trees [18], which resorted to unrolling the obvious stateful program into a pure state-transforming function in order to conduct proofs.

One strength of functional programming is the support it provides for *reasoning* about programs: the techniques of simple high-school algebra suffice, and one can reason directly in the language of programs, rather than having to extract verification conditions from the programs and then reason indirectly in predicate calculus. In that respect, functional programming has a similar motivation to Hoare's "programs are predicates" work [16], Hehner's predicative programming [13], and Morgan's refinement calculus [37]—namely, to avoid where possible the distinction between syntax and semantics, and to remove the layer of interpretation that translates from the former to the latter.

The other main strength of functional programming is the tools it provides for *abstraction*: for defining 'embedded domain-specific languages' in terms of existing language constructs such as algebraic datatypes, higher-order functions, and lazy evaluation, rather than having to step outside the existing language to define a new one. In that respect, functional programming goes beyond predicative programming and refinement calculus, which are not expressive enough to support such extension. (Of course, embedded DSLs have their limits. Sometimes a desired feature cannot be defined conveniently, if at all, in terms of existing constructs; then the best approach is to relent and to define a new language after all.)

9.1 Nondeterminism and Probability in Program Calculi

Dijkstra [6] argued forcefully for the centrality of nondeterminism in programming calculi, particularly in order to support underspecification and program development by stepwise refinement. That impetus led to the development of the refinement calculus [37,1] for imperative programming. However, although functional programming is an excellent setting in which to calculate with programs, it does not support refinement well—for that, one has to make the step from functions to relations [3]. Nevertheless, functional programming is very convenient for manipulating collections of elements, and collection types such as lists and sets form monads; so collection-oriented programming does fit the functional view well [51,4].

Lawvere [27,11] pointed out that probability distributions form a monad too; this has led to a slow but steady stream of functional programming approaches to probabilistic computation [20,44,9,21]. Independently, Kozen [24] presented a semantics for while-programs with probabilistic choice; but it was a longstanding challenge to integrate this semantics with nondeterministic choice. There was a flurry of work in the early 1990s addressing this issue within the process algebra setting [55,29,39]. He *et al.* [12] used Jones' probabilistic powerdomain construction to provide a semantics for a guarded command language with both probabilistic and nondeterministic choice; in fact, they defined two semantics—one like ours, in which, operationally speaking, demonic nondeterminism is resolved at run-time whenever a nondeterministic choice is executed, and another in which nondeterminism is resolved at compile-time, but which sacrifices idempotence of conditional. The first of He *et al.*'s semantics is the basis of the 'demonic/probabilistic' approach taken by Morgan [31]. Varacca [49], citing a personal correspondence with Gordon Plotkin, shows that although the composition of the powerset and probability distribution monads do not directly form a monad, this is fixed by taking the convex closure—giving rise to essentially the model we have in Section 5.2.

The combination of nondeterminism and probability and the selection of distributivity properties that we have presented here are not new; they are fairly well established in work on program calculi [12,31,32,34]. Curiously, however, not all authors settle on the same distributivity properties; some [55,39] have nondeterministic choice distributing over probabilistic, the opposite of the approach we take. Choosing this law sacrifices the intuitively reasonable *arbcoin* example; by the same line of reasoning as in Section 5.2, one can show under this alternative distributivity regime that, for arbitrary w,

$$arbcoin\ v = (arb \triangleleft w \triangleright return\ False) \triangleleft w \triangleright (return\ True \triangleleft w \triangleright arb)$$

That is, with probability $w^2 + \overline{w}^2$ (independent of v!) the outcome is an arbitrary choice, and otherwise it is determined probabilistically. Worse, having nondeterministic choice distribute over probabilistic is inconsistent with idempotence—by similar reasoning again, using idempotence and commutativity of $\square$ and of $\triangleleft\triangleright$, and distributivity of $\square$ over $\triangleleft\triangleright$, one can show that

$$coin = coin \triangleleft {}^{1}\!/_{2} \triangleright arb$$

which seems a most unwelcome property: even a fair coin can be subverted. One might argue (as Mislove [35] does) that idempotence is a fundamental property of nondeterminism, and that this consequence for *coin* is untenable, and that therefore the alternative distributivity property should be avoided.

Similarly, Deng *et al.* [5] show that taking the perspective of testing equivalences on a probabilistic version of CSP—that is, attempting to distinguish two CSP processes by exhibiting different outcomes when they are each run in parallel with a common test process—eliminates many of the otherwise reasonable equivalences; in particular, they give counterexamples to either distributivity property between nondeterministic ('internal') and probabilistic choice; however, distributivity of CSP's 'external' choice over probabilistic choice does still survive.

However, we emphasize that our approach is agnostic as to the particular axiomatization. It is perfectly possible to impose distributivity of nondeterministic over probabilistic choice, obtaining the consequences for *arbcoin* and *coin* above; or to impose no distributivity law at all, in which case there are simply fewer program equivalences. The approach still works; whether it faithfully models intuition or reality is a separate question.

9.2 Beyond Finite Support

The approach we have presented here really only tells the story for finitely supported probability distributions. By exploiting recursive definitions, one might hope to be able to build distributions with infinite support; for example, with

$$\begin{array}{l} \mathit{naturals} :: \mathit{MonadProb}\ m \Rightarrow \mathit{Integer} \rightarrow m\ \mathit{Integer} \\ \mathit{naturals}\ n = \mathit{return}\ n \lhd 1/2 \rhd \mathit{naturals}\ (n+1) \end{array}$$

one might hope that *naturals* 0 returns result i with probability $1/2^{i+1}$, possibly returning any of the naturals. This works in a lazy language like Haskell, provided that the definition of $\lhd\rhd$ is non-strict in its right argument; for example, for an implementation based on possibly infinite weighted lists as in Section 8.1, it yields

$$[(0, 1/2), (1, 1/4), (2, 1/8), (3, 1/16), (4, 1/32), (5, 1/64), \ldots]$$

as expected. We are optimistic that the 'free monad' technique from Section 8.2 might be extended to give a more disciplined explanation of such cases. In related work [41], we have been using free monads to model a generic framework for tracing execution. In the case of nonterminating computations, one will in general get an infinite trace; to account for that case, one needs a coalgebraic rather than an algebraic reading of the tracing datatype. Perhaps this can all be conveniently captured in a 'strong functional programming' [48] or constructive type theory [33] setting, carefully distinguishing between terminating functions from algebraic datatypes and productive functions to coalgebraic codatatypes (in which case the constructions are technically no longer 'free' monads), or perhaps it really requires a shift from SET to CPO.

But none of these extensions will help when it comes to dealing with continuous probability distributions—say, a uniform choice among reals in the unit interval. Any particular real result will have probability zero; if represented using the free monad *DistT*, all the leaves will have to be infinitely deep in the tree, and no useful computation can be done. There is no fundamental reason why one cannot deal with such distributions; after all, continuous probability distributions form a monad too [27,11,20]. But it requires an approach based on measure theory and Lebesgue integrals rather than point masses: distributions must be represented as mappings from measurable sets of outcomes to probabilities, rather than from individual outcomes. We leave this for future work.

For both reasons—possible nontermination and continuous distributions—the lightweight, embedded approach of unifying the 'syntactic' programming notation with the 'semantic' reasoning framework, which is one of the great appeals of functional programming, has its limitations. An approach that separates syntax and semantics pays the cost of two distinct domains of discourse, but does not suffer from the same limitation.

9.3 Lawvere Theories

The axiomatic approach to reasoning about effectful functional programs that we have used here derives from our earlier paper [10]. It should come as no surprise that algebraic theories—consisting of a signature for the operations, together with laws that the operations are required to satisfy, but abstracting away from specific models of the theory—are convenient for equational reasoning about programs; after all, algebraic specifications have long been espoused as a useful technique for isloating the interface of a module from its possible implementations, separating the concerns of the module provider and consumer [7].

What did come as a surprise, at least to us, was that computational effects such as nondeterminism and probabilistic choice are amenable to algebraic specifications. But history [19] tells us that this is only to be expected: algebraic theories were introduced in Lawvere's PhD thesis [26] as a category-theoretic formulation of universal algebra; Linton [28] showed the equivalence between such 'Lawvere theories' and monads (every Lawvere theory has a category of models that is isomorphic to the category of algebras of some monad, unique up to isomorphism), which arise as adjoint pairs of functors [8,22]; and Moggi [36] and Wadler [54] showed that monads are precisely what is needed to encapsulate effects in pure functional languages. Indeed, this is precisely how impure effects are implemented in a pure functional programming language such as Haskell: pure evaluation is used to construct a term in the algebraic theory, which is subsequently interpreted—with possible side-effects—by the impure run-time system. In some ways, the algebraic theory approach to effects is more appealing than the monadic approach, since it places the additional operations and their properties front and centre; nevertheless, monads and Haskell's **do** notation do provide a rather elegant programming notation.

On the other hand, not all the additional operations we have discussed technically fit into the algebraic theory framework. Specifically, the bind operator $\gg\!=$ should distribute over every such operation [42], as for example it does over probabilistic choice:

$$\textbf{do}\ \{x \leftarrow (p \lhd w \rhd q)\ ; k\ x\} = \textbf{do}\ \{x \leftarrow p\ ; k\ x\} \lhd w \rhd \textbf{do}\ \{x \leftarrow q\ ; k\ x\}$$

But as we saw in Section 7, bind does not distribute over *catch*. Plotkin and Pretnar [43] call operations like *catch* 'effect handlers'; they are not 'algebraic effects', and need a different treatment.

Acknowledgements. We are grateful to members of the *Algebra of Programming* research group at Oxford and of IFIP Working Groups 2.1 and 2.8, and to the referees of this and the earlier paper [10], all of whom have made helpful suggestions. Nicolas Wu suggested the subsequences example in Section 3.1, and Ralf Hinze provide much useful advice. This work was supported by the UK EPSRC grant *Reusability and Dependent Types*.

References

1. Back, R.J., von Wright, J.: Refinement Calculus: A Systematic Introduction. Springer (1998), graduate Texts in Computer Science
2. Beck, J.: Distributive laws. In: Seminar on Triples and Categorical Homology Theory. Lecture Notes in Mathematics, vol. 80, pp. 119–140. Springer (1969)
3. Bird, R., de Moor, O.: Algebra of Programming. Prentice-Hall (1997)
4. Dean, J., Ghemawat, S.: MapReduce: Simplified data processing on large clusters. In: Operating Systems Design & Implementation, pp. 137–150. USENIX Association (2004)
5. Deng, Y., van Glabbeek, R., Hennessy, M., Morgan, C., Zhang, C.: Remarks on testing probabilistic processes. Electronic Notes in Theoretical Computer Science 172, 359–397 (2007)
6. Dijkstra, E.W.: A Discipline of Programming. Prentice-Hall Series in Automatic Computation. Prentice-Hall (1976)
7. Ehrig, H., Mahr, B.: Fundamentals of Algebraic Specification. Springer (1985)
8. Eilenberg, S., Moore, J.C.: Adjoint functors and triples. Illinois Journal of Mathematics, 381–398 (1965)
9. Erwig, M., Kollmansberger, S.: Probabilistic functional programming in Haskell. Journal of Functional Programming 16(1), 21–34 (2006)
10. Gibbons, J., Hinze, R.: Just do it: Simple monadic equational reasoning. In: Danvy, O. (ed.) International Conference on Functional Programming, pp. 2–14. ACM, New York (2011)
11. Giry, M.: A categorical approach to probability theory. In: Categorical Aspects of Topology and Analysis. Lecture Notes in Mathematics, vol. 915, pp. 68–85. Springer (1981)
12. He, J., Seidel, K., McIver, A.: Probabilistic models for the Guarded Command Language. Science of Computer Programming 28, 171–192 (1997)
13. Hehner, E.C.R.: Predicative programming, parts I and II. Communications of the ACM 27(2), 134–151 (1984)
14. Hinze, R.: Deriving backtracking monad transformers. In: International Conference on Functional Programming, pp. 186–197 (2000)
15. Hoare, C.A.R.: A couple of novelties in the propositional calculus. Zeitschrift für mathematische Logik und Grundlagen der Mathematik 31(2), 173–178 (1985)
16. Hoare, C.A.R., Hanna, F.K.: Programs are predicates. Philosophical Transactions of the Royal Society, Part A 312(1522), 475–489 (1984)

17. Hoare, C.A.R., He, J.: Unifying Theories of Programming. Prentice Hall (1998)
18. Hutton, G., Fulger, D.: Reasoning about effects: Seeing the wood through the trees. In: Preproceedings of Trends in Functional Programming (May 2008)
19. Hyland, M., Power, J.: The category theoretic understanding of universal algebra: Lawvere theories and monads. Electronic Notes in Theoretical Computer Science 172, 437–458 (2007)
20. Jones, C., Plotkin, G.: A probabilistic powerdomain of evaluations. In: Logic in Computer Science, pp. 186–195 (1989)
21. Kiselyov, O., Shan, C.-c.: Embedded Probabilistic Programming. In: Taha, W.M. (ed.) DSL 2009. LNCS, vol. 5658, pp. 360–384. Springer, Heidelberg (2009)
22. Kleisli, H.: Every standard construction is induced by a pair of adjoint functors. Proceedings of the American Mathematical Society 16, 544–546 (1965)
23. Knuth, D.E., Yao, A.C.C.: The complexity of nonuniform random number generation. In: Traub, J.F. (ed.) Algorithms and Complexity: New Directions and Recent Results, pp. 357–428. Academic Press (1976); reprinted in Selected Papers on Analysis of Algorithms (CSLI 2000)
24. Kozen, D.: Semantics of probabilistic programs. J. Comput. Syst. Sci. 22, 328–350 (1981)
25. Launchbury, J.: Lazy imperative programming. In: ACM SIGPLAN Workshop on State in Programming Languages (June 1993)
26. Lawvere, F.W.: Functorial Semantics of Algebraic Theories. Ph.D. thesis, Columbia University, also available with commentary as Theory and Applications of Categories Reprint 5 (1963), `http://www.tac.mta.ca/tac/reprints/articles/5/tr5abs.html`
27. Lawvere, F.W.: The category of probabilistic mappings (1962) (preprint)
28. Linton, F.E.J.: Some aspects of equational theories. In: Categorical Algebra, pp. 84–95. Springer, La Jolla (1966)
29. Lowe, G.: Representing nondeterministic and probabilistic behaviour in reactive processes (1993) (manuscript) Oxford University Computing Laboratory
30. Mac Lane, S.: Categories for the Working Mathematician. Springer (1971)
31. McIver, A., Morgan, C.: Abstraction, Refinement and Proof for Probabilistic Systems. Springer (2005)
32. McIver, A.K., Weber, T.: Towards Automated Proof Support for Probabilistic Distributed Systems. In: Sutcliffe, G., Voronkov, A. (eds.) LPAR 2005. LNCS (LNAI), vol. 3835, pp. 534–548. Springer, Heidelberg (2005)
33. McKinna, J.: Why dependent types matter. In: Principles of Programming Languages, p. 1. ACM (2006), full paper available at, `http://www.cs.nott.ac.uk/~txa/publ/ydtm.pdf`
34. Meinicke, L., Solin, K.: Refinement algebra for probabilistic programs. Formal Aspects of Computing 22, 3–31 (2010)
35. Mislove, M.W.: Nondeterminism and Probabilistic Choice: Obeying the Laws. In: Palamidessi, C. (ed.) CONCUR 2000. LNCS, vol. 1877, pp. 350–364. Springer, Heidelberg (2000)
36. Moggi, E.: Notions of computation and monads. Information and Computation 93(1) (1991)
37. Morgan, C.: Programming from Specifications, 2nd edn. Prentice-Hall (1994)
38. Morgan, C.: Elementary Probability Theory in the Eindhoven Style. In: Gibbons, J., Nogueira, P. (eds.) MPC 2012. LNCS, vol. 7342, pp. 48–73. Springer, Heidelberg (2012)
39. Morgan, C., McIver, A., Seidel, K., Sanders, J.W.: Refinement-oriented probability for CSP. Formal Aspects of Computing 8(6), 617–647 (1996)

40. Peyton Jones, S.: Tackling the awkward squad: Monadic input/output, concurrency, exceptions, and foreign-language calls in Haskell. In: Hoare, T., Broy, M., Steinbruggen, R. (eds.) Engineering Theories of Software Construction, pp. 47–96. IOS Press (2001)
41. Piróg, M., Gibbons, J.: Tracing monadic computations and representing effects. In: Mathematically Structured Functional Programming (March 2012)
42. Plotkin, G., Power, J.: Notions of Computation Determine Monads. In: Nielsen, M., Engberg, U. (eds.) FOSSACS 2002. LNCS, vol. 2303, pp. 342–356. Springer, Heidelberg (2002)
43. Plotkin, G., Pretnar, M.: Handlers of Algebraic Effects. In: Castagna, G. (ed.) ESOP 2009. LNCS, vol. 5502, pp. 80–94. Springer, Heidelberg (2009)
44. Ramsey, N., Pfeffer, A.: Stochastic lambda calculus and monads of probability distributions. In: Principles of Programming Languages, pp. 154–165 (2002)
45. Rosenhouse, J.: The Monty Hall Problem: The Remarkable Story of Math's Most Contentious Brain Teaser. Oxford University Press (2009)
46. Spivey, M.: A functional theory of exceptions. Science of Computer Programming 14, 25–42 (1990)
47. Spivey, M., Seres, S.: Combinators for logic programming. In: Gibbons, J., de Moor, O. (eds.) The Fun of Programming, pp. 177–200. Cornerstones in Computing, Palgrave (2003)
48. Turner, D.A.: Total functional programming. Journal of Universal Computer Science 10(7), 751–768 (2004)
49. Varacca, D., Winskel, G.: Distributing probability over nondeterminism. Mathematical Structures in Computer Science 16, 87–113 (2006)
50. Vos Savant, M.: Ask Marilyn. Parade Magazine (September 9th, 1990), `http://www.marilynvossavant.com/articles/gameshow.html`
51. Wadler, P.: How to Replace Failure by a List of Successes: A Method for Exception Handling, Backtracking, and Pattern Matching in Lazy Functional Languages. In: Jouannaud, J.-P. (ed.) FPCA 1985. LNCS, vol. 201, pp. 113–128. Springer, Heidelberg (1985), `http://dx.doi.org/10.1007/3-540-15975-4_33`
52. Wadler, P.: Theorems for free? In: Functional Programming Languages and Computer Architecture, pp. 347–359. ACM (1989), `http://doi.acm.org/10.1145/99370.99404`
53. Wadler, P.: Comprehending monads. Mathematical Structures in Computer Science 2(4), 461–493 (1992)
54. Wadler, P.: Monads for functional programming. In: Broy, M. (ed.) Program Design Calculi: Proceedings of the Marktoberdorf Summer School (1992)
55. Yi, W., Larsen, K.G.: Testing probabilistic and nondeterministic processes. In: Linn Jr., R.J., Uyar, M.Ü. (eds.) Protocol Specification, Testing and Verification, pp. 47–61. North-Holland (1992)

Circus Time with Reactive Designs

Kun Wei, Jim Woodcock, and Ana Cavalcanti

Department of Computer Science, University of York, York, YO10 5GH, UK
{kun.wei,jim.woodcock,ana.cavalcanti}@york.ac.uk

Abstract. The UTP theories for CSP and *Circus* can be built by the combination of the theories of designs and reactive processes. Defining the CSP operators using reactive design provides a more concise, readable and uniform UTP semantics, and, more importantly, exposes the pre-postcondition semantics of the operators. For *Circus Time*, a few operators have been defined as reactive designs, but some important operators are still be considered. In this paper, we develop the reactive design semantics of sequential composition, hiding and recursion within *Circus Time*, and show how to prove some subtle laws using the new semantics.

Keywords: Circus Time, UTP, reactive designs.

1 Introduction

Circus [3,17,18] is a comprehensive combination of Z [15], CSP [5,10] and Morgan's refinement calculus [8], so that it can define both data and behavioural aspects of a system. Over the years, *Circus* has developed into a family of languages for specification, programming and verification. *Circus Time* is an extension of a subset of *Circus* with some time operators added to the notion of actions in *Circus*. The semantics of *Circus Time* is defined using the UTP by introducing time observation variables. The *Circus Time* UTP theory is a discrete time model, and time operators are very similar to that in Timed CSP [11]. Compared to the original *Circus Time* [12] and Timed CSP, we have recently developed a new version of *Circus Time* [13] that provides more time operators such as deadlines. Using various languages in the *Circus* family, we have proposed an approach in [1] for stepwise development of safety-critical Java programs [7]. In the new *Circus Time* theory, besides some new time operators, each action is expressed as a reactive design for a more concise, readable and uniform UTP semantics. In the UTP, Hoare and He provide many sub-theories by adopting different healthiness conditions. For example, the theory of designs can describe some sequential programming languages, and the theory of reactive processes allows communications between processes. The theory of CSP is traditionally built upon the theory of reactive processes by imposing extra healthiness conditions. However, there is no uniform pattern of the semantics for CSP primitive processes and various operators. Hoare and He have, however, proposed an approach to generate the theory of CSP by embedding the theory of designs in the theory of reactive processes. This means that each process in CSP can be expressed as a reactive design. The importance of this semantics is that it exposes the pre-postcondition semantics.

B. Wolff, M.-C. Gaudel, A. Feliachi (Eds.): UTP 2012, LNCS 7681, pp. 68–87, 2013.

The work in [2,9] have provided the reactive design semantics to some operators in CSP. On the other hand, sequential composition, recursion, hiding and so on are still to be considered. In this paper, based on our new *Circus Time* model, we develop the reactive design semantics of these operators in a timed environment, and also demonstrate how we can easily to prove some very tricky laws using the new semantics. This paper has the following structure. Section 2 gives a brief introduction to *Circus Time* and related UTP theories. We show how to deduce the reactive design semantics of those operators from their original UTP definitions in Section 3. We then give a demonstration to show how to prove some algebraic laws using the new semantics in Section 4. Finally in Section 5 we present some conclusions and summarize future work. We assume knowledge of CSP.

2 UTP and *Circus Time*

In the UTP, a relation P is a predicate with an alphabet αP, composed of *undashed* variables $(a, b, ...)$ and *dashed* variables $(a', x', ...)$. The former, written as $in\alpha P$, stands for initial observations, and the latter, $out\alpha P$, for intermediate or final observations. The relation is then called *homogeneous* if $out\alpha P = in\alpha P'$, where $in\alpha P'$ is simply obtained by putting a dash on all the variables of $in\alpha P$. A *condition* has an empty output alphabet.

The program constructors in the theory of relations include sequential composition $(P \,;\, Q)$, conditional $(P \lhd b \rhd Q)$, assignment $(x := e)$, non-determinism $(P \sqcap Q)$ and recursion $(\mu X \bullet C(X))$. The correctness of a program P with respect to a specification S is denoted by $S \sqsubseteq P$ (P refines S), and is defined as follows:

$$S \sqsubseteq P \textit{ iff } [P \Rightarrow S]$$

where the square bracket is universal quantification over all variables in the alphabet. In other words, the correctness of P is proved by establishing that every observation that satisfies P must also satisfy S. Moreover, the set of relations with a particular alphabet is a complete lattice under the refinement ordering. Its bottom element is the weakest relation **true**, which behaves arbitrarily $([\mathbf{true} \sqsubseteq P])$, and the top element is the strongest relation **false**, which behaves miraculously and satisfies any specification $([P \sqsubseteq \mathbf{false}])$. The bottom and top elements in this complete lattice are usually called **CHAOS** and **Miracle** respectively.

2.1 Designs

A design in the UTP is a relation that can be expressed as a pre-postcondition pair in combination with a boolean variable, called *ok*. In designs, *ok* records that the program has started, and *ok′* records that it has terminated. If a precondition

P and a postcondition Q are predicates, a design with P and Q, written as $P \vdash Q$, is defined as follows:

$$P \vdash Q \mathrel{\widehat=} ok \land P \Rightarrow ok' \land Q$$

which means that if a program starts in a state satisfying P, then it must terminate, and whenever it terminates, it must satisfy Q.

Healthiness conditions of a theory in the UTP are a collection of some fundamental laws that must be satisfied by relations belonging to the theory. These laws are expressed in terms of monotonic idempotent functions. The healthy relations are the fixed points of these functions. There are four healthiness conditions identified by Hoare and He in the theory of designs and here we introduce only two of them.

$$\mathbf{H1} \quad P = ok \Rightarrow P \qquad \mathbf{H2} \quad [P[false/ok'] \Rightarrow P[true/ok']]$$

The first healthiness means that observations of a predicate P can only be made after the program has started. **H2** states that a design cannot require non-termination, since if P is satisfied when ok' is false, it must also be satisfied when ok' is true. A predicate is **H1** and **H2** if, and only if, it is a design; the proof is in [6]. A useful law about designs, which is used later, is given as below.

Law 1. *Suppose P and Q are predicates and b is a condition,*

$$((P_1 \vdash P_2) \lhd b \rhd (Q_1 \vdash Q_2)) = ((P_1 \lhd b \rhd Q_1) \vdash (P_2 \lhd b \rhd Q_2))$$

This states that conditionals distribute through designs. A proof of this law can be found in [6].

The purpose of the theory of designs is to exclude relations that do not satisfy the zero laws, $\mathbf{true}\,; P = \mathbf{true} = P\,; \mathbf{true}$. For example, the relations that satisfy the equation $\mathbf{true}\,; P = P$ should not be included in the theory of designs. The program **true** behaves arbitrarily. For instance, the least fixed-point semantics of a non-terminating loop in the theory of relations is **true**, and it, when followed by an assignment like $x := c$, behaves like the assignment. In practice, it means that a program can recover from the non-terminating loop. For a tutorial introduction to designs, the reader is referred to [6,16].

2.2 Reactive Processes

A reactive process in the UTP is a program whose behaviour may depend on interactions with its environment. To represent intermediate waiting states, a boolean variable *wait* is introduced to the alphabet of a reactive process. For example, if $wait'$ is true, then the process is in an intermediate state. If *wait* is true, it denotes an intermediate observation of its predecessor. Thus, we are able to represent any states of a process by combining the values of *ok* and *wait*. If ok' is false, the process diverges. If ok' is true, the state of the process depends on the value of $wait'$. If $wait'$ is true, the process is in an intermediate state; otherwise it has successfully terminated. Similarly, the values of undashed variables represent the states of a process's predecessor.

Apart from ok, ok', $wait$ and $wait'$, another two pairs of observational variables, tr and ref, and their dashed counterparts, are introduced. The variable tr records the events that have occurred until the last observation, and tr' contains all the events until the next observation. Similarly, ref records the set of events that could be refused in the last observation, and ref' records the set of events that may be refused in the next observation. The reactive identity, $I\!I_{rea}$, is defined as follows:

$$I\!I_{rea} \mathrel{\widehat=} (\neg\, ok \wedge tr \le tr') \vee (ok' \wedge wait' = wait \wedge tr' = tr \wedge ref' = ref)$$

As a result, a reactive process must satisfy the following healthiness conditions:

R1 $P = P \wedge tr \le tr'$
R2 $P(tr, tr') = P(\langle\rangle, tr' - tr)$
R3 $P = I\!I_{rea} \lhd wait \rhd P$

If a relation P describes a reactive process behaviour, **R1** states that it never changes history, or the trace is always increasing. The second, **R2**, states that the history of the trace tr has no influence on the behaviour of the process. The final, **R3**, requires that a process should leave the state unchanged ($I\!I_{rea}$) if it is in a waiting state ($wait = true$) of its predecessor. A reactive process is a relation whose alphabet includes ok, $wait$, tr and ref, and their dashed counterparts, and that satisfies the composition **R** where $\mathbf{R} \mathrel{\widehat=} \mathbf{R1} \circ \mathbf{R2} \circ \mathbf{R3}$. In other words, a process P is a reactive process if, and only if, it is a fixed point of **R**. Since each of $\mathbf{R}i$ is idempotent and any two of them commuted, **R** is also idempotent. For a more detailed introduction to the theory of reactive designs, the reader is referred to the tutorial [2].

2.3 CSP Processes

In the UTP, the theory of CSP is built by applying extra healthiness conditions to reactive processes. For example, a reactive process is also a CSP process if and only if, it satisfies the following healthiness conditions:

CSP1 $P = P \vee (\neg\, ok \wedge tr \le tr')$ **CSP2** $P = P\, ;\, J$

where $J = (ok \Rightarrow ok') \wedge wait' = wait \wedge tr' = tr \wedge ref' = ref$. The first healthiness condition requires that, in case of divergence of the predecessor, the extension of the trace and should be the only guaranteed property. The second one means that P cannot require non-termination, so that it is always possible to terminate. The CSP theory introduced in the UTP book is different from any standard models of CSP [5,10] which have more restrictions or satisfy more healthiness conditions. There are more healthiness conditions, **CSP3-CSP5**, given in UTP to further restrict behaviours of reactive processes.

A CSP process can also be obtained by applying the healthiness condition **R** to a design. This follows from the theorem in [6], that, for every CSP process P, $P = \mathbf{R}(\neg P^f_f \vdash P^t_f)$. This theorem gives a new style of specification for CSP processes in which a design describes the behaviour when its predecessor has terminated and not diverged, and the other situations of its behaviour are left to **R**. Note that P^a_b is an abbreviation of $P[a, b / ok', wait]$, and it is often used in this paper. Motivated by the above theorem, the work in [2,9] provide reactive design definitions for some constructs of CSP such as $STOP$, $SKIP$, $CHAOS$, external choice, and so on. The reactive design definitions of more operators, such as sequential composition, hiding and recursion, will be developed in this paper.

2.4 *Circus Time*

We give a brief introduction to *Circus Time* because the reactive design semantics is developed within this timed model presented in this paper. In *Circus Time*, an action is described as an alphabetised predicate whose observational variables include ok, $wait$, tr, ref, $state$ and their dashed counterparts.

- $ok, ok' : Boolean$
- $wait, wait' : Boolean$
- $state, state' : N \nrightarrow Value$
- $tr, tr' : seq^+(seq\ Event)$
- $ref, ref' : seq^+(\mathbb{P}\ Event)$

Here, ok, ok', $wait$ and $wait'$ are the same variables used in the theory of reactive processes. The traces, tr and tr', are defined to be non-empty (seq^+), and each element in the trace represents a sequence of events that have occurred over one time unit. Also, ref and ref' are non-empty sequences where each element is a refusal at the end of a time unit. Thus, time is actually hidden in the length of traces. In addition, $state$ and $state'$ records a set of local variables and their values. N is a set of names of these variables.

Both the original *Circus Time* and Timed CSP use the concept of failures, each of which consists of a trace and a refusal. This structure, however, is hard to manipulate: a trace is no longer a sequence of events, but a sequence of pairs containing a sequence of events and a refusal set. In the new *Circus Time* model, we split a failure as shown above to record sequences of traces and a refusals, and use their indices (which start at 1) to match related pairs. However, the decomposition of the failures results in a little bit inconvenience, since we have to ensure the equality of the lengths of tr and ref, or tr' and ref'. This is achieved by imposing an extra constraint on the healthiness conditions.

Although a trace in the new model is a sequence of sequences, the standard operations on sequences defined in Z can still be used here such as $head$, $tail$, $front$, $last$, $\#$(length), $^\frown$(concatenation), $^\frown/$(flattening), $-$(difference) and $\leq$(prefix). Additionally, it is unnecessary that $last(tr) = tr'(\#tr)$. An expanding relation between traces is defined as follows, requiring that $front(tr)$ and $last(tr)$ are the prefixes of tr' and $tr'(\#tr)$ respectively.

$$tr \preccurlyeq tr' \mathrel{\widehat{=}} front(tr) \leq tr' \land last(tr) \leq tr'(\#tr) \tag{1}$$

An action in *Circus Time* must satisfy the healthiness conditions, $\mathbf{R1_t}$-$\mathbf{R3_t}$ and $\mathbf{CSP1_t}$-$\mathbf{CSP5_t}$. These healthiness conditions have similar meanings as those in the CSP theory, but are changed to accommodate discrete time. For the sake of a simpler proof, we focus on the healthiness conditions, $\mathbf{R1_t}$ and $\mathbf{R3_t}$, as follows (the properties including other healthiness conditions are usually straightforward to be proven). The detailed introduction to other healthiness conditions can be found in [13].

$$\mathbf{R1_t}(X) \mathrel{\widehat{=}} X \land RT \qquad \mathbf{R3_t}(X) \mathrel{\widehat{=}} I\!I_t \lhd wait \rhd X$$

where the predicate RT, $I\!I^{-ok}$ (the identity without ok) and the timed reactive identity $I\!I_t$ are given as

$$RT \mathrel{\widehat{=}} tr \preccurlyeq tr' \land front(ref) \leq ref' \land \#diff(tr', tr) = \#(ref' - front(ref))$$
$$I\!I^{-ok} \mathrel{\widehat{=}} \big(tr' = tr \land front(ref') = front(ref) \land wait' = wait \land state' = state\big)$$
$$I\!I_t \mathrel{\widehat{=}} (\neg\, ok \land RT) \lor (ok' \land I\!I^{-ok})$$

Note that we impose a restriction, $\#ref' = \#tr'$ and $\#ref = \#tr$, to ensure that the lengths of ref and ref' are always the same as those of tr and tr' respectively. This is a consequence of splitting traces and refusals as already explained. Rather than recording the refusals only at the end of traces in CSP, *Circus Time* records the refusals at the end of each time unit. In other words, we need to keep the history of refusals. However, we are usually not interested in the refusals of the last time unit after an action terminates. Therefore, we use $front(ref) \leq ref'$ and $front(ref') = front(ref)$ in these healthiness conditions, instead of $ref \leq ref'$ and $ref' = ref$ because we have to maintain the consistency among $\mathbf{R_t} \mathrel{\widehat{=}} \mathbf{R1_t} \circ \mathbf{R2_t} \circ \mathbf{R3_t}$ and $\mathbf{CSP1_t}$-$\mathbf{CSP5_t}$. In addition, by means of a result in [13], each action in *Circus Time* can also be described as a reactive design.

Theorem 1. *For every action P in Circus Time,*

$$P = \mathbf{R_t}(\neg\, P^f_f \vdash P^t_f)$$

Another useful law about $\mathbf{R1_t}$, which is used later, is given and its detailed proof can be found in [13].

Law 2

$$\mathbf{R1_t}(P \lor Q) = \mathbf{R1_t}(P) \lor \mathbf{R1_t}(Q)$$

The full syntax, definitions and detailed explanations of *Circus Time* can be found in [13]. Here, we briefly introduce some operators that are used in the following sections. The action *Skip* terminates immediately without changing anything,

Chaos is the worst action (the bottom element in the refinement ordering) whose behaviour is arbitrary, but satisfies $\mathbf{R_t}$. The action *Miracle* is the top element that expresses an unstarted process. This action is not included in the standard failures-divergences model of CSP. The definition and properties of *Miracle* are discussed in Section 4. The delay action $Wait\ d$ does nothing except that it requires d time units to elapse before it terminates. The sequential composition $P;\ Q$ behaves like P until P terminates, and then behaves as Q. The prefix action $c.e \rightarrow P$ is usually constructed by a composition of a simple prefix and P itself, written as $(c.e \rightarrow Skip);\ P$. The hiding action $P \setminus CS$ will behave like P, but the events within the set CS become invisible. The recursive action $\mu X \bullet P$ behaves like P with every occurrence of the variable X in P representing a recursive invocation. The recursive call takes no time.

3 Reactive Designs for *Circus Time*

In this section, we calculate the reactive design semantics of sequential composition, hiding and recursion from their original UTP semantics (which have been slightly changed to contain time) in terms of Theorem 1.

3.1 Sequential Composition

The definition of sequential composition in the UTP is given as follows:

$$P;\ Q \mathrel{\widehat=} \exists\, obs_0 \bullet P[obs_0/obs'] \wedge Q[obs_0/obs]$$

To deduce the reactive design of sequential composition, we first give some auxiliary laws that have been proven in [13].

Law 3. *Suppose P is $\mathbf{R1_t}$ and $\mathbf{CSP1_t}$,*

$$\mathbf{R1_t}(\neg\, ok)\,;\, P = \mathbf{R1_t}(\neg\, ok)$$

Law 4. *Suppose P is a predicate and Q is $\mathbf{R1_t}$ and $\mathbf{R3_t}$,*

$$\mathbf{R3_t}(P)\,;\, Q = \mathbf{R3_t}(P\,;\, Q)$$

Below, we characterise the behaviour of the sequential composition of two $\mathbf{R1_t}$-healthy predicates.

Law 5. *Suppose P, Q, R and S are predicates (ok,ok' are not in αP, αQ, αR and αS),*

$$\mathbf{R1_t}(P \vdash Q)\;;\;\mathbf{R1_t}(R \vdash S) = \mathbf{R1_t}\left(\begin{array}{c}\neg\,(\mathbf{R1_t}(\neg\, P)\,;\,\mathbf{R1_t}(true)) \wedge \neg\,(\mathbf{R1_t}(Q)\,;\,\mathbf{R1_t}(\neg\, R)) \\ \vdash \\ \mathbf{R1_t}(Q)\,;\,\mathbf{R1_t}(S)\end{array}\right)$$

Proof

$$
\begin{array}{lr}
\mathbf{R1_t}(P \vdash Q) \mathbin{;} \mathbf{R1_t}(R \vdash S) & [\text{def of design}] \\
= \mathbf{R1_t}(\neg\, ok \lor \neg\, P \lor (ok' \land Q)) \mathbin{;} \mathbf{R1_t}(\neg\, ok \lor \neg\, R \lor (ok' \land S)) & \\
 & [\text{Law 2 and rel. cal.}] \\
= \mathbf{R1_t}(\neg\, ok) \mathbin{;} \mathbf{R1_t}(\neg\, ok \lor \neg\, R \lor (ok' \land S)) \lor & [\text{Law 3}] \\
\quad \mathbf{R1_t}(\neg\, P) \mathbin{;} \mathbf{R1_t}(\neg\, ok \lor \neg\, R \lor (ok' \land S)) \lor & \\
\quad \mathbf{R1_t}(ok' \land Q) \mathbin{;} \mathbf{R1_t}(\neg\, ok \lor \neg\, R \lor (ok' \land S)) & \\
= \mathbf{R1_t}(\neg\, ok) \lor \mathbf{R1_t}(\neg\, P) \mathbin{;} R1_t(\neg\, ok \lor \neg\, R \lor (ok' \land S)) \lor & \\
\quad \mathbf{R1_t}(ok' \land Q) \mathbin{;} \mathbf{R1_t}(\neg\, ok \lor \neg\, R \lor (ok' \land S)) & \\
 & [\text{def of ; and case split on } ok] \\
= \mathbf{R1_t}(\neg\, ok) \lor & [\text{propositional calculus}] \\
\quad \mathbf{R1_t}(\neg\, P)[false/ok'] \mathbin{;} \mathbf{R1_t}(\neg\, ok \lor \neg\, R \lor (ok' \land S))[false/ok] \lor & \\
\quad \mathbf{R1_t}(\neg\, P)[true/ok'] \mathbin{;} \mathbf{R1_t}(\neg\, ok \lor \neg\, R \lor (ok' \land S))[true/ok] \lor & \\
\quad \mathbf{R1_t}(ok' \land Q) \mathbin{;} \mathbf{R1_t}(\neg\, ok \lor \neg\, R \lor (ok' \land S)) & \\
= \mathbf{R1_t}(\neg\, ok) \lor \mathbf{R1_t}(\neg\, P) \mathbin{;} \mathbf{R1_t}(true) \lor & [\text{rel. calculus and Law 2}] \\
\quad \mathbf{R1_t}(\neg\, P) \mathbin{;} \mathbf{R1_t}(\neg\, R \lor (ok' \land S)) \lor & \\
\quad \mathbf{R1_t}(ok' \land Q) \mathbin{;} \mathbf{R1_t}(\neg\, ok \lor \neg\, R \lor (ok' \land S)) & \\
= \mathbf{R1_t}(\neg\, ok) \lor \mathbf{R1_t}(\neg\, P) \mathbin{;} \mathbf{R1_t}(true) \lor & [\text{propositional calculus}] \\
\quad \mathbf{R1_t}(ok' \land Q) \mathbin{;} \mathbf{R1_t}(\neg\, ok \lor \neg\, R \lor (ok' \land S)) & \\
= \mathbf{R1_t}(\neg\, ok) \lor \mathbf{R1_t}(\neg\, P) \mathbin{;} \mathbf{R1_t}(true) \lor & [\text{rel. calculus and Law 2}] \\
\quad \mathbf{R1_t}(ok' \land Q) \mathbin{;} \mathbf{R1_t}(\neg\, ok \lor (ok \land \neg\, R) \lor (ok \land ok' \land S)) & \\
= \mathbf{R1_t}(\neg\, ok) \lor & [\text{def of ;}] \\
\quad \mathbf{R1_t}(\neg\, P) \mathbin{;} \mathbf{R1_t}(true) \lor \mathbf{R1_t}(ok' \land Q) \mathbin{;} \mathbf{R1_t}(\neg\, ok) \lor & \\
\quad \mathbf{R1_t}(ok' \land Q) \mathbin{;} \mathbf{R1_t}(ok \land \neg\, R) \lor \mathbf{R1_t}(ok' \land Q) \mathbin{;} \mathbf{R1_t}(ok \land ok' \land S) & \\
= \mathbf{R1_t}(\neg\, ok) \lor & [\text{Law 2 and prop. calculus}] \\
\quad \mathbf{R1_t}(\neg\, P) \mathbin{;} \mathbf{R1_t}(true) \lor \mathbf{R1_t}(ok' \land Q) \mathbin{;} \mathbf{R1_t}(\neg\, ok) \lor & \\
\quad \mathbf{R1_t}(Q) \mathbin{;} \mathbf{R1_t}(ok \land \neg\, R) \lor \mathbf{R1_t}(Q) \mathbin{;} \mathbf{R1_t}(ok \land ok' \land S) & \\
= \mathbf{R1_t}(\neg\, ok) \lor & [\text{def of ;}] \\
\quad \mathbf{R1_t}(\neg\, P) \mathbin{;} \mathbf{R1_t}(true) \lor \mathbf{R1_t}(ok' \land Q) \mathbin{;} \mathbf{R1_t}(\neg\, ok) \lor & \\
\quad \mathbf{R1_t}(Q) \mathbin{;} \mathbf{R1_t}(\neg\, R) \lor \mathbf{R1_t}(Q) \mathbin{;} \mathbf{R1_t}(ok' \land S) & \\
= \mathbf{R1_t}(\neg\, ok) \lor \mathbf{R1_t}(\neg\, P) \mathbin{;} \mathbf{R1_t}(true) \lor false \lor & [\text{rel. calculus}] \\
\quad \mathbf{R1_t}(Q) \mathbin{;} \mathbf{R1_t}(\neg\, R) \lor \mathbf{R1_t}(Q) \mathbin{;} \mathbf{R1_t}(ok' \land S) & \\
= \mathbf{R1_t}(\neg\, ok) \lor \mathbf{R1_t}(\neg\, P) \mathbin{;} \mathbf{R1_t}(true) \lor & [\text{def of design}] \\
\quad \mathbf{R1_t}(Q) \mathbin{;} \mathbf{R1_t}(\neg\, R) \lor (ok' \land (\mathbf{R1_t}(Q) \mathbin{;} \mathbf{R1_t}(S))) & \\
= \mathbf{R1_t}\left(\begin{array}{c} \neg\, (\mathbf{R1_t}(\neg\, P) \mathbin{;} \mathbf{R1_t}(true)) \land \neg\, (\mathbf{R1_t}(Q) \mathbin{;} \mathbf{R1_t}(\neg\, R)) \vdash \\ \mathbf{R1_t}(Q) \mathbin{;} \mathbf{R1_t}(S) \end{array} \right) &
\end{array}
$$

However, the timed reactive identity $I\!I_t$ is not a design, and hence $\mathbf{R3_t}(P)$ is not, even if P is a design. Therefore, Woodcock in [14] introduces a new healthiness condition to replace **R3**, in order to make a design behave like the identity design when waiting. And here we have a similar healthiness condition, $\mathbf{R3j_t}(P) \mathrel{\widehat{=}} I\!I_D \lhd wait \rhd P$ where $I\!I_D = true \vdash I\!I$. We also have a useful law about the new healthiness condition whose proof can be found in [13].

Law 6

$$\mathbf{R1_t} \circ \mathbf{R3j_t} = \mathbf{R1_t} \circ \mathbf{R3_t}$$

Finally, we are ready to deduce the reactive design of sequential composition from its original definition.

Theorem 2. *Suppose P and Q are two Circus Time actions,*

$$P\,;\,Q = \mathbf{R_t}\left(\begin{array}{c}\neg\,(\mathbf{R1_t}(P_f^f)\,;\,\mathbf{R1_t}(true)) \wedge \neg\,(\mathbf{R1_t}(P_f^t)\,;\,\mathbf{R1_t}(\neg\,wait \wedge Q_f^f)) \\ \vdash \\ \mathbf{R1_t}(P_f^t)\,;\,\mathbf{R1_t}(I\!I \lhd wait \rhd Q_f^t)\end{array}\right)$$

Proof

$$\begin{array}{lr}
P\,;\,Q & [\text{Theorem 1}] \\
=\mathbf{R_t}(\neg\,P_f^f \vdash P_f^t)\,;\,\mathbf{R_t}(\neg\,Q_f^f \vdash Q_f^t) & [\text{def of } \mathbf{R_t}] \\
=\mathbf{R3_t} \circ \mathbf{R1_t}(\neg\,P_f^f \vdash P_f^t)\,;\,\mathbf{R1_t} \circ \mathbf{R3_t}(\neg\,Q_f^f \vdash Q_f^t) & [\text{Law 4}] \\
=\mathbf{R3_t} \circ (\mathbf{R1_t}(\neg\,P_f^f \vdash P_f^t)\,;\,\mathbf{R1_t} \circ \mathbf{R3_t}(\neg\,Q_f^f \vdash Q_f^t)) & [\text{Law 6}] \\
=\mathbf{R3_t} \circ (\mathbf{R1_t}(\neg\,P_f^f \vdash P_f^t)\,;\,\mathbf{R1_t} \circ \mathbf{R3j_t}(\neg\,Q_f^f \vdash Q_f^t)) & [\text{def of } \mathbf{R3j_t}] \\
=\mathbf{R3_t} \circ (\mathbf{R1_t}(\neg\,P_f^f \vdash P_f^t)\,;\,\mathbf{R1_t}(I\!I_D \lhd wait \rhd \neg\,Q_f^f \vdash Q_f^t)) & [\text{def of } I\!I_D] \\
=\mathbf{R3_t} \circ (\mathbf{R1_t}(\neg\,P_f^f \vdash P_f^t)\,;\,\mathbf{R1_t}(true \vdash I\!I \lhd wait \rhd \neg\,Q_f^f \vdash Q_f^t)) & [\text{Law 1}] \\
=\mathbf{R3_t} \circ (\mathbf{R1_t}(\neg\,P_f^f \vdash P_f^t)\,;\,\mathbf{R1_t}((true \lhd wait \rhd \neg\,Q_f^f) \vdash (I\!I \lhd wait \rhd Q_f^t))) & \\
 & [\text{rel. cal.}] \\
=\mathbf{R3_t} \circ (\mathbf{R1_t}(\neg\,P_f^f \vdash P_f^t)\,;\,\mathbf{R1_t}((wait \vee \neg\,Q_f^f) \vdash (I\!I \lhd wait \rhd Q_f^t))) & \\
 & [\text{Law 5}] \\
=\mathbf{R3_t} \circ \mathbf{R1_t}\left(\begin{array}{c}\neg\,(\mathbf{R1_t}(P_f^f)\,;\,\mathbf{R1_t}(true)) \wedge \neg\,(\mathbf{R1_t}(P_f^t)\,;\,\mathbf{R1_t}(\neg\,wait \wedge Q_f^f)) \\ \vdash \\ \mathbf{R1_t}(P_f^t)\,;\,\mathbf{R1_t}(I\!I \lhd wait \rhd Q_f^t)\end{array}\right) & \\
 & [\text{def of } \mathbf{R_t}] \\
=\mathbf{R_t}\left(\begin{array}{c}\neg\,(\mathbf{R1_t}(P_f^f)\,;\,\mathbf{R1_t}(true)) \wedge \neg\,(\mathbf{R1_t}(P_f^t)\,;\,\mathbf{R1_t}(\neg\,wait \wedge Q_f^f)) \\ \vdash \\ \mathbf{R1_t}(P_f^t)\,;\,\mathbf{R1_t}(I\!I \lhd wait \rhd Q_f^t)\end{array}\right) &
\end{array}$$

This theorem shows that, if P does not diverge and Q does not diverge after P terminates, $P\,;\,Q$ behaves like the sequential composition of the terminations of P and Q.

3.2 Hiding

Similar to the CSP hiding operator in the UTP [6], the hiding operator in *Circus Time* is defined as follows:

$$
\begin{aligned}
&P \setminus CS \mathrel{\widehat=} \mathbf{R_t}(\exists\, s, r \bullet P[s, r/tr', ref'] \wedge L_t)\,;\, Skip\\
&L_t \mathrel{\widehat=} diff(tr', tr) = diff(s, tr) \downarrow_t (\Sigma - CS) \wedge\\
&\qquad\qquad r - front(ref) = ((ref' - front(ref)) \cup_t CS)\\
&diff(tr', tr) \mathrel{\widehat=} \langle tr'(\#tr) - last(tr)\rangle \frown tail(tr' - front(tr))
\end{aligned}
\tag{2}
$$

where *diff* is the difference of two traces, and two special operators, $\downarrow_t$ and $\cup_t$, are defined to restrict timed traces and complement refusals respectively.

$$
\begin{aligned}
&tr_1 = (tr_2 \downarrow_t CS) \Leftrightarrow \forall\, i : 1..\#tr_1 \bullet tr_1(i) = (tr_2(i) \downarrow CS) \wedge \#tr_1 = \#tr_2\\
&ref_1 = (ref_2 \cup_t CS) \Leftrightarrow \forall\, i : 1..\#ref_1 \bullet ref_1(i) = (ref_2(i) \cup CS) \wedge \#ref_1 = \#ref_2
\end{aligned}
$$

Clearly, this definition is not a reactive design. As usual, three useful laws are given and their proof can be found in [13].

Law 7

$$Skip^f = \mathbf{R1_t}(\neg\, ok)$$

Law 8

$$Skip^t = \mathbf{R1_t}(\neg\, ok) \vee (ok \wedge I\!I)$$

Law 9

$$\mathbf{R1_t}(\exists\, s, r \bullet L_t) = \exists\, s, r \bullet L_t$$

Law 10 *Suppose P is a Circus Time action,*

$$(P \setminus CS)^f_f = (\exists\, s, r \bullet P^f_f[s, r/tr', ref'] \wedge L_t)\,;\, \mathbf{R1_t}(true)$$

Proof

$$
\begin{aligned}
&(P \setminus CS)^f_f && [\text{def of } \setminus]\\
=&(\mathbf{R_t}(\exists\, s, r \bullet P[s, r/tr', ref'] \wedge L_t)\,;\, Skip)^f_f && [\text{relational calculus}]\\
=&(\mathbf{R_t}(\exists\, s, r \bullet P[s, r/tr', ref'] \wedge L_t))_f\,;\, Skip^f && [\text{Law 7}]\\
=&(\mathbf{R_t}(\exists\, s, r \bullet P[s, r/tr', ref'] \wedge L_t))_f\,;\, \mathbf{R1_t}(\neg\, ok) && [\text{case split on } ok']\\
=&((\mathbf{R_t}(\exists\, s, r \bullet P[s, r/tr', ref'] \wedge L_t))^f_f\,;\, \mathbf{R1_t}(\neg\, ok)) \vee && [\text{relational calculus}]\\
&((\mathbf{R_t}(\exists\, s, r \bullet P[s, r/tr', ref'] \wedge L_t))^t_f\,;\, \mathbf{R1_t}(\neg\, ok))\\
=&((\mathbf{R_t}(\exists\, s, r \bullet P[s, r/tr', ref'] \wedge L_t))^f_f\,;\, \mathbf{R1_t}(\neg\, ok)) \vee false\\
& && [\mathbf{R3_t} \text{ and } wait \text{ is } false]
\end{aligned}
$$

$$=(\mathbf{R1_t}(\exists\, s, r \bullet P[s, r/tr', ref'] \wedge L_t))_f^f \,;\, \mathbf{R1_t}(\neg\, ok)$$
[P and L_t, Law 9 and predicate calculus]

$$=(\exists\, s, r \bullet P[s, r/tr', ref'] \wedge L_t)_f^f \,;\, \mathbf{R1_t}(\neg\, ok)$$
[relational calculus]

$$=(\exists\, s, r \bullet P[s, r/tr', ref'] \wedge L_t)_f^f \,;\, \mathbf{R1_t}(true)$$
[predicate calculus]

$$=(\exists\, s, r \bullet P_f^f[s, r/tr', ref'] \wedge L_t) \,;\, \mathbf{R1_t}(true)$$

Law 11. *Suppose P is a Circus Time action,*

$$(P \setminus E)_f^t = \begin{pmatrix} (\exists\, s, r \bullet P_f^f[s, r/tr', ref'] \wedge L_t) \,;\, \mathbf{R1_t}(true) \\ \vee\, (\exists\, s, r \bullet P_f^t[s, r/tr', ref'] \wedge L_t) \end{pmatrix}$$

Proof

$$(P \setminus E)_f^t$$
[def of \]

$$= (\mathbf{R_t}(\exists\, s, r \bullet P[s, r/tr', ref'] \wedge L_t) \,;\, Skip)_f^t$$
[relational calculus]

$$= (\mathbf{R_t}(\exists\, s, r \bullet P[s, r/tr', ref'] \wedge L_t))_f \,;\, Skip^t$$
[Law 8]

$$= (\mathbf{R_t}(\exists\, s, r \bullet P[s, r/tr', ref'] \wedge L_t))_f \,;\, (\mathbf{R1_t}(\neg\, ok) \vee (ok \wedge I\!I))$$
[relational cal.]

$$= (\mathbf{R_t}(\exists\, s, r \bullet P[s, r/tr', ref'] \wedge L_t))_f \,;\, \mathbf{R1_t}(\neg\, ok) \vee (\mathbf{R_t}(\exists\, s, r \bullet P[s, r/tr', ref'] \wedge L_t))_f \,;\, (ok \wedge I\!I)$$
[Step 4 in Law 10]

$$= (\exists\, s, r \bullet P_f^f[s, r/tr', ref'] \wedge L_t) \,;\, \mathbf{R1_t}(true) \vee (\mathbf{R_t}(\exists\, s, r \bullet P[s, r/tr', ref'] \wedge L_t))_f \,;\, (ok \wedge I\!I)$$
[P is $\mathbf{R1_t}$ and *wait* is *false*]

$$= (\exists\, s, r \bullet P_f^f[s, r/tr', ref'] \wedge L_t) \,;\, \mathbf{R1_t}(true) \vee (\exists\, s, r \bullet P[s, r/tr', ref'] \wedge L_t)_f \,;\, (ok \wedge I\!I)$$
[relational calculus]

$$= (\exists\, s, r \bullet P_f^f[s, r/tr', ref'] \wedge L_t) \,;\, \mathbf{R1_t}(true) \vee (\exists\, s, r \bullet P_f^t[s, r/tr', ref'] \wedge L_t) \,;\, I\!I$$
[unit law]

$$= (\exists\, s, r \bullet P_f^f[s, r/tr', ref'] \wedge L_t) \,;\, \mathbf{R1_t}(true) \vee (\exists\, s, r \bullet P_f^t[s, r/tr', ref'] \wedge L_t)$$

Now, the reactive design of hiding can be deduced in terms of the above laws.

Theorem 3. *Suppose P is a Circus Time action,*

$$P \setminus CS = \mathbf{R_t}\begin{pmatrix} \neg\, ((\exists\, s, r \bullet P_f^f[s, r/tr', ref'] \wedge L_t) \,;\, \mathbf{R1_t}(true)) \\ \vdash (\exists\, s, r \bullet P_f^t[s, r/tr', ref'] \wedge L_t) \end{pmatrix}$$

Proof.

$$P \setminus CS$$
[Theorem 1]

$$= \mathbf{R_t}(\neg\, (P \setminus CS)_f^f \vdash (P \setminus CS)_f^t)$$
[def of design]

$$= \mathbf{R_t}(ok \wedge \neg\, (P \setminus CS)_f^f \Rightarrow ok' \wedge (P \setminus CS)_f^t)$$
[Law 10 and Law 11]

$$= \mathbf{R_t}\begin{pmatrix} ok \wedge \neg\, ((\exists\, s, r \bullet P_f^f[s, r/tr', ref'] \wedge L_t) \,;\, \mathbf{R1_t}(true)) \Rightarrow \\ ok' \wedge \begin{pmatrix} (\exists\, s, r \bullet P_f^f[s, r/tr', ref'] \wedge L_t) \,;\, \mathbf{R1_t}(true) \\ \vee\, (\exists\, s, r \bullet P_f^t[s, r/tr', ref'] \wedge L_t) \end{pmatrix} \end{pmatrix}$$
[prop. cal.]

$$= \mathbf{R_t}\begin{pmatrix} ok \wedge \neg\, ((\exists\, s, r \bullet P_f^f[s, r/tr', ref'] \wedge L_t)\, ;\, \mathbf{R1_t}(true)) \Rightarrow \\ ok' \wedge (\exists\, s, r \bullet P_f^t[s, r/tr', ref'] \wedge L_t) \end{pmatrix} \quad \text{[def-design]}$$

$$= \mathbf{R_t}\begin{pmatrix} \neg\, ((\exists\, s, r \bullet P_f^f[s, r/tr', ref'] \wedge L_t)\, ;\, \mathbf{R1_t}(true)) \\ \vdash (\exists\, s, r \bullet P_f^t[s, r/tr', ref'] \wedge L_t) \end{pmatrix}$$

Note that $\mathbf{R1_t}(true)$ in the precondition captures the observation that leads to a divergence.

3.3 Recursion

The semantics of recursion is the same as that in the UTP [6]: weakest fixed point. Given a monotonic function F, the semantics of recursion is the weakest fixed point of F.

$$\mu X \bullet F(X) \mathrel{\widehat{=}} \bigsqcap\{X \mid F(X) \sqsubseteq X\} \tag{3}$$

The strongest fixed point of $F(X)$ is defined as the dual of the weakest.

$$\nu F \mathrel{\widehat{=}} \neg\, \mu X \bullet \neg\, F(\neg\, X) \tag{4}$$

To express a recursion as a reactive design, we have to calculate the precondition and postcondition of a recursively defined design. For that, we can use the definition of a recursive design and some theorems on linking theories in [6]. In the theory of designs, any monotonic function of designs can be expressed in terms of a pair of function that apply separately to the precondition and the postcondition, for example

$$F(P, Q) \vdash G(P, Q)$$

Here, P and Q are predicates representing the precondition and postcondition of a design, F is monotonic in P and antimonotonic in Q, whereas G is monotonic in Q and antimonotonic in P. Thus, as described in the theory of designs, the weakest fixed point is given by a mutually recursive formula, that we reproduce below.

Law 12

$$\begin{aligned} &\mu(X, Y) \bullet (F(X, Y) \vdash G(X, Y)) = P(Q) \vdash Q \\ \text{where}\ \ &P(Y) = \nu X \bullet F(X, Y) \\ \text{and}\ \ &Q = \mu\, Y \bullet (P(Y) \Rightarrow G(P(Y), Y)) \end{aligned}$$

As shown in Theorem 1, if X is a reactive design, $X = \neg\, X_f^f \vdash X_f^t$. Hence, based on Law 12, we have the following theorem for recursively reactive designs.

Theorem 4

$$\mu(X, Y) \bullet (\mathbf{R_t}(F(X, Y) \vdash G(X, Y))) = \mathbf{R_t}(\mu(X, Y) \bullet (F(X, Y) \vdash G(X, Y))$$

To prove Theorem 4, we directly adopt an important theorem from the linking theories of the UTP book, which can be described here.

Theorem 5. *Let D and E be monotonic functions. If there exists a function R such that $R \circ D = E \circ R$, then $R(\mu\, D) = \mu\, E$.*

As a result, the proof of Theorem 4 can be established as follows.

Proof

$$\begin{aligned} \text{Let } & D(X \vdash Y) = F(X,Y) \vdash G(X,Y) \ \ \textit{and} \\ & E(\mathbf{R_t}(X \vdash Y)) = \mathbf{R_t}(F(X,Y) \vdash G(X,Y)) \end{aligned}$$

$$\begin{aligned} \text{then } & E \circ \mathbf{R_t}(X \vdash Y) && \text{[def of } E\text{]} \\ =& \mathbf{R_t}(F(X,Y) \vdash G(X,Y)) && \text{[def of } D\text{]} \\ =& \mathbf{R_t}(D(X \vdash Y)) && \text{[def of composition]} \\ =& \mathbf{R_t} \circ D(X \vdash Y) \end{aligned}$$

$$\text{therefore } \ \mu(X,Y) \bullet E(\mathbf{R_t}(X \vdash Y)) = \mathbf{R_t}(\mu(X,Y) \bullet D(X \vdash Y))$$

4 Applications of Reactive Designs

The reactive design semantics can help us understand the exact behaviours of some complex processes. For example, the reactive design of a simple prefix, which is based on the semantics in [2], has been worked out in [13].

$$c.e \rightarrow \mathit{Skip} \mathrel{\widehat{=}} \mathbf{R_t}(\mathit{true} \vdash \mathit{wait\_com}(c) \lor \mathit{terminating\_com}(c.e)) \tag{5}$$

$$\mathit{wait\_com}(c) \mathrel{\widehat{=}} \mathit{wait}' \land \mathit{possible}(\mathit{ref}, \mathit{ref}', c) \land {}^\frown/\mathit{tr}' = {}^\frown/\mathit{tr} \tag{6}$$

$$\mathit{possible}(\mathit{ref}, \mathit{ref}', c) \mathrel{\widehat{=}} \forall\, i : \#\mathit{ref}..\#\mathit{ref}' \bullet c \notin \mathit{ref}'(i) \tag{7}$$

$$\mathit{term\_com}(c.e) \mathrel{\widehat{=}} \begin{pmatrix} \neg\, \mathit{wait}' \land \mathit{diff}(\mathit{tr}', \mathit{tr}) = \langle\langle c.e \rangle\rangle \\ \land\, \mathit{front}(\mathit{ref}') = \mathit{front}(\mathit{ref}) \end{pmatrix} \tag{8}$$

$$\mathit{terminating\_com}(c.e) \mathrel{\widehat{=}} \begin{pmatrix} \mathit{wait\_com}(c);\, \mathit{term\_com}(c.e) \\ \lor\, \mathit{term\_com}(c.e) \end{pmatrix} \tag{9}$$

Such a process never diverges since its precondition is true, and, as described by its postcondition, behaves in three different ways: it waits for interaction from its environment, or it waits for a while and then terminates with a fired event, or it simply executes the event immediately. The action *Miracle*, expressed as $\mathbf{R_t}(\mathit{true} \vdash \mathit{false})$, has miraculous behaviour that simply denotes an unstarted action. Therefore, it should never appear during an execution of a process. The exact behaviour of the combination of the two actions can be easily figured out using our newly established reactive design of sequential composition.

Theorem 6

$$c.e \rightarrow Miracle = \mathbf{R_t}(true \vdash wait' \wedge {}^\frown/tr' = {}^\frown/tr \wedge possible(tr, tr', c))$$

Proof

$$\begin{aligned}
& c.e \rightarrow Miracle && \text{[def of prefix]}\\
&= (c.e \rightarrow Skip) \,;\, Miracle && \text{[def 5 and } Miracle\text{]}\\
&= \mathbf{R_t}(true \vdash wait_com(c) \vee terminating_com(c.e)) \,;\, \mathbf{R_t}(true \vdash false) && \text{[Theorem 2]}\\
&= \mathbf{R_t}\left(\begin{array}{c} \neg\,(\mathbf{R1_t}(false) \,;\, \mathbf{R1_t}(true)) \wedge \\ \neg\,(\mathbf{R1_t}((wait_com(c) \vee terminating_com(c.e))^t_f) \,;\, \mathbf{R1_t}(\neg\, wait \wedge false)) \\ \vdash \\ \mathbf{R1_t}(wait_com(c) \vee terminating_com(c.e)) \,;\, \mathbf{R1_t}(I\!I \lhd wait \rhd false) \end{array}\right) && \text{[rel. cal.]}\\
&= \mathbf{R_t}(true \vdash \mathbf{R1_t}(wait_com(c) \vee terminating_com(c.e)) \,;\, \mathbf{R1_t}(I\!I \wedge wait)) && \text{[rel. cal.]}\\
&= \mathbf{R_t}\left(true \vdash \left(\begin{array}{c} \mathbf{R1_t}(wait_com(c)) \,;\, \mathbf{R1_t}(I\!I \wedge wait) \vee \\ \mathbf{R1_t}(terminating_com(c.e)) \,;\, \mathbf{R1_t}(I\!I \wedge wait) \end{array}\right)\right) && \text{[def 9]}\\
&= \mathbf{R_t}\left(true \vdash \left(\begin{array}{l} \mathbf{R1_t}(wait_com(c)) \,;\, \mathbf{R1_t}(I\!I \wedge wait) \vee \\ \left(\begin{array}{c} \mathbf{R1_t}(wait_com(c) \,;\, term_com(c.e) \\ \vee\, term_com(c.e) \end{array}\right) ;\, \mathbf{R1_t}(I\!I \wedge wait) \end{array}\right)\right) && \text{[} wait' \text{ in } term_com \text{ is false]}\\
&= \mathbf{R_t}(true \vdash (\mathbf{R1_t}(wait_com(c)) \,;\, \mathbf{R1_t}(I\!I \wedge wait) \vee false)) && \text{[def 6]}\\
&= \mathbf{R_t}(true \vdash \mathbf{R1_t}(wait' \wedge {}^\frown/tr' = {}^\frown/tr \wedge possible(tr, tr', c)) \,;\, \mathbf{R1_t}(I\!I \wedge wait)) && \text{[rel. cal.]}\\
&= \mathbf{R_t}(true \vdash \mathbf{R1_t}(wait' \wedge {}^\frown/tr' = {}^\frown/tr \wedge possible(tr, tr', c)) && \text{[}\mathbf{R1_t} \text{ is idempotent]}\\
&= \mathbf{R_t}(true \vdash wait' \wedge {}^\frown/tr' = {}^\frown/tr \wedge possible(tr, tr', c))
\end{aligned}$$

This theorem states that, if this action starts, it waits for interaction with its environment, but never actually perform any event even if the event $c.e$ has been offered. This process is different from that of the standard CSP failures-divergences model in which one of the assumptions requires that, if an event is not in the refusal set, the process is always willing to execute the event.

There is a very subtle law in the CSP theory about hiding and recursion as $(\mu\, X \bullet c \rightarrow X) \setminus \{c\} = Chaos$, which is difficult to be proved using their original UTP definitions. However, the reactive designs of the two operators allow us to prove this law straightforwardly. To prove this law, we use the *Kleene* theorem rather than the traditional definition of the weakest fixed point to calculate the recursive design in the recursively reactive design.

Theorem 7 (Kleene fixed point theorem)
If F is continuous [1], *then* $\mu X \bullet F(X) = \bigsqcup_{n=0}^{\infty} F^n(true)$ *where* $F^0(X) \mathrel{\widehat=} true$, *and* $F^{n+1} \mathrel{\widehat=} F(F^n(X))$.

This theorem states a normal form for programs that contain recursion. First of all, the behaviour of a recursive program is expressed as an *infinite* sequence of predicates $\{F^i \mid i \in \mathbb{N}\}$ and each F^i is a finite normal form. Since each F^{i+1} is defined by its previous expression, F^{i+1} is potentially stronger if $F^i \sqsubseteq F^{i+1}$. If i is large enough, the exact behaviour of the program can be captured by the *least upper bound* of the infinite sequence, written $\bigsqcup_{n=0}^{\infty} F^n(true)$.

In addition, we are able to prove a similar theorem for the strongest fixed point of F.

Theorem 8. *If F is continuous,* $\nu X \bullet F(X) = \bigsqcap_{n=0}^{\infty} F^n(false)$

Proof

$$
\begin{aligned}
& \nu X \bullet F(X) && \text{[def of } \nu] \\
=& \neg\, \mu X \bullet \neg\, F(\neg\, X) && \text{[Theorem 7]} \\
=& \neg \bigsqcup_{n=0}^{\infty} (\lambda X \bullet \neg\, F(\neg\, X))^n(true) && \text{[relational calculus]} \\
=& \bigsqcap_{n=0}^{\infty} \neg\, (\lambda X \bullet \neg\, F(\neg\, X))^n(true) && \text{[predicate calculus]} \\
=& \bigsqcap_{n=0}^{\infty} F^n(false)
\end{aligned}
$$

Now, firstly, we calculate the reactive design of a single call of $\mu X \bullet c \rightarrow X$. The procedure is similar to Theorem 6, and the proof can be found in [13].

Law 13

$$
c \rightarrow X = \mathbf{R_t}\left(\begin{array}{c} \neg\,(terminating\_com(c)\,;\, \mathbf{R1_t}(\neg\, wait \wedge X_f^f)) \\ \vdash \\ wait\_com(c) \vee (terminating\_com(c)\,;\, \mathbf{R1_t}(X_f^t)) \end{array}\right)
$$

Secondly, in terms of Theorem 4 and Law 13, we let

$$X = \neg\, X_f^f \text{ and } Y = X_f^t, \text{ then} \tag{10}$$

$$F(X, Y) = \neg\,(terminating\_com(c)\,;\, \mathbf{R1_t}(\neg\, wait \wedge \neg\, X)) \tag{11}$$

$$G(X, Y) = wait\_com(c) \vee (terminating\_com(c)\,;\, \mathbf{R1_t}(Y)) \tag{12}$$

As a result, the weakest fixed point of $(\mu X \bullet c \rightarrow X) \setminus \{c\}$ can be calculated by the following law.

[1] A function is *continuous* only if its value at a limit point can be determined from its values on a sequence converging to that point. Also, a continuous function is monotonic.

Law 14

$$\mu(X,Y) \bullet E(\mathbf{R_t}(X \vdash Y)) = \mathbf{R_t}((\nu X \bullet F(X,Y)) \vdash Q)$$

Proof

$$\begin{aligned} & \mu(X,Y) \bullet E(\mathbf{R_t}(X \vdash Y)) && \text{[Theorem 4]} \\ =& \mathbf{R_t}(\mu(X,Y) \bullet D(X \vdash Y)) && \text{[Law 12]} \\ =& \mathbf{R_t}((\nu X \bullet F(X,Y)) \vdash Q) \end{aligned}$$

Note that, since the postcondition of D has no influence on the final result, we here simply use Q to denote the postcondition and never unfold it in the later proof.

Next, we calculate the strongest fixed point of F by means of the *Kleene* theorem. Before starting to prove the law before, we give some useful properties. Some proofs can be found in [13], and some leave to the reader.

Property 1

L1. $\mathbf{R1_t}(\mathit{terminating\_com}(c)) = \mathit{terminating\_com}(c)$

L2. $\mathit{terminating\_com}(c);\ \mathbf{R1_t}(\mathit{true}) \wedge \mathit{terminating\_com}(c)^2;\ \mathbf{R1_t}(\mathit{true})$
$= \mathit{terminating\_com}(c)^2;\ \mathbf{R1_t}(\mathit{true})$

L3. $\mathit{terminating\_com}(c)^n \sqsubseteq \mathit{term\_com}(c)^n$

L4. $\mathit{diff}(tr', tr) = \langle\langle c\rangle\rangle \Leftrightarrow \mathit{front}(tr') = \mathit{front}(tr) \wedge \mathit{last}(tr') - \mathit{last}(tr) = \langle c\rangle$

L5. $((\mathit{front}(\mathit{ref}') = \mathit{front}(\mathit{ref}));\ (\mathit{front}(\mathit{ref}') = \mathit{front}(\mathit{ref})))$
$\Leftrightarrow \mathit{front}(\mathit{ref}') = \mathit{front}(\mathit{ref})$

Law 15

$$\nu(X) \bullet F(X,Y) = \neg \left(\begin{array}{c} \mathbf{R1_t}\left(\begin{array}{c} \mathit{front}(tr) \frown \langle \mathit{last}(tr) \frown \langle c\rangle^n \rangle \preccurlyeq tr' \\ \wedge\ \mathit{front}(\mathit{ref}) \leq \mathit{ref}' \end{array} \right) \\ \vee\ (\mathit{terminating\_com}(c)^n\,;\ \mathbf{R1_t}(\mathit{true})) \end{array} \right)$$

Proof

$$\begin{aligned} & \nu(X) \bullet F(X,Y) && \text{[Theorem 8]} \\ =& \prod_{n=0}^{\infty} F^n(\mathit{false}) && \text{[unfold } \textstyle\prod\text{]} \\ =& F^0(\mathit{false}) \sqcap F^1(\mathit{false}) \sqcap F^2(\mathit{false}) \ldots \sqcap F^n(\mathit{false}) && \text{[unfold } F \text{(def 11)]} \\ =& \mathit{false} \sqcap \neg\, (\mathit{terminating\_com}(c)\,;\ \mathbf{R1_t}(\neg\, \mathit{wait} \wedge \neg\, \mathit{false}))\ldots \\ & \sqcap \neg \left(\begin{array}{c} \mathit{terminating\_com}(c) \\ ; \\ \mathbf{R1_t}(\neg\, \mathit{wait} \wedge (\mathit{terminating\_com}(c)\,;\ \mathbf{R1_t}(\neg\, \mathit{wait} \wedge \neg\, \mathit{false}))) \end{array} \right) \ldots \\ & \sqcap F^n(\mathit{false}) && \text{[relational calculus } (\neg\, \mathit{wait} \text{ is absorbed by } \mathit{terminating\_com})] \end{aligned}$$

$$= \mathit{false} \sqcap \neg\,(\mathit{terminating\_com}(c)\,;\mathbf{R1_t}(\mathit{true}))$$
$$\sqcap \neg\,(\mathit{terminating\_com}(c)\,;\mathbf{R1_t}((\mathit{terminating\_com}(c)\,;\mathbf{R1_t}(\mathit{true}))) ...$$
$$\sqcap F^n(\mathit{false}) \qquad \text{[Property 1-L1 and } \mathbf{R1_t} \text{ is idempotent and rel. cal.]}$$
$$= \mathit{false} \sqcap \neg\,(\mathit{terminating\_com}(c)\,;\mathbf{R1_t}(\mathit{true})) \qquad [\text{property of } \textstyle\bigsqcap]$$
$$\sqcap \neg\,(\mathit{terminating\_com}(c)^2\,;\mathbf{R1_t}(\mathit{true})) ...$$
$$\sqcap \neg\,(\mathit{terminating\_com}(c)^n\,;\mathbf{R1_t}(\mathit{true}))$$
$$= \bigsqcap_{n=1}^{\infty} (\neg\,(\mathit{terminating\_com}(c)^n\,;\mathbf{R1_t}(\mathit{true}))) \qquad [\text{property of } \textstyle\bigsqcup]$$
$$= \neg \bigsqcup_{n=1}^{\infty} (\mathit{terminating\_com}(c)^n\,;\mathbf{R1_t}(\mathit{true})) \qquad [\text{unfold } \textstyle\bigsqcup]$$
$$= \neg \begin{pmatrix} (\mathit{terminating\_com}(c)\,;\mathbf{R1_t}(\mathit{true})) \wedge \\ (\mathit{terminating\_com}(c)^2\,;\mathbf{R1_t}(\mathit{true})) \wedge \\ .... \wedge \\ (\mathit{terminating\_com}(c)^n\,;\mathbf{R1_t}(\mathit{true})) \end{pmatrix} \qquad \text{[Property 1-L2 and Induction]}$$
$$= \neg\,(\mathit{terminating\_com}(c)^n\,;\mathbf{R1_t}(\mathit{true})) \qquad \text{[def 9]}$$
$$= \neg\,((\mathit{wait\_com}(c)\,;\mathit{term\_com}(c) \vee \mathit{term\_com}(c))^n\,;\mathbf{R1_t}(\mathit{true}))$$
$$\text{[Property 1-L3]}$$
$$= \neg \left(\begin{pmatrix} (\mathit{wait\_com}(c)\,;\mathit{term\_com}(c) \vee \mathit{term\_com}(c))^n \\ \vee\ \mathit{term\_com}(c)^n \end{pmatrix} ;\mathbf{R1_t}(\mathit{true}) \right) \qquad \text{[def 9]}$$
$$= \neg\,((\mathit{term\_com}(c)^n \vee \mathit{terminating\_com}(c)^n)\,;\mathbf{R1_t}(\mathit{true})) \qquad \text{[def 8]}$$
$$= \neg \left(\begin{pmatrix} \begin{pmatrix} \neg\,\mathit{wait}' \wedge \mathit{diff}(tr', tr) = \langle\langle c \rangle\rangle \\ \wedge\ \mathit{front}(\mathit{ref}') = \mathit{front}(\mathit{ref}) \end{pmatrix}^n \\ \vee\ \mathit{terminating\_com}(c)^n \end{pmatrix} ;\mathbf{R1_t}(\mathit{true}) \right) \qquad \text{[Property 1-L4]}$$
$$= \neg \left(\begin{pmatrix} \begin{pmatrix} \neg\,\mathit{wait}' \wedge \mathit{last}(tr') - \mathit{last}(tr) = \langle c \rangle \\ \wedge\ \mathit{front}(tr') = \mathit{front}(tr) \wedge \mathit{front}(\mathit{ref}') = \mathit{front}(\mathit{ref}) \end{pmatrix}^n \\ \vee\ \mathit{terminating\_com}(c)^n \end{pmatrix} ;\mathbf{R1_t}(\mathit{true}) \right)$$
$$\text{[Property 1-L5 and Induction]}$$
$$= \neg \left(\begin{pmatrix} \begin{pmatrix} \neg\,\mathit{wait}' \wedge (\mathit{last}(tr') - \mathit{last}(tr) = \langle c \rangle)^n \wedge \\ \mathit{front}(tr') = \mathit{front}(tr) \wedge \mathit{front}(\mathit{ref}') = \mathit{front}(\mathit{ref}) \end{pmatrix} \\ \vee\ \mathit{terminating\_com}(c)^n \end{pmatrix} ;\mathbf{R1_t}(\mathit{true}) \right)$$
$$\text{[rel. cal.]}$$
$$= \neg \begin{pmatrix} \begin{pmatrix} \neg\,\mathit{wait}' \wedge \mathit{diff}(tr' - tr) = \langle\langle c \rangle^n\rangle \\ \wedge\ \mathit{front}(\mathit{ref}') = \mathit{front}(\mathit{ref}) \end{pmatrix} ;\mathbf{R1_t}(\mathit{true}) \\ \vee\ \mathit{terminating\_com}(c)^n\,;\mathbf{R1_t}(\mathit{true}) \end{pmatrix}$$
$$\text{[def of 2 and relational calculus]}$$
$$= \neg \begin{pmatrix} \begin{pmatrix} \neg\,\mathit{wait}' \wedge \\ \langle tr'(\#tr) - \mathit{last}(tr)\rangle ^\frown \mathit{tail}(tr' - \mathit{front}(tr)) = \langle\langle c \rangle^n\rangle \\ \wedge\ \mathit{front}(\mathit{ref}') = \mathit{front}(\mathit{ref}) \end{pmatrix} ;\mathbf{R1_t}(\mathit{true}) \\ \vee\ \mathit{terminating\_com}(c)^n\,;\mathbf{R1_t}(\mathit{true}) \end{pmatrix}$$
$$\text{[relational calculus]}$$

$$= \neg \left(\begin{array}{c} \mathbf{R1_t}(front(tr) ^\frown \langle last(tr) ^\frown \langle c \rangle^n \rangle \preccurlyeq tr' \wedge front(ref) \leq ref') \\ \vee\ terminating\_com(c)^n \,;\, \mathbf{R1_t}(true) \end{array} \right)$$

Finally, we are ready to prove the law, $(\mu X \bullet c \to X) \setminus \{c\} = Chaos$, and the proof is simply the combination of the laws and theorems above.

Theorem 9

$$(\mu X \bullet c \to X) \setminus \{c\} = Chaos$$

Proof

$$\begin{array}{ll}
(\mu X \bullet c \to X) \setminus \{c\} & \text{[Theorem 3]} \\
= \mathbf{R_t}(\neg\, ((\exists\, s, r \bullet (\mu X \bullet c \to X)^f_f[s, r/tr', ref'] \wedge L_t);\ \mathbf{R1_t}(true)) \vdash EE^2) & \\
& \text{[def of } \vdash \text{ and merge unused proof]} \\
= \mathbf{R_t}(((\exists\, s, r \bullet (\mu X \bullet c \to X)^f_f[s, r/tr', ref'] \wedge L_t);\ \mathbf{R1_t}(true)) \vee EE) & \\
& \text{[Theorem 4]} \\
= \mathbf{R_t} \left(\begin{array}{l} ((\exists\, s, r \bullet (\mu(X, Y) \bullet E(\mathbf{R_t}(X \vdash Y)))^f_f[s, r/tr', ref'] \wedge L_t);\ \mathbf{R1_t}(true)) \\ \vee\ EE \end{array} \right) & \\
& \text{[Law 14]} \\
= \mathbf{R_t} \left(\begin{array}{l} ((\exists\, s, r \bullet (\neg\, \nu X \bullet F(X, Y))[s, r/tr', ref'] \wedge L_t);\ \mathbf{R1_t}(true)) \\ \vee\ EE \end{array} \right) & \text{[Law 15]} \\
= \mathbf{R_t} \left(\begin{array}{c} \left(\exists\, s, r \bullet \left(\begin{array}{c} \mathbf{R1_t} \left(\begin{array}{c} front(tr) ^\frown \langle last(tr) ^\frown \langle c \rangle^n \rangle \preccurlyeq tr' \\ \wedge\ front(ref) \leq ref' \end{array} \right) \\ \vee\ terminating_com(c)^n \,;\, \mathbf{R1_t}(true) \end{array} \right) [s, r/tr', ref'] \wedge L_t \right) \\ ;\, \mathbf{R1_t}(true) \\ \vee\ EE \end{array} \right) & \\
& \text{[merge } (terminating_com(c)^n \,;\, \mathbf{R1_t}(true)) \text{ to } EE] \\
= \mathbf{R_t} \left(\begin{array}{c} \left(\exists\, s, r \bullet \mathbf{R1_t} \left(\begin{array}{c} front(tr) ^\frown \langle last(tr) ^\frown \langle c \rangle^n \rangle \preccurlyeq tr' \\ \wedge\ front(ref) \leq ref' \end{array} \right) [s, r/tr', ref'] \wedge L_t \right) \\ ;\, \mathbf{R1_t}(true) \\ \vee\ EE \end{array} \right) & \\
& \text{[only } tr' = tr \wedge front(ref) \leq ref' \text{ can satisfy } L_t] \\
= \mathbf{R_t}((\mathbf{R1_t}(tr' = tr \wedge front(ref) \leq ref') \,;\, \mathbf{R1_t}(true)) \vee EE) & \text{[rel. calculus]} \\
= \mathbf{R_t}(\mathbf{R1_t}(true) \vee EE) & \text{[prop. calculus]} \\
= \mathbf{R_t}(true) & \text{[def of design]} \\
= \mathbf{R_t}(false \vdash true) & \text{[def of } Chaos] \\
= Chaos &
\end{array}$$

[2] We simply use EE to denote the unused part of the proof. This abbreviation continuously collects unused parts during the proof and it is changing at each step of this proof.

The proof of the above law shows one of the cases to result in *Chaos*. If c happens immediately at each call, the hiding operator is able to make this recursion become divergent at once when it starts.

5 Conclusion

In this paper we develop the reactive design semantics of three important CSP operators, sequential composition, hiding and recursion; this complements the early work in [2,9]. Compared to the original CSP semantics in UTP, the reactive designs provides us with a more concise, readable and uniform semantics, which can help us to exactly understand the behaviours of some subtle processes. In addition, this reactive design semantics is developed in a timed context, *Circus Time*, and the full version can be found in [13]. So far, this semantics and related laws have been proved by hand. In our short-term goal, we will mechanise them in a new *Circus* tool, Isabelle/Circus [4], to underpin their correctness.

Acknowledgments. This work was fully supported by hiJaC project funded by EPSRC(EP/H017461/1).

References

1. Cavalcanti, A., Wellings, A., Woodcock, J., Wei, K., Zeyda, F.: Safety-critical Java in Circus. In: Proceedings of the 9th International Workshop on Java Technologies for Real-Time and Embedded Systems, JTRES 2011, pp. 20–29. ACM, New York (2011)
2. Cavalcanti, A., Woodcock, J.: A Tutorial Introduction to CSP in *Unifying Theories of Programming*. In: Cavalcanti, A., Sampaio, A., Woodcock, J. (eds.) PSSE 2004. LNCS, vol. 3167, pp. 220–268. Springer, Heidelberg (2006)
3. Cavalcanti, A., Sampaio, A., Woodcock, J.: A Refinement Strategy for *Circus*. Formal Aspects of Computing 15(2-3), 146–181 (2003)
4. Feliachi, A., Gaudel, M.-C., Wolff, B.: Isabelle/Circus: a Process Specification and Verification Environment. Technical Report 1547, LRI, Université Paris-Sud XI (November 2011), `http://www.lri.fr/Rapports-internes`
5. Hoare, C.A.R.: Communicating Sequential Processes. Prentice-Hall International (1985)
6. Hoare, C.A.R., Jifeng, H.: Unifying Theories of Programming. Prentice-Hall International (1998)
7. Locke, D., et al.: Safety Critical Java Specification. First Release 0.76, The Open Group, UK (2010)
8. Morgan, C.: Programming from specifications. Prentice-Hall, Inc., Upper Saddle River (1990)
9. Oliveira, M., Cavalcanti, A., Woodcock, J.: A UTP Semantics for *Circus*. Formal Aspects of Computing 21(1), 3–32 (2007)
10. Roscoe, A.W.: The Theory and Practice of Concurrency. Prentice-Hall International (1998)
11. Schneider, S.A.: Concurrent and real-time systems: the CSP approach. John Wiley & Sons (1999)

12. Sherif, A., Cavalcanti, A.L.C., Jifeng, H., Sampaio, A.C.A.: A process algebraic framework for specification and validation of real-time systems. Formal Aspects of Computing 22(2), 153–191 (2010)
13. Wei, K., Woodcock, J., Cavalcanti, A.: New Circus Time. Technical report, Department of Computer Science, University of York, UK (March 2012), `http://www.cs.york.ac.uk/circus/hijac/publication.html`
14. Woodcock, J.: The Miracle of Reactive Programming. In: Butterfield, A. (ed.) UTP 2008. LNCS, vol. 5713, pp. 202–217. Springer, Heidelberg (2010)
15. Woodcock, J., Davies, J.: Using Z: specification, refinement, and proof. Prentice-Hall, Inc., Upper Saddle River (1996)
16. Woodcock, J., Cavalcanti, A.: A Tutorial Introduction to Designs in Unifying Theories of Programming. In: Boiten, E.A., Derrick, J., Smith, G.P. (eds.) IFM 2004. LNCS, vol. 2999, pp. 40–66. Springer, Heidelberg (2004)
17. Woodcock, J., Cavalcanti, A.: A concurrent language for refinement. In: Butterfield, A., Pahl, C. (eds.) IWFM 2001: 5th Irish Workshop in Formal Methods, BCS Electronic Workshops in Computing, Dublin, Ireland (July 2001)
18. Woodcock, J., Cavalcanti, A.: The Semantics of \$*Circus*\$. In: Bert, D., Bowen, J.P., Henson, M.C., Robinson, K. (eds.) B 2002 and ZB 2002. LNCS, vol. 2272, pp. 184–203. Springer, Heidelberg (2002)

Algebra Unifies Operational Calculi

Stephan van Staden[1] and Tony Hoare[2]

[1] ETH Zurich, Switzerland
Stephan.vanStaden@inf.ethz.ch
[2] Microsoft Research, Cambridge, United Kingdom

Abstract. We survey the well-known algebraic laws of sequential programming, and propose some less familiar laws for concurrent programming. On the basis of these laws, we derive a general calculus of program execution. The basic judgment of the theory is a quintuple, and we deduce its rules by algebraic reasoning. The general calculus can be specialised to obtain more familiar operational calculi, such as the structural operational semantics of Plotkin, process calculus semantics of Milner, reduction semantics with evaluation contexts of Felleisen and Hieb, and the natural semantics of Kahn. The algebra unifies these calculi, as it is simpler than each calculus derived from it, and stronger than all of them put together.

1 Introduction

The purpose of an operational calculus is to demonstrate an abstract implementation of a programming language, and thereby provide guidance on its practical implementations. There are many flavours of operational calculi, also known as operational semantics, that have been successfully applied in human and mechanical reasoning about program execution. Examples include structural operational semantics [1], natural semantics [2], and reduction semantics with evaluation contexts [3]. This paper derives the central rules of these and several other operational calculi from a handful of algebraic laws that abstractly characterize program behaviour.

The basic ideas and content of the algebraic laws of sequential programming are familiar [4]. That paper treated the main program structuring operators, including sequential composition, choice, and recursion. This paper introduces additional laws to deal with concurrency. The formulation is purely algebraic and lacks negative statements, so all the earlier axioms and theorems survive the introduction of additional laws.

The variables (P, Q, R, s) that occur in our algebraic laws may stand for computational states, assertions about the state, programs, program designs, and program specifications. We regard them all as descriptions of the events that occur in and around a computer that is executing a program. The program itself is the most precise description of its own execution. The most abstract description is the user specification, which mentions only aspects of execution that are observable and controllable by the user. A computational state can be regarded

B. Wolff, M.-C. Gaudel, A. Feliachi (Eds.): UTP 2012, LNCS 7681, pp. 88–104, 2013.

as a description of all executions that end in that state. An assertion describes a set of states that satisfy it, i.e., the union of all executions ending in such a state. Each of these examples has a different role in program development and execution, and they are usually expressed in different notations. But we ignore the distinctions between them, because they all obey the same algebraic laws.

The main novel content of the paper is a unifying treatment of a varied collection of programming calculi, which have been proposed as formalisations of the operational meaning of sequential and concurrent programming languages. To this end, we first outline a general operational calculus whose basic judgement is defined in terms of the algebra. The inference rules of the general calculus all follow as theorems from the algebraic laws. Other operational calculi can then be derived by specialising the general calculus. Such a specialisation involves defining the judgement(s) of the calculus in terms of the general judgment, and deriving its rules from a subset of the general rules. We claim that the algebra unifies operational calculi because of its simplicity and its strength, i.e. its ability to elegantly describe and explain a range of operational calculi.

We make no claims that our algebraic laws are actually true of the operators of any particular programming language. We rely on the readers' good will to check the individual laws against their intuitive understanding and experience of the essential concepts of programming. The demonstration that these properties are true of many historic programming calculi gives some independent evidence that the algebra is potentially useful, and that it corresponds to a widely held common understanding of the meaning of programs.

All theorems of the paper have been formally checked with Isabelle/HOL. A proof script is available online [5].

Outline. Section 2 surveys the algebraic laws of programming. Section 3 proposes a general operational calculus whose rules all follow as theorems from the laws. Section 4 shows that various familiar operational calculi are specialisations of the general calculus. Section 5 concludes the presentation.

2 Laws of Programming

The descriptions of program behaviour are clearly propositions, and they may be connected by the normal operators and relations of the propositional calculus. They are ordered by logical implication, often called refinement: $P \subseteq Q$ indicates that P refines Q. This refinement has several meanings. For example, it can say that the program P is more determinate than program Q (i.e. all behaviours of P are also behaviours of Q) or that the specification P is stronger than the specification Q (i.e. P implies Q). Generally, a description is more abstract or general compared to the descriptions that refine it. Refinement obeys three laws that make it a partial order:

- $P \subseteq P$
- $P \subseteq Q \quad \& \quad Q \subseteq R \quad \Rightarrow \quad P \subseteq R$
- $P \subseteq Q \quad \& \quad Q \subseteq P \quad \Rightarrow \quad P = Q$

The simplest terms of an algebra are its constants, in this case *skip*, $\bot$ and $\top$. The constant *skip* is a basic program that does nothing but terminate successfully. Bottom $\bot$ represents the False predicate: it describes no execution. Considered as a program, $\bot$ describes the meaning of a program containing a fault like a syntax violation, which the implementation is required to detect, and to prevent the program from running. Top $\top$ is a program containing a generic error like subscript overflow, which the implementation is not required to detect, and which may have unbounded consequences. As a proposition, it can be identified with the predicate True. It is the programmer's responsibility to avoid submitting such a program for execution.

Apart from the constant descriptions, there are operators for forming descriptions in terms of others. The operators are likewise drawn from programming languages and propositional logic. For example, sequential composition (;) and concurrent composition ($\|$) are binary operators from programming: the formula $P\,;Q$ describes the sequential composition of P and Q, while $P \parallel Q$ is a description of their concurrent behaviour. In each case, their execution involves execution of both the operands.

Conjunction ($\wedge$) and disjunction ($\vee$) are operators from propositional logic. Considered as a program, $P \vee Q$ is the nondeterministic choice between the program components P and Q. The choice may be determined at some later stage in the design trajectory of the program, or by a specified condition tested at run time; failing this, it may be determined by an implementation of the language at compile time, or even nondeterministically at run time. It satisfies the following laws:

- $P \subseteq P \vee Q$ and $Q \subseteq P \vee Q$.
- Whenever $P \subseteq R$ and $Q \subseteq R$, then $P \vee Q \subseteq R$.

These laws say that ($\vee$) is the least upper bound with respect to the refinement order. Conjunction is its dual and corresponds to the greatest lower bound.

The logical operators, or connectives, satisfy familiar algebraic laws. For instance, conjunction and disjunction are both associative and commutative. Programming operators enjoy similar algebraic properties. For example, saying that $(P\,;Q)\,;R$ and $P\,;(Q\,;R)$ describe the same computation is the same as stating that sequential composition is associative. The properties of most of the operators considered here are described and intuitively justified in [4]. Table 1 summarizes how the binary operators behave in isolation from each other.

In addition to such laws, distribution laws state the relationships between two (or more) operators. All the binary operators in the table distribute leftward and rightward through ($\vee$), i.e. for $\circ \in \{\vee, \wedge, ;, \|\}$ we have:

- $P \circ (Q \vee R) = (P \circ Q) \vee (P \circ R)$
- $(P \vee Q) \circ R = (P \circ R) \vee (Q \circ R)$

The most unfamiliar law reported in this paper is analogous to the exchange law of category theory. It specifies how sequential and concurrent composition interact:

Table 1. Basic properties of the operators

	$\vee$	$\wedge$	;	$\|$
Commutative	yes	yes	no	yes
Associative	yes	yes	yes	yes
Idempotent	yes	yes	no	no
Unit	$\bot$	$\top$	*skip*	*skip*
Zero	$\top$	$\bot$	$\bot$	$\bot$

- $(P \parallel Q) ; (R \parallel S) \subseteq (P ; R) \parallel (Q ; S)$

This is a form of mutual distribution between the two operators, where different components of each operand distribute through to different components of the other operand. The refinement in the law reflects the fact that concurrency introduces nondeterminism, whereas sequential composition does not. It says that the program $(P \parallel Q) ; (R \parallel S)$ has fewer behaviours than $(P ; R) \parallel (Q ; S)$.

But is the law in fact true of implementations of concurrency in real computers and in usable programming languages? Yes, it is true for all implementations which interleave the independent actions from the constituent threads; or implementations which are sequentially consistent, in that they successfully simulate such an interleaving. Here is an informal proof. The right-hand side of the inclusion describes all interleavings of an execution of $(P ; R)$ with an execution of $(Q ; S)$. The left hand side describes all interleavings which synchronise at the two semicolons displayed in $(P ; R)$ and $(Q ; S)$. Thus the left hand side contains $<p_1, q, p_2, r_1, s, r_2>$, but it does not contain $<p_1, q, s, p_2, r_1, r_2>$, which is an interleaving of the right side (here the lower case letters denote sub-executions of the executions of the corresponding upper case programs).

The exchange law can be exploited in a divide-and-conquer algorithm to compute one (or all) of the interleavings of two strings. If one of the arguments is empty, deliver the other argument as result. Otherwise, split each string arbitrarily into two parts $P ; R$ and $Q ; S$. Then (recursively) find an interleaving of P with Q and an interleaving of R with S. Concatenate the two results.

Iteration is another common programming construct. This unary operator is typically written as a postfix Kleene star: P^* describes the iteration where P is performed zero or more times in sequence. Iteration interacts with the other operators according to laws from Kleene algebra [6]:

- $\mathit{skip} \vee (P ; P^*) \subseteq P^*$
- $P \vee (Q ; R) \subseteq R \quad \Rightarrow \quad Q^* ; P \subseteq R$
- $\mathit{skip} \vee (P^* ; P) \subseteq P^*$
- $P \vee (R ; Q) \subseteq R \quad \Rightarrow \quad P ; Q^* \subseteq R$

The first law says that P^* has more behaviours than *skip*, and more behaviours than $P ; P^*$. A valid implementation of an iteration can therefore start by unfolding it into two cases, one of which does no iterations, and the other of which does at least one iteration. The second law implies that iteration is the least solution of the first inequation. It permits inductive proofs of the properties of an iteration. The last two laws simply swap the arguments of (;).

2.1 Theorems

A binary operator that distributes through ($\vee$) is monotone in both arguments. So for $\circ \in \{\vee, \wedge, ;, \|\}$:

($\circ$Monotone) $$P \subseteq P' \ \& \ Q \subseteq Q' \ \Rightarrow \ P \circ Q \subseteq P' \circ Q'$$

Also, the exchange law has several consequences that can be proved as theorems with the help of the properties in Table 1. In particular, two small exchange laws hold, and sequential composition refines concurrent composition (i.e. it is a special case thereof):

(SmallExchange$_1$) $$P ; (Q \| R) \subseteq (P ; Q) \| R$$
(SmallExchange$_2$) $$(P \| Q) ; R \subseteq P \| (Q ; R)$$
(SeqRefinesConc) $$P ; Q \subseteq P \| Q$$

Although exchange is a less familiar form of distribution law, there are also other cases where operators exchange. For example, it follows as a theorem that (;) exchanges with ($\wedge$):[1]

(ConjExchange) $$(P \wedge Q) ; (R \wedge S) \subseteq (P ; R) \wedge (Q ; S)$$

An interesting property of all our algebraic laws is that (like many laws in physics) they remain true when the direction of time is reversed. In other words, they preserve the symmetry of time-reversal. Formally expressed, each law remains valid when sequential composition is replaced by backward sequential composition ($\breve{;}$), defined

$$P \breve{;} Q \stackrel{\text{def}}{=} Q ; P$$

As a consequence, every theorem of our algebra also respects time-reversal: swapping the arguments of every (;) in a theorem yields another theorem for free. Swapping the arguments of (;) once again will result in the original theorem, so time-reversal is a duality.

Of course, there are useful and realistic laws that do not respect time-reversal. For example, if *abort* stands for a program that never terminates and never has any interaction with its environment, it could realistically be stated to satisfy:

$$P \neq \bot \ \Rightarrow \ abort ; P = abort$$

[1] The same theorem holds when (;) is replaced by ($\|$) or any other monotonic operator. The dual property, where ($\vee$) replaces ($\wedge$) and the refinement order is reversed, also holds.

Such a law could be added to our algebra, but it would not respect time-reversal.

The algebra embodies other algebraic structures used in computer science. For example, if $\mathbb{D}$ is the set of descriptions, then:

- $(\mathbb{D}, \vee, ;, ^*, \bot, \mathit{skip})$ is a Kleene algebra [6].
- $(\mathbb{D}, \vee, ;, \bot, \mathit{skip})$ is an idempotent semiring.
- $(\mathbb{D}, \vee, \wedge, \bot, \top)$ is a bounded lattice.
- When the lattice is complete and (;) and ($\|$) distribute through arbitrary suprema, then $(\mathbb{D}, \vee, \bot, \|, ;, \mathit{skip})$ is a concurrent Kleene algebra [7].

3 A General Operational Calculus

The general operational calculus uses a quintuple $\langle P,\, s\rangle \xrightarrow{Q} \langle P',\, s'\rangle$ as the basic judgement. It says that the configuration $\langle P,\, s\rangle$ can evolve to $\langle P',\, s'\rangle$ in a single step by performing the action Q. Here P and s describe the initial program and computational state respectively, and P' describes the remaining program and s' the resulting computational state. Formally:

$$\langle P,\, s\rangle \xrightarrow{Q} \langle P',\, s'\rangle \;\stackrel{\mathbf{def}}{=}\; Q \in \mathit{Actions} \;\;\&\;\; P \supseteq Q\,;P' \;\;\&\;\; s\,;Q \supseteq s'$$

The set *Actions* contains descriptions of primitive actions. Since actions are executed in a single step, an operational semantics can choose a step size by defining *Actions* appropriately. For example, a big-step calculus can put everything in the *Actions* set, while a small-step calculus can confine the set to atomic actions such as *skip*, communications, tests and assignments. Our only requirement is that *Actions* shall include *skip*.

The second conjunct in the definition says that it is possible to refine a program P into a pair consisting of the prefix action Q and remainder program P'. Hence one possible way of executing P is by doing Q first and then executing P'. The direction of refinement reflects the fact that execution may reduce or resolve the nondeterminism in a program under execution.

The third conjunct says that if s describes a machine state before doing Q, then s' describes a possible state thereafter. We have associated a state with an execution history, or more generally, a set of possible execution histories. Then $s\,;Q$ describes the full set of possible execution histories that result from doing Q in state s. A state s' describes a possible final state of the execution when it is contained in $s\,;Q$, i.e. every execution history that s' describes as possible is indeed possible for $s\,;Q$.

The conjuncts in the definition of the general quintuple embody an important separation of concerns. The second conjunct describes how an action relates before/after programs, and the third conjunct describes how an action relates before/after states. Combining these notions in a single judgement makes it straightforward later on to derive the rules of familiar calculi from the general ones.

The inference rules of the general calculus all follow from the algebraic laws and are therefore theorems. Some rules are shared among the small-step and big-step calculi that we treat in the next section, for example:

(Gaction) $P \in \mathit{Actions} \;\Rightarrow\; \langle P,\, s\rangle \xrightarrow{P} \langle \mathit{skip},\, s\,;P\rangle$

(Gskip) $\langle \mathit{skip},\, s\rangle \xrightarrow{\mathit{skip}} \langle \mathit{skip},\, s\rangle$

(Gchoice1) $\langle P,\, s\rangle \xrightarrow{Q} \langle P',\, s'\rangle \;\Rightarrow\; \langle P \vee P'',\, s\rangle \xrightarrow{Q} \langle P',\, s'\rangle$

(Gchoice2) $\langle P',\, s\rangle \xrightarrow{Q} \langle P'',\, s'\rangle \;\Rightarrow\; \langle P \vee P',\, s\rangle \xrightarrow{Q} \langle P'',\, s'\rangle$

(Giter) $\langle P^*,\, s\rangle \xrightarrow{\mathit{skip}} \langle \mathit{skip},\, s\rangle$

Small-step calculi use several additional rules, such as:

(GSseq1) $\langle P,\, s\rangle \xrightarrow{Q} \langle P',\, s'\rangle \;\Rightarrow\; \langle P\,;P'',\, s\rangle \xrightarrow{Q} \langle P'\,;P'',\, s'\rangle$

(GSseq2) $\langle P,\, s\rangle \xrightarrow{Q} \langle \mathit{skip},\, s'\rangle \;\Rightarrow\; \langle P\,;P',\, s\rangle \xrightarrow{Q} \langle P',\, s'\rangle$

(GSchoice1) $\langle P \vee P',\, s\rangle \xrightarrow{\mathit{skip}} \langle P,\, s\rangle$

(GSchoice2) $\langle P \vee P',\, s\rangle \xrightarrow{\mathit{skip}} \langle P',\, s\rangle$

(GSiter) $\langle P^*,\, s\rangle \xrightarrow{\mathit{skip}} \langle P\,;P^*,\, s\rangle$

(GSconc1) $\langle P,\, s\rangle \xrightarrow{Q} \langle P',\, s'\rangle \;\Rightarrow\; \langle P \parallel P'',\, s\rangle \xrightarrow{Q} \langle P' \parallel P'',\, s'\rangle$

(GSconc2) $\langle P,\, s\rangle \xrightarrow{Q} \langle \mathit{skip},\, s'\rangle \;\Rightarrow\; \langle P \parallel P',\, s\rangle \xrightarrow{Q} \langle P',\, s'\rangle$

Rules for executing the second operand of a concurrent composition follow from (GSconc1) and (GSconc2) by the commutativity of $(\parallel)$.

Big-step calculi such as Kahn's natural semantics have judgements that execute programs to completion. This behaviour is captured by general rules that only use judgements of the form $\langle P,\, s\rangle \xrightarrow{Q} \langle \mathit{skip},\, s'\rangle$. The following examples of big-step rules all have as additional premisses $\langle P,\, s\rangle \xrightarrow{Q} \langle \mathit{skip},\, s'\rangle$ and $Q\,;Q' \in \mathit{Actions}$:

(GBseq) $\langle P',\, s'\rangle \xrightarrow{Q'} \langle \mathit{skip},\, s''\rangle \;\Rightarrow\; \langle P\,;P',\, s\rangle \xrightarrow{Q;Q'} \langle \mathit{skip},\, s''\rangle$

(GBiter) $\langle P^*,\, s'\rangle \xrightarrow{Q'} \langle \mathit{skip},\, s''\rangle \;\Rightarrow\; \langle P^*,\, s\rangle \xrightarrow{Q;Q'} \langle \mathit{skip},\, s''\rangle$

(GBconc1) $\langle P',\, s'\rangle \xrightarrow{Q'} \langle \mathit{skip},\, s''\rangle \;\Rightarrow\; \langle P \parallel P',\, s\rangle \xrightarrow{Q;Q'} \langle \mathit{skip},\, s''\rangle$

(GBconc2) $\langle P',\, s'\rangle \xrightarrow{Q'} \langle \mathit{skip},\, s''\rangle \;\Rightarrow\; \langle P' \parallel P,\, s\rangle \xrightarrow{Q;Q'} \langle \mathit{skip},\, s''\rangle$

4 Specialisations

Various familiar operational calculi follow from the general calculus. Each derived calculus bases its judgement(s) on the general quintuple, and uses a subset of the general rules.

4.1 Structural Operational Semantics

The structural operational semantics[2] of Plotkin [1] is a small-step semantics that leaves computer actions implicit. An existential quantifiers hides the action in its fundamental judgement:

$$\langle P, s\rangle \longrightarrow \langle P', s'\rangle \stackrel{\mathbf{def}}{=} \exists Q : \langle P, s\rangle \stackrel{Q}{\longrightarrow} \langle P', s'\rangle$$

For the special case where a program is executed to completion in a single step, it uses a judgement with three arguments:

$$\langle P, s\rangle \longrightarrow s' \stackrel{\mathbf{def}}{=} \exists Q : \langle P, s\rangle \stackrel{Q}{\longrightarrow} \langle \mathit{skip}, s'\rangle$$

Using these definitions, it is simple to show that the inference rules of structural operational semantics follow from general rules and hence hold as theorems. For example:

(Pskip)	$\langle \mathit{skip}, s\rangle \longrightarrow s$
(Pseq1)	$\langle P, s\rangle \longrightarrow \langle P', s'\rangle \;\Rightarrow\; \langle P ; P'', s\rangle \longrightarrow \langle P' ; P'', s'\rangle$
(Pseq2)	$\langle P, s\rangle \longrightarrow s' \;\Rightarrow\; \langle P ; P', s\rangle \longrightarrow \langle P', s'\rangle$
(Pchoice1)	$\langle P \vee P', s\rangle \longrightarrow \langle P, s\rangle$
(Pchoice2)	$\langle P \vee P', s\rangle \longrightarrow \langle P', s\rangle$
(Piter1)	$\langle P^*, s\rangle \longrightarrow s$
(Piter2)	$\langle P^*, s\rangle \longrightarrow \langle P ; P^*, s\rangle$
(Pconc1)	$\langle P, s\rangle \longrightarrow \langle P', s'\rangle \;\Rightarrow\; \langle P \parallel P'', s\rangle \longrightarrow \langle P' \parallel P'', s'\rangle$
(Pconc2)	$\langle P, s\rangle \longrightarrow s' \;\Rightarrow\; \langle P \parallel P', s\rangle \longrightarrow \langle P', s'\rangle$

4.2 Process Calculus Semantics

This style of operational semantics was introduced by Milner for CCS in [8], and has also been used to specify the operational meaning of other process calculi. It uses small execution steps to accommodate concurrency, and hides machine states in its fundamental judgement:

$$P \stackrel{Q}{\longrightarrow} P' \stackrel{\mathbf{def}}{=} \forall s : \exists s' : \langle P, s\rangle \stackrel{Q}{\longrightarrow} \langle P', s'\rangle$$

An alternative but equivalent characterization of $P \stackrel{Q}{\longrightarrow} P'$ says that one possible way of executing the program P is by doing the action Q first and then executing the program P':

$$P \stackrel{Q}{\longrightarrow} P' \quad\Leftrightarrow\quad Q \in \mathit{Actions} \;\;\&\;\; P \supseteq Q ; P'$$

[2] Also called *transition* semantics.

The next theorem shows that the state components can equivalently be made implicit with existential quantifiers:

$$P \xrightarrow{Q} P' \quad \Leftrightarrow \quad \exists s, s' : \langle P,\, s\rangle \xrightarrow{Q} \langle P',\, s'\rangle$$

By using this equivalence, it is simple to see that operational inference rules of process calculi follow as theorems from general operational rules.

(Maction) $\qquad P \in \mathit{Actions} \quad \Rightarrow \quad P \xrightarrow{P} \mathit{skip}$

The judgement $P \xrightarrow{Q} \mathit{skip}$ says that P can be completely executed in a single step by doing Q, since it remains to do nothing (*skip*). This is sometimes written $P \xrightarrow{Q} \surd$ in process calculi (e.g. [9]), so the above rule states that $P \xrightarrow{P} \surd$ holds when $P \in \mathit{Actions}$.

(Mseq1) $\qquad P \xrightarrow{Q} P' \quad \Rightarrow \quad P ; P'' \xrightarrow{Q} P' ; P''$

(Mseq2) $\qquad P \xrightarrow{Q} \mathit{skip} \quad \Rightarrow \quad P ; P' \xrightarrow{Q} P'$

CCS uses prefixing – a restricted form of sequential composition in which the first operand must be an action. Combining (Maction) and (Mseq2) gives Milner's rule:

(Mprefixing) $\qquad P \in \mathit{Actions} \quad \Rightarrow \quad P ; P' \xrightarrow{P} P'$

A judgement $P \xrightarrow{\mathit{skip}} P'$ says that without doing real work, the program P can be validly rearranged/rewritten as P', which is then executed instead. The notation $P \longrightarrow P'$ abbreviates $P \xrightarrow{\mathit{skip}} P'$ and is equivalent to $P \supseteq P'$. Hence rearrangement is simply refinement – a reduction in the program's nondeterminism. Resolving a nondeterministic choice and unfolding an iteration are example rearrangements.

(Mchoice1) $\qquad P \vee P' \longrightarrow P$

(Mchoice2) $\qquad P \vee P' \longrightarrow P'$

(Miter1) $\qquad P^* \longrightarrow \mathit{skip}$

(Miter2) $\qquad P^* \longrightarrow P ; P^*$

(Mconc1) $\qquad P \xrightarrow{Q} P' \quad \Rightarrow \quad P \parallel P'' \xrightarrow{Q} P' \parallel P''$

(Mconc2) $\qquad P \xrightarrow{Q} \mathit{skip} \quad \Rightarrow \quad P \parallel P' \xrightarrow{Q} P'$

Almost all process calculi include features for communication. A communication in CCS combines actions from two or more concurrent processes in a single action. Since the participating actions must happen together, the communication achieves a rendezvous among the processes. For example, CCS allows a process performing an input action a and a concurrent process performing output action $\bar{a}$ to communicate, and doing so yields the internal action τ:

$$P \xrightarrow{a} P' \quad \& \quad R \xrightarrow{\overline{a}} R' \quad \Rightarrow \quad P \parallel R \xrightarrow{\tau} P' \parallel R'$$

By requiring that $\tau \subseteq a \parallel \overline{a}$, it is generalized by the theorem:

$$P \xrightarrow{Q} P' \quad \& \quad R \xrightarrow{Q'} R' \quad \& \quad Q'' \in \mathit{Actions} \quad \& \quad Q'' \subseteq Q \parallel Q'$$
$$\Rightarrow \quad P \parallel R \xrightarrow{Q''} P' \parallel R'$$

Note that the participating actions are combined in a concurrent composition that forms the basis of the communication action. Instead of requiring $\tau \subseteq a \parallel \overline{a}$, the calculus can define τ_a as $a \parallel \overline{a}$ and adopt the convention that τ stands for τ_a for some a. However, such choices fall outside the scope of the current paper, which does not treat specific basic actions apart from *skip*.

4.3 Reduction Semantics with Evaluation Contexts

This flavour of operational semantics was originally presented by Felleisen and Hieb [3] for a functional language, but is readily adapted to imperative settings (see e.g. [10]). It combines the notion of an explicit evaluation context with aspects of Milner and Plotkin semantics to provide a compact operational calculus. It uses two judgements: the $P \longrightarrow P'$ reduction/rearrangement judgement of the Milner calculus, and Plotkin's judgement $\langle P, s\rangle \longrightarrow \langle P', s'\rangle$.

The idea of an explicit evaluation context is central to the calculus. There are two kinds of evaluation context: program contexts and configuration contexts. A program context is a program with a hole where another program can be plugged in. An execution step of any plugged-in program must also be a step of the context plus program combination, so holes indicate which program components may be executed next. Formally, a program context is any function $pc \in \mathbb{D} \to \mathbb{D}$ (where $\mathbb{D}$ is the set of all descriptions) such that

$$P \xrightarrow{Q} P' \quad \Rightarrow \quad pc(P) \xrightarrow{Q} pc(P')$$

The identity function is the empty program context, and it is evident from the Milner rules that $\lambda x.\,(x\,;P)$, $\lambda x.\,(x \parallel P)$ and $\lambda x.\,(P \parallel x)$ are also valid program contexts. The last two show that there might be more than one way to factor a program into a context-program pair, i.e. it is possible that two or more of its components are ready for execution.

The functional composition of two program contexts is again a program context, so e.g. $\lambda x.\,((P \parallel (x \parallel P'))\,; P'')$ is also a program context.

The second kind of evaluation context is a configuration context. A configuration context is a construct of the form $\langle pc, s\rangle$ which maps descriptions to configurations: $\langle pc, s\rangle(P) = \langle pc(P), s\rangle$. In summary, an evaluation context ec is a function in $\mathbb{D} \to (\mathbb{D} \cup \mathit{Configurations})$ that is either a program context or a configuration context.

In contrast to the Plotkin and Milner calculi, the calculus has only one inference rule with a premise. It states that if a program P reduces to P', then this reduction is valid inside any evaluation context:

$$\text{(Rmain)} \qquad P \longrightarrow P' \quad \Rightarrow \quad ec(P) \longrightarrow ec(P')$$

Apart from specifying contexts and this rule, the calculus has a small set of rules of the form $P \longrightarrow P'$ and a small set of rules of the form $\langle P,\, s\rangle \longrightarrow \langle P',\, s'\rangle$. By using (Rmain), it becomes possible to derive more complicated judgements of the form $P \longrightarrow P'$ and additional judgements of the form $\langle P,\, s\rangle \longrightarrow \langle P',\, s'\rangle$.

Reduction rules of the form $P \longrightarrow P'$ that the calculus adopts as axioms include the Milner rules for nondeterministic choice and iteration, as well as trivial rules for sequential composition and concurrency:

$$\text{(Rseq)} \qquad skip\,; P \longrightarrow P$$
$$\text{(Rconc1)} \qquad skip \parallel P \longrightarrow P$$
$$\text{(Rconc2)} \qquad P \parallel skip \longrightarrow P$$

Here are examples of how (Rmain) and these rules support reasoning about program execution. Since $\lambda x.\, \langle (P \parallel (x \parallel P'))\,; P'',\, s\rangle$ is a valid evaluation context, one can use (Rmain) with (Mchoice1), (Miter2) and (Rseq) respectively to deduce the judgements:

- $\langle (P \parallel ((P_1 \vee P_2) \parallel P'))\,; P'',\, s\rangle \longrightarrow \langle (P \parallel (P_1 \parallel P'))\,; P'',\, s\rangle$
- $\langle (P \parallel ((P_1{}^*) \parallel P'))\,; P'',\, s\rangle \longrightarrow \langle (P \parallel ((P_1\,; P_1{}^*) \parallel P'))\,; P'',\, s\rangle$
- $\langle (P \parallel ((skip\,; P_1) \parallel P'))\,; P'',\, s\rangle \longrightarrow \langle (P \parallel (P_1 \parallel P'))\,; P'',\, s\rangle$

The calculus typically includes one or more rules of the form $\langle P,\, s\rangle \longrightarrow \langle P',\, s'\rangle$ for each action. If Q is an action, and s' faithfully records the effect of Q on s, i.e. Plotkin's judgement $\langle Q,\, s\rangle \longrightarrow s'$ holds, then it is justified to adopt the rule:

$$\langle pc,\, s\rangle(Q) \longrightarrow \langle pc,\, s'\rangle(skip)$$

which can also be written as:

$$\langle pc(Q),\, s\rangle \longrightarrow \langle pc(skip),\, s'\rangle$$

As Milner triples are available in our setting, and $Q \xrightarrow{Q} skip$ for all actions Q, the idea is generalized by the theorem:

$$P \xrightarrow{Q} P' \;\;\&\;\; \langle Q,\, s\rangle \longrightarrow s' \quad \Rightarrow \quad \langle pc(P),\, s\rangle \longrightarrow \langle pc(P'),\, s'\rangle$$

which in turn follows from the equivalence:

$$P \xrightarrow{Q} P' \;\;\&\;\; \langle Q,\, s\rangle \longrightarrow s' \quad \Leftrightarrow \quad (\forall pc : \langle pc(P),\, s\rangle \xrightarrow{Q} \langle pc(P'),\, s'\rangle)$$

Because its right side is equivalent to $\langle P,\, s\rangle \xrightarrow{Q} \langle P',\, s'\rangle$, the theorem illustrates the reversible decomposition of a quintuple into a Milner transition and a state transformation:

$$\langle P,\, s\rangle \xrightarrow{Q} \langle P',\, s'\rangle \quad \Leftrightarrow \quad P \xrightarrow{Q} P' \quad \& \quad \langle Q,\, s\rangle \longrightarrow s'$$

4.4 A Small-Step Semantics with Implicit States and Implicit Actions

In [11], Plotkin considers Milner's presentation of operational rules for CCS, and observes that "for an imperative language, one could also leave the state component implicit". He also gives an example of such a rule:

$$\text{(Oseq1)} \qquad P \to P' \quad \Rightarrow \quad P\,;P'' \to P'\,;P''$$

This calculus is based on structural operational semantics, so it uses small execution steps. The state components of the Plotkin judgement are hidden by quantifiers:

$$P \to P' \overset{\text{def}}{=} \forall s : \exists s' : \langle P,\, s\rangle \longrightarrow \langle P',\, s'\rangle$$

The next theorem shows that the state components can equivalently be made implicit with existential quantifiers:

$$P \to P' \quad \Leftrightarrow \quad \exists s, s' : \langle P,\, s\rangle \longrightarrow \langle P',\, s'\rangle$$

There is also a direct relationship with the Milner judgement:

$$P \to P' \quad \Leftrightarrow \quad \exists Q : P \xrightarrow{Q} P'$$

Using the first equivalence, it is simple to derive additional rules of the calculus from the Plotkin ones. The same is true for the second equivalence and the Milner rules. For example:

$$\begin{array}{ll} \text{(Oseq2)} & P \to \mathit{skip} \quad \Rightarrow \quad P\,;P' \to P' \\ \text{(Ochoice1)} & P \vee P' \to P \\ \text{(Oiter2)} & P^* \to P\,;P^* \\ \text{(Oconc1)} & P \to P' \quad \Rightarrow \quad P \parallel P'' \to P' \parallel P'' \end{array}$$

If a rule of the Milner calculus had the same action in its premise and conclusion judgements, then it is justified to think that in its implicit action counterpart here, the effect on the implicit state in the premise judgement may also be attributed to the conclusion judgement. In (Oconc1), for example, if evolving P into P' has a certain effect on the implicit state, then evolving $P \parallel P''$ into

$P' \parallel P''$ can have the same effect on the implicit state. Of course, (Oconc1) also says that evolving $P \parallel P''$ into $P' \parallel P''$ is valid if P can evolve to P'.

4.5 The Chemical Abstract Machine

The chemical abstract machine (cham) of Berry and Boudol [12] uses a chemical metaphor to specify the operational semantics of concurrent languages. According to [12]:

> Unlike some other models, the Γ and cham models are operational in character and handle (true) concurrency as *the* primitive built-in notion.

A chemical solution is the fundamental structuring concept that models concurrency in a cham. It abbreviates the concurrent composition of its comprising molecules (descriptions):

$$\{\!|P_1, \ldots, P_n|\!\} \stackrel{\text{def}}{=} P_1 \parallel \cdots \parallel P_n$$

Cham postulates that chemical solutions behave like multisets, i.e. that concurrency is commutative, associative and has a unit. These assumptions are validated by our algebraic laws. Thus the multiset union $\uplus$ of chemical solutions is $(\parallel)$, and the unit of $\uplus$, the empty solution $\{\!|\,|\!\}$, is *skip*. These facts can be used together with the rules of our general operational theory to derive the cham rules as theorems.

Chemical solutions encapsulate molecules and can be structured hierarchically. To interact with its environment, a nested solution can expose one of its molecules in a reversible way with an airlock operator. We define a generalized airlock operator[3], whose second argument is a program context, as follows:

$$P \blacktriangleleft pc \stackrel{\text{def}}{=} pc(P)$$

The cham's standard airlock is defined in terms of the general one:

$$P \triangleleft P' \stackrel{\text{def}}{=} P \blacktriangleleft \lambda x.\,(x \parallel P')$$

Cham has three judgements: a heating judgement $\rightharpoonup$, a cooling judgement $\rightharpoondown$, and a reaction judgement $\rightarrow$. Heating and cooling differ only conceptually – both are defined as the Milner judgement $P \stackrel{skip}{\longrightarrow} P'$:

$$\begin{array}{lll} P \rightharpoonup P' & \stackrel{\text{def}}{=} & P \longrightarrow P' \\ P \rightharpoondown P' & \stackrel{\text{def}}{=} & P \longrightarrow P' \end{array}$$

The symbol $\rightleftharpoons$ abbreviates a heating/cooling judgement pair:

$$P \rightleftharpoons P' \stackrel{\text{def}}{=} P \rightharpoonup P' \;\;\&\;\; P' \rightharpoondown P$$

---

[3] The definition and use of the general airlock operator was inspired by the treatment in [10] and the manipulation of heavy ions in [12].

Such pairs express manipulations that do not alter a solution or molecule in a fundamental way: $P \rightleftharpoons P'$ is equivalent to $P = P'$.

Reaction judgements are unlabeled transitions that can specify real work. The reaction judgement $P \rightarrow P'$ was defined in the previous section and is equivalent to $\exists Q : P \xrightarrow{Q} P'$. Heating and cooling are special kinds of reactions.

Cham has only two rules with premisses: the chemical rule and the solution rule[4]. For $\leadsto$ in $\{\rightharpoonup, \rightharpoondown, \rightleftharpoons, \rightarrow\}$:

(Cchemical)	$P \leadsto P' \quad \Rightarrow \quad P \uplus P'' \leadsto P' \uplus P''$
(Csolution)	$P \leadsto P' \quad \Rightarrow \quad \{\!\|pc(P)\|\!\} \leadsto \{\!\|pc(P')\|\!\}$

The other cham rules are premise-free and also hold as theorems:

(CgeneralAirlock)	$\{\!\|pc(P)\|\!\} \rightleftharpoons \{\!\|P \blacktriangleleft pc\|\!\}$
(Cairlock)	$\{\!\|P\|\!\} \uplus P' \rightleftharpoons \{\!\|P \lhd P'\|\!\}$
(Cseq)	$\{\!\|(P\,;P') \lhd P''\|\!\} \rightleftharpoons \{\!\|P \blacktriangleleft \lambda x.\,((x\,;P') \lhd P'')\|\!\}$
(Cconc)	$\{\!\|P \parallel P'\|\!\} \rightleftharpoons \{\!\|P, P'\|\!\}$
(Cchoice1)	$\{\!\|(P \vee P') \blacktriangleleft pc\|\!\} \rightarrow \{\!\|P \blacktriangleleft pc\|\!\}$
(Cchoice2)	$\{\!\|(P \vee P') \blacktriangleleft pc\|\!\} \rightarrow \{\!\|P' \blacktriangleleft pc\|\!\}$
(Citer1)	$\{\!\|P^* \blacktriangleleft pc\|\!\} \rightarrow \{\!\|\mathit{skip} \blacktriangleleft pc\|\!\}$
(Citer2)	$\{\!\|P^* \blacktriangleleft pc\|\!\} \rightarrow \{\!\|(P\,;P^*) \blacktriangleleft pc\|\!\}$
(Cdropskip)	$\{\!\|(\mathit{skip}\,;P) \blacktriangleleft pc\|\!\} \rightarrow \{\!\|P \blacktriangleleft pc\|\!\}$
(Cskip)	$\{\!\|\mathit{skip}\|\!\} \rightharpoonup \{\!\|\ \|\!\}$

Here is an example computation with cham showing that $(Q\,;P) \parallel P^*$ can reduce to P under the assumption $\{\!|Q \blacktriangleleft pc|\!\} \rightarrow \{\!|\mathit{skip} \blacktriangleleft pc|\!\}$:

$$
\begin{array}{ll}
 & \{\!|(Q\,;P) \parallel P^*|\!\} \\
\rightharpoonup & \text{(Cconc)} \\
 & \{\!|Q\,;P, P^*|\!\} \\
\rightharpoonup & \text{(Cairlock)} \\
 & \{\!|(Q\,;P) \lhd \{\!|P^*|\!\}|\!\} \\
\rightharpoonup & \text{(Cseq)} \\
 & \{\!|Q \blacktriangleleft \lambda x.\,((x\,;P) \lhd \{\!|P^*|\!\})|\!\} \\
\rightarrow & \text{(Csolution) with (Citer1)} \\
 & \{\!|Q \blacktriangleleft \lambda x.\,((x\,;P) \lhd \{\!|\mathit{skip}|\!\})|\!\} \\
\rightarrow & \text{Assumption} \\
 & \{\!|\mathit{skip} \blacktriangleleft \lambda x.\,((x\,;P) \lhd \{\!|\mathit{skip}|\!\})|\!\} \\
\rightharpoondown & \text{(Cseq)} \\
 & \{\!|(\mathit{skip}\,;P) \lhd \{\!|\mathit{skip}|\!\}|\!\} \\
\rightarrow & \text{(Cdropskip)}
\end{array}
$$

[4] The solution rule is called the *membrane rule* in [12]. The membrane operator $\{\!|\_, \ldots, \_|\!\}$ corresponds to iterated concurrent composition. Applying a membrane to molecules results in a chemical solution.

$\{\!|P \lhd \{\!|skip|\!\}|\!\}$
$\rightharpoondown$ (Cairlock)
$\{\!|P, skip|\!\}$
$\rightharpoonup$ (Cchemical) with (Cskip)
$\{\!|P|\!\}$

This example and the ones in [12] chain simple judgements to show a reduction. However, the solution and chemical rules makes cham a "truly concurrent" calculus according to [12]:

> A cham is an intrinsically parallel machine: one can simultaneously apply several rules to a solution provided that their premisses are not conflicting, i.e. that no molecule is involved in more than one rule; one can also transform subsolutions in parallel.

Berry and Boudol do not adopt a particular evaluation scheme, and state that "a nonconflicting parallel application of rules is equivalent, up to permutations, to any sequence of the individual rules" [12].

True concurrency can be made explicit by allowing concurrent actions, i.e. closing *Actions* under $(\|)$:

$$Q \in Actions \quad \& \quad Q' \in Actions \quad \Rightarrow \quad Q \parallel Q' \in Actions$$

and generalizing a program context to be any n-ary function $pc \in \mathbb{D}^n \to \mathbb{D}$ that satisfies:

$$P_1 \xrightarrow{Q_1} P_1' \quad \& \quad \ldots \quad \& \quad P_n \xrightarrow{Q_n} P_n' \quad \Rightarrow \quad pc(P_1, \ldots, P_n) \xrightarrow{Q_1 \| \ldots \| Q_n} pc(P_1', \ldots, P_n')$$

This also suggests the possibility of adapting other operational calculi to implement the cham notion of true concurrency.

4.6 Natural Semantics

The natural semantics[5] of Kahn [2] was originally presented for a functional language. The idea is readily adapted to imperative settings (see e.g. [13]), where the fundamental judgement involves a program, an input and an output state. The calculus allows arbitrarily big execution steps by including every description in the set *Actions*. All programs are executed to completion and machine actions are left implicit.

$$\langle P, s\rangle \longrightarrow s' \stackrel{\text{def}}{=} \exists Q : \langle P, s\rangle \xrightarrow{Q} \langle skip, s'\rangle$$

As expected, $\langle P, s\rangle \longrightarrow s'$ asserts that s' describes a possible final machine state after program P has been executed in initial state s:

$$\langle P, s\rangle \longrightarrow s' \quad \Leftrightarrow \quad s\,; P \supseteq s'$$

[5] Also called *evaluation* semantics.

The inference rules of natural semantics follow from the general rules and are therefore theorems. For instance:

(Kskip)	$\langle skip,\, s\rangle \longrightarrow s$
(Kseq)	$\langle P,\, s\rangle \longrightarrow s' \;\;\&\;\; \langle P',\, s'\rangle \longrightarrow s'' \;\;\Rightarrow\;\; \langle P\,;P',\, s\rangle \longrightarrow s''$
(Kchoice1)	$\langle P,\, s\rangle \longrightarrow s' \;\;\Rightarrow\;\; \langle P \vee P',\, s\rangle \longrightarrow s'$
(Kiter1)	$\langle P^*,\, s\rangle \longrightarrow s$
(Kiter2)	$\langle P,\, s\rangle \longrightarrow s' \;\;\&\;\; \langle P^*,\, s'\rangle \longrightarrow s'' \;\;\Rightarrow\;\; \langle P^*,\, s\rangle \longrightarrow s''$
(Kconc1)	$\langle P,\, s\rangle \longrightarrow s' \;\;\&\;\; \langle P',\, s'\rangle \longrightarrow s'' \;\;\Rightarrow\;\; \langle P \parallel P',\, s\rangle \longrightarrow s''$
(Kconc2)	$\langle P',\, s\rangle \longrightarrow s' \;\;\&\;\; \langle P,\, s'\rangle \longrightarrow s'' \;\;\Rightarrow\;\; \langle P \parallel P',\, s\rangle \longrightarrow s''$

The rules for concurrency are trivial and not very interesting. As Nielson and Nielson remark [13, p. 50], "in a natural semantics the execution of the immediate constituents [of a parallel composition] is an atomic entity so we cannot express interleaving of computations". In contrast to this, the small-step calculi can easily express interleaving.

Because of this problem, a big-step version of Milner semantics (where *Actions* contain all descriptions and all judgements have the form $P \xrightarrow{Q} skip$, i.e. programs are executed to completion) is not very useful for process calculi with concurrency. We do not pursue such a calculus further here, and leave its construction to interested readers.

5 Conclusion

This paper concentrates on the unification of a wide range of existing operational calculi by a simple algebra. The same algebraic laws form the basis of other calculi of programming such as Hoare logic, Dijkstra's weakest precondition calculus, the Back/Morgan refinement calculus and Jones' rely-guarantee calculus - see for example [14,7]. This provides additional evidence that the algebra corresponds to a widely held common understanding of the meaning of programs, and that it can serve as a foundation for more ambitious unification.

The algebraic laws that a calculus needs provide a succinct summary of the properties of programs it relies on. This can form the basis for investigating the differences and commonalities of various calculi. For example, none of the calculi in this paper uses the distribution law $P\,;(P' \vee P'') = (P\,;P') \vee (P\,;P'')$. They rely at most on the weaker property that (;) is monotone in its second argument, i.e. $P\,;(P' \vee P'') \supseteq (P\,;P') \vee (P\,;P'')$. This commonality between the operational calculi contrasts sharply with the deductive Hoare calculus, which requires the law $P\,;(P' \vee P'') \subseteq (P\,;P') \vee (P\,;P'')$ for its rule for nondeterministic choice [7]:

$$P\,\{Q\}\,R \;\;\&\;\; P\,\{Q'\}\,R \;\;\Rightarrow\;\; P\,\{Q \vee Q'\}\,R$$

Algebra is simple, elegant and abstract. One can specify properties of interest without commitment to a particular model. This generality enables reuse in different settings and encourages an incremental style of formalisation, where additional operators and laws are introduced when and if needed. The study of algebra has made an immense contribution to the advancement of mathematics and engineering; and there is now a good prospect that it may also assist in reasoning about the execution and correctness of computer programs.

Acknowledgements. For useful comments and suggestions we are grateful to Thomas Dinsdale-Young, Sophia Drossopoulou, Peter O'Hearn, Rasmus Petersen, Andreas Podelski, Vlad Scherbina, Georg Struth, Jim Woodcock, Hongseok Yang. We are grateful also to other attendants at the meeting of IFIP WG 2.3, held in Winchester 18–23 September, 2011; also the Separation logic Workshop held in Queen Mary University, London, 5–6 October 2011. Van Staden was supported by ETH Research Grant ETH-15 10-1.

References

1. Plotkin, G.D.: A structural approach to operational semantics. Technical Report DAIMI FN-19, Computer Science Department, Aarhus University, Aarhus, Denmark (September 1981)
2. Kahn, G.: Natural Semantics. In: Brandenburg, F.J., Wirsing, M., Vidal-Naquet, G. (eds.) STACS 1987. LNCS, vol. 247, pp. 22–39. Springer, Heidelberg (1987)
3. Felleisen, M., Hieb, R.: The revised report on the syntactic theories of sequential control and state. Theor. Comput. Sci. 103(2), 235–271 (1992)
4. Hoare, C.A.R., Hayes, I.J., Jifeng, H., Morgan, C.C., Roscoe, A.W., Sanders, J.W., Sorensen, I.H., Spivey, J.M., Sufrin, B.A.: Laws of programming. Commun. ACM 30, 672–686 (1987)
5. Isabelle/HOL proofs (2012), `http://se.inf.ethz.ch/people/vanstaden/AlgebraUnifiesOperationalCalculi.thy`
6. Kozen, D.: A completeness theorem for Kleene algebras and the algebra of regular events. Inf. Comput. 110, 366–390 (1994)
7. Tony Hoare, C.A.R., Möller, B., Struth, G., Wehrman, I.: Concurrent Kleene Algebra. In: Bravetti, M., Zavattaro, G. (eds.) CONCUR 2009. LNCS, vol. 5710, pp. 399–414. Springer, Heidelberg (2009)
8. Milner, R.: A Calculus of Communication Systems. LNCS, vol. 92. Springer, Heidelberg (1980)
9. Fokkink, W.: Introduction to Process Algebra, 1st edn. Springer-Verlag New York, Inc., New York (2000)
10. Roşu, G.: Programming Languages: A Rewriting Approach, `http://fsl.cs.uiuc.edu/pub/pl.pdf`
11. Plotkin, G.D.: The origins of structural operational semantics. Journal of Logic and Algebraic Programming 60-61, 3–15 (2004)
12. Berry, G., Boudol, G.: The chemical abstract machine. Theoretical Computer Science 96(1), 217–248 (1992)
13. Nielson, H.R., Nielson, F.: Semantics with Applications: A Formal Introduction, Revised edn. (July 1999), `http://www.daimi.au.dk/~bra8130/Wiley_book/wiley.html`; Original edition published by John Wiley & Sons (1992)
14. Wehrman, I., Hoare, C.A.R., O'Hearn, P.W.: Graphical models of separation logic. Inf. Process. Lett. 109(17), 1001–1004 (2009)

A Probabilistic Theory of Designs Based on Distributions

Riccardo Bresciani and Andrew Butterfield*

Foundations and Methods Group,
Trinity College Dublin,
Dublin, Ireland
{bresciar,butrfeld}@scss.tcd.ie

Abstract. We present a theory of designs based on functions from the state space to real numbers, which we term *distributions*. This theory uses predicates, in the style of UTP, based on homogeneous relations between distributions, and is richer than the standard UTP theory of designs as it allows us to reason about probabilistic programs; the healthiness conditions H1–H4 of the standard theory are implicitly accounted for in the distributional theory we present. In addition we propose a Galois connection linkage between our distribution-based model of probabilistic designs, and the standard UTP model of (non-probabilistic) designs.

1 Introduction

The Unifying Theories of Programming (UTP) aims at a semantic framework where programs and specifications can be modelled as alphabetised relational predicates, capturing the semantic models normally used for their formal description [HJ98, DS06, But10, Qin10]: the advantage of this common framework is that of enabling formal reasoning on the integration of the different languages.

UTP relies on untyped predicate calculus: programs are expressed by means of logical predicates (programs are predicates! [Heh84, Hoa85]), and different theories can be given a UTP semantics, and here we focus on the theory of designs: this theory allows us to reason about the total correctness of programs from the perspective of what preconditions must be met in order to reach some given postconditions.

A challenging research question is how to add probability to the picture, and in particular how to integrate it in a framework where non-determinism is present: we use a framework based on distributions over the state space, where the predicates used involve a homogeneous relation between before- and after-distributions. This allows us to define a probabilistic theory of designs, which can handle programs where both probabilistic and non-deterministic choice co-exist.

This paper is structured as follows: we describe the background to UTP, with particular focus on the standard theory of designs in that framework (§2);

* The present work has emanated from research supported by Science Foundation Ireland grant 08/RFP/CMS1277 and, in part, by Science Foundation Ireland grant 03/CE2/I303_1 to Lero – the Irish Software Engineering Research Centre.

B. Wolff, M.-C. Gaudel, A. Feliachi (Eds.): UTP 2012, LNCS 7681, pp. 105–123, 2013.

introduce a probabilistic framework based on distributions over the state space (§3); present a probabilistic theory of designs in this new framework (§4) and discuss its application to a well-known example (§5); and conclude (§6).

2 Background

2.1 UTP

UTP uses second-order predicates to represent programs: they are used to express relations among a set of *observable variables* which constitute their alphabet.

Observable variables usually occur as both undecorated and decorated with a dash $'$: the former refer to states before the program starts (*before-states*), whereas the latter refer to the final states reached after the program has run (*after-states*).

For example, a program using two variables x and y might be characterised by having the set $\{x, x', y, y'\}$ as an alphabet, and the meaning of the assignment $x := y + 3$ would be described by the predicate

$$x' = y + 3 \wedge y' = y.$$

In effect UTP uses predicate calculus in a disciplined way to build up a relational calculus for reasoning about programs.

In addition to observations of the values of program variables, often we need to introduce observations of other aspects of program execution via so-called auxiliary variables. For example the theory of reactive programs uses three auxiliary variables — namely ok, $wait$, tr, ref — to keep track of information concerning the current program run, such as termination, reach of a stable state, refusals, ...

A key notion in UTP is that of *healthiness conditions*: they are usually characterised as monotonic idempotent predicate transformers whose fixpoints characterise sensible (healthy) predicates. In other words they outlaw all arbitrary predicate calculus statements that describe predicates with no sense — an example is $\neg ok \Rightarrow ok'$, which describes a "program" that must terminate when not started.

This notion is closely related to that of *refinement*, defined as the universal closure[1] of reverse implication:

$$S \sqsubseteq P \mathrel{\hat=} [P \Rightarrow S]$$

Healthy predicates form a lattice under the ordering induced by the refinement relation.

The refinement calculus enables the derivation of an implementation P from a specification S: such derivation can be proven correct if P is a valid refinement of S.

[1] Square brackets denote universal closure, *i.e.* $[P]$ asserts that P is true for all values of its free variables.

Most UTP theories developed so far deal only with non-deterministic choice, nevertheless the introduction of a probabilistic choice operator is beneficial to many application requiring a quantitative approach, for example to evaluate reliability of programs.

Nevertheless some lines of research are moving along this direction. In [HS06] the authors present an approach to unification of probabilistic choice with standard constructs. They provide an example of how the laws of pGCL could be captured in UTP as predicates about program equivalence and refinement. However only an axiomatic semantics was presented, and the laws were justified via a Galois connection to an expectation-based semantic model.

The approach presented in [CS09] is that of decomposing non-deterministic choice into a combination of pure probabilistic choice and a unary operator that accounted for its non-deterministic behaviour . It is worth underlining a comment of theirs, on how still unsatisfactory theories are with respect to the issue of having probabilistic and demonic choice to coexist.

The UTP model described in [He10], which is used to give a UTP-style semantics to a probabilistic BPEL-like language, relates an initial state to a final probability distribution over states, rather than relating before-variables to corresponding after-variables of the same type.

We have previously presented an encoding of the semantics of the probabilistic guarded command language (pGCL) in the UTP framework [BB11, BB12]. This encoding captures pGCL programs as predicate-transformers, on predicates over probability before- and after-distributions.

In §3 we will present the underlying distributional framework, which we subsequently use in order to obtain a probabilistic theory of designs.

2.2 The Standard Theory of Designs

Now that we have given a general overview of the UTP framework, we are going to focus on the theory of designs and present its UTP semantics.

The theory of designs patches the relational theory, in the sense that predicates from the relational theory fail to satisfy the following equality:

$$\mathit{true} ; \mathcal{P} = \mathit{true}$$

In fact according to the relational theory true is a left identity of the sequential composition operator:

$$\begin{aligned} \mathit{true} ; \mathcal{P} &\equiv \exists \underline{v}_m \bullet \mathit{true}\{\underline{v}_m/\underline{v}'\} \wedge \mathcal{P}\{\underline{v}_m/\underline{v}\} \\ &\equiv \exists \underline{v}_m \bullet \mathit{true} \wedge \mathcal{P}\{\underline{v}_m/\underline{v}\} \\ &\equiv \exists \underline{v}_m \bullet \mathcal{P}\{\underline{v}_m/\underline{v}\} \end{aligned}$$

Which reduces to true if $\underline{v} \in fv(\mathcal{P})$, or to $\mathcal{P}$ otherwise.

This has disastrous consequences, as this enables us to show that a program can recover from a never-ending loop:

$$\mathit{true} * \mathit{skip} \equiv \mu X \bullet X \equiv \bot \equiv \mathit{true}$$

...which is surprising, to say the least.

The theory of designs uses an additional auxiliary variable ok (along with its dashed version ok') to record start (and termination) of a program.

A design (specification) is made of a precondition Pre that has to be met when the program starts, and if so the program establishes $Post$ upon termination, which is guaranteed:

$$ok \wedge Pre \Rightarrow ok' \wedge Post$$

for which we use the following shorthand:

$$Pre \vdash Post$$

The semantics of the assignment $x := y + 3$ in this theory is the following:

$$true \vdash x' = y + 3 \wedge y' = y$$

(if started, it will terminate, and the final value of x will equal the initial value of y plus three, with y unchanged).

The behaviour of $true$ with respect to sequential composition is the desirable one, as now we have:

$$\begin{aligned} true; (Pre \vdash Post) &\equiv true; ok \wedge Pre \Rightarrow ok' \wedge Post \\ &\equiv \exists ok_m, \underline{v}_m \bullet true\{ok_m/ok'\}\{\underline{v}_m/\underline{v}'\} \wedge (ok_m \wedge Pre\{\underline{v}_m/\underline{v}\} \Rightarrow ok' \wedge Post) \\ &\equiv \exists ok_m, \underline{v}_m \bullet true \wedge (ok_m \wedge Pre\{\underline{v}_m/\underline{v}\} \Rightarrow ok' \wedge Post) \\ &\equiv \exists ok_m, \underline{v}_m \bullet ok_m \wedge Pre\{\underline{v}_m/\underline{v}\} \Rightarrow ok' \wedge Post \\ &\equiv true \end{aligned}$$

and therefore $true$ is a left zero for sequential composition.

Designs form a lattice, whose bottom and top elements are respectively:

$$abort \triangleq false \vdash false \equiv false \vdash true$$

and

$$miracle \triangleq true \vdash false \equiv \neg ok$$

It should be noted that $miracle$ is a (infeasible) program that cannot be started.

Valid designs are predicates R which comply with four healthiness conditions [HJ98]. The first one (*unpredictability*, H1) excludes from observation all programs that have not started, and therefore restricts valid relations to those such that:

$$R = (ok \Rightarrow R)$$

All H1-healthy predicates satisfy the left zero and left unit laws:

$$true; R = true \qquad \text{and} \qquad skip; R = R$$

The second one (*possible termination*, H2) states that a valid relation cannot require nontermination:

$$R\{false/ok'\} \Rightarrow R\{true/ok'\}$$

The third one (*dischargeable assumptions*, H3) states that preconditions cannot use dashed variables. All H3-healthy predicates satisfy the right unit law:

$$R; \mathit{skip} = R$$

The fourth one (*feasibility* or *excluded miracle*, H4) requires the existence of final values for the dashed variables that satisfy the relation:

$$\exists ok', \underline{v}' \bullet R = \mathit{true}$$

H4 excludes *miracle* from the valid designs, and this implies that all H4-healthy predicates satisfy the right zero law:

$$R; \mathit{true} = \mathit{true}$$

This condition cannot be expressed as an idempotent healthiness transformer, and does not preserve the predicate lattice structure. It serves solely to identify and/or eliminate predicates that characterise infeasible behaviour.

Through our distributional framework (§4) we obtain a richer theory where corresponding healthiness conditions hold (§4.1), even without the introduction of the auxiliary variables ok, ok'. Moreover the use of distributions enables us to evaluate the probability both of termination and of meeting a set of arbitrary postconditions as a function of the initial distribution (which determines the probability of meeting any required precondition).

3 The Distributional Framework

In [BB11] we have presented a UTP framework to deal with demonic probabilistic programs.

This framework relies on the concept of *distributions* over the state space: a generic distribution is a real-valued function $\chi : \mathcal{S} \to \mathbb{R}$ that assigns a *weight* x_i (a real number) to each state σ_i in the state space $\mathcal{S}$. The mathematics we employ is valid provided the probabilities constitute what is known as a measure space [Hal50]. If the state is not finite, then the limitation we face is that property predicates (pre- and post-expectations, for example) can only talk about probabilities associated with sets of observations, rather than single ones — in effect χ has to be interpreted as a probability density function.

A state σ bundles all the information regarding program variables into a single observation, in a style shared with many presentations of *Circus*-like languages: program variable values are modelled with a single state observation $\sigma : \mathcal{V} \to \mathcal{W}$, which is treated as a finite map from variables ($\mathcal{V}$) to values ($\mathcal{W}$). This choice simplifies the treatment of alphabets to a considerable degree.

The weight of a distribution is defined as:

$$\|\chi\| \triangleq \sum_{\sigma \in \operatorname{dom} \chi} \chi(\sigma)$$

This operation can be lifted to a set $\mathcal{X}$ of distributions:

$$\|\mathcal{X}\| \triangleq \{\|\chi\| \mid \chi \in \mathcal{X}\}$$

Among all generic distributions, the following two sub-classes play important roles in our framework:

- a *weighting distribution* π has the property that for every state σ we have $0 \leq \pi(\sigma) \leq 1$ — we define two particular weighting distributions, ϵ and ι, as the ones mapping every state to 0 and 1 respectively. There is no limit for the distribution weight;
- a *probability distribution* δ is a weighting distribution with the additional property that $\|\delta\| \leq 1$.

We will use the term *sub-distribution* to refer to a probability distribution where $\|\delta\| < 1$ and the term *full distribution* to refer to a probability distribution where $\|\delta\| = 1$.

Generally speaking, it is possible to operate on distributions by lifting pointwise operators such as addition, multiplication and multiplication by a scalar. Analogously we can lift pointwise all traditional relations and functions on real numbers[2].

In the case of pointwise multiplication, it is interesting to see it as a way of "re-weighting" a distribution. We have a particular interest in the case when one of the operands is a weighting distribution π, as we will use this operation to give semantics to choice constructs. We opt for a postfix notation to write this operation, as this is an effective way of marking when pointwise multiplication happens in the operational flow: for example if we multiply the probability distribution δ by the weighting distribution π, we write this as $\delta\langle\pi\rangle$. We use notation ϵ and ι to denote the everywhere zero and unit distributions, respectively:

$$\epsilon(\sigma) = 0 \wedge \iota(\sigma) = 1, \qquad \text{for all } \sigma$$

Given a condition (predicate on state) c, we can define the weighting distribution that maps every state where c evaluates to true to 1, and every other state to 0: as the value of each state can be seen as the boolean value of c in that state multiplied by 1, we overload the above notation and note this distribution as $\iota\langle c\rangle$. In general whenever we have the multiplication of a distribution by $\iota\langle c\rangle$, we can use the postfix operator $\langle c\rangle$ for short, instead of using $\langle\iota\langle c\rangle\rangle$. It is worth pointing out that if we multiply a probability distribution δ by $\iota\langle c\rangle$, we obtain a distribution whose weight $\|\delta\langle c\rangle\|$ is exactly the probability of being in a state satisfying c.

3.1 Assignment

A challenge we have faced has been describing how assignment, which is very much oriented towards individual variables, is given a semantics in terms of a

[2] Distributions form a vector space, which we have explored elsewhere. We omit discussion of this aspect of our theory for clarity and brevity.

distribution that involves complete entanglement of those variables. In effect an assignment statement $x := e$ involves a partial entanglement of variable x with the variables mentioned in e. In general as we build up larger programs using single assignment as the basic component we observe an increasing degree of entanglement, which can often be captured as an appropriate simultaneous assignment, so we shall work at this level here.

Given a simultaneous assignment $\underline{v} := \underline{e}$, where underlining indicates that we have lists of variables and expressions of the same length, we denote its effect on an initial probability distribution δ by $\delta\{\!|\underline{e}/\underline{v}|\!\}$. The postfix operator $\{\!|\underline{e}/\underline{v}|\!\}$ reflects the modifications introduced by the assignment — the intuition behind this, roughly speaking, is that all states σ where the expression $\underline{e}$ evaluates to the same value $\underline{w} = \text{eval}_\sigma(\underline{e})$ are replaced by a single state $\sigma' = (\underline{v} \mapsto \underline{w})$ that maps to a probability that is the sum of the probabilities of the states it replaces.

$$(\delta\{\!|\underline{e}/\underline{v}|\!\})(\sigma') \triangleq (\sum \delta(\sigma) \mid \sigma' = \sigma \dagger \{\underline{v} \mapsto \text{eval}_\sigma(\underline{e})\})$$

Here we treat the state as a map, where $\dagger$ denotes map override; this operator essentially implements the concept of "push-forward" used in measure theory, and is therefore a linear operator. An example is given in Figure 1.

Assignment preserves the overall weight of a probability distribution if $\underline{e}$ can be evaluated in every state, and if not the assignment returns a sub-distribution, where the "missing" weight accounts for the assignment failing on some states (this failure prevents a program from proceeding and causes non-termination).

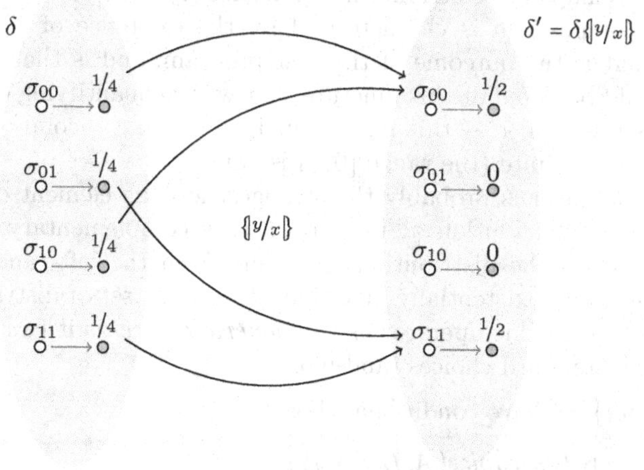

Fig. 1. The assignment $x := y$ from an initial uniform distribution on the state space $\mathcal{S} = \{0,1\} \times \{0,1\}$

$$
\begin{array}{rcl}
\mathit{abort} & \triangleq & \|\delta'\| \le \|\delta\| \\
\mathit{miracle} & \triangleq & (\delta = \epsilon) \wedge (\delta' = \epsilon) \\
\mathit{skip} & \triangleq & \delta' = \delta \\
\underline{v} := \underline{e} & \triangleq & \delta' = \delta\{\!|\underline{e}/\underline{v}|\!\} \\
A;B & \triangleq & \exists \delta_m \bullet A(\delta, \delta_m) \wedge B(\delta_m, \delta') \\
\mathit{choice}(A, B, \mathcal{X}) & \triangleq & \exists \pi, \delta_A, \delta_B \bullet \pi \in \mathcal{X} \wedge A(\delta\langle\pi\rangle, \delta_A) \wedge B(\delta\langle\bar{\pi}\rangle, \delta_B) \wedge \delta' = \delta_A + \delta_B \\
c * A & \triangleq & \mu X \bullet \mathit{choice}((A;X), \mathit{skip}, \{\iota\langle c\rangle\})
\end{array}
$$

Fig. 2. UTP semantics for different programming constructs

3.2 Programming Constructs

The semantic definitions of various programming constructs are based on a homogeneous relation between distributions and are listed in Figure 2; we will now proceed to discuss each one.

The failing program abort is represented by the predicate $\|\delta'\| \le \|\delta\|$, which captures the fact that it is maximally unpredictable, given that it cannot increase distribution weight. Such an increase would describe a program whose probability of termination was higher than that of it starting, and is infeasible.

The miraculous program $\mathit{miracle}$ is defined as $(\delta = \epsilon) \wedge (\delta' = \epsilon)$: this is a difference in comparison with the standard UTP theory, where it is simply false. This definition coincides with the standard one for most pairs of before- and after-distributions, with the exception of (ϵ, ϵ): this makes sure that $\mathit{miracle}$ is a unit for nondeterministic choice.

Program skip makes no changes and immediately terminates.

Assignment remaps the distribution as has already been discussed in §3.1.

Sequential composition is characterised by the existence of a "mid-point" distribution that is the outcome of the first program, and is then fed into the second. It should be noted at this juncture that we are quantifying over function quantities, such as δ or π — this makes our logic at least second-order, even if the state spaces are finite (the range $[0,1]$ is not).

The choice operator is probably the strangest-looking element of the list: it takes a weighting distribution π, uses it with its complementary distribution $\bar{\pi} = \iota - \pi)$ to weigh the distributions resulting from the left- and right-hand side respectively, and existentially quantifies it over the set of distributions $\mathcal{X} \subseteq \mathcal{D}_w$. We have termed this operator as the *generic choice* as it can emulate the behaviour of all standard choices (and more):

- for $\mathcal{X} = \{\iota\langle c\rangle\}$ we have conditional choice:

$$
\begin{aligned}
A \lhd c \rhd B &= \mathit{choice}(A, B, \{\iota\langle c\rangle\}) \\
&= \exists \delta_A, \delta_B \bullet A(\delta\langle c\rangle, \delta_A) \wedge B(\delta\langle \neg c\rangle, \delta_B) \wedge \delta' = \delta_A + \delta_B
\end{aligned}
$$

- for $\mathcal{X} = \{p \cdot \iota\}$ we have probabilistic choice:

$$
\begin{aligned}
A \;{}_p\!\oplus B &= \mathit{choice}(A, B, \{p \cdot \iota\}) \\
&= \exists \delta_A, \delta_B \bullet A(p \cdot \delta, \delta_A) \wedge B((1-p) \cdot \delta, \delta_B) \wedge \delta' = \delta_A + \delta_B
\end{aligned}
$$

– for $\mathcal{X} = \mathcal{D}_w$ we have non-deterministic choice:

$$\begin{aligned} A \sqcap B &= \mathit{choice}(A, B, \mathcal{D}_w) \\ &= \exists \pi, \delta_A, \delta_B \bullet A(\delta\langle\pi\rangle, \delta_A) \wedge B(\delta\langle\bar{\pi}\rangle, \delta_B) \wedge \delta' = \delta_A + \delta_B \end{aligned}$$

The usual notations for conditional, probabilistic and non-deterministic choice will be used as syntactic sugar in the remainder of this document. Program abort is a zero for non-deterministic choice, as entering $\|\delta'\| \le \|\delta\|$ for B in the definition, results in

$$\exists \pi, \delta_A, \delta_B \bullet A(\delta\langle\pi\rangle, \delta_A) \wedge \|\delta_B\| \le \|\delta\langle\bar{\pi}\rangle\| \wedge \delta' = \delta_A + \delta_B$$

which, after the one-point rule with $\delta_B = \delta' - \delta_A$ reduces to

$$\exists \pi, \delta_A \bullet A(\delta\langle\pi\rangle, \delta_A) \wedge \|\delta' = \delta_A\| \le \|\delta\langle\bar{\pi}\rangle\|$$

We can take $\pi = \epsilon$ as a witness, which forces $\delta_A = \epsilon$ (by healthiness condition Dist1, see Section 3.3) and we obtain

$$(A(\epsilon, \epsilon) \wedge \|\delta' - \epsilon\| \le \|\delta\|) \vee \exists \pi, \delta_A \bullet \ldots$$

A consequence of Dist1 is that $A(\epsilon, \epsilon)$ is always true for healthy A so this reduces to $\|\delta'\| \le \|\delta\|$ in a disjunction with a predicate that it subsumes, and hence equivalent to abort.

As commonly seen in UTP, disjunction of two programs is a kind of choice (usually non-deterministic, in other theories), which here can be defined using generic choice:

$$A \vee B = \mathit{choice}(A, B, \{\epsilon, \iota\}).$$

Disjunction is the usual semantics for non-deterministic choice, but here we see that non-deterministic choice has a richer behaviour as it exhibits more variability. Nevertheless with the appropriate definition of refinement we can introduce a concept of equivalence (*i.e.* two programs mutually refine each other), that restores the equivalence between disjunction and non-deterministic choice. [BB11]

Using the customary notation for conditional choice enlightens the definition of while-loops, which can be rewritten in a more familiar fashion as:

$$c * A \mathrel{\hat{=}} \mu X \bullet (A; X) \lhd c \rhd \mathit{skip}$$

They are characterized as fixpoints of the appropriate functional, with respect to the ordering defined by the refinement relation, details of which can be found in [MM04, BB11] and are beyond the scope of this paper.

These are the most significant elements and constructs that characterise our framework: this has been a presentation from a fairly high level, and it should have provided the reader with a working knowledge of the framework; a formal and rigorous definition of the elements presented so far is beyond the scope of this paper and can be found in [BB11], along with some soundness proofs.

3.3 Healthiness Conditions

Before moving further on, we are going to list quickly the healthiness conditions that characterise this framework.

The first one (*feasibility*, Dist1) assures that for any program $\mathcal{P}(\delta, \delta')$ the probability of termination cannot be greater than that of having started:

$$\|\delta'\| \leq \|\delta\|$$

Another healthiness condition (*monotonicity*, Dist2), states that, for any deterministic program $\mathcal{P}$, increasing δ implies that the resulting δ' increases as well:

$$\mathcal{P}(\delta_1, \delta_1') \wedge \mathcal{P}(\delta_2, \delta_2') \wedge \delta_2 > \delta_1 \Rightarrow \delta_2' \geq \delta_1'$$

A third healthiness conditions is that multiplication by a (not too large and non-negative[3]) constant distributes through commands (*scaling*, Dist3):

$$\forall a \in \mathbb{R}^+ \wedge \|a \cdot \delta\| \leq 1 \bullet \mathcal{P}(\delta, \delta') \Leftrightarrow \mathcal{P}(a \cdot \delta, a \cdot \delta')$$

Finally the purely random non-deterministic model adopted in the distributional framework yields a fourth healthiness condition Dist4 (*convexity*):

$$(\mathcal{P}_1 \sqcap \mathcal{P}_2)(\delta, \delta') \Rightarrow \delta' \geq \min\big(\mathcal{P}_1(\delta) \cup \mathcal{P}_2(\delta)\big)$$

Here $\mathcal{P}_1(\delta)$ denotes the set of all δ' that satisfy $\mathcal{P}_1(\delta, \delta')$.

This poses restrictions on the space of possible program images, which is strictly a subset of $\wp\mathcal{D}$: this is analogous to the set $\mathbb{H}S$ from [MM04].

4 A Probabilistic Theory of Designs

A distinguishing characteristic of designs is the use of the auxiliary variables ok and ok'. They are not sufficient in a probabilistic setting, as we need to be able to express quantitative information about the program also in terms of it having started or finished. We argue that this information is embedded in the distributions used to express programming constructs.

In fact the variable δ records implicitly if the program has started, as for each state σ it gives a precise probability that the program is in that initial state.

If δ is a full distribution (*i.e.* $\|\delta\| = 1$), then the program has started with probability 1: in some sense we can translate the statement $ok = true$ with the statement $\|\delta\| = 1$. Conversely a program for which $\delta = \epsilon$ has not started. Obviously there are all situations in between, where the fact of δ being a sub-distribution accounts for the program having started with probability $\|\delta\| < 1$.

Similarly if δ' is a full distribution, then the program terminates with probability 1: coherently we can translate the statement $ok' = true$ with the statement $\|\delta'\| = 1$. In general the weight of δ' is the probability of termination: if the program reaches an after-distribution whose weight is strictly less than 1, then termination is not guaranteed (and in particular if $\delta' = \epsilon$ it is certain that it will not terminate).

[3] Mathematically the relation holds also if this is not met, but in that case $a \cdot \delta$ is not a probability distribution.

4.1 From Standard Designs to Probabilistic Designs

Given a standard design $\mathcal{P}re \vdash \mathcal{P}ost$ we can easily derive the corresponding probabilistic design by using the observation above:

$$\begin{aligned}\mathcal{P}re \vdash \mathcal{P}ost &\equiv ok \wedge \mathcal{P}re \Rightarrow ok' \wedge \mathcal{P}ost\\ &\equiv \|\delta\| = 1 \wedge \mathcal{P}re \Rightarrow \|\delta'\| = 1 \wedge \mathcal{P}ost\\ &\equiv \|\delta\langle\mathcal{P}re\rangle\| = 1 \Rightarrow \|\delta'\langle\mathcal{P}ost\rangle\| = 1\end{aligned}$$

This expression tells us that we have a valid design if whenever the before-distribution δ is a full distribution which is null everywhere $\mathcal{P}re$ is not satisfied (and therefore $\delta = \delta\langle\mathcal{P}re\rangle$), then the resulting after-distribution δ' is a full distribution which is null everywhere $\mathcal{P}ost$ is not satisfied (and therefore $\delta' = \delta'\langle\mathcal{P}ost\rangle$).

We can easily redefine assignment, in the same style as it has been redefined to make it a valid construct according to the theory of designs:

$$\begin{aligned}\underline{v} := \underline{e} &\mathrel{\hat=} true \vdash \delta' = \delta\{\!|\underline{e}/\underline{v}|\!\}\\ &\equiv ok \wedge true \Rightarrow ok' \wedge \delta\{\!|\underline{e}/\underline{v}|\!\}\\ &\equiv \|\delta\| = 1 \Rightarrow \|\delta'\| = 1 \wedge \delta' = \delta\{\!|\underline{e}/\underline{v}|\!\}\end{aligned}$$

This states that an assignment is a valid design only if the expression e is defined everywhere in the state space: in fact undefinedness of e causes $\delta\{\!|\underline{e}/\underline{v}|\!\}$ to be a sub-distribution and therefore $\underline{v} :=$ e reduces to *false*.

We can redefine *skip* in a similar way:

$$\begin{aligned}skip &\mathrel{\hat=} true \vdash \delta' = \delta\\ &\equiv ok \wedge true \Rightarrow ok' \wedge \delta\\ &\equiv \|\delta\| = 1 \Rightarrow \|\delta'\| = 1 \wedge \delta' = \delta\\ &\equiv \|\delta\| = 1 \Rightarrow \delta' = \delta\end{aligned}$$

This new version of *skip* states that the after-distribution is the same as the before-distribution (and therefore it does not alter the weight, so this can be left implicit), but as any other design it reduces to *true* if δ is not a full distribution.

The bottom of the lattice is *abort*, which is again *true* as in the standard theory:

$$\begin{aligned}abort &\mathrel{\hat=} false \vdash false\\ &\equiv ok \wedge false \Rightarrow ok' \wedge false\\ &\equiv false \Rightarrow false\\ &\equiv true\\ &\equiv false \Rightarrow true\\ &\equiv ok \wedge false \Rightarrow ok' \wedge true\\ &\equiv false \vdash true\end{aligned}$$

The standard definition of the construct *chaos* is

$$\begin{aligned} \mathit{chaos} &\mathrel{\hat=} \mathit{true} \vdash \mathit{true} \\ &\equiv \mathit{ok} \wedge \mathit{true} \Rightarrow \mathit{ok}' \wedge \mathit{true} \\ &\equiv \mathit{ok} \Rightarrow \mathit{ok}' \\ &\equiv \|\delta\| = 1 \Rightarrow \|\delta'\| = 1 \end{aligned}$$

This is a program that guarantees termination, but in an unspecified state. It is equivalent to:

$$\mathit{chaos} \equiv \mathit{true} \vdash \mathit{abort}_R\,,$$

where the subscript R indicates that we are talking of the relational version of *abort*, from Figure 2.

The top of the lattice is *miracle*:

$$\begin{aligned} \mathit{miracle} &\mathrel{\hat=} \mathit{true} \vdash \mathit{false} \\ &\equiv \mathit{ok} \wedge \mathit{true} \Rightarrow \mathit{ok}' \wedge \mathit{false} \\ &\equiv \mathit{ok} \Rightarrow \mathit{false} \\ &\equiv \neg \mathit{ok} \\ &\equiv \neg(\|\delta\| = 1) \\ &\equiv \|\delta\| < 1 \end{aligned}$$

This is equivalent to

$$\mathit{miracle} \equiv \mathit{true} \vdash \mathit{miracle}_R\,.$$

Healthiness Conditions These new definitions relying on the distributional framework satisfy the healthiness conditions H1–H4 as well (§2.2).

We can in fact prove that the following laws hold:

– left unit law:

$$\begin{aligned} \mathit{skip}; \mathit{Pre} \vdash \mathit{Post} &\equiv (\|\delta\| = 1 \Rightarrow \delta' = \delta); (\|\delta(\mathit{Pre})\| = 1 \Rightarrow \|\delta'(\mathit{Post})\| = 1) \\ &\equiv \exists \delta_m \bullet (\|\delta\| = 1 \Rightarrow \delta_m = \delta) \ \wedge\ (\|\delta_m(\mathit{Pre})\| = 1 \Rightarrow \|\delta'(\mathit{Post})\| = 1) \\ &\equiv \|\delta(\mathit{Pre})\| = 1 \Rightarrow \|\delta'(\mathit{Post})\| = 1 \\ &\equiv \mathit{Pre} \vdash \mathit{Post} \end{aligned}$$

– right unit law:

$$\begin{aligned} \mathit{Pre} \vdash \mathit{Post}; \mathit{skip} &\equiv (\|\delta(\mathit{Pre})\| = 1 \Rightarrow \|\delta'(\mathit{Post})\| = 1); (\|\delta\| = 1 \Rightarrow \delta' = \delta) \\ &\equiv \exists \delta_m \bullet (\|\delta(\mathit{Pre})\| = 1 \Rightarrow \|\delta_m(\mathit{Post})\| = 1) \ \wedge\ (\|\delta_m\| = 1 \Rightarrow \delta' = \delta_m) \\ &\equiv \|\delta(\mathit{Pre})\| = 1 \Rightarrow \|\delta'(\mathit{Post})\| = 1 \\ &\equiv \mathit{Pre} \vdash \mathit{Post} \end{aligned}$$

– left zero law:

$$\begin{aligned} \mathit{true}; \mathcal{P}re \vdash \mathcal{P}ost &\equiv \mathit{true}; (\|\delta(\mathcal{P}re)\| = 1 \Rightarrow \|\delta'(\mathcal{P}ost)\| = 1) \\ &\equiv \exists \delta_m \bullet \mathit{true} \wedge (\|\delta_m(\mathcal{P}re)\| = 1 \Rightarrow \|\delta'(\mathcal{P}ost)\| = 1) \\ &\equiv \exists \delta_m \bullet \|\delta_m(\mathcal{P}re)\| = 1 \Rightarrow \|\delta'(\mathcal{P}ost)\| = 1 \\ &\equiv \mathit{true} \end{aligned}$$

– right zero law:

$$\begin{aligned} \mathcal{P}re \vdash \mathcal{P}ost; \mathit{true} &\equiv (\|\delta(\mathcal{P}re)\| = 1 \Rightarrow \|\delta'(\mathcal{P}ost)\| = 1); \mathit{true} \\ &\equiv \exists \delta_m \bullet (\|\delta(\mathcal{P}re)\| = 1 \Rightarrow \|\delta_m(\mathcal{P}ost)\| = 1) \wedge \mathit{true} \\ &\equiv \exists \delta_m \bullet \|\delta(\mathcal{P}re)\| = 1 \Rightarrow \|\delta_m(\mathcal{P}ost)\| = 1 \\ &\equiv \mathit{true} \end{aligned}$$

4.2 Recasting Total Correctness

The reason that led to the standard theory of designs was that programs fail to satisfy the left zero law in the relational theory.

In the distributional framework programming constructs do satisfy this law, as for any programming construct $\mathcal{P}$ other than *miracle* it is never the case that $\delta \notin fv(\mathcal{P})$.

For this reason we have:

$$\begin{aligned} \mathit{true}; \mathcal{P}(\delta, \delta') &\equiv \exists \delta_m \bullet \mathit{true} \wedge \mathcal{P}(\delta_m, \delta') \\ &\equiv \exists \delta_m \bullet \mathcal{P}(\delta_m, \delta') \\ &\equiv \mathit{true} \end{aligned}$$

Similarly the right zero law is satisfied as well, along with the left and right unit laws: healthiness conditions equivalent to H1–H4 hold here as well.

Following this observation it appears that restricting the reasoning to programs with guaranteed termination is somehow limiting, as guaranteed termination is not an actual real-world feature of programs: programs must be reasonably reliable, but failure is always a possibility.

The reason for this may be inherent to the fact that programs are run on hardware which is susceptible of failure, as well as being imputable to the way a program is designed (for example the implementation of a probabilistic algorithm where termination is probabilistic as well).

We can fully exploit the potential of the distributional framework towards modelling these situations by removing the constraints on the weights of the before- and after-distributions — so we use the programming constructs in Figure 2 exactly with the semantics presented there.

The role of preconditions and postconditions is that of restricting the range of acceptable before- and after-distributions (and therefore act as restrictions to be applied to δ and δ' respectively) — this allows us to express desirable characteristics of a program in great detail, for example:

- $\mathcal{P} \wedge \|\delta'\| = 1$ requires $\mathcal{P}$ to guarantee termination;
- $\mathcal{P} \wedge \|\delta'\| > 0.95$ requires $\mathcal{P}$ to terminate with at least 95% probability;
- $\mathcal{P} \wedge \|\delta'(\mathcal{Post})\| > 0.95$ requires $\mathcal{P}$ to terminate with at least 95% probability in a state satisfying $\mathcal{Post}$;
- $\mathcal{Pre} \Rightarrow \mathcal{P} \wedge \|\delta'(\mathcal{Post})\| > 0.95$ requires $\mathcal{P}$ to terminate with at least 95% probability in a state satisfying $\mathcal{Post}$ whenever it starts in a state satisfying $\mathcal{Pre}$;
- $\|\delta(\mathcal{Pre})\| > 0.98 \Rightarrow \mathcal{P} \wedge \|\delta'(\mathcal{Post})\| > 0.95$ requires $\mathcal{P}$ to terminate with at least 95% probability in a state satisfying $\mathcal{Post}$ whenever the probability of $\mathcal{Pre}$ being satisfied at the beginning is at least 0.98;
- ...

All healthiness conditions deriving from the distributional framework (Dist1–Dist4) obviously hold here as well; with a small modification we can recast the notion of total correctness by restricting Dist1 to a variant Dist1-TC (which implies Dist1), stating that:

$$\|\delta\| = \|\delta'\|$$

This requires a program to terminate with the same probability p with which it has started:

$$\|\delta\| = p \wedge \mathcal{Pre} \Rightarrow \|\delta'\| = p \wedge \mathcal{Post}$$

4.3 Link with the Standard Model

Standard designs have observations ok, ok', σ, σ'.

$$ok, ok' : \mathbb{B}$$
$$\sigma, \sigma' : \mathcal{S}$$

A standard design is a predicate $\mathcal{P}_S(\sigma, \sigma', ok, ok')$ that states that a program started (if ok is true) in the state σ ends (if ok' is true) in the state σ'.

Probabilistic designs have observations δ, δ'

$$\delta, \delta' : \mathcal{S} \to [0, 1]$$

A probabilistic design is a predicate $\mathcal{P}_D(\delta, \delta')$ stating that a before-distribution δ will be transformed into the after-distribution δ'.

Informally we require the two approaches to yield the same results when we are dealing with point distributions, *i.e.* when the probability of being in a given state is 1.

In order to formalise the link between these two worlds, we define the linking predicate L as:

$$L((\delta, \delta'), (\sigma, \sigma', ok, ok')) \triangleq ok \Leftrightarrow (\|\delta'\| = 1) \wedge ok' \Leftrightarrow (\|\delta'\| = 1)$$
$$\wedge \delta = \eta_\sigma \wedge \delta' = \eta_{\sigma'}$$

Here the notation η_σ denotes the point distribution returning 1 for state σ, and 0 elsewhere.

This linking predicate allows us to introduce the following *Galois connections*; first we define the weakest probabilistic design corresponding to a standard design $\mathcal{P}_S$:

$$\forall \sigma, \sigma', ok, ok' \bullet L((\delta, \delta'), (\sigma, \sigma', ok, ok')) \Rightarrow \mathcal{P}_S(\sigma, \sigma', ok, ok')$$

Analogously, the strongest standard design corresponding to a probabilistic design $\mathcal{P}_D$ is:

$$\exists \delta, \delta' \bullet L((\delta, \delta'), (\sigma, \sigma', ok, ok')) \wedge \mathcal{P}_D(\delta, \delta')$$

It is easy to see that all programming constructs from the probabilistic theory that have homologue ones in the standard theory are linked to them, with the restriction of operating only on point distributions, otherwise they reduce to *abort*.

Weakening the Link. This linking predicate is a bit too strong, as it maps many interesting program constructs to the aborting program: an example is that of generic choice, which has no homologue in the standard theory. Ideally a better option would be to relax some constraints and to map generic choice to non-deterministic choice rather than to *abort*.

In other words we are aiming at a link that loses all probabilistic information about the possible after-states and flattens it to a mere list of them.

This is not straightforward, as the linking predicate L in some sense verifies consistency of δ with respect to σ, ok and of δ' with respect to σ', ok': when the support[4] of the distribution has more than one element, the relation between δ and a state from its domain is too weak to be useful.

The situation is similar to that of a 3D-space, where dots are characterised by their x, y, z coordinates: a transformation creates a space with coordinates x', y', z', whose relation with the undashed coordinates cannot in general be captured by a relation that mentions only one undashed and one dashed coordinate.

So far we have seen standard designs as relations:

$$\mathcal{P}_S : \mathcal{S} \times \mathbb{B} \rightarrow \mathcal{S} \times \mathbb{B}$$

but in order to build a more useful link we turn to this other interpretation:

$$\mathcal{P}_{\wp S} : \mathcal{S} \times \mathbb{B} \rightarrow \wp\mathcal{S} \times \mathbb{B}$$

which maps a state to what we may term its program image $\mathcal{P}(\sigma)$ (as it is a similar concept to that of program image introduced in §3), which contains all of the possible after-states reachable from a given before-state:

$$\mathcal{P}(\sigma) = \{\sigma' \mid \mathcal{P}_S(\sigma, \sigma')\}$$

All deterministic standard constructs map a state to a singleton set, whereas non-deterministic choice maps it to larger sets.

[4] We remind the reader that the support of a function is the set of points where the function is not zero-valued: $\text{supp}(\delta) \triangleq \text{dom}(\delta) \setminus \ker(\delta)$.

The interpretation of the predicate $\mathcal{P}_{\wp S}(\sigma, \alpha', ok, ok')$ is therefore that $\mathcal{P}$ has started (if ok is true) in the state σ and has ended (if ok' is true) in a state $\sigma' \in \alpha'$:

$$\mathcal{P}_{\wp S}(\sigma, \alpha', ok, ok') \equiv \bigvee_{\sigma' \in \alpha'} \mathcal{P}_S(\sigma, \sigma', ok, ok')$$

With this in mind we can define the following linking predicate:

$$L_{\wp}((\delta, \delta'), (\sigma, \alpha', ok, ok')) \triangleq ok \Leftrightarrow (\|\delta'\| = 1) \wedge ok' \Leftrightarrow (\|\delta'\| = 1) \\ \wedge \delta = \eta_\sigma \wedge \mathrm{supp}(\delta') = \alpha'$$

We can state the variants of the Galois connections above as:

$$\forall \sigma, \alpha', ok, ok' \bullet L_{\wp}((\delta, \delta'), (\sigma, \alpha', ok, ok')) \Rightarrow \mathcal{P}_{\wp S}(\sigma, \alpha', ok, ok') \\ \exists \delta, \delta' \bullet L_{\wp}((\delta, \delta'), (\sigma, \alpha', ok, ok')) \wedge \mathcal{P}_D(\delta, \delta')$$

5 An Example: Interaction of Probabilistic and Non-deterministic Choice

This brief classical example is meant to show the interaction and the difference between probabilistic and non-deterministic choice: we will use this to show the effect of projecting the probabilistic design on the space of standard designs.

Let us take these two simple programs:

$$A \triangleq x := 0 \sqcap x := 1 \ ; \ y := 0 \ {}_{\frac{1}{2}}\!\oplus y := 1 \\ B \triangleq x := 0 \ {}_{\frac{1}{2}}\!\oplus x := 1 \ ; \ y := 0 \sqcap y := 1$$

In Figure 3 we have worked out parametric expression for the final distribution for each program — they are parametric in the weighting distribution π which accounts for the non-deterministic choice performed in both programs:

$$\delta'_A(\pi) \triangleq 1/2 \cdot \left(\delta\langle\pi\rangle\{\!\!\{0/x\}\!\!\}\{\!\!\{0/y\}\!\!\} + \delta\langle\bar{\pi}\rangle\{\!\!\{1/x\}\!\!\}\{\!\!\{0/y\}\!\!\} + \delta\langle\pi\rangle\{\!\!\{0/x\}\!\!\}\{\!\!\{1/y\}\!\!\} + \delta\langle\bar{\pi}\rangle\{\!\!\{1/x\}\!\!\}\{\!\!\{1/y\}\!\!\}\right) \\ \delta'_B(\pi) \triangleq 1/2 \cdot \left(\delta\{\!\!\{0/x\}\!\!\}\langle\pi\rangle\{\!\!\{0/y\}\!\!\} + \delta\{\!\!\{1/x\}\!\!\}\langle\pi\rangle\{\!\!\{0/y\}\!\!\} + \delta\{\!\!\{0/x\}\!\!\}\langle\bar{\pi}\rangle\{\!\!\{1/y\}\!\!\} + \delta\{\!\!\{1/x\}\!\!\}\langle\bar{\pi}\rangle\{\!\!\{1/y\}\!\!\}\right)$$

The two after-distributions are very similar, but with one crucial difference: the position of $\langle\pi\rangle$, which clearly marks when the non-deterministic choice was made; this is reflected in the different after-distributions reached by each program:

- $\forall \pi \bullet \|\delta'_A(\pi)\langle x = y\rangle\| = 1/2$, *i.e.* regardless of the non-deterministic choice and of the initial distribution program A terminates in a state satisfying the condition $x = y$ with probability $1/2$, whereas in program B we cannot remove the dependence on π so if we turn to a worst-case analysis (in the non-deterministic choice the left-hand side $y := 0$ is picked whenever $x = 1$, *i.e.* $\pi = \iota\langle x = 1\rangle$) we have that $\|\delta'_B(\iota\langle x = 1\rangle)\langle x = y\rangle\| = 0$ and therefore the minimum guaranteed probability that $x = y$ is 0;

$$\begin{array}{lll}
A & \triangleq & x := 0 \sqcap x := 1 \;;\; y := 0 \;{}_{\frac{1}{2}}\!\oplus y := 1 \\
 & \equiv & \exists \pi \bullet \delta' = \delta\langle\pi\rangle\{\!|0/x|\!\} + \delta\langle\bar{\pi}\rangle\{\!|1/x|\!\} \;;\; \delta' = 1/2 \cdot \delta\{\!|0/y|\!\} + 1/2 \cdot \delta\{\!|1/y|\!\} \\
 & \equiv & \exists \pi, \delta_m \bullet \delta_m = \delta\langle\pi\rangle\{\!|0/x|\!\} + \delta\langle\bar{\pi}\rangle\{\!|1/x|\!\} \;\wedge\; \delta' = 1/2 \cdot \delta_m\{\!|0/y|\!\} + 1/2 \cdot \delta_m\{\!|1/y|\!\} \\
 & \equiv & \exists \pi \bullet \delta' = 1/2 \cdot \left(\delta\langle\pi\rangle\{\!|0/x|\!\} + \delta\langle\bar{\pi}\rangle\{\!|1/x|\!\}\right)\{\!|0/y|\!\} + \\
 & & \qquad + 1/2 \cdot \left(\delta\langle\pi\rangle\{\!|0/x|\!\} + \delta\langle\pi\rangle\{\!|1/x|\!\}\right)\{\!|1/y|\!\} \\
 & \equiv & \exists \pi \bullet \delta' = \delta'_A(\pi) \;\wedge\; \delta'_A(\pi) \triangleq 1/2 \cdot \delta\langle\pi\rangle\{\!|0/x|\!\}\{\!|0/y|\!\} + 1/2 \cdot \delta\langle\bar{\pi}\rangle\{\!|1/x|\!\}\{\!|0/y|\!\} + \\
 & & \qquad + 1/2 \cdot \delta\langle\pi\rangle\{\!|0/x|\!\}\{\!|1/y|\!\} + 1/2 \cdot \delta\langle\bar{\pi}\rangle\{\!|1/x|\!\}\{\!|1/y|\!\}
\end{array}$$

$$\begin{array}{lll}
B & \triangleq & x := 0 \;{}_{\frac{1}{2}}\!\oplus x := 1 \;;\; y := 0 \sqcap y := 1 \\
 & \equiv & \delta' = 1/2 \cdot \delta\{\!|0/x|\!\} + 1/2 \cdot \delta\{\!|1/x|\!\} \;;\; \exists \pi \bullet \delta' = \delta\langle\pi\rangle\{\!|0/y|\!\} + \delta\langle\bar{\pi}\rangle\{\!|1/y|\!\} \\
 & \equiv & \exists \pi, \delta_m \bullet \delta_m = 1/2 \cdot \delta\{\!|0/x|\!\} + 1/2 \cdot \delta\{\!|1/x|\!\} \;\wedge\; \delta' = \delta_m\langle\pi\rangle\{\!|0/y|\!\} + \delta_m\langle\bar{\pi}\rangle\{\!|1/y|\!\} \\
 & \equiv & \exists \pi \bullet \delta' = \left(1/2 \cdot \delta\{\!|0/x|\!\} + 1/2 \cdot \delta\{\!|1/x|\!\}\right)\langle\pi\rangle\{\!|0/y|\!\} + \\
 & & \qquad + \left(1/2 \cdot \delta\{\!|0/x|\!\} + 1/2 \cdot \delta\{\!|1/x|\!\}\right)\langle\bar{\pi}\rangle\{\!|1/y|\!\} \\
 & \equiv & \exists \pi \bullet \delta' = \delta'_B(\pi) \;\wedge\; \delta'_B(\pi) \triangleq 1/2 \cdot \delta\{\!|0/x|\!\}\langle\pi\rangle\{\!|0/y|\!\} + 1/2 \cdot \delta\{\!|1/x|\!\}\langle\pi\rangle\{\!|0/y|\!\} + \\
 & & \qquad + 1/2 \cdot \delta\{\!|0/x|\!\}\langle\bar{\pi}\rangle\{\!|1/y|\!\} + 1/2 \cdot \delta\{\!|1/x|\!\}\langle\bar{\pi}\rangle\{\!|1/y|\!\}
\end{array}$$

Fig. 3. Programs A and B

- viceversa for program B we can show that $\forall \pi \bullet \|\delta'_B(\pi)\langle x = 1\rangle\| = 1/2$ similarly as above, and so the probability that $x = 1$ after program B is $1/2$, whereas if we take program A we can see that if $\pi = \iota$ (*i.e.* in the non-deterministic choice the left-hand side $x := 0$ is always picked) than we have that $\|\delta'_A(\iota)\langle x = 1\rangle\| = 0$, so the minimum guaranteed probability that $x = 1$ is 0.

We are now going to derive the strongest standard design corresponding to A and B using the linking predicate $L_\wp$:

$$\exists \delta, \delta' \bullet L_\wp((\delta, \delta'), (\sigma, \alpha', ok, ok')) \wedge A(\delta, \delta')$$

$\equiv$ Definition of $L_\wp$

$$\exists \delta, \delta' \bullet \left(ok \Leftrightarrow (\|\delta'\| = 1) \wedge ok' \Leftrightarrow (\|\delta'\| = 1) \wedge \delta = \eta_\sigma \wedge \mathrm{supp}(\delta') = \alpha'\right) \wedge A(\delta, \delta')$$

$\equiv$ A and B return after-distributions with the same support

$$\exists \delta, \delta' \bullet \left(ok \Leftrightarrow (\|\delta'\| = 1) \wedge ok' \Leftrightarrow (\|\delta'\| = 1) \wedge \delta = \eta_\sigma \wedge \mathrm{supp}(\delta') = \alpha'\right) \wedge B(\delta, \delta')$$

The last line of this derivation clearly shows the effect of the link, which flattens out all probabilistic information and as a result the programs A and B are mapped to the same program in the world of standard designs: such a program records that a choice[5] was made, but there is no discrimination among choices of different kind. Moreover what matters is the set of possible after-states and this is also not affected by altering the order in which the choices are made.

[5] Conditional choice is excluded, as it is not really a choice but rather a different evolution of the program which was determined by the current program state.

6 Conclusion

We have presented a probabilistic theory of designs, which relies on a UTP-style framework based on distributions over the state space.

We have shown that we are able to embed the standard UTP theory by requiring guaranteed termination from all program constructs, and treating them as the aborting program otherwise.

We have later relaxed this constraint to be able to reason about probabilistic programs: the advantages of this richer approach is that it allows us to express in fine detail the desired behaviour of a program, including its probabilistic aspects.

References

[BB11] Bresciani, R., Butterfield, A.: Towards a UTP-style framework to deal with probabilities. Technical Report TCD-CS-2011-09, FMG, Trinity College Dublin, Ireland (August 2011)

[BB12] Bresciani, R., Butterfield, A.: A UTP Semantics of pGCL as a Homogeneous Relation. In: Derrick, J., Gnesi, S., Latella, D., Treharne, H. (eds.) IFM 2012. LNCS, vol. 7321, pp. 191–205. Springer, Heidelberg (2012)

[But10] Butterfield, A. (ed.): UTP 2008. LNCS, vol. 5713. Springer, Heidelberg (2010)

[CS09] Chen, Y., Sanders, J.W.: Unifying Probability with Nondeterminism. In: Cavalcanti, A., Dams, D.R. (eds.) FM 2009. LNCS, vol. 5850, pp. 467–482. Springer, Heidelberg (2009)

[DS06] Dunne, S., Stoddart, B. (eds.): UTP 2006. LNCS, vol. 4010. Springer, Heidelberg (2006)

[Hal50] Halmos, P.R.: Measure Theory. University Series in Higher Mathematics. D. Van Nostrand Company, Inc., Princeton (1950)

[He10] He, J.: A probabilistic bpel-like language. In: Qin [Qin10], pp. 74–100

[Heh84] Hehner, E.C.R.: Predicative programming part i & ii. Commun. ACM 27(2), 134–151 (1984)

[HJ98] Hoare, C.A.R., He, J.: Unifying Theories of Programming. Prentice Hall International Series in Computer Science (1998)

[Hoa85] Hoare, C.A.R.: Programs are predicates. In: Proceedings of a Discussion Meeting of the Royal Society of London on Mathematical Logic and Programming Languages, pp. 141–155. Prentice-Hall, Upper Saddle River (1985)

[HS06] He, J., Sanders, J.W.: Unifying probability. In: Dunne and Stoddart [ds06], pp. 173–199

[MM04] McIver, A., Morgan, C.: Abstraction, Refinement and Proof For Probabilistic Systems. Monographs in Computer Science. Springer (2004)

[Qin10] Qin, S. (ed.): UTP 2010. LNCS, vol. 6445. Springer, Heidelberg (2010)

A Keisli Composition

Assume a semantic model of the form $S \to \mathbb{F}S$ where $\mathbb{F}$ is a type constructor (functor). The question that naturally arises is how to compose such functions, i.e., given $p : S \to \mathbb{F}T$ and $q : T \to \mathbb{F}U$, how do we compose these to get $(p;q) :$

$S \to \mathbb{F}U$? The standard solution for this is Kleisli lifting and composition which involves two functions with the following signatures:

$$\eta_S : S \to \mathbb{F}S \qquad \_^* : (S \to \mathbb{F}T) \to (\mathbb{F}S \to \mathbb{F}T)$$

that obey the following laws:

$$\eta_S^* = id_{\mathbb{F}S} \qquad p^* \circ \eta_S = p \qquad (q^* \circ p)^* = q^* \circ p^*$$

The intuition behind these is best understood in a diagram:

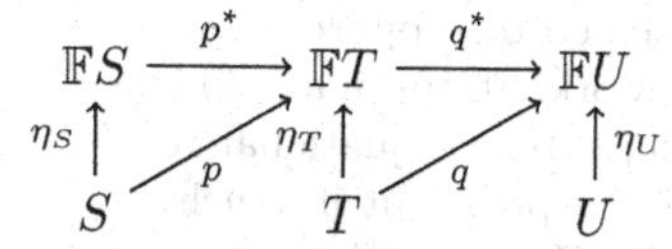

The Kleisli composition of p and q is given by $q^* \circ p$, where $\circ$ denotes regular function composition.

In this paper $\mathbb{F}S = \mathbb{C}(S \to [0,1])$, and we do not use the full lifting (which results in $\mathbb{C}(S \to [0,1]) \to \mathbb{C}(S \to [0,1])$), but instead lift partway to get $((S \to [0,1]) \to \mathbb{C}(S \to [0,1]))$. This "partway" lifting is one of the stages in giving an explicit definition of the full lifting.

The Logic of $U\cdot(TP)^{2*}$

Andrew Butterfield

Lero@TCD, Trinity College Dublin
butrfeld@tcd.ie

Abstract. $U\cdot(TP)^2$ is a theorem prover developed to support the Unifying Theories of Programming (UTP) framework. Its primary design goal was to support the higher-order logic, alphabets, equational reasoning and "programs as predicates" style that is prevalent in much of the UTP literature, from the seminal work by Hoare & He onwards. In this paper we focus on the underlying logic of the prover, emphasising those aspects that are tailored to support the style of proof so often used for UTP foundational work. These aspects include support for alphabets, type-inferencing, explicit substitution notation, and explicit meta-notation for general variable-binding lists in quantifiers. The need for these features is illustrated by a running example that develops a theory of UTP designs. We finish with a discussion of issues regarding the soundness of the proof tool, and linkages to existing "industrial strength" provers such as Isabelle, PVS or CoQ.

1 Introduction

Unifying Theories of Programming (UTP) [HH98], is a framework that uses alphabetised predicates to define language semantics in a relational calculus style, in a way that facilitates the unification of otherwise disjoint semantic theories, either by merging them, or using special linking predicates that form a Galois connection. The framework is designed to cover the spectrum from abstract specifications all the way down to near-machine level descriptions, and as a consequence the notion of refinement plays a key role.

Typically the development of a UTP theory involves determining the key observational variables, so fixing the alphabet, then defining healthiness conditions to characterise the predicates that describe feasible behaviour, introducing the language under study as a signature, and giving meaning to that signature using healthy predicates. Algebraic laws of the language can then be developed.

In [But10] we gave an overview of the Unifying Theories of Programming Theorem Prover ($U\cdot(TP)^2$) that we are developing to support such theory development work[1]. The prover is an interactive tool, with a graphical user-interface,

* This research was supported by grants 07-RFP-CMSF186 and 08-RFP-CMS1277 from Science Foundation Ireland, as well as partial support from Lero, the Irish Software Engineering Research Centre.

[1] In that paper it was called SAOITHÍN, but the name has since changed to $U\cdot(TP)^2$.

B. Wolff, M.-C. Gaudel, A. Feliachi (Eds.): UTP 2012, LNCS 7681, pp. 124–143, 2013.

designed to make it easy to define a UTP theory and to experiment and perform the key foundational proofs. The motivation for developing this tool, rather than using an existing one has been discussed in some detail in [But10]. We do not repeat it here in the introduction, but this paper effectively gives a technical underpinning to that motivation. In this paper we describe the logic behind $U\cdot(TP)^2$, starting from 1st-order equational logic [Tou01], and gradually exposing the extensions required to facilitate the kind of reasoning we require for foundational work. In effect this paper explores the proof infrastructure needed to reason about a theory of a simple imperative language (*While*), built upon a theory of "Designs", itself layered on top of a generic UTP base theory. We start at the bottom looking at the logic and work up until we can see what is needed for the *While* language.

This paper assumes that the reader is familiar with the basic ideas behind UTP, and does not give an introduction to the subject. A good introduction is the key textbook written by C.A.R. Hoare and He Jifeng [HH98], which is free to download from `unifyingtheories.org`.

In the rest of this paper, we use the term "user" to refer to a UTP practitioner involved in the development of new UTP theories, and not a software developer who might want to employ a formal method whose underlying semantics derive from UTP.

1.1 Structure of This Paper

Section 2 talks about theories, and gives a visual outline of much of this paper in Figure 1. Section 3 introduces the logic of $U\cdot(TP)^2$, and Section 4 gives us an introduction to definitions common to most theories. In Section 5, and Section 6, we describe how `Theory`s can be layered up to present a UTP Theory of Designs, as well as a theory for a simple While programming language built as an extension on top of Designs. Section 7 and Section 8 discuss issues to do with the trustworthiness and usefulness of $U\cdot(TP)^2$, and finally, Section 9 concludes. A collection of relevant rules can be found in Appendix A.

2 Theories

A UTP theory is a coherent collection of the following items: an alphabet defining the observations that can be made; a set of healthiness conditions that characterise predicates that describe realistic/feasible systems; a signature that defines the abstract syntax of the language being defined; definitions of the language constructs as healthy predicates; and laws that relate the behaviours of the various language components. In $U\cdot(TP)^2$ we use the term "`Theory`" to refer to such collections, along with various other pieces of ancillary information, as well as subsets of a full theory. The ancillary information includes components to support language parsing, local and temporary definitions, as well as proof support in the form of conjectures, theorems and laws. In effect a UTP theory may be constructed in $U\cdot(TP)^2$ as a layering of `Theory` "slices", each looking at a small part of the whole.

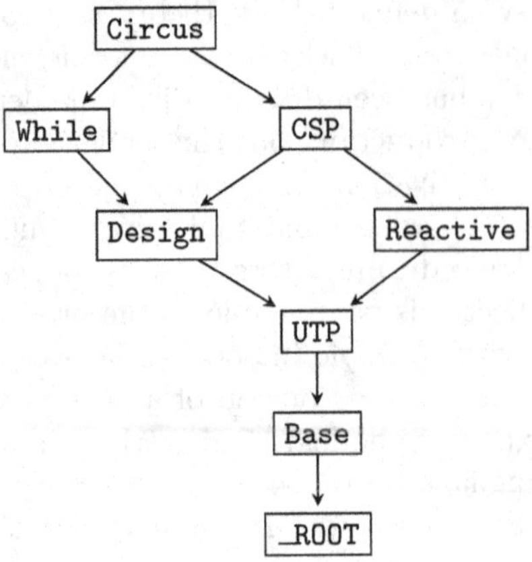

Fig. 1. A Hierarchy of `Theory`s

As an example, consider Figure 1. Here we see theory slices organised as an acyclic directed graph, where each slice inherits material from those below it. At the bottom we have the `_ROOT Theory` (slice), which is hardwired in[2], and simply contains just the axioms of the underlying logic. On top of this a full set of laws of predicate calculus are built (by positing conjectures and proving them), as well as useful theories about equality, and various datatypes, such as numbers, sets and sequences. In $U\cdot(TP)^2$ these are presented as a layer of `Theory` slices, but here we simply imagine them all encapsulated into the `Base Theory`, that sits on top of `_ROOT`. On top of this we construct a slice (`UTP`) that presents the language constructs that are common to most UTP theories, e.g. sequential composition, and non-deterministic choice. We then branch: a theory of Designs is implemented by building a `Design Theory` slice on top of `UTP`, and hence incorporating `Base` and `_ROOT`. Similarly, we can define, independently of `Design`, a `Reactive Theory` slice over `UTP`. It is this ability to re-use common material that motivates the splitting of UTP theories into $U\cdot(TP)^2$ Theory slices. Figure 1 also shows how further slices allow us to build a theory of a simple imperative language (`While`) on top of `Design`, as well as fusing `Design` and `Reactive` to get `CSP` [Ros97]. A similar fusing of `While` with `CSP` gives `Circus`[OCW09].

In the sequel we shall no longer distinguish between "proper" UTP theories and $U\cdot(TP)^2$'s `Theory` slices, simply referring to them all as "theories". We do not give details of the contents of a theory here, but instead elucidate these details as we go through the paper.

[2] `_ROOT` is the only thing hardwired—all other slices and their hierarchy can be custom-built to suit the user.

3 Logic

The logic of $U\cdot(TP)^2$ is an adaptation of the first-order equational logic described by Tourlakis [Tou01], that fully formalises the logic of Dijkstra, Gries and Schneider [GS93].

3.1 $U\cdot(TP)^2$ Logic Syntax

We define our logic syntax over a collection of given sets characterising different name-spaces:

$$
\begin{array}{lll}
x, y, z \in \mathit{Var} & (\mathit{given}) & \text{Obs. Variables} \\
k \in \mathit{Const} & (\mathit{given}) & \text{Constants} \\
f, g, h \in \mathit{Name} & (\mathit{given}) & \text{(Function) Names} \\
E, F, G \in \mathit{EName} & (\mathit{given}) & \text{Expression Metavariable Names} \\
P, Q, R \in \mathit{PName} & (\mathit{given}) & \text{Predicate Metavariable Names}
\end{array}
$$

Variables, constants and function names are as one would expect in a logic with associated equational theories, but we also have explicit meta-variables for expressions and predicates, in the object logic, as many UTP laws are expressed using such.

Expressions and Predicates are defined by mutual induction, because both may contain instances of the other. Expressions denote values in the "world of discourse" (observations) and are typed. Expressions whose type is boolean ($c \in \mathit{Expr}$) form the class of *atomic predicates*:

$$
\begin{array}{rll}
c, e \in \mathit{Expr} ::= & k \mid x & \text{Expressions} \\
\mid & f\ e & \text{Applications} \\
\mid & \lambda\, x \bullet e & \text{Obs. Abstraction} \\
\mid & \Lambda E \bullet e & \text{E-var. Abstraction} \\
\mid & \Lambda P \bullet e & \text{P-var. Abstraction} \\
\mid & \{x \mid p \bullet e\} & \text{Comprehension} \\
\mid & E & \text{Explicit Metavariable}
\end{array}
$$

Predicates are defined much as expected:

$$
\begin{array}{rll}
p, q, r \in \mathit{Pred} ::= & \mathit{True} \mid \mathit{False} & \text{Constant Predicates} \\
\mid & e & \text{Atomic Predicate (Boolean-valued Expr.)} \\
\mid & \neg\, p & \text{Negation} \\
\mid & p \maltese q & \text{Composites, } \maltese \in \{\wedge, \vee, \Rightarrow, \equiv\} \\
\mid & P & \text{Explicit Metavariable} \\
\mid & \yen x \bullet p & \text{1st-order Quantifiers, } \yen \in \{\forall, \exists, \exists!\} \\
\mid & \yen P \bullet p & \text{higher-order Quantifiers, } \yen \in \{\forall, \exists\} \\
\mid & \yen E \bullet p & \text{higher-order Quantifiers, } \yen \in \{\forall, \exists\} \\
\mid & [p] & \text{Universal Closure (over observations)}
\end{array}
$$

The axioms of the logic are shown in Appendix A (A.1, A.3). The axioms are stored in the hardwired _ROOT theory, in the *laws* component of the theory, which maps law-names to laws, where a law is a predicate and a side-condition. Side-conditions are a conjunction of zero or more basic conditions, which typically capture relationships between given variables and the free variables (fv) of given predicates.

$$\begin{aligned}
\mathit{Theory} &= \textbf{record} \\
&\qquad \mathit{laws} : \mathit{Name} \rightsquigarrow \mathit{Law} \\
&\qquad \ldots\textbf{end} \\
\mathit{Law} &= \mathit{Pred} \times \mathit{Side} \\
\mathit{Side} &= x \notin \mathsf{fv}.P \mid \{x, y, \ldots\} = \mathsf{fv}.P \mid \{x, y, \ldots\} \supseteq \mathsf{fv}.P \mid \ldots
\end{aligned}$$

Here the notation $A \rightsquigarrow B$ denotes a partial finite function from A to B, and so is effectively a table using a key of type A to lookup a value of type B.

The inference rules (A.2) are implemented, in the main, by a pattern matching mechanism that takes a current proof goal and sees which laws can apply, and a process that allows the user to select and apply the desired one, storing the changed goal in a list that is assumed to be chained together by logical equivalence. The basic structural match has a judgement $\Gamma \vdash P \ddagger T \mid \beta$ that asserts that, given matching environment Γ, test predicate T matches pattern predicate P, with resulting bindings β. Bindings map variables to well-formed expressions or predicates, as appropriate. If we ignore Γ for now, then a representative collection of structural matching rules are:

$$\Gamma \vdash x \ddagger e \mid \{x \mapsto e\} \qquad \langle\!\langle \text{MATCH-VAR} \rangle\!\rangle$$

$$\frac{\Gamma \vdash P_i \ddagger T_i \mid \beta_i \qquad \beta_1 \cong \beta_2}{\Gamma \vdash P_1 \wedge P_2 \ddagger T_1 \wedge T_2 \mid \beta_1 \uplus \beta_2} \qquad \langle\!\langle \text{MATCH-}\wedge \rangle\!\rangle$$

$$\frac{P \ddagger Q \mid \beta_1 \qquad xs \ddagger ys \mid \beta_2 \qquad \beta_1 \cong \beta_2}{\forall\, xs \bullet P \ddagger \forall\, ys \bullet P \mid \beta_1 \uplus \beta_2} \qquad \langle\!\langle \text{MATCH-}\forall \rangle\!\rangle$$

The $\cong$ predicate asserts that two bindings do not map the same variable to different things. The $\uplus$ operator merges two bindings, provided they satisfy $\cong$. An attempted match of T against P fails if no rules apply, or an attempt is made to apply $\uplus$ to two bindings that do not satisfy $\cong$.

In order to facilitate proof, the theory has two components, one for conjectures, which can be viewed as aspirant laws (posited, hopefully true, but not yet proven), and theorems, which are conjectures with proofs:

$$
\begin{aligned}
\mathit{Theory} &= \textbf{record} \ldots \\
&\qquad \mathit{conjs} : \mathit{Name} \rightsquigarrow \mathit{Law} \\
&\qquad \mathit{thms} : \mathit{Name} \rightsquigarrow \mathit{Proof} \\
&\qquad \ldots \textbf{end} \\
\mathit{Proof} &= \textbf{record} \\
&\qquad \mathit{goal} : \mathit{Pred} \\
&\qquad \mathit{sc} : \mathit{Side} \\
&\qquad \mathit{done} : \mathbb{B} \\
&\qquad \ldots \textbf{end}
\end{aligned}
$$

The workflow is as follows: conjectures can be entered by the user and accumulated in *conjs*. A proof can then be started by selecting a conjecture, which creates a corresponding entry in *thms*, with *goal*, *sc* set to match the conjectured law, and the *done* flag set to false. More than one proof can be active at any one time. A proof is carried out using all the *laws* accessible from the theory. Once a proof is complete, the *done* flag is set true, the corresponding conjecture is deleted, and, usually, a corresponding entry is made into *laws*.

The mechanism as described so far is adequate for proving all and any conjectures based on propositional logic. However it needs extensions to cater for non-propositional logic, and the datatype theories. We will address the non-propositional extensions in the next section on generic UTP. Here we discuss briefly some practical issues with datatype theories. We can define a theory of natural number arithmetic using Peano axioms, for example—the tool supports the creation of a new named empty theory, and the addition of appropriate axiomsby the user into the *laws* table. Operations on natural numbers can be defined axiomatically by adding further laws as required. From this it is possible to prove a range of theorems about natural number operations, e.g. $m + 0 = m$. A similar exercise can be done for sets, and sequences, resulting in laws like $S \cup \emptyset = S$ and $s \frown \langle\rangle = s$. The problem is that we do not just match against whole laws, but can also match against just the lefthand or righthand sides of an equality or equivalence—so the righthand sides of all three laws above will match an arbitrary expression e, offering $e+0$, $e \cup \emptyset$ and $e \frown \langle\rangle$ as replacements. To prevent such spurious matches, we introduce a type system for expressions, and a type-inference engine, that uses context information to deduce the types of expressions like e, and serves to reduce spurious matches to a considerable degree. A theory contains tables to support this feature:

$$
\begin{aligned}
\mathit{Theory} &= \textbf{record} \ldots \\
&\qquad \mathit{type} : \mathit{Name} \rightsquigarrow \mathit{Type} \\
&\qquad \ldots \textbf{end} \\
t \in \mathit{Type} &::= \mathbb{B} \mid \mathbb{Z} \mid \tau \mid \mathcal{P}t \mid \ldots
\end{aligned}
$$

The *Names* in *type* are typically names of variables or functions.

4 UTP

Some key concepts are common to most UTP theories, namely sequential composition ($\fatsemi$), non-deterministic choice ($\sqcap$), refinement ($\sqsubseteq$) and conditional ($\lhd c \rhd$). Importantly, in most theories these all have the same definition:

$$\begin{aligned} P \fatsemi Q &\mathrel{\widehat=} \exists\, Obs_m \bullet P[Obs_m/Obs'] \land Q[Obs_m/Obs] \\ P \sqcap Q &\mathrel{\widehat=} P \lor Q \\ P \sqsubseteq Q &\mathrel{\widehat=} [Q \Rightarrow P] \\ P \lhd c \rhd Q &\mathrel{\widehat=} c \land P \lor \neg c \land Q \end{aligned}$$

The definitions for $\sqcap$, $\sqsubseteq$ and $\lhd c \rhd$ are unproblematical, and are easily handled by the existing machinery, with one key extension. The definition of $\fatsemi$ not only makes use of explicit substitution notation, but also raises the question of how to interpret Obs_m, Obs' and Obs. Clearly they stand for the obervational variables of a UTP theory along with appropriate decorations, but how do we support this? In particular, how can we arrange matters so that we only define $\fatsemi$ once, in such a way that it can be used by many different theories? We will first address the key extension alluded to above, and then return to the problem of sequential composition.

4.1 Defining Your Own Language in $U{\cdot}(TP)^2$

A key aspect of a UTP theory is the signature that captures the abstract syntax of the language being defined. This means that $U{\cdot}(TP)^2$ needs to support user-defined languages. This is achieved by having a table-driven parser for entering predicates, and providing a facility for the user to add new entries to the relevant tables:

$$\begin{aligned} Theory = \mathbf{record} \ldots & \\ & precs : Name \leadsto Precedence \\ & lang : Name \leadsto LangSpec \\ & \ldots \mathbf{end} \end{aligned}$$

The *precs* table maps the name of an infix operator to information about its parsing precedence and its associativity. The *lang* table maps a language construct name to a language specification (*LangSpec*) that describes the concrete syntactical structure of that construct. A language specification is a mix of keywords denoting syntactical components like variables (V) , expressions (E) , predicates (P), or various lists of such, interspersed with concrete syntax symbols. We won't give a full definition here but present some examples to give the idea:

– Refinement: we specify this as "`P |= P`", which states that `|=` is an infix operator between two predicates. When this is entered into the *lang* table, a corresponding entry is automatically created in the *precs* table with default

values (mid-range precedence, non-associative) which can then be edited by the user to suit. Also entered is a dummy definition for the construct into the *laws* table, which itself then needs to be edited.
- Assignment: specified as "`V := E`", stating that `:=` is an infix operator in-between a variable and expression, resulting in a predicate.

In general defining a language construct (resulting in a predicate) involves adding entries to the *lang* and *laws* tables, and possibly also to the *types* and *precs* tables, depending on the precise nature of the construct. Infix expression operators do not have *lang* entries but require *laws*, *precs* and *types* entries.

When we talk about developing a theory of Designs (Section 5), we shall give a worked-out example of a language definition.

4.2 The Problem with $\fatsemi$

The definition of sequential composition,

$$P \fatsemi Q \mathrel{\widehat{=}} \exists\, Obs_m \bullet P[Obs_m/Obs'] \wedge Q[Obs_m/Obs]$$

says in effect that for each observation, x, say, in Obs, we replace any free occurrence of x' in p by x_m and any free occurrence of x in q by Obs_m, and use existential quantification to hide x_m. In effect the rule above is really a rule-schema, characterising an infinite number of rules, one for each possible alphabet represented by Obs. However, we don't want to repeatedly instantiate this rule and reason about its consequences for each specific alphabet we use. In fact, we want to use the definition in cases where only part of the alphabet is known (Designs again, Section 5). We would prefer to be able to do proofs with the definition as given above, only instantiating Obs where necessary, and then perhaps only partially. In fact, we want to support the following proof (of the associativity of $\fatsemi$) which does not require any instantation of Obs:

$$\begin{aligned}
& P;\ (Q;\ R) \\
\equiv\ & \exists\, Obs_m \bullet P[Obs_m/Obs'] \wedge (Q;\ R)[Obs_m/Obs] \\
\equiv\ & \exists\, Obs_m \bullet P[Obs_m/Obs'] \wedge (\exists\, Obs_n \bullet Q[Obs_n/Obs'] \wedge R[Obs_n/Obs])[Obs_m/Obs] \\
\equiv\ & \exists\, Obs_m, Obs_n \bullet P[Obs_m/Obs'] \wedge Q[Obs_n/Obs'][Obs_m/Obs] \wedge R[Obs_n/Obs][Obs_m/Obs] \\
\equiv\ & \exists\, Obs_m, Obs_n \bullet P[Obs_m/Obs'][Obs_n/Obs'] \wedge Q[Obs_n, Obs_m/Obs', Obs] \wedge R[Obs_n/Obs] \\
\equiv\ & \exists\, Obs_n \bullet (\exists\, Obs_m \bullet P[Obs_m/Obs'][Obs_n/Obs'] \wedge Q[Obs_m/Obs][Obs_n/Obs']) \\
& \qquad \wedge R[Obs_n/Obs] \\
\equiv\ & \exists\, Obs_n \bullet (\exists\, Obs_m \bullet P[Obs_m/Obs'] \wedge Q[Obs_m/Obs])[Obs_n/Obs'] \wedge R[Obs_n/Obs] \\
\equiv\ & \exists\, Obs_n \bullet (P;\ Q)[Obs_n/Obs'] \wedge R[Obs_n/Obs] \\
\equiv\ & (P;\ Q);\ R
\end{aligned}$$

In effect we want to reason within our logic about "schematic" variables like Obs and treat the substitution notation as part of the object logic, rather than meta-notation describing the behaviour of an inference rule.

To achieve this we have to add another linguistic innovation to the logic. A common shorthand in most presentations of logic is to view $\forall x, y, z \bullet p$ (say) as a shorthand for $\forall x \bullet \forall y \bullet \forall z \bullet p$. Our innovation is not only to add the former as a full part of the logic syntax, but also a further extension. We want to be able to have quantifier variables (e.g. *Obs*) that represent lists of "ordinary" quantifier variables. We do this by splitting the list into two parts, separated by a semi-colon, with those in the first part being ordinary, whilst those in the second part denote lists of variables. The revised syntax of $\forall$ is now:

$$\forall x_1, \ldots, x_m ; xs_1, \ldots, xs_m \bullet P \qquad m \geq 0, n \geq 0, m + n \geq 1$$

Other observation (1st-order) quantifiers are modified similarly. The x_i and xs_j above are "quantifier variables", and will be disambiguated were necessary by referring to the x_i (before the ; sysmbol) as "single variables" and the xs_j (after ; as "list variables"). A list where $m = 0$ is referred to as an "ordinary list". The meaning of a quantifier variable list of the form $x_1, \ldots, x_m ; xs_1, \ldots, xs_m$ is that it matches an ordinary list of the form $y_1, \ldots, y_{m+k}, k \geq 0$ where each x_i binds to one y_j, each xs_i binds to zero or more y_j, and every y_j is bound exactly once. In principle the bindings associated with a variable like xs_i are non-deterministic, albeit they must be consistent with bindings derived from the match as a whole, i.e. the wider context in which that variable occurs. In practice, heuristics are used in the implementation to select a binding that is hopefully as "good" as possible.

As our proof above largely depended on properties of (explicit) substitution, we have to add it into our logic as well. So we revise our syntax for predicates:

$p, q, r \in Pred$	$::= \ldots$	
	$\mid\ ¥ qvs \bullet p$	1st-order Quantifiers, $¥ \in \{\forall, \exists, \exists!\}$
	$\mid\ p[e/x]$	Explicit Obs. Substitution
	$\mid\ p[e/E]$	Explicit E-var. Substitution
	$\mid\ p[p/P]$	Explicit P-var. Substitution
$qvs \in QVars$		Quantifier Variable lists
	$::= x_1, \ldots, x_m ; xs_1, \ldots, xs_m$	$m \geq 0, n \geq 0, m + n \geq 1$

Explicit substitutions are also added to expressions as well. Laws regarding explicit substitutions also need to be developed, e.g.

$$p[e/x][f/y] = p[e, f/x, y], \quad x \neq y, y \notin \mathsf{fv}.e$$

but we do not list these here.

This extension allows us to introduce axioms like:

$$(\forall x ; xs \bullet p) \Rightarrow (\forall ; xs \bullet p[e/x]) \qquad \ll\text{AX-}\forall x\text{-INST}\gg$$

rather than relying on a simple single quantifier axiom and the usual conventions regarding the $\forall x, y, z$ shorthand. In essence what we have done is to formalise and automate this convention.

To support the definition of $\fatsemi$ we need one further step. The list variable *Obs* does not stand for an arbitrary list of single variables, but is instead intended to stand for precisely those un-dashed variables that are present in the alphabet of the current theory, even if that alphabet has not been fully described. Similarly, *Obs'* stands for all the dashed variables, and Obs_m denotes the decoration of all the *Obs* variables. In effect we designate certain list variables (like *Obs*) as having a special meaning.

The basic matcher described in Section 3, has to be enhanced to perform appropriate matching where non-ordinary quantifier lists are present. To make this work, we need to extend theories to have a table that records the theory alphabet:

$$\begin{aligned} \mathit{Theory} = \mathbf{record} \ldots & \\ \mathit{obs} : \mathit{Name} \rightsquigarrow \mathit{Type} & \\ \ldots \mathbf{end} & \end{aligned}$$

The *obs* table needs to become part of the matching context Γ, and we introduce rules for matching quantifier lists:

$$\frac{}{\Gamma \vdash {;}Obs \ddagger {;}Obs \mid \varepsilon}$$

$$\frac{Obs(\Gamma) = \{o_1, \ldots, o_n\}}{\Gamma \vdash {;}Obs \ddagger \{o_1, \ldots, o_n\} \mid \{Obs \mapsto \{o_1, \ldots, o_n\}\}}$$

The first rule allows *Obs* to match itself, and so we can do proofs that do not require it to be expanded to an ordinary list. Note also that in this case an empty binding (ε) is returned. Other matching rules not shown here, take care of decorations, ensuring that *Obs* matches x, y, z, if appropriate, but not x', y', z'.

We can now define sequential composition in our revised logic as:

$$P \fatsemi Q \mathrel{\widehat{=}} \exists {;}Obs_m \bullet P[Obs_m/Obs'] \wedge Q[Obs_m/Obs]$$

and produce a proof as shown earlier. There is an additional extension required to the logic to do this, but we shall motivate and introduce it in the section on Designs (Section 5).

5 Designs

The UTP theory of Designs [HH98, Chp 3] introduces two boolean observation variables (ok, ok') to model program start and termination, and new notation $P \vdash Q$ to represent a predicate with pre and post-conditions:

$$\begin{aligned} ok, ok' &: \mathbb{B} \\ P \vdash Q &\mathrel{\widehat{=}} ok \wedge P \Rightarrow ok' \wedge Q, \qquad ok, ok' \notin \mathsf{fv}.P \cup \mathsf{fv}.Q \end{aligned}$$

A key feature to note is that in this theory we do not specify the entire alphabet, but only stipulate that whatever it is, it must contain ok and ok'. In this light we see an even stronger need for special list-variables like Obs as already introduced.

We can already capture this with our theories as described so far:

$$\begin{aligned}
obs(ok) &= \mathbb{B} \\
obs(ok') &= \mathbb{B} \\
lang(\vdash) &= P \vdash P \\
prec(\vdash) &= (n, NonAssoc), \quad n \text{ is desired precedence} \\
laws(\vdash\!-\!DEF) &= (P \vdash Q \equiv ok \land P \Rightarrow ok' \land Q, ok, ok' \notin \mathsf{fv}.P \cup \mathsf{fv}.Q)
\end{aligned}$$

Here we see some side-conditions that assert that neither P nor Q should mention either ok or ok'. These are important side-conditions, without which we do not obtain the desired behaviours (algebraic laws) for designs. However, in proving properties of designs in UTP, we find that the side-conditions play a more active role than encountered in more traditional presentations of logic. In many logics, side-conditions about free variables are syntactic in nature and can always be checked/discharged when applying a rule to a predicate in the logic. In particular, when applying a rule like the one above, both P and Q will have been instantiated to concrete predicates, and so it will be easy to establish the truthfulness of these side-conditions. However in a UTP proof about the properties of designs, we work with explicit meta-variables P and Q for which it is not possible to compute side-condition rules at rule-application time.

Instead, we have to add a post processing stage to law matching. Assuming that a target predicate match involving a law has succeeded returning a binding, We use that binding to translate any side-condition with the law to a corresponding one in the target world. We then need to show that the translated law-side condition is a consequence of any side-conditions associated with the conjecture goal.

In effect, in addition to a syntax for side-conditions, we have to implement a side-condition inference engine that can deduce when one side-condition implies another. Let psc denote the translated pattern side-condition, and tsc denote the side-condition associated with the conjecture being proven. We have to demonstrate that $tsc \Rightarrow psc$. As side-conditions are a conjunction of a few basic primitive side-conditions, we simply take both tsc and $tsc \land psc$, reduce both to a canonical normal form, and check for equality.

To illustrate all of this, here is a proof that $R \vdash S \equiv R \vdash R \land S$, given that $ok, ok' \notin \mathsf{fv}.R \cup \mathsf{fv}.S$. Here we deliberately state our conjecture using different meta-variables to those used to define designs, to show the translation aspect at work. Our proof strategy will be to take the lefthand side and transform it into the righthand side[3].

The first step proceeds when a match of $R \vdash S$ succeeds against pattern $P \vdash Q$ returning the binding $[P \mapsto R, Q \mapsto S]$. However, we need to discharge the side-condition $ok, ok' \notin \mathsf{fv}.P \cup \mathsf{fv}.Q$. We use the bindings to translate this

[3] The strategy in play is noted in the *Proof* record.

to $ok, ok' \notin \mathsf{fv}.R \cup \mathsf{fv}.S$. This then has to be implied by our conjecture side-condition, which in this case is identical to the law condition, so we can deduce that it holds. The proof then proceeds as follows:

$$\begin{array}{ll}
 & R \vdash S \\
\equiv & \quad \text{“ as just discussed above ”} \\
 & ok \land R \Rightarrow ok' \land S \\
\equiv & ok \Rightarrow (R \Rightarrow ok' \land S) \\
\equiv & ok \Rightarrow (R \Rightarrow R \land ok' \land S) \\
\equiv & ok \land R \Rightarrow ok' \land S \land R \\
\equiv & \quad \text{“ see below ”} \\
 & R \vdash R \land S
\end{array}$$

The last step up is similar to the first, as the matching of righthand sides succeeds, and the bindings and translation are the same. This raises a new and important issue to do with observational variables. The variables *ok* and *ok'* mentioned above are not arbitrary, but denote specific observations, and so it is important for UTP that they only match themselves in laws, unlike general variables that can match arbitrary expressions (including other variables). This leads to the need to indicate that certain variables in patterns stand for themselves. Such variables are described as being “known”. All *obs* variables are known, and there is also a facility for a user to give names to constants and expressions, and so those names would also be considered “known”. We will not give further details here.

The structural matching rule for variable patterns needs to be modified, using the context Γ to check if a variable is known, here written as $x \in \Gamma$:

$$\frac{x \in \Gamma}{\Gamma \vdash x \ddagger x}$$

$$\frac{x \notin \Gamma}{\Gamma \vdash x \ddagger v \mid \{x \mapsto v\}}$$

$$\frac{x \notin \Gamma}{\Gamma \vdash x \ddagger e \mid \{x \mapsto e\}}$$

Note that when a known variable matches against itself, no binding entry is produced.

At this point, given the hierarchy of Figure 1, we have a theory called `Design`, which has access to the laws of logic, equality, arithmetic and sets, as well as the definitions and associated laws of $;$, $\sqcap$, $\sqsubseteq$, $\lhd c \rhd$ and $\vdash$, as well as the known observation variables *ok* and *ok'*. In particular, we stress that by being linked in the hierarchy shown, the `Design` theory inherits all the material defined in `UTP`, and all its ancestors. This is quite abstract at this point, so now we move to ground it all a little more.

5.1 Healthiness Conditions

A key feature of UTP is the use of healthiness conditions, expressed typically as monotonic idempotent predicate transformers. To support this in $U\cdot(TP)^2$ we need to extend the predicate syntax to include notation for functions over predicates, and the application of those to predicates, and appropriate axiomatisation:

$$\begin{aligned} p, q, r \in Pred ::= & \ldots \\ & \mid \Lambda P \bullet p, \quad \text{Predicate Abstraction} \\ & \mid p(q), \quad \text{Predicate Application} \\ (\Lambda P \bullet p)(r) \equiv & \; p[r/P] \end{aligned}$$

It is at this point that we definitely leave 1st-order logic behind and move up towards 2nd- and higher-orders of logic. At this point it is useful to have a facility to give names to frequently used constructs like healthiness conditions or common predicate fragments, such as the predicates called II, B and J used in the definition of the Reactive theory [HH98, Chp. 8]. In effect we want to give definitions like the following (not necessarily from the theory of Designs):

$$\begin{aligned} \mathbf{H1} &\mathrel{\widehat{=}} \Lambda P \bullet ok \Rightarrow P \\ J &\mathrel{\widehat{=}} (ok \Rightarrow ok') \wedge wait = wait \wedge tr' = tr \wedge ref' = ref \end{aligned}$$

We achieve this by adding in tables into a theory that allow us to write such definitions, and modifying the matching algorithm to treat all names in those tables as "known":

$$\begin{aligned} Theory = \mathbf{record} & \ldots \\ & preds : Name \rightsquigarrow Pred \\ & exprs : Name \rightsquigarrow Expr \\ & \ldots \mathbf{end} \end{aligned}$$

So, for example, in this theory of Designs we have $preds(\mathbf{H1}) = \Lambda P \bullet ok \Rightarrow P$. The rest of the $U\cdot(TP)^2$ machinery can then be used to reason about and use these healthiness conditions in the normal way, so for example, $\mathbf{H1}(q)$ can be converted into $ok \Rightarrow q$, and vice-versa.

6 Programs

To get concrete, we are now going to define the semantics for a simple imperative programming language (a.k.a. *While*), as a UTP Design. To keep things simple for now, we assume the language has exactly three program variables: x, y, and z (we look at the issue of many variables below in Section 6.1).

$$
\begin{array}{rcll}
u, w \in \mathit{While} & ::= & \mathit{Skip} & \text{do nothing} \\
& | & v := e & \text{Assignment, } v \in \{x, y, z\}, \mathsf{fv}.e \subseteq \{x, y, z\} \\
& | & u \mathbin{;} w & \text{Sequential Composition} \\
& | & u \lhd c \rhd w & \text{Conditional, } \mathsf{fv}.c \subseteq \{x, y, z\} \\
& | & c \circledast w & \text{While-loop, } \mathsf{fv}.c \subseteq \{x, y, z\}
\end{array}
$$

The alphabet of this theory now contains x, y, z, x', y', z' in addition to ok, ok' inherited from the Design theory. Also inherited are the definitions of $;$ and $\lhd c \rhd$, where now *Obs* can bind to $ok, x, y, z, ok', x', y', z'$ in pattern matching. We can use the language specification facility to introduce the syntax to $U(TP)^2$, so in *While.lang* we have:

$$\mathit{Skip} \mapsto \texttt{Skip}$$

$$:= \mapsto \texttt{V := E}$$

$$\mathit{whl} \mapsto \texttt{E ** P}$$

6.1 The $U\cdot(TP)^2$ Semantics of *Skip* and $x := e$

We start to define the semantics of *Skip*, and we could immediately write:

$$\mathit{Skip} \mathrel{\widehat{=}} \mathit{True} \vdash x' = x \wedge y' = y \wedge z' = z$$

While correct, we may worry about what happens if the number of variables increases, or if we want to have some dynamism regarding the number and names of program variables. While we discuss another possible approach to program variables later, for now let's see what we can do to improve things. We could try to use special list variable *Obs*, to get

$$\mathit{Skip} \mathrel{\widehat{=}}?\ \mathit{True} \vdash \mathit{Obs}' = \mathit{Obs}$$

but this is not satisfactory, as *Obs* (Obs') includes *ok* (ok') and these cannot occur in the design predicates, as per the side-condition used in the Design theory.

The solution here is realise that in many UTP theories we actually have two classes of observations: those associated with the values of variables in the program text under consideration (here x, y and z), and those that capture overall program properties, independent of any program variable (here *ok* and ok', denoting termination). We shall refer to the former as script variables and the latter as model variables, and add in two new special list-variables called *Scr* and *Mdl* to match against the two classes. So in this theory, *Scr* can match x, y, z, while *Mdl* matches *ok*. Also *Obs* can now match *Scr*, *Mdl*, or combinations such as *Scr*, *ok*. This requires us to modify the *obs* table in a theory slightly as we must now record observation class, as well as its type:

$$
\begin{array}{rcl}
\mathit{Theory} & = & \textbf{record}\ldots \\
& & \quad \mathit{obs} : \mathit{Name} \leadsto \mathit{Type} \times \mathit{OClass} \\
& & \ldots\textbf{end} \\
\mathit{OClass} & ::= & \mathit{Model} \mid \mathit{Script}
\end{array}
$$

So, for example, in theory `Design` we have $obs(ok) = (\mathbb{B}, Model)$, while in theory `While` we have $obs(x) = (t, Script)$, where t is some type. We can now define the semantics of *Skip* as:

$$Skip \mathrel{\widehat{=}} True \vdash Scr' = Scr$$

This definition will now work in a range of theories, provided the observations are classified appropriately. However it does also require a further extension of the law matching algorithm. This has to be modified to allow a pattern like $Scr' = Scr$, given bindings $Scr \mapsto x, y, z$ and $Scr' \mapsto x', y', z'$, to match against a predicate fragment like $x' = x \wedge y' = y \wedge z' = z$. This feature is quite easily implemented as part of the structural matcher.

We now turn our attention to the definition of assignment. The following is *not* satisfactory:

$$x := e \mathrel{\widehat{=}}?\ True \vdash x' = e \wedge Scr' = Scr$$

First, as x is known, this rule will only match assignments whose variable is x, so we would need a different definition for each program variable—not a good idea! Secondly, $Scr' = Scr$ will match $x' = x \wedge y' = y \wedge z' = z$ as already described, and so we can match $x' = e \wedge x' = x$ which reduces to $x = e$, and then probably *False*. We could try to make the matching of $Scr' = Scr$ against $x' = x \wedge y' = y \wedge z' = z$ "context sensitive", only matching an equality if both sides do not appear "elsewhere", but it is currently very unclear if this is at all feasible. Instead, we extend the list-variable notation to allow modifiers, so we can write the following satisfactory definition for assignment:

$$v := e \mathrel{\widehat{=}} True \vdash v' = e \wedge (Scr' \setminus v') = (Scr \setminus v)$$

The law/pattern variable v is not known, so it will match any of x, y or z, and even ok. However as ok cannot appear in the predicates in a design, any matching of v to ok will lead to a proof that eventually freezes up because the side-condition defining $\vdash$ won't be satisfiable. Imagine we are matching the righthand side of the above definition with $y' = f \wedge x' = x \wedge z' = z$. The matching algorithm will attempt match y' against v', returning a binding $v' \mapsto y'$. This binding gives us enough information to be able to match $(Scr' \setminus v') = (Scr \setminus v)$ against $x' = x \wedge z' = z$.

A further complication arises when we try to prove laws such as:

$$(v := e \mathbin{;} v := f) \equiv (v := f[e/v])$$
$$(u := e \mathbin{;} v := f) \equiv (v := f[e/u] \mathbin{;} u := e), \quad v \notin \mathsf{fv}.e$$

We will not elaborate on details here, but we find the need to use special list variables like *Scr* and *Scr'* in substitutions, so the matching algorithm needs to handle those cases as well.

6.2 Merging Program Variables

Another way to handle program variables is to group them together into an environment, a mapping from variable names to values:

$$\rho \in Env = Var \rightsquigarrow Val$$

We can then introduce *Model* variables called *state* and *state'*. This simplifies the alphabet handling, as it is now fixed, and we can model variable declarations with map extensions. In effect we have no script variables, just model ones, with the consequence that the theory of the alphabet is now independent of the program script. The added complexity now emerges in the type system, because *Val* needs to include all types in *Type*, and the definition of assignment now requires an *eval* function of type $Env \rightarrow Expr \rightsquigarrow Val$ (here $\oplus$ denotes map override):

$$v := e \mathrel{\widehat{=}} True \vdash state' = state \oplus \{v \mapsto eval(state)(e)\}$$

$U{\cdot}(TP)^2$ can support either style of program variable handling, although the environment-based approach requires a theory of finite maps, and laws defining *eval* for every expression construct, with an added complication of having to handle explicit expression *syntax* in laws. However, the provision of such an *eval* function is not quite as onerous as it sounds as laws providing the meaning of all expression constructs are required in any case.

We are not going to elaborate too much on how to give a semantics to the while-loop construct here, apart from noting that it requires a fixpoint construct in the logic syntax, and an appropriate axiomatisation of fixpoint theory. Then the loop can be defined as the least fixed point of the appropriate functional.

$$\begin{aligned} p, q, r \in Pred &::= \ldots \\ &\mid \mu P \bullet F(P) \qquad \text{Fixpoint Operator} \\ c \circledast w &\mathrel{\widehat{=}} \mu W \bullet (w \mathbin{;} W) \lhd c \rhd Skip \end{aligned}$$

7 Soundness

Is $U{\cdot}(TP)^2$ sound? For now, the simple answer is no, due mainly to two reasons.

Firstly, users can add their own laws (axioms), and this always leads to the risk of defining a theory that is inconsistent. As we consider the typical user to be a UTP practitioner with experience in logic and axiomatics, developing foundational theories, we feel it is reasonable to expect such (power) users to be able to use their judgement to avoid such pitfalls. Having said that, it will probably make sense in future versions of the tool to support users at different levels of experience, with the more advanced and dangerous features disabled for novices.

Secondly, the underlying proof engine is very complex, reflecting the complexity of the logic required. At present we are not in a position to guarantee soundness of every action that can be invoked. However, in mitigation, we do point out that the outcome of each basic proof step is highly visible in the tool's GUI. It is clear that eventually we will have to pay serious attention to ensuring the prover is sound (modulo any inconsistencies introduced via user-defined axioms). We envisage two possible approaches:

1. Identifying a very small core from which the whole logic can be developed conservatively, and producing a small piece of prover kernel code that can then be verified. This is the LCF approach adopted for prover systems like HOL[NPW02] and Coq[The08].
2. Developing an encoding of the $U{\cdot}(TP)^2$ logic into the logic of a system with a verified kernel, such as HOL or CoQ, and using those systems to do automated proof checks, possibly even for each proof step as it is done.

8 Exploitation

Assuming that we have addressed the soundness of the implementation of $U{\cdot}(TP)^2$, and have used it to develop a nice theory of an interesting language, how useful will the results be if we try to apply them to a real problem? In principle, we could use $U{\cdot}(TP)^2$ to prove properties of a program written in the language described by our theory. In fact some work has already been done exploring a feature that allows us to take a predicate-transformer theory (e.g. weakest precondition, as per [HH98, Chp. 2, p66]), and a program, and automatically generate proof obligations. However, $U{\cdot}(TP)^2$ is an interactive proof assistant, designed to support UTP theory development, rather than theory use. In practise, there is no way that $U{\cdot}(TP)^2$ can realistically compete with existing industrial-strength tools that can both generate and discharge such proof obligations with a high degree of efficiency.

However what does seem to be feasible, is to develop a facility whereby a UTP theory, once complete, can be translated and exported as a theory useable by just such industrial-strength provers. We are currently exploring building such a theorem-prover link to HOL, as recent work has looked at encoding UTP in ProofPower/HOL[OCW06, ZC08], or Isabelle/HOL [FGW10, FGW12]. We hope to be able to make use of these results to build such a $U{\cdot}(TP)^2$-to-HOL bridge.

9 Conclusions

We can, in effect, summarise the paper by giving a requirements list summarising all the special logic features we desire for $U{\cdot}(TP)^2$: predicate and expression meta-variables; user language definitions; quantifier list variables, with specials to identify alphabets; explicit substitutions; "semantic" side-conditions; and predicate transformers.

All the above could be implemented using Isabelle, or CoQ, or PVS, or pretty much any higher-order theorem prover. However any algorithm can, in principle, be written in the pure lambda calculus, or expressed as a Turing machine, but this does not make it feasible, desirable or practical to use those notations. Similarly we feel that encoding our requirements into one of the above higher-order systems, at least to the extent that it would be visible to the user, is not the way to meet our requirement for machine-assisted support for UTP foundational reasoning.

The resulting logic is quite large, and space limitations have prevented us from giving a complete description here. More details can be found in a draft of the $U{\cdot}(TP)^2$ Reference Manual [But12].

References

[But10] Butterfield, A.: Saoithín: A Theorem Prover for UTP. In: Qin, S. (ed.) UTP 2010. LNCS, vol. 6445, pp. 137–156. Springer, Heidelberg (2010)

[But12] Butterfield, A.: $U.(TP)^2$ reference manual (draft, ongoing). Technical report, School of Computer Science and Statistics, Trinity College Dublin (July 2012), `https://www.scss.tcd.ie/Andrew.Butterfield/Saoithin/`

[FGW10] Feliachi, A., Gaudel, M.-C., Wolff, B.: Unifying Theories in Isabelle/HOL. In: Qin, S. (ed.) UTP 2010. LNCS, vol. 6445, pp. 188–206. Springer, Heidelberg (2010)

[FGW12] Feliachi, A., Gaudel, M.-C., Wolff, B.: Isabelle/circus: A Process Specification and Verification Environment. In: Joshi, R., Müller, P., Podelski, A. (eds.) VSTTE 2012. LNCS, vol. 7152, pp. 243–260. Springer, Heidelberg (2012)

[GS93] Gries, D., Schneider, F.B.: A Logical Approach to Discrete Math. Texts and Monographs in Computer Science. Springer, Berlin (1993)

[HH98] Hoare, C.A.R., He, J.: Unifying Theories of Programming. Prentice-Hall (1998)

[NPW02] Nipkow, T., Paulson, L.C., Wenzel, M.T.: Isabelle/HOL - A Proof Assistant for Higher-Order Logic. LNCS, vol. 2283. Springer, Heidelberg (2002)

[OCW06] Oliveira, M., Cavalcanti, A., Woodcock, J.: Unifying Theories in ProofPower-Z. In: Dunne, S., Stoddart, B. (eds.) UTP 2006. LNCS, vol. 4010, pp. 123–140. Springer, Heidelberg (2006)

[OCW09] Oliveira, M., Cavalcanti, A., Woodcock, J.: A UTP semantics for circus. Formal Asp. Comput 21(1-2), 3–32 (2009)

[Ros97] rOSCOE, A.W.: The Theory and Practise of Concurrency. Prentice-Hall, Pearson (1997); revised to 2000 and lightly revised to 2005

[The08] The Coq Development Team. The coq proof assistant, reference manual, version 8.2. Technical report, INRIA, Roquencourt, France (2008)

[Tou01] Tourlakis, G.: On the soundness and completeness of equational predicate logics. J. Log. Comput. 11(4), 623–653 (2001)

[ZC08] Zeyda, F., Cavalcanti, A.: Encoding *Circus* Programs in ProofPower-Z. In: Butterfield, A. (ed.) UTP 2008. LNCS, vol. 5713, pp. 218–237. Springer, Heidelberg (2010)

A Rules

A.1 Propositional Axioms

$((P \equiv Q) \equiv R) \equiv (P \equiv (Q \equiv R))$	≪Ax-≡-assoc≫
$P \equiv Q \equiv Q \equiv P$	≪Ax-≡-symm≫
$true \equiv Q \equiv Q$	≪Ax-≡-id≫
$false \equiv \neg true$	≪Ax-*false*-def≫
$\neg(P \equiv Q) \equiv \neg P \equiv Q$	≪Ax-¬-≡-distr≫
$P \vee Q \equiv Q \vee P$	≪Ax-∨-symm≫
$(P \vee Q) \vee R \equiv P \vee (Q \vee R)$	≪Ax-∨-assoc≫
$P \vee P \equiv P$	≪Ax-∨-idem≫
$P \vee (Q \equiv R) \equiv P \vee Q \equiv P \vee R$	≪Ax-∨-≡-distr≫
$P \vee \neg P$	≪Ax-Excl-Mdl≫
$P \wedge Q \equiv P \equiv Q \equiv P \vee Q$	≪Ax-Golden-Rule≫
$P \Rightarrow Q \equiv P \vee Q \equiv Q$	≪Ax-⇒-def≫

A.2 Inference Rules

$$\frac{P}{P[Q := R]} \quad \text{(Substitution)}$$

$$\frac{P \equiv Q}{R[S := P] \equiv R[S := Q]} \quad \text{(Leibniz)}$$

$$\frac{P, P \equiv Q}{Q} \quad \text{(Equanimity)}$$

A.3 Non-propositional Axioms

$p \lor (\forall ;xs, ys \bullet q)$ ≪AX-∨-∀ x-SCOPE≫
$\equiv (\forall ;xs \bullet p \lor (\forall ;ys \bullet q)), \quad xs \notin p$
$p \lor (\forall ;Es, Fs \bullet q)$ ≪AX-∨-∀ E-SCOPE≫
$\equiv (\forall ;Es \bullet p \lor (\forall ;Fs \bullet q)), \quad Es \notin p$
$p \lor (\forall ;Ps, Qs \bullet q)$ ≪AX-∨-∀ P-SCOPE≫
$\equiv (\forall ;Ps \bullet p \lor (\forall ;Qs \bullet q)), \quad Ps \notin p$

$(\forall ;xs \bullet p \land q) \equiv (\forall ;xs \bullet p) \land (\forall ;xs \bullet q)$ ≪AX-∀ x-DISTR≫
$(\forall ;Es \bullet p \land q) \equiv (\forall ;Es \bullet p) \land (\forall ;Es \bullet q)$ ≪AX-∀ E-DISTR≫
$(\forall ;Ps \bullet p \land q) \equiv (\forall ;Ps \bullet p) \land (\forall ;Ps \bullet q)$ ≪AX-∀ P-DISTR≫

$(\forall x ; xs \bullet p) \Rightarrow (\forall ;xs \bullet p[e/x])$ ≪AX-∀ x-INST≫
$(\forall E ; Es \bullet p) \Rightarrow (\forall ;Es \bullet p[e/E])$ ≪AX-∀ E-INST≫
$(\forall P ; Ps \bullet p) \Rightarrow (\forall ;Ps \bullet p[q/P])$ ≪AX-∀ P-INST≫

$(\exists ;xs \bullet p) \equiv \neg (\forall ;xs \bullet \neg p)$ ≪AX-∃ x-DEF≫
$(\exists ;Es \bullet p) \equiv \neg (\forall ;Es \bullet \neg p)$ ≪AX-∃ E-DEF≫
$(\exists ;Ps \bullet p) \equiv \neg (\forall ;Ps \bullet \neg p)$ ≪AX-∃ P-DEF≫
$\exists! ; xs \bullet p$ ≪AX-∃!x-DEF≫
$\equiv (\exists ;xs \bullet p) \land \exists ;ys \bullet p[ys/ ; xs] \Rightarrow ys = xs$

$e = e$ ≪AX-=-REFL≫
$(e = \theta x \bullet p)$ ≪AX-θ-DEF≫
$\equiv p[e/x] \land (\forall y \bullet p[y/x] \Rightarrow y = e), \; x \notin e$

$(\lambda x ; xs \bullet e)f = (\lambda ;xs \bullet e)[f/x]$ ≪AX-β-OREDUCE≫
$(\Lambda E ; Es \bullet q)e \equiv (\Lambda ; Es \bullet q)[e/E]$ ≪AX-β-EREDUCE≫
$(\Lambda P ; Ps \bullet q)r \equiv (\Lambda ; Ps \bullet q)[r/P]$ ≪AX-β-PREDUCE≫

$(\bigwedge_{i=1}^{n} x_i = e_i) \Rightarrow (p \equiv p[e/x]), \quad x_i$ distinct, ≪AX-LEIBNIZ≫
x_i distinct

$p[x := e] \equiv p[e/x]$ ≪AX-OSUBST≫
$p[e/Es] \equiv p[Es := e]$ ≪AX-ESUBST≫
$p[q/Ps] \equiv p[Ps := q]$ ≪AX-PSUBST≫
$true[e/x] \equiv true$ ≪AX-*true*-OSUBST≫
$true[e/Es] \equiv true$ ≪AX-*true*-ESUBST≫
$true[q/Ps] \equiv true$ ≪AX-*true*-PSUBST≫
$false[e/x] \equiv false$ ≪AX-*false*-OSUBST≫
$false[e/Es] \equiv false$ ≪AX-*false*-ESUBST≫
$false[q/Ps] \equiv false$ ≪AX-*false*-PSUBST≫

Conscriptions: A New Relational Model for Sequential Computations

Steve Dunne

School of Computing
University of Teesside, Middlesbrough, UK
stevedunne47@gmail.com

Abstract. We define a new class of UTP homogeneous binary relations called *conscriptions*, which like prescriptions provide a general-correctness model of sequential computations. Their novelty is that the skip conscription is a right unit of sequential composition for all conscriptions, including even those whose assumptions refer to the after-state as well as before-state; they thus improve on prescriptions by providing a less restricted, and hence more expressive, general-correctness model for sequential computations. We also exploit our conscription concept to derive two new enriched sequential models, *extended conscriptions* and *timed conscriptions*, which differentiate between aborting and non-terminating computations.

1 Introduction

Existing models of sequential programs in Unifying Theories of Programming (UTP), such as designs [7, chap. 2] or prescriptions [1], characterise such programs as homogeneous binary relations which can be structurally decomposed into subrelation pairs, whose first subrelation is known as its *assumption* and second as its *commitment*. We contend that any realistic model of sequential computation must provide that its skip program is both a left and right unit of sequential composition.

In this paper we define a new class of UTP homogeneous binary relations called *conscriptions* which, like prescriptions, provide a general-correctness model of sequential computations. Their advantage over prescriptions is that the skip conscription is structurally guaranteed to be a right unit of sequential composition for the entire class of conscriptions without placing any restriction on the form of their assumptions. Conscriptions therefore exhibit all the usual algebraic properties we would wish, but without the restrictions on expressive power which are the price of securing the skip right-unit property in other UTP sequential models such as designs or prescriptions. They also provide a basis for richer sequential models analogous to extended and timed designs [5,6], but with fewer restrictions on their expressive capabilities, and therefore able to express a wider range of computational behaviours in their respective domains.

The rest of the paper is organised as follows. In §2 we summarise our notion of an alphabetised relation together with its associated operators and properties. In §3 we outline Möller's linear-algebra approach to reasoning about UTP

B. Wolff, M.-C. Gaudel, A. Feliachi (Eds.): UTP 2012, LNCS 7681, pp. 144–163, 2013.

designs and prescriptions which represents them as matrices. In §4 we introduce *conscriptions* and employ matrix algebra to establish their properties. In §5 we address sequential programming models which distinguish between abortion and non-termination, in the process introducing *extended conscriptions*. In §6 we address *timed* sequential programming models, in the process introducing *timed conscriptions* and showing that these provide greater expressivity than timed designs. Finally, in §7 we summarise the various conscription-based models we have presented.

2 Alphabetised Relations

Each of the UTP models we present in this paper comprises a characteristic family of alphabetised homogeneous binary relations on a given alphabet of variables, which is closed under relational union and relational composition. In this preliminary section we describe the relational concepts and properties which our work relies. We begin by defining our hierarchy of relation types.

Definition 1 (Alphabetised Relation). *An alphabetised relation is characterised by a pair (p, A) where A is an alphabet of variables and p is a predicate all of whose free variables belong to A.*

When the alphabet A of an alphabetised relation $P = (p, A)$ can be inferred from the context we will often use its predicate p as a proxy for the relation P itself.

Definition 2 (Binary Relation). *An alphabetised relation (p, A) is binary if its alphabet A is partitioned into subalphabets inA and $outA$, called respectively its input and output alphabets.*

Definition 3 (Homogeneous Binary Relation). *A binary relation is homogeneous if its output alphabet comprises dashed versions of the variables of its input alphabet. Thus such a relation is of the form $(p, \{w, w'\})$, where w and w' are corresponding lists of undashed and dashed variables.*

We note that to determine the alphabet of a homogeneous binary relation only its input alphabet need be given, since its output alphabet is then derived by systematic dashing of its input variables.

We next define two important relational operators: union and composition. A key principle of UTP is that relational union always expresses the nondeterministic choice between computations, and relational composition their sequential composition.

Definition 4 (Relational Union). *The relational union $P \sqcap Q$ of alphabetised relations $P = (p, A)$ and $Q = (q, A)$ over the same alphabet A, is defined as*

$$P \sqcap Q \;\widehat{=}\; (p \vee q, A) \,.$$

Definition 5 (Relational Composition). *The relational composition of homogeneous binary relations* $(p, \{w, w'\})$ *and* $(q, \{w, w'\})$ *over the same alphabet* $\{w, w'\}$ *is the relation* $(p\,;q\ ,\ \{w, w'\})$*, in which*

$$p\,;q \ \widehat{=}\ \exists\, w''\,.\ p[w''/w'] \wedge q[w''/w]$$

where w'' *is the list of fresh variables obtained by systematically double-dashing those of* w.

We give relational composition a lower precedence than relational union. Thus for example, $P \sqcap Q\,;R$ means the same as $(P \sqcap Q)\,;R$ and $P\,;Q \sqcap R$ means the same as $P\,;(Q \sqcap R)$.

Relational composition distributes through relational union in either of its arguments. That is to say, for any homogeneous binary relations p, q, r, s over the same alphabet, we have that

$$p\,;(r \vee s) \ = \ (p\,;r) \vee (p\,;s)\ , \qquad (1)$$
$$(p \vee q)\,;r \ = \ (p\,;r) \vee (q\,;r)\ . \qquad (2)$$

Certain homogeneous binary relations are idempotent with respect to relational composition. For example, the maximal relation $\mathrm{T} = (\mathrm{true}\,, \{w, w'\})$ is such that

$$\mathrm{T}\,;\mathrm{T} \ = \ \mathrm{T}\ . \qquad (3)$$

By virtue of relational composition's distributive properties T is absorptive, in the sense that for any homogeneous binary relations $P = (p\,, \{w, w'\})$ and $Q = (q\,, \{w, w'\})$ we have that

$$(p\,;\mathrm{T}) \vee (p\,;q) \ = \ p\,;\mathrm{T}\ . \qquad (4)$$

The identity relation $((w = w')\,, \{w, w'\})$ is a left and right unit of relational composition. Thus for any homogeneous binary relation $P = (p\,, \{w, w'\})$ we have that

$$p\,;(w = w') \ = \ p \ = \ (w = w')\,;p\ . \qquad (5)$$

Similarly, the vacuous relation $\mathrm{F} = (\mathrm{false}\,, \{w, w'\})$ is a left and right zero of relational composition. Thus for any homogeneous binary relation $P = (p\,, \{w, w'\})$ we have that

$$p\,;\mathrm{F} \ = \ \mathrm{F} \ = \ \mathrm{F}\,;p\ . \qquad (6)$$

Finally, the extreme relations F and T have their obvious logical properties with respect to relational union. Thus for any homogeneous binary relation $P = (p\,, \{w, w'\})$ we have that

$$p \vee \mathrm{F} \ = \ p \qquad \text{and} \qquad p \vee \mathrm{T} \ = \ \mathrm{T}\ . \qquad (7)$$

Whenever we express properties of our models by logical formulae denoting predicates, these should be understood as being universally quantified over all their free variables.

3 Linear Algebra of UTP

UTP designs [7, chap. 2] express sequential computations from a total-correctness perspective, whereby those circumstances admitting abortive or non-terminating behaviour are always deemed to admit otherwise-arbitrary terminating behaviour too. The philosophy embodied by total correctness is that abortive or non-terminating behaviour is the worst of all behaviours, so that wherever a specification allows this there is no point in its excluding any other behaviour. The UTP design with assumption p and commitment r is denoted by $p \vdash r$, where

$$p \vdash r \;\; \widehat{=} \;\; ok \wedge p \Rightarrow r \wedge ok' \;.$$

The predicate on the right-hand side of the definition can be informally interpreted as saying that if the program's execution starts and satisfies its assumption p then it must terminate in a final state satisfying its commitment r.

Möller [8] represents UTP designs as 2×2 matrices by partitioning them into the four subrelations corresponding to each of the possible value-combinations of the boolean variables ok and ok'. Thus, for example, the design $p \vdash r$ is represented by the matrix

	$\neg\, ok'$	ok'
$\neg\, ok$	T	T
ok	$\neg\, p$	$\neg\, p \vee r$

(8)

The T entries in the top rows of matrix (8) are entirely dictated by the definition of a UTP design, and are therefore known as *structural* entries. On the other hand, the entry $\neg\, p$ in the bottom of the left-hand column of the matrix characterises all this design's possible aborting/non-terminating behaviour; likewise, the entry $\neg\, p \vee r$ in the bottom of the right-hand column characterises all its possible terminating behaviour. We note that the left-hand $\neg\, p$ is contained in the right-hand $\neg\, p \vee r$, reflecting the total-correctness perspective of UTP designs.

Möller's crucial insight was that by representing UTP designs in this way, matrix algebra can then be employed to model program combinators such as non-deterministic choice and sequential composition. For example, the non-deterministic choice of two designs is modelled by "matrix addition" and the sequential composition of two such designs by "matrix multiplication", in which the underlying component addition is interpreted as relational union (disjunction) and component multiplication as relational composition. By this means it is straightforward to show that

$$(p \vdash r)\,;(q \vdash s) \;\; = \;\; \neg\,(\neg\, p\,;\mathrm{T}) \wedge \neg\,(r\,;\neg\, q) \;\; \vdash \;\; (r\,;s)\;. \tag{9}$$

Prescriptions [1] are the general-correctness analogue of UTP designs. The philosophy underlying general correctness is that requirements concerning abortive or non-terminating behaviour are separate from those concerning terminating behaviour. The prescription with assumption p and commitment r is denoted by $p \Vdash r$, where

$$p \Vdash r \;\widehat{=}\; (ok \land p \Rightarrow ok') \land (ok' \Rightarrow r \land ok) .$$

The predicate on the right-hand side of this definition can be informally interpreted as saying that if the program's execution starts and satisfies its assumption p then it must terminate, and if it terminates it must do so in a final state satisfying its commitment r and it must have started.

Neither UTP designs nor prescriptions discriminate between abortion and non-termination, each of these behaviours being signified by the same observation $\neg\, ok'$ in both models. Prescriptions, like designs, can be represented by 2×2 matrices: the prescription $p \Vdash r$ is represented by the matrix

	$\neg\, ok'$	ok'
$\neg\, ok$	T	F
ok	$\neg\, p$	r

(10)

We note in matrix (10) that the entry $\neg\, p$ in the bottom of the left-hand column, which characterises the aborting or non-terminating behaviour of the prescription, is independent of the entry r in the bottom of the right-hand column which characterises its terminating behaviour.

Matrix algebra can be used to establish that prescriptions are closed under sequential composition, by showing that

$$(p \Vdash r) ; (q \Vdash s) \;=\; \neg\,(\neg\, p ; \mathrm{T}) \land \neg\,(r ; \neg\, q) \Vdash (r ; s) . \qquad (11)$$

The term $\neg\,(\neg\, p ; \mathrm{T})$ which occurs in the right-hand sides of both (9) and (11) prevents skip being a right unit of composition for either designs or prescriptions in general. However, if p refers only to the before-state then $\neg\,(\neg\, p ; \mathrm{T})$ reduces to p. Only such restricted designs and prescriptions (known as H3 designs and normal prescriptions) have skip as a right unit of composition.

4 Conscriptions

We can derive a new UTP relational model of sequential computations by strengthening prescriptions with an extra conjunct $\neg\, ok \Rightarrow v' = v$ requiring that if the computation does not start then it must conserve the existing values of the regular program variables. We call such a strengthened version of a prescription a *conscription*–for *con*serving pre*scription*– and we denote the conscription with assumption p and commitment r by $p \Vvdash r$.

Definition 6 (Conscription). *A conscription is a homogeneous binary relation with input alphabet $\{v, ok\}$, which is characterised by the following predicate, where p and r can each refer to $\{v, v'\}$:*

$$p \Vvdash r \;\widehat{=}\; (ok \land p \Rightarrow ok') \land (ok' \Rightarrow r \land ok) \land (\neg\, ok \Rightarrow v' = v) .$$

The predicate on the right-hand side of Definition 6 can be informally interpreted as saying that if the program's execution satisfies its assumption p then it must terminate, and if it terminates it must satisfy its commitment r and it must have started; on the other hand, if it fails to execute at all then the values of the regular program variables v will be unchanged.

Like designs and prescriptions, conscriptions do not discriminate between abortion and non-termination, and can be represented by 2×2 matrices: for example, the conscription $p \Vvdash r$ is represented by the matrix

	$\neg\, ok'$	ok'
$\neg\, ok$	$v = v'$	F
ok	$\neg\, p$	r

(12)

The two following lemmas establish that conscriptions have the necessary closure properties for an effective sequential model.

Lemma 1 (Nondeterministic Choice of Conscriptions). *Conscriptions are closed under nondeterministic choice. For arbitrary conscriptions* $p \Vvdash r$ *and* $q \Vvdash s$ *over the same alphabet we have that*

$$(\; p \Vvdash r \;) \sqcap (\; q \Vvdash s \;) \quad = \quad p \wedge q \;\Vvdash\; r \vee s \;.$$

Proof. We note that $q \Vvdash s$ is represented by the matrix

	$\neg\, ok'$	ok'
$\neg\, ok$	$v = v'$	F
ok	$\neg\, q$	s

(13)

To derive the matrix representation of $(\; p \Vvdash r \;) \sqcap (\; q \Vvdash s \;)$ we therefore disjoin corresponding entries of matrices (12) and (13) to obtain

	$\neg\, ok'$	ok'
$\neg\, ok$	$v = v'$	F
ok	$\neg\, p \vee \neg\, q$	$r \vee s$

which is the matrix representation of the conscription

$$p \wedge q \;\Vvdash\; r \vee s \;.$$

Lemma 2 (Sequential Composition of Conscriptions). *Conscriptions are closed under sequential composition. For arbitrary conscriptions* $p \Vvdash r$ *and* $q \Vvdash s$ *over the same alphabet we have that*

$$(\; p \Vvdash r \;);(\; q \Vvdash s \;) \quad = \quad p \wedge \neg\, (r\,;\neg\, q) \;\Vvdash\; (r\,;s) \;.$$

Proof. To derive the matrix representation of $(\, p \Vdash r \,) ; (\, q \Vdash s \,)$ we multiply matrix (12) by matrix (13) in that order to obtain the product matrix

	$\neg\, ok'$	ok'
$\neg\, ok$	$(v = v' \,; v = v') \vee (\mathrm{F} \,; \neg\, q)$	$(v = v' \,; \mathrm{F}) \vee (\mathrm{F} \,; s)$
ok	$(\neg\, p \,; v = v') \vee (r \,; \neg\, q)$	$(\neg\, p \,; \mathrm{F}) \vee (r \,; s)$

which simplifies by properties (5) and (6) to

	$\neg\, ok'$	ok'
$\neg\, ok$	$v = v'$	F
ok	$\neg\, p \vee (r \,; \neg\, q)$	$r \,; s$

which is the matrix representation of the conscription

$$p \wedge \neg\, (r \,; \neg\, q) \;\Vdash\; (r \,; s)\,.$$

Extreme Conscriptions. The following special cases of conscriptions are of interest:

$$\begin{array}{rcl} \mathbf{skip}_{\mathsf{c}} & \widehat{=} & \mathrm{true} \Vdash v = v' \\ \mathbf{abort}_{\mathsf{c}} & \widehat{=} & \mathrm{false} \Vdash \mathrm{false} \\ \mathbf{anarchy}_{\mathsf{c}} & \widehat{=} & \mathrm{false} \Vdash \mathrm{true} \\ \mathbf{magic}_{\mathsf{c}} & \widehat{=} & \mathrm{true} \Vdash \mathrm{false} \\ \mathbf{chaos}_{\mathsf{c}} & \widehat{=} & \mathrm{true} \Vdash \mathrm{true}\,. \end{array}$$

Our operational interpretations of these are as follows:

- $\mathbf{skip}_{\mathsf{c}}$ terminates with unchanged program variables;
- $\mathbf{abort}_{\mathsf{c}}$ aborts or fails to terminate;
- $\mathbf{anarchy}_{\mathsf{c}}$ either aborts or fails to terminate, or else terminates with unconstrained program variables;
- $\mathbf{magic}_{\mathsf{c}}$ is the everywhere-miraculous prescription, which is infeasible;
- $\mathbf{chaos}_{\mathsf{c}}$ terminates with unconstrained program variables.

The next lemma reveals that conscriptions have a remarkably simple algebraic characterisation.

Lemma 3 (Algebraic Characterisation of Conscriptions). *A homogeneous binary relation A with input alphabet $\{v, ok\}$ is a conscription if and only if it satisfies*

$$\mathbf{abort}_{\mathsf{c}} \,; A \quad = \quad \mathbf{abort}_{\mathsf{c}} \qquad (14)$$

and in that case we have that

$$A \quad = \quad \neg\, A_{\mathsf{tf}} \Vdash A_{\mathsf{tt}}$$

where A_{tf} is $A[\mathrm{true}, \mathrm{false}/ok, ok']$ and A_{tt} is $A[\mathrm{true}, \mathrm{true}/ok, ok']$.

Proof. Let A be an arbitrary homogeneous binary relation with input alphabet $\{v, ok\}$. Then A is represented by the matrix

	$\neg\, ok'$	ok'
$\neg\, ok$	A_{ff}	A_{ft}
ok	A_{tf}	A_{tt}

(15)

We also have that **abort**$_c$ is represented by the matrix

	$\neg\, ok'$	ok'
$\neg\, ok$	$v' = v$	F
ok	T	F

(16)

Multiplying matrix (16) by matrix (15) in that order yields the product matrix

	$\neg\, ok'$	ok'
$\neg\, ok$	$(v = v' \,;\, A_{ff}) \vee (\mathrm{F} \,;\, A_{tf})$	$(v = v' \,;\, A_{ft}) \vee (\mathrm{F} \,;\, A_{tt})$
ok	$(\mathrm{T} \,;\, A_{ff}) \vee (\mathrm{F} \,;\, A_{tf})$	$(\mathrm{T} \,;\, A_{ft}) \vee (\mathrm{F} \,;\, A_{tt})$

which simplifies by properties (5) and (6) to

	$\neg\, ok'$	ok'
$\neg\, ok$	A_{ff}	A_{ft}
ok	$\mathrm{T} \,;\, A_{ff}$	$\mathrm{T} \,;\, A_{ft}$

(17)

Thus (14) holds if and only if matrix (17) is equal to matrix (16), which is the case if and only if A_{ff} is $v' = v$ and A_{ft} is F. In that case that A's matrix (15) can be re-written as

	$\neg\, ok'$	ok'
$\neg\, ok$	$v' = v$	F
ok	A_{tf}	A_{tt}

(18)

which is the matrix representation of the conscription $\neg\, A_{tf} \Vdash A_{tt}$. This concludes the proof of Lemma 3.

The next lemma shows that the skip conscription is both a left and right unit of sequential composition for all conscriptions, including even those whose assumptions refer to dashed program variables:

Lemma 4 (Conscription Unit of Composition). *For any conscription A*

$$\mathbf{skip}_c \,;\, A \quad = \quad A \quad = \quad A \,;\, \mathbf{skip}_c \,.$$

Proof. Since $\mathbf{skip_c}$ is true $\Vdash v' = v$, its matrix representation is

	$\neg ok'$	ok'
$\neg ok$	$v' = v$	F
ok	F	$v' = v$

which is clearly both a left and right identity of matrix multiplication.

4.1 Why Not Condesigns?

Given how conscriptions are derived from prescriptions, one might reasonably ask whether the same could be done for UTP designs: that is, could UTP designs be strengthened with the conjunct $\neg\, ok \Rightarrow v = v'$ so as to obtain "condesigns" (conserving designs)?

In fact, if we strengthen for example the design $p \vdash r$ in such a way, we obtain a relation whose matrix represntation is

	$\neg ok'$	ok'
$\neg ok$	$v = v'$	$v = v'$
ok	$\neg\, p$	$\neg\, p \vee r$

(19)

Unfortunately, as can readily by shown by matrix algebra, the form of (19) is not closed under sequential composition. An obvious way to remedy this deficiency is to strengthen the extra conjunct to $\neg\, ok \Rightarrow v = v' \wedge \neg\, ok'$, which yields a relation whose matrix representation is

	$\neg ok'$	ok'
$\neg ok$	$v = v'$	F
ok	$\neg\, p$	$\neg\, p \vee r$

(20)

whose form is indeed closed under sequential composition. But we recognise (20) as the matrix representation of the conscription $p \Vdash (p \Rightarrow r)$, so our attempt to devise an effective conserving design has merely led us back to a conscription.

5 Abortion *versus* Non-termination

Extended designs [5,6] were proposed by Hayes *et al* to provide a relational model of sequential programs which distinguishes between abortion and non-termination. It does so by employing a second boolean auxiliary variable *term* in addition to *ok*, to record whether or not a non-aborting computation terminates ($term' = \text{true}$) or runs forever ($term' = \text{false}$). Extended designs are therefore a class of homogeneous binary relations with input alphabet $\{v, term, ok\}$.

The extended design with assumption p and commitment r, where p can refer only to $\{v\}$ and r to $\{v, v', term'\}$, is denoted by $p \vdash_X r$, where

$$\begin{aligned} p \vdash_X r \;\widehat{=}\; & (ok \wedge term \wedge p \Rightarrow r \wedge ok') \wedge (term' \Rightarrow term) \\ & \wedge (\neg\, term \Rightarrow ok) \wedge (\neg\, term' \Rightarrow ok')\,. \end{aligned} \tag{21}$$

Furthermore, p and r must satisfy

$$p \wedge \neg\, term' \Rightarrow (r \Leftrightarrow \forall\, v'\,.\, r) \tag{22}$$

which ensures that the after-values v' of the regular program variables are unconstrained under under non-termination.

The first conjunct $ok \wedge term \wedge p \Rightarrow r \wedge ok'$ on the right-hand side of (21) asserts that if its predecessor has terminated normally and thus allowed the current program to start from an initial state in which its assumption p holds, then it will establish its commitment r and will not abort. The second conjunct $term' \Rightarrow term$ asserts that if the current program terminates its predecessor must have done so too. The third conjunct $\neg\, term \Rightarrow ok$ asserts that if the predecessor does not terminate then it does not abort, and the fourth conjunct $\neg\, term' \Rightarrow ok'$ makes a corresponding assertion about the current program.

Guttmann [3,4,2] has characterised extended designs algebraically by means of matrix algebra. An extended design can specify the circumstances in which non-termination is allowed or even required, and also those when abortion is allowed, but it can never actually *require* the computation to abort.

We can analogously define another class of homogeneous binary relations with input alphabet $\{v, term, ok\}$, which we call *extended conscriptions.* We denote the extended conscription with assumption p and commitment r by $p \Vdash\!\vdash_X r$.

Definition 7 (Extended Conscription). *An extended conscription is a homogeneous binary relation with input alphabet $\{v, ok, term\}$, which is characterised by the following predicate, where p can refer to $\{v, v'\}$, and r can refer to $\{v, v', term'\}$ and is such that $\neg\, term' \Rightarrow (r \Leftrightarrow \forall\, v'\,.\, r)$:*

$$\begin{aligned} p \Vdash\!\vdash_X r \;\widehat{=}\; & (ok \wedge term \wedge p \Rightarrow ok') \wedge (ok' \wedge term \Rightarrow r \wedge ok) \\ & \wedge (\neg\, ok \Rightarrow v = v' \wedge term = term') \wedge (term' \Rightarrow term) \\ & \wedge (\neg\, term \Rightarrow ok) \wedge (\neg\, term' \Rightarrow ok')\,. \end{aligned}$$

We note that the assumption p of the extended conscription $p \Vdash\!\vdash_X r$, unlike that of an extended design, can refer to the after-values v' of the program variables as well as their before-values v. The healthiness condition

$$\neg\, term' \Rightarrow (r \Leftrightarrow \forall\, v'\,.\, r) \tag{23}$$

on r ensures that the after-values v' of the regular program variables are unconstrained under non-termination.

The predicate on the right-hand side of Definition 7 can be interpreted as follows. The first conjunct $ok \wedge term \wedge p \Rightarrow ok'$ asserts that if its predecessor has terminated and the current program's execution satisfies p then it cannot abort.

The second conjunct $ok' \wedge term \Rightarrow r \wedge ok$ asserts that if its predecessor terminated and the current program executes without aborting then it must satisfy r and it must have started. The third conjunct $\neg\, ok \Rightarrow v = v' \wedge term = term'$ asserts that if the current program fails to start at all then the regular program variables v and the auxiliary variable *term* remain unchanged. The fourth conjunct $term' \Rightarrow term$ asserts that that if the current program has terminated then its predecessor must have done so too. The fifth conjunct $\neg\, term \Rightarrow ok$ asserts that if the predecessor does not terminate then it does not abort, and the sixth conjunct $\neg\, term' \Rightarrow ok'$ makes a corresponding assertion about the current program.

An extended conscription can be represented by a 3×3 matrix[1]. For example, $p \Vdash_X r$ is represented by the matrix

	$\neg\, ok' \wedge term'$	$ok' \wedge \neg\, term'$	$ok' \wedge term'$
$\neg\, ok \wedge term$	$v = v'$	F	F
$ok \wedge \neg\, term$	F	T	F
$ok \wedge term$	$\neg\, p$	r_{f}	r_{t}

(24)

where r_{f} is $r[\text{false}/term']$ and r_{t} is $r[\text{true}/term']$. We note that all the entries in the first and second rows of matrix (24) are structural, while the three non-structural entries in its bottom row are mutually independent.

The next two lemmas, whose proofs are given in Appendix A, establish that extended conscriptions have the appropriate closure properties for a sequential model.

Lemma 5 (Nondeterminstic Choice of Extended Conscriptions). *Extended conscriptions are closed under nondeterministic choice. For arbitrary extended conscriptions $p \Vdash_X r$ and $q \Vdash_X s$ over the same alphabet, we have that*

$$(p \Vdash_X r) \sqcap (q \Vdash_X s) \quad = \quad p \wedge q \;\; \Vdash_X \;\; r \vee s \,.$$

Lemma 6 (Composition of Extended Conscriptions). *Extended conscriptions are closed under sequential composition. For arbitrary extended conscriptions $p \Vdash_X r$ and $q \Vdash_X s$ over the same alphabet, we have that*

$$(p \Vdash_X r) \,;\, (q \Vdash_X s) \quad = \quad p \wedge \neg\, (r_{\mathsf{t}} \,;\, \neg\, q) \;\; \Vdash_X \;\; r_{\mathsf{f}} \vee (r_{\mathsf{t}} \,;\, s) \,.$$

Extreme Extended Conscriptions. The following special cases of extended conscriptions are of interest:

$$\begin{aligned} \mathbf{skip}_{\mathsf{xc}} \;\; &\widehat{=} \;\; \text{true} \Vdash_X \; v = v' \wedge term' \\ \mathbf{abort}_{\mathsf{xc}} \;\; &\widehat{=} \;\; \text{false} \Vdash_X \; \text{false} \end{aligned}$$

[1] A fourth row and column, corresponding to the respective combinations ($\neg\, ok \wedge \neg\, term$) and ($\neg\, ok' \wedge \neg\, term'$), are omitted from the matrix since all their entries are F*s* and thus invariant under matrix addition and multiplication.

$$
\begin{aligned}
\mathbf{anarchy}_{\mathsf{xc}} &\mathrel{\widehat{=}} \text{false} \Vdash\!\!\vdash_X \text{true} \\
\mathbf{magic}_{\mathsf{xc}} &\mathrel{\widehat{=}} \text{true} \Vdash\!\!\vdash_X \text{false} \\
\mathbf{chaos}_{\mathsf{xc}} &\mathrel{\widehat{=}} \text{true} \Vdash\!\!\vdash_X \text{true} \\
\mathbf{terminate}_{\mathsf{xc}} &\mathrel{\widehat{=}} \text{true} \Vdash\!\!\vdash_X \mathit{term}' \\
\mathbf{forever}_{\mathsf{xc}} &\mathrel{\widehat{=}} \text{true} \Vdash\!\!\vdash_X \neg\, \mathit{term}' \\
\mathbf{mortal}_{\mathsf{xc}} &\mathrel{\widehat{=}} \text{false} \Vdash\!\!\vdash_X \mathit{term}' \\
\mathbf{noterm}_{\mathsf{xc}} &\mathrel{\widehat{=}} \text{false} \Vdash\!\!\vdash_X \neg\, \mathit{term}' \,.
\end{aligned}
$$

Our operational interpretations of these are as follows:

- $\mathbf{skip}_{\mathsf{xc}}$ terminates with the program variables unchanged;
- $\mathbf{abort}_{\mathsf{xc}}$ aborts;
- $\mathbf{anarchy}_{\mathsf{xc}}$ either aborts, or runs forever, or terminates with unconstrained program variables;
- $\mathbf{magic}_{\mathsf{xc}}$ is the everywhere-miraculous extended conscription which cannot be implemented;
- $\mathbf{chaos}_{\mathsf{xc}}$ either runs forever or else terminates with unconstrained program variables;
- $\mathbf{terminate}_{\mathsf{xc}}$ terminates with unconstrained program variables;
- $\mathbf{forever}_{\mathsf{xc}}$ runs forever;
- $\mathbf{mortal}_{\mathsf{xc}}$ either aborts or terminates with unconstrained program variables;
- $\mathbf{noterm}_{\mathsf{xc}}$ either aborts or runs forever.

Corollary 1 (Algebraic properties of extended conscriptions). *Every extended conscription A satisfies the following algebraic properties:*

$$
\begin{aligned}
\mathbf{skip}_{\mathsf{xc}}\,; A \;&=\; A \;=\; A\,; \mathbf{skip}_{\mathsf{xc}} \\
\mathbf{abort}_{\mathsf{xc}}\,; A \;&=\; \mathbf{abort}_{\mathsf{xc}} \\
\mathbf{forever}_{\mathsf{xc}}\,; A \;&=\; \mathbf{forever}_{\mathsf{xc}} \,.
\end{aligned}
$$

Proof. From Lemma 6 and the definitions of $\mathbf{skip}_{\mathsf{xc}}$, $\mathbf{abort}_{\mathsf{xc}}$ and $\mathbf{forever}_{\mathsf{xc}}$.

6 Sequential Models Incorporating Time

The timed-design model [5,6] was introduced by Hayes *et al* as a further refinement of their extended-design model, wherein an observation τ recording the current time replaces the *term* observation. The domain of time values can be either natural numbers or real numbers, in each case supplemented by infinity (∞) to represent non-termination. The timed design with assumption p and commitment r, where p can to refer to $\{v, \tau, \tau'\}$ and r to $\{v, v', \tau, \tau'\}$, is denoted by $p \vdash_T r$ where

$$
\begin{aligned}
p \vdash_T r \;\mathrel{\widehat{=}}\; & (ok \wedge \tau < \infty \wedge p \Rightarrow ok' \wedge r) \wedge (\tau \leq \tau') \\
& \wedge (\tau = \infty \Rightarrow ok) \wedge (\tau' = \infty \Rightarrow ok') \,.
\end{aligned}
$$

Furthermore, p and r must satisfy the following conditions:

$$\tau \neq \infty \wedge p \wedge \tau' = \infty \Rightarrow (r \Leftrightarrow \forall v' . r) , \tag{25}$$

$$\tau \leq \tau'' < \tau' \wedge p \Rightarrow p[\tau''/\tau'] . \tag{26}$$

Condition (25) ensures that the after-values v' of the program variables are unconstrained under non-termination. Condition (26) requires that if the computation is safe from risk of aborting at time τ' it must also be safe at all prior times τ'' from the start τ of its execution ($\tau \leq \tau'' < \tau'$). This is necessary to ensure that timed designs satisfy the skip-right-unit law $A ; \mathbf{skip}_{\mathsf{xc}} = A$, but unfortunately it precludes constructions such as

$$\tau < \tau' \ \vdash_T \ \tau' = \infty \tag{27}$$

by which we might wish to specify the computation which may abort immediately ($\tau' = \tau$ being outside its assumption), but which, providing it manages to avoid succumbing to that immediate risk, is thereafter guaranteed to run forever (commitment $\tau' = \infty$).

We can analogously define the notion of a timed conscription, denoting the timed conscription with assumption p and commitment r by $p \Vdash\!\!\vdash_T r$, as follows:

Definition 8 (Timed Conscription). *A timed conscription is a homogeneous binary relation with input alphabet $\{v, ok, \tau\}$, which is characterised by the following predicate, where p and r can both refer to $\{v, v', \tau, \tau'\}$ and r is such that $\tau < \tau' = \infty \ \Rightarrow \ (r \Leftrightarrow \forall v' . r)$:*

$$\begin{aligned} p \Vdash\!\!\vdash_T r \ \ \widehat{=} \ \ & (ok \wedge \tau < \infty \wedge p \ \Rightarrow \ ok') \wedge (ok' \wedge \tau < \infty \ \Rightarrow \ r \wedge ok) \\ & \wedge (\neg\, ok \ \Rightarrow \ v = v' \wedge \tau = \tau') \wedge (\tau \leq \tau') \\ & \wedge (\tau = \infty \ \Rightarrow \ ok) \wedge (\tau' = \infty \ \Rightarrow \ ok') . \end{aligned}$$

The healthiness condition

$$\tau < \tau' = \infty \ \Rightarrow \ (r \Leftrightarrow \forall v' . r) \tag{28}$$

on r ensures that the after-values v' of the regular program variables are unconstrained under non-termination. We note, however, that there is no healthiness condition for timed conscriptions which corresponds to (26) on the assumption of a timed design.

The predicate on the right-hand side of Definition 8 can be interpreted as follows. The first conjunct $ok \wedge \tau < \infty \wedge p \Rightarrow ok'$ asserts that if its predecessor has terminated and the current program's own execution satisfies p then it cannot have aborted. The second conjunct $ok' \wedge \tau < \infty \Rightarrow r \wedge ok$ asserts that if its predecessor terminated and the current program has executed without aborting then that execution must have started and must satisfy r. The third conjunct $\neg\, ok \Rightarrow v = v' \wedge \tau = \tau'$ asserts that if the current program fails to execute at all then the program variables v and the time auxiliary variable τ remain unchanged. The fourth conjunct $\tau \leq \tau'$ asserts that time must run forwards. The fifth conjunct $\tau = \infty \Rightarrow ok$ asserts that if the predecessor does not terminate then it does not abort, and the sixth conjunct $\tau' = \infty \Rightarrow ok'$ makes the corresponding assertion for the current program.

A timed conscription can be represented by a 3×3 matrix[2]. For example, $p \Vvdash_{\mathrm{T}} r$ is represented by the following matrix:

	$\neg\, ok' \wedge \tau' < \infty$	$ok' \wedge \tau' = \infty$	$ok' \wedge \tau' < \infty$
$\neg\, ok \wedge \tau < \infty$	$v = v' \wedge$ $\tau = \tau' < \infty$	F	F
$ok \wedge \tau = \infty$	F	$\tau = \tau' = \infty$	F
$ok \wedge \tau < \infty$	$\neg\, p \wedge$ $\tau \leq \tau' < \infty$	$r \wedge$ $\tau < \tau' = \infty$	$r \wedge$ $\tau \leq \tau' < \infty$

(29)

The next two lemmas, whose proofs are given in Appendix B, show that timed conscriptions have the necessary closure properties for a sequential model.

Lemma 7 (Nondeterministic Choice of Timed Conscriptions). *For arbitrary timed conscriptions $p \Vvdash_{\mathrm{T}} r$ and $q \Vvdash_{\mathrm{T}} s$ over the same alphabet,*

$$(p \Vvdash_{\mathrm{T}} r) \sqcap (q \Vvdash_{\mathrm{T}} s) \quad = \quad p \wedge q \;\; \Vvdash_{\mathrm{T}} \;\; r \vee s\ .$$

To express the next lemma succinctly, we first define the following special variant of relational composition for homogeneous binary relations whose input alphabet includes the time variable τ.

Definition 9 (Timed Composition). *For homogeneous binary relations A and B whose input alphabet includes τ, we define their* timed composition $A\ ;_\tau\ B$ *by*

$$A\ ;_\tau\ B \;\;\widehat{=}\;\; A \wedge \tau \leq \tau' < \infty\ ;\ B \wedge \tau \leq \tau'\ .$$

Lemma 8 (Composition of Timed Conscriptions). *For arbitrary timed conscriptions $p \Vvdash_{\mathrm{T}} r$ and $q \Vvdash_{\mathrm{T}} s$ over the same alphabet, we have that*

$$(p \Vvdash_{\mathrm{T}} r)\ ;\ (q \Vvdash_{\mathrm{T}} s) \quad = \quad p \wedge \neg\,(r\ ;_\tau\ \neg\, q) \;\; \Vvdash_{\mathrm{T}} \;\; (r \wedge \tau' = \infty) \vee (r\ ;_\tau\ s)\ .$$

Extreme Timed Conscriptions. The following special cases of timed conscriptions are of interest:

$$\begin{aligned}
\mathbf{skip}_{\mathrm{tc}} \;&\widehat{=}\; \mathrm{true} \Vvdash_{\mathrm{T}} v = v' \wedge \tau = \tau' \\
\mathbf{idle}_{\mathrm{tc}} \;&\widehat{=}\; \mathrm{true} \Vvdash_{\mathrm{T}} v = v' \wedge \tau' < \infty \\
\mathbf{boneidle}_{\mathrm{tc}} \;&\widehat{=}\; \mathrm{true} \Vvdash_{\mathrm{T}} \tau' < \infty \Rightarrow v = v'
\end{aligned}$$

[2] Once again, a fourth row and column, this time corresponding to the respective combinations ($\neg\, ok \wedge \tau = \infty$) and ($\neg\, ok' \wedge \tau' = \infty$), are omitted from the matrix since all their entries are Fs and are thus invariant under matrix addition and multiplication.

$$\begin{array}{rcl}
\mathbf{eagerabort}_{\mathrm{tc}} & \mathrel{\widehat{=}} & \tau < \tau' \;\Vdash_{\mathrm{T}}\; \text{false} \\
\mathbf{lazyabort}_{\mathrm{tc}} & \mathrel{\widehat{=}} & \text{false} \;\Vdash_{\mathrm{T}}\; \text{false} \\
\mathbf{anarchy}_{\mathrm{tc}} & \mathrel{\widehat{=}} & \text{false} \;\Vdash_{\mathrm{T}}\; \text{true} \\
\mathbf{magic}_{\mathrm{tc}} & \mathrel{\widehat{=}} & \text{true} \;\Vdash_{\mathrm{T}}\; \text{false} \\
\mathbf{chaos}_{\mathrm{tc}} & \mathrel{\widehat{=}} & \text{true} \;\Vdash_{\mathrm{T}}\; \text{true} \\
\mathbf{terminate}_{\mathrm{tc}} & \mathrel{\widehat{=}} & \text{true} \;\Vdash_{\mathrm{T}}\; \tau' < \infty \\
\mathbf{forever}_{\mathrm{tc}} & \mathrel{\widehat{=}} & \text{true} \;\Vdash_{\mathrm{T}}\; \tau' = \infty \\
\mathbf{mortal}_{\mathrm{tc}} & \mathrel{\widehat{=}} & \text{false} \;\Vdash_{\mathrm{T}}\; \tau' < \infty \\
\mathbf{noterm}_{\mathrm{tc}} & \mathrel{\widehat{=}} & \text{false} \;\Vdash_{\mathrm{T}}\; \tau' = \infty \,.
\end{array}$$

Our operational interpretations of these are as follows:

- $\mathbf{skip}_{\mathrm{tc}}$ terminates immediately with unchanged program variables;
- $\mathbf{idle}_{\mathrm{tc}}$ terminates eventually with unchanged program variables;
- $\mathbf{boneidle}_{\mathrm{tc}}$ either terminates eventually with unchanged program variables or else runs forever;
- $\mathbf{eagerabort}_{\mathrm{tc}}$ aborts immediately;
- $\mathbf{lazyabort}_{\mathrm{tc}}$ aborts eventually;
- $\mathbf{anarchy}_{\mathrm{tc}}$ aborts eventually, or runs forever, or terminates eventually with unconstrained program variables;
- $\mathbf{magic}_{\mathrm{tc}}$ is the everywhere-miraculous timed conscription which cannot be implemented;
- $\mathbf{chaos}_{\mathrm{tc}}$ either runs forever or else terminates eventually with unconstrained program variables;
- $\mathbf{terminate}_{\mathrm{tc}}$ terminates eventually with unconstrained program variables;
- $\mathbf{forever}_{\mathrm{tc}}$ runs forever;
- $\mathbf{mortal}_{\mathrm{tc}}$ either aborts eventually or terminates eventually with unconstrained program variables;
- $\mathbf{noterm}_{\mathrm{tc}}$ either aborts eventually or else runs forever.

Corollary 2 (Algebraic proerties of timed conscriptions). *Every timed conscription A satisfies the following algebraic properties:*

$$\begin{array}{rcl}
\mathbf{skip}_{\mathrm{tc}}\,;A \;=\; A & = & A\,;\mathbf{skip}_{\mathrm{tc}} \\
\mathbf{eagerabort}_{\mathrm{tc}}\,;A & = & \mathbf{eagerabort}_{\mathrm{tc}} \\
\mathbf{lazyabort}_{\mathrm{tc}}\,;A & = & \mathbf{lazyabort}_{\mathrm{tc}} \\
\mathbf{forever}_{\mathrm{tc}}\,;A & = & \mathbf{forever}_{\mathrm{tc}} \,.
\end{array}$$

Proof. From Lemma 8 and the definitions of $\mathbf{skip}_{\mathrm{tc}}$, $\mathbf{eagerabort}_{\mathrm{tc}}$, $\mathbf{lazyabort}_{\mathrm{tc}}$ and $\mathbf{forever}_{\mathrm{tc}}$.

Timed conscriptions enable us to express a wider range of timed sequential computations than timed designs. For example, the legitimate timed conscription

$$\tau < \tau' \;\Vdash_{\mathrm{T}}\; \tau' = \infty$$

expresses precisely the computation we originally sought to express with (27). That is to say, it specifies a computation which may either abort immediately ($\tau' = \tau$ being outside its assumption) or else run forever (commitment $\tau' = \infty$).

7 Conclusion

We have introduced conscriptions as a new homogeneous binary relational model of sequential programs which upholds all the expected algebraic properties of such a model, and moreover does so without needing to restrict their assumptions for the sake of the skip-right-unit property. In this way conscriptions are an improvement on both designs and prescriptions. We have also shown how this basic conscription model can be extended into one which distinguishes between abortion and non-termination in a similar way to the extended-design model of Hayes *et al*. Likewise, we have developed timed conscriptions as the conscription counterpart of Hayes *et al*'s timed designs, and we have shown how these are more expressive than the latter in permitting a wider range of behaviours to be specified.

Definitions 7 (Extended Conscriptions) and 8 (Timed Conscriptions) are each elaborate enough to prompt the question: how can we be certain that we have defined them appropriately? In response, we would contend that the properties we have deduced from these definitions, as represented by the lemmas and corollaries we have presented, are precisely what one should expect of these two models, and this gives us our confidence in them. In short, they work!

Acknowledgements. I thank the anonymous referees for their valuable comments on the original draft of this paper.

References

1. Dunne, S.E.: Recasting Hoare and He's unifying theory of programs in the context of general correctness. In: Butterfield, A., Strong, G., Pahl, C. (eds.) Proceedings of the 5th Irish Workshop in Formal Methods, IWFM 2001, Workshops in Computing. British Computer Society (2001), `http://ewic.bcs.org/conferences/2001/5thformal/papers`
2. Guttmann, W.: Algebras for iteration and infinite computations. Acta Informatica (2012), doi: 10.1007/s00236-012-0162-2
3. Guttmann, W.: Extended designs algebraically. Science of Computer Programming (to appear, 2012)
4. Guttmann, W.: Unifying Correctness Statements. In: Gibbons, J., Nogueira, P. (eds.) MPC 2012. LNCS, vol. 7342, pp. 198–219. Springer, Heidelberg (2012)
5. Hayes, I.J., Dunne, S.E., Meinicke, L.: Unifying Theories of Programming That Distinguish Nontermination and Abort. In: Bolduc, C., Desharnais, J., Ktari, B. (eds.) MPC 2010. LNCS, vol. 6120, pp. 178–194. Springer, Heidelberg (2010)
6. Hayes, I.J., Dunne, S.E., Meinicke, L.: Linking unifying theories of program refinement. Science of Computer Programming (to appear, 2012)
7. Hoare, C.A.R., He, J.: Unifying Theories of Programming. Prentice Hall (1998)
8. Möller, B.: The Linear Algebra of UTP. In: Uustalu, T. (ed.) MPC 2006. LNCS, vol. 4014, pp. 338–358. Springer, Heidelberg (2006)

A Proofs of Lemmas 5 and 6

Lemma 5 (Nondeterministic Choice of Extended Conscriptions). *Extended conscriptions are closed under nondeterministic choice. For arbitrary extended conscriptions $p \Vvdash_X r$ and $q \Vvdash_X s$ over the same alphabet, we have that*

$$(p \Vvdash_X r) \sqcap (q \Vvdash_X s) \quad = \quad p \wedge q \;\; \Vvdash_X \;\; r \vee s \; .$$

Proof. We note that $q \Vvdash_X s$ is represented by the matrix

	$\neg\, ok' \wedge term'$	$ok' \wedge \neg\, term'$	$ok' \wedge term'$
$\neg\, ok \wedge term$	$v = v'$	F	F
$ok \wedge \neg\, term$	F	T	F
$ok \wedge term$	$\neg\, q$	s_{f}	s_{t}

(30)

To derive the matrix representation of $(p \Vvdash_X r) \sqcap (q \Vvdash_X s)$ we therefore disjoin corresponding entries of matrices (24) and (30) to obtain the matrix

	$\neg\, ok' \wedge term'$	$ok' \wedge \neg\, term'$	$ok' \wedge term'$
$\neg\, ok \wedge term$	$v = v'$	F	F
$ok \wedge \neg\, term$	F	T	F
$ok \wedge term$	$\neg\, p \vee \neg\, q$	$r_{\mathsf{f}} \vee s_{\mathsf{f}}$	$r_{\mathsf{t}} \vee s_{\mathsf{t}}$

which can be re-expressed as

	$\neg\, ok' \wedge term'$	$ok' \wedge \neg\, term'$	$ok' \wedge term'$
$\neg\, ok \wedge term$	$v = v'$	F	F
$ok \wedge \neg\, term$	F	T	F
$ok \wedge term$	$\neg\, (p \wedge q)$	$(r \vee s)_{\mathsf{f}}$	$(r \vee s)_{\mathsf{t}}$

which is the matrix representation of the extended conscription

$$p \wedge q \;\; \Vvdash_X \;\; r \vee s \; .$$

Lemma 6 (Composition of Extended Conscriptions). *Extended conscriptions are closed under sequential composition. For arbitrary extended conscriptions $p \Vvdash_X r$ and $q \Vvdash_X s$ over the same alphabet, we have that*

$$(p \Vvdash_X r) \,;\, (q \Vvdash_X s) \quad = \quad p \wedge \neg\, (r_{\mathsf{t}} \,;\, \neg\, q) \;\; \Vvdash_X \;\; r_{\mathsf{f}} \vee (r_{\mathsf{t}} \,;\, s) \; .$$

Proof. Multiplying matrix (24) by matrix (30) in that order yields the product matrix

	$\neg\, ok' \wedge term'$	$ok' \wedge \neg\, term'$	$ok' \wedge term'$
$\neg\, ok \wedge term$	$(v = v' \,;\, v = v')$ $\vee\ (\mathrm{F} \,;\, \mathrm{F})$ $\vee\ (\mathrm{F} \,;\, \neg\, q)$	$(v = v' \,;\, \mathrm{F})$ $\vee\ (\mathrm{F} \,;\, \mathrm{T})$ $\vee\ (\mathrm{F} \,;\, s_{\mathrm{f}})$	$(v = v' \,;\, \mathrm{F})$ $\vee\ (\mathrm{F} \,;\, \mathrm{F})$ $\vee\ (\mathrm{F} \,;\, s_{\mathrm{t}})$
$ok \wedge \neg\, term$	$(\mathrm{F} \,;\, v = v')$ $\vee\ (\mathrm{T} \,;\, \mathrm{F})$ $\vee\ (\mathrm{F} \,;\, \neg\, q)$	$(\mathrm{F} \,;\, \mathrm{F})$ $\vee\ (\mathrm{T} \,;\, \mathrm{T})$ $\vee\ (\mathrm{F} \,;\, s_{\mathrm{f}})$	$(\mathrm{F} \,;\, \mathrm{F})$ $\vee\ (\mathrm{T} \,;\, \mathrm{F})$ $\vee\ (\mathrm{F} \,;\, s_{\mathrm{t}})$
$ok \wedge term$	$(\neg\, p \,;\, v = v')$ $\vee\ (r_{\mathrm{f}} \,;\, \mathrm{F})$ $\vee\ (r_{\mathrm{t}} \,;\, \neg\, q)$	$(\neg\, p \,;\, \mathrm{F})$ $\vee\ (r_{\mathrm{f}} \,;\, \mathrm{T})$ $\vee\ (r_{\mathrm{t}} \,;\, s_{\mathrm{f}})$	$(\neg\, p \,;\, \mathrm{F})$ $\vee\ (r_{\mathrm{f}} \,;\, \mathrm{F})$ $\vee\ (r_{\mathrm{t}} \,;\, s_{\mathrm{t}})$

which simplifies by properties (3), (5), (6) and healthiness condition (23) to

	$\neg\, ok' \wedge term'$	$ok' \wedge \neg\, term'$	$ok' \wedge term'$
$\neg\, ok \wedge term$	$v = v'$	F	F
$ok \wedge \neg\, term$	F	T	F
$ok \wedge term$	$\neg\, p \vee (r_{\mathrm{t}} \,;\, \neg\, q)$	$r_{\mathrm{f}} \vee (r_{\mathrm{t}} \,;\, s_{\mathrm{f}})$	$r_{\mathrm{t}} \,;\, s_{\mathrm{t}}$

which, by $(r_{\mathrm{t}} \,;\, s_{\mathrm{f}}) = (r_{\mathrm{t}} \,;\, s)_{\mathrm{f}}$ and $(r_{\mathrm{t}} \,;\, s_{\mathrm{t}}) = (r_{\mathrm{t}} \,;\, s)_{\mathrm{t}}$, is a matrix representation of the extended conscription

$$p \wedge \neg\, (r_{\mathrm{t}} \,;\, \neg\, q) \ \Vdash\!\!\vdash_{X}\ r_{\mathrm{f}} \vee (r_{\mathrm{t}} \,;\, s)\ ,$$

which concludes the proof of Lemma 6.

B Proofs of Lemmas 7 and 8

Lemma 7 (Nondeterministic Choice of Timed Conscriptions). *For arbitrary timed conscriptions $p \Vdash\!\!\vdash_{\mathrm{T}} r$ and $q \Vdash\!\!\vdash_{\mathrm{T}} s$ over the same alphabet, we have that*

$$(p \Vdash\!\!\vdash_{\mathrm{T}} r) \sqcap (q \Vdash\!\!\vdash_{\mathrm{T}} s) \quad = \quad p \wedge q \quad \Vdash\!\!\vdash_{\mathrm{T}} \quad r \vee s\ .$$

Proof. We note that $q \Vdash\!\!\vdash_{\mathrm{T}} s$ is represented by the matrix

	$\neg\, ok' \wedge \tau' < \infty$	$ok' \wedge \tau' = \infty$	$ok' \wedge \tau' < \infty$	
$\neg\, ok \wedge \tau < \infty$	$v = v' \wedge$ $\tau = \tau' < \infty$	F	F	
$ok \wedge \tau = \infty$	F	$\tau = \tau' = \infty$	F	(31)
$ok \wedge \tau < \infty$	$\neg\, q \wedge$ $\tau \le \tau' < \infty$	$s \wedge$ $\tau < \tau' = \infty$	$s \wedge$ $\tau \le \tau' < \infty$	

To derive the matrix representation of $(p \Vdash\!\!\vdash_T r) \sqcap (q \Vdash\!\!\vdash_T s)$ we therefore disjoin corresponding entries of matrices (29) and (31) to obtain the matrix

	$\neg\, ok' \wedge \tau' < \infty$	$ok' \wedge \tau' = \infty$	$ok' \wedge \tau' < \infty$
$\neg\, ok \wedge \tau < \infty$	$v = v' \wedge$ $\tau = \tau' < \infty$	F	F
$ok \wedge \tau = \infty$	F	$\tau = \tau' = \infty$	F
$ok \wedge \tau < \infty$	$(\neg\, p \vee \neg\, q) \wedge$ $\tau \leq \tau' < \infty$	$(r \vee s) \wedge$ $\tau < \tau' = \infty$	$(r \vee s) \wedge$ $\tau \leq \tau' < \infty$

which is the matrix representation of the timed conscription

$$p \wedge q \;\; \Vdash\!\!\vdash_T \;\; r \vee s \; .$$

Lemma 8 (Composition of Timed Conscriptions).
For arbitrary timed conscriptions $p \Vdash\!\!\vdash_T r$ *and* $q \Vdash\!\!\vdash_T s$ *over the same alphabet, we have that*

$$(p \Vdash\!\!\vdash_T r) \,;\, (q \Vdash\!\!\vdash_T s) \quad = \quad p \wedge \neg\,(r \;;_\tau\; \neg\, q) \;\; \Vdash\!\!\vdash_T \;\; (r \wedge \tau' = \infty) \vee (r \;;_\tau\; s) \; .$$

Proof. Multiplying matrix (29) by matrix (31) in that order yields a product matrix whose entries are as follows:

- (row 1, col 1) is
  $(v = v' \wedge \tau = \tau' < \infty \;\; ; \;\; v = v' \wedge \tau = \tau' < \infty) \vee (\mathrm{F} \,;\, \mathrm{F})$
  $\vee\, (\mathrm{F} \,;\, \neg\, q \wedge \tau \leq \tau' < \infty)$
  which simplifies by properties (6), (7) and Definition 5 to
  $v = v' \wedge \tau = \tau' < \infty$.
- (row 1, col 2) is
  $(v = v' \wedge \tau = \tau' < \infty \;\; ; \mathrm{F}) \vee (\mathrm{F} \,;\, \tau = \tau' = \infty) \vee (\mathrm{F} \,;\, q \wedge \tau < \tau' = \infty)$
  which simplifies by properties (6) and (7) to F .
- (row 1, col 3) is
  $(v = v' \wedge \tau = \tau' < \infty \;\; ; \mathrm{F}) \vee (\mathrm{F} \,;\, \mathrm{F}) \vee (\mathrm{F} \,;\, s \wedge \tau \leq \tau' < \infty)$
  which simplifies by properties (6) and (7) to F .
- (row 2, col 1) is
  $(\mathrm{F} \,;\, v = v' \wedge \tau = \tau' < \infty) \vee (\tau = \tau' = \infty \,;\, \mathrm{F}) \vee (\mathrm{F} \,;\, \neg\, q \wedge \tau \leq \tau' < \infty)$
  which simplifies by properties (6) and (7) to F .
- (row 2, col 2) is
  $(\mathrm{F} \,;\, \mathrm{F}) \vee (\tau = \tau' = \infty \,;\, \tau = \tau' = \infty) \vee (\mathrm{F} \,;\, s \wedge \tau < \tau' = \infty)$
  which simplifies by properties (5), (6) and (7) to $\tau = \tau' = \infty$.
- (row 2, col 3) is
  $(\mathrm{F} \,;\, \mathrm{F}) \vee (\tau = \tau' = \infty \,;\, \mathrm{F}) \vee (\mathrm{F} \,;\, s \wedge \tau \leq \tau' < \infty)$
  which simplifies by properties (6) and (7) to F .

- (row 3, col 1) is
  $(\neg\, p \wedge \tau \leq \tau' < \infty\,;\, v = v' \wedge \tau = \tau' < \infty) \vee (r \wedge \tau < \tau' = \infty\,;\, \mathrm{F})$
  $\vee\, (r \wedge \tau \leq \tau' < \infty\,;\, \neg\, q \wedge \tau \leq \tau' < \infty)$
  which reduces by properties (5), (6), (7) and Definition 9 to
  $(\neg\, p \vee (r\, ;_\tau\, \neg\, q)) \wedge \tau \leq \tau' < \infty$.
- (row 3, col 2) is
  $(\neg\, p \wedge \tau \leq \tau' < \infty\,;\, \mathrm{F}) \vee (r \wedge \tau < \tau' = \infty\,;\, \tau = \tau' = \infty)$
  $\vee\, (r \wedge \tau \leq \tau' < \infty\,;\, s \wedge \tau < \tau' = \infty)$
  which simplifies by properties (5), (6), (7) and Definition 9 to
  $(r \vee (r\, ;_\tau\, s)) \wedge \tau \leq \tau' = \infty$.
- (row 3, col 3) is
  $(\neg\, p \wedge \tau \leq \tau' < \infty\,;\, \mathrm{F}) \vee (r \wedge \tau < \tau' = \infty\,;\, \mathrm{F})$
  $\vee\, (r \wedge \tau \leq \tau' < \infty\,;\, s \wedge \tau \leq \tau' < \infty)$
  which simplifies by properties (6), (7) and Definition 9 to
  $(r\, ;_\tau\, s) \wedge \tau \leq \tau' < \infty$.

The product matrix we obtain is thus

	$\neg\, ok' \wedge \tau' < \infty$	$ok' \wedge \tau' = \infty$	$ok' \wedge \tau' < \infty$
$\neg\, ok \wedge \tau < \infty$	$v = v' \wedge$ $\tau = \tau' < \infty$	F	F
$ok \wedge \tau = \infty$	F	$\tau = \tau' = \infty$	F
$ok \wedge \tau < \infty$	$(\neg\, p \vee (r\, ;_\tau\, \neg\, q))$ $\wedge\, \tau \leq \tau' < \infty$	$(r \vee (r\, ;_\tau\, s))$ $\wedge\, \tau < \tau' = \infty$	$(r\, ;_\tau\, s) \wedge$ $\tau \leq \tau' < \infty$

which is the matrix representation of the timed conscription

$$p \wedge \neg\, (r\, ;_\tau\, \neg\, q) \;\; ⧺_{\mathrm{T}} \;\; (r \wedge \tau' = \infty) \vee (r\, ;_\tau\, s)\ .$$

Mechanical Approach to Linking Operational Semantics and Algebraic Semantics for Verilog Using Maude

Huibiao Zhu[1], Peng Liu[1], Jifeng He[1], and Shengchao Qin[2]

[1] Shanghai Key Laboratory of Trustworthy Computing
East China Normal University, Shanghai 200062, China
{hbzhu,liup,jifeng}@sei.ecnu.edu.cn

[2] School of Computing, University of Teesside
Middlesbrough TS1 3BA, UK
s.qin@tees.ac.uk

Abstract. Verilog is a hardware description language (HDL) that has been standardized and widely used in industry. It contains interesting features such as event-driven computation and shared-variable concurrency. This paper considers how the algebraic semantics links with the operational semantics for Verilog. Our approach is to apply the equational and rewriting logic system Maude in exploring the linking theories. Firstly we present the algebraic semantics for Verilog. We introduce the concept of head normal form and every program is expressed as a guarded choice with location status. Secondly we present the strategy of deriving operational semantics from algebraic semantics. Our mechanical approach using Maude can visually show the head normal form of each program, as well as the execution steps of a program based on the derivation strategy. Finally we also mechanize the derived operational semantics. The results mechanized from the second and third exploration indicate that the transition system of the derived operational semantics is the same as the one based on the derivation strategy.

1 Introduction

Modern hardware design typically uses a hardware description language (HDL) to express designs at various levels of abstraction. An HDL is a high level programming language with the usual programming constructs such as assignments, conditionals, iterations, together with the appropriate extensions for real-time, concurrency and data structures suitable for modelling hardware. Verilog is an HDL that has been standardized and widely used in industry [9, 10].

Verilog programs can exhibit a rich variety of behaviours, including event-driven computation, shared-variable concurrency and simulator-based interpretation. Verilog also has real-time features [17], through the time delay statement and the event-driven computation feature.

The semantics for Verilog is very important because it is widely used in industry. The denotational semantics [22] has been investigated using Duration

B. Wolff, M.-C. Gaudel, A. Feliachi (Eds.): UTP 2012, LNCS 7681, pp. 164–185, 2013.

Calculus [19] in order to describe its real-time features. Various operational semantics have also been studied [5, 6, 11]. Besides the operational and denotational semantics, a set of algebraic laws can also represent the meaning of a language. These three semantics should provide the same understanding of the language from different viewpoints and they should be consistent. Therefore, the linking of these three semantics is a challenging task. Below is the diagram for linking Verilog semantics.

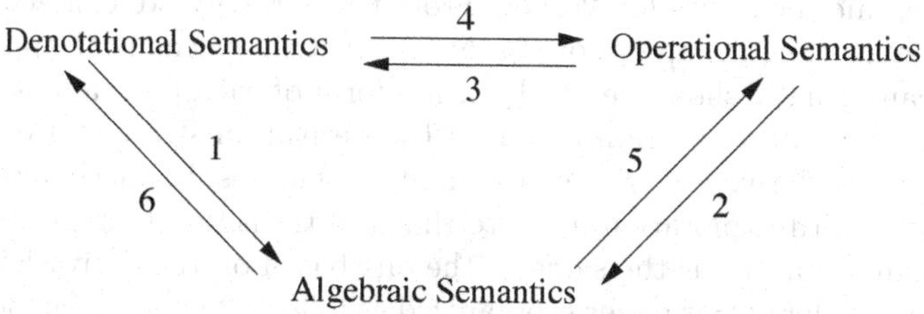

(1) The aim of this step is to generate a set of algebraic laws. These laws can be proved via the achievement of the denotational semantics for Verilog [22].
(2) The aim of this step is also to generate a set of algebraic laws. Compared with step (1), the approach here is based on the operational semantics via bisimulation [15, 16].
(3) Denotational and operational semantics give the meaning for the same language. How can we prove the equivalence and consistency of these two semantics? This step is to derive the denotational semantics from the operational semantics for Verilog.
(4) This aim of this step is to derive the operational semantics from the denotational semantics for Verilog. This gives another way for considering the equivalence and consistency of denotational and operational semantics.
(5) Algebraic semantics also represents the meaning of programs. The aim of this step is to derive the operational semantics from the algebraic semantics.
(6) This step is to derive the denotational semantics back from the algebraic semantics.

Regarding the above linking work of Verilog semantics. Some of them have already been achieved (shown as step (1) to (4), and step (6) in the above diagram). The algebraic laws for Verilog has been verified via the denotational semantics in [22]. These algebraic laws can also be validated based on the operational semantics via bisimulation [6, 11]. Further studies have investigated how the operational semantics relates with denotational semantics for Verilog [20, 21, 23]. We have already investigated the derivation of denotational semantics from operational semantics and algebraic semantics for Verilog respectively [21, 23]. We also derived the operational semantics for Verilog from its denotational semantics [20].

This paper studies how the algebraic semantics for Verilog links with its operational semantics (shown as step (5) in the above diagram). Our approach is to derive Verilog operational semantics from its algebraic semantics, which can show that the operational semantics is sound and complete with respect to the algebraic laws. We apply the mechanical method to support the semantic linking by using the equational and rewriting logic system Maude [1, 2]. Firstly we present the algebraic semantics for Verilog. We introduce the concept of head normal form and every program is expressed as a guarded choice with location status. In order to investigate the parallel expansion laws, a sequence is introduced, which can indicate an instantaneous action is due to which exact parallel component. Secondly we provide a strategy for deriving operational semantics from algebraic semantics for Verilog. From this strategy, we can achieve a transition system (i.e., an operational semantics). Our mechanical approach using Maude can visually show the head normal form of each program, as well as the execution steps of a program based on the derivation strategy. Finally we also mechanize the derived operational semantics. The results mechanized from the second and third exploration indicate that the transition system of the derived operational semantics is the same as the one based on the derivation strategy.

The remainder of this paper is organized as follows. Section 2 introduces Hardware Description Language Verilog and, as well as Equation and Rewriting Logic system Maude. Section 3 presents a set of algebraic laws, where every program can be represented as a guarded choice with location status. In section 4, we introduce the concept of head normal form and we encode the head normal form of each program in Maude. Section 5 investigates the derivation of the operational semantics from the algebraic semantics. We mechanize the derivation strategy in Maude system. Every program can be executed based on the derivation strategy. For the derived operational semantics, we also explore its mechanical approach. The mechanical approaches from the derivation strategy and the derived operational semantics support the claim that the transition system of the derived operational semantics is the same as the one based on the derivation strategy. Section 6 concludes the paper and provides some future work.

2 Hardware Description Language Verilog and Equational and Rewriting Logic System Maude

2.1 Hardware Description Language Verilog

The Verilog Hardware Description Language (Verilog HDL) became as an IEEE standard in 1995 as IEEE std 1364-1995 [9, 10]. It has many interesting features, such as event-driven computation, shared-variable concurrency and simulator-based interpretation. The syntax of Verilog is expressed in a way that is closer to the syntax of a traditional programming language. Verilog contains the following categories of syntactic elements and is similar to the one introduced by Gordon [3, 4].

$$\begin{aligned} P ::= PC \mid P\,;\,P \mid \textbf{if } b \textbf{ then } P \textbf{ else } P \mid \textbf{while } b \textbf{ do } P \\ \mid c\,P \mid P \,\|\, P \end{aligned}$$

where:

- PC ranges over primitive commands.

  $PC ::= x := e \mid$ **Skip** $\mid @(x := e)$, where

  $x := e$ is the assignment, which is executed exactly once. **Skip** behaves the same as $x := x$. $x := e$ (also **Skip**) is not considered as an atomic action, which is a fragment of an atomic action (i.e., a statement of an atomic action).

  On the other hand, $@(x := e)$ is considered as an atomic action, which is called as atomic assignment.

- $P \; ; \; Q$ is the sequential composition.
- $P \parallel Q$ is the parallel composition, where its mechanism is an interleaving shared-variable concurrency model. The parallel composition can not only be at the outside level, but also can appear at any place.
- $c \; P$ denotes a timing control statement, and c is a time control used for scheduling.

  $$c ::= \#n \mid @(g)$$

  where, $$g ::= \eta \mid g \; or \; g \mid g \; and \; g \mid g \; and \; \neg g$$

  $$\eta ::= v \mid \uparrow v \mid \downarrow v, \quad n \geq 1$$

  (1) Time delay $\#n$ suspends the execution for exactly n time units, where n is treated as an integer in this paper.

  (2) An event guard $@(\uparrow v)$ is fired by the increase of the value of v, whereas $@(\downarrow v)$ is triggered by a decrease in v. Any change of v awakes the guard $@(v)$.

  (3) $@(g_1 \; or \; g_2)$ becomes enabled if $@(g_1)$ or $@(g_2)$ is fired.

  (4) $@(g_1 \; and \; g_2)$ is triggered if both $@(g_1)$ and $@(g_2)$ are awakened simultaneously.

  (5) $@(g_1 \; and \; \neg g_2)$ becomes fired if $@(g_2)$ remains idle and $@(g_1)$ is awakened.

2.2 Equational and Rewriting Logic System Maude

Rewriting logic has been introduced as a general semantic and logical framework [12–14, 18]. Many applications are implemented in the Maude system [1] and have revealed inspiring results.

In Maude, the fundamental unit can be a functional module or a system module. They can be declared by the following syntax: `fmod NAME is ... endfm` (or `mod NAME is ... endm`) . Here the dots denote the declarations of importing options, sorts, subsorts, operations, equations and rules (only in system modules). First, we take the Peano notation of natural numbers as an example to show the structure of functional modules.

```
fmod PEANO-NATURAL is including BOOL .
```

```
        sorts NzNat Nat .
        subsort NzNat < Nat .
        op 0 : -> Nat [ctor] .
        op s(_) : Nat -> NzNat [ctor] .
        op _+_ : Nat Nat -> Nat .
        vars N M : Nat .
        eq 0 + N = N .
        eq s(M) + N = s(M + N) .
        op _>_ : Nat Nat -> Bool .
        eq s(N) > 0 = true .
        ceq s(N) > s(M) = true if N > M .
        eq N > M = false [owise] .
endfm
```

Defined modules can be reused, as the precluded module `BOOL` is imported into the `PEANO-NATURAL`. Two sorts `NzNat` and `Nat` are declared to represent non-zero natural numbers and natural numbers, and `NzNat` is declared as a `subsort` of `Nat`. `ops` are keywords to define operators on defined sorts. Here, 0 is defined with no operands thus it can be treated as a constant of sort `Nat`. `s(_)` is an operator to define the successor of a natural number, so the result is of sort `NzNat`. We associate the attribute `ctor` (abbreviated for constructor) with these two operators, which means that they are the fundamental operations for defining the canonical forms of the resulting sort. However the operator `+` is not defined as a constructor, because it is not necessary for defining natural numbers. Attributes such as `assoc` and `comm` can also be attached to `ops`, representing that the operator satisfies associative and commutative laws. Variables are declared using the keyword `var(s)` with the sort following behind the name. Equations are defined as simplification rules towards a canonical form. They are declared using the keywords `eq` (i.e., equation) and `ceq` (i.e., conditional equation). We can use the command `red(uce)` to compute the canonical form simplified by equations. When typing in Maude `red s(0) + s(s(0))`, the result will be `s(s(s(0)))`.

In system modules, rewriting rules are declared by keyword `rl` (`crl` for conditional one). Rewriting rules reflect nondeterministic and concurrent transitions of systems. Suppose we define a list of natural numbers as following:

```
mod MY-LIST is including PEANO-NATURAL .
        sorts Elt List .
        subsort Nat < Elt < List .
        op null : -> List [ctor] .
        op _ _ : List List -> List [ctor assoc id: null] .
        vars A B : Elt .
        crl [swap] : A B => B A if A > B .
endm
```

The rule `swap` will make the smaller numbers swap to the left. Any part of the list satisfying this rule will do the transition concurrently. Using the command `rew(rite)` we can see the result of the transitions. `rew s(s(0)) s(s(s(0))) s(0) 0` shows the result as `0 s(0) s(s(0)) s(s(s(0)))`.

As rules in system modules can be nondeterministic and concurrent, rewrite command only shows one of the possible multiple results. Maude provides `search` and `show path` commands to display all possible results. We can see how to use them in later sections.

3 Generating Algebraic Semantics

3.1 Pre-emption Point and Atomic Action

In Verilog, $x := e$, **Skip** and $@(x := e)$ are considered as instantaneous actions. We first introduce the concept of pre-emption point. Only at a pre-emption point does the scheduler make a decision whether the environment gets a chance to make its contribution or the program itself continues to execute.

A pre-emption point can be one of the cases: (1) the two points before and after a timing control statement; (2) the two points before and after a parallel process; (3) for a process that is a component of a parallel process, the two points before and after the process are also pre-emption points. For a sequence of instantaneous actions, if its beginning and ending points are two pre-emption points and there are no pre-emption points appearing inside the sequence, then this sequence is called an atomic action. $x := e$ is not an atomic action. It is a fragment of an atomic action, whereas $@(x := e)$ is an atomic action.

At each pre-emption point for a process, both the process itself and its environment can get the control to do its atomic action. The scheduling between them is non-deterministic. If an instantaneous action is at the beginning of an atomic action, this instantaneous action can be scheduled to execute immediately. Alternatively, the environment can also perform its instantaneous behaviours. After the first instantaneous action in an atomic action terminates, the following actions in the atomic action must be executed sequentially and uninterruptedly. This indicates that the execution of an atomic action is uninterrupted. Regarding the triggering case, a guard can be triggered by its atomic action that has just completed. If there are no cases like this, the guard waits for its environment to trigger it. At some particular points of execution, if the process itself and the environment cannot do any instantaneous action, then time may advance.

Example 3.1.
(1) Consider the program $P_1 =_{df} @(\uparrow x)\ ;\ x := 0\ ;\ x := x + 1\ ;\ y := x + 1\ ;\ \#1$. There are four pre-emption points; i.e., the points before and after the event guard $@(\uparrow x)$ and the two points before and after time delay $\#1$.
(2) Consider the program $P \parallel Q$ when $P =_{df} (x := 0\ ;\ y := x + 1\ ;\ z := x + 1)$ and $Q =_{df} x := 2$. For process P, there are two pre-emption points; i.e., the point before the assignment $x := 0$ and the point after $z := x + 1$. For process Q, the pre-emption points are the points just before and after $x := 2$.
(3) Consider the program $P =_{df} @(\uparrow x)\ ;\ x := 1\ ;\ y := x + 1\ ;\ @(x := 0)\ ;\ z := x + 1\ ;\ \#1$. The assignment guard $@(x := 0)$ not only assigns a value to x, but also indicates that the previous instantaneous sequence forms an atomic action and itself is an atomic action. This means "$x := 1\ ;\ y := x + 1$", "$@(x := 0)$" and "$z := x + 1$" are three atomic actions inside program P. □

3.2 Locality of Instantaneous Action and Guarded Choice with Location Status

In order to model the scheduling policy for parallel processes, we use a thread sequence *seq* to index the currently active sub-process in a nested parallel composition. A thread sequence can be $\langle\rangle$ or a non-empty thread sequence, where $\langle\rangle$ indicates that there is only one thread for the action that has just been executed.

Example 3.2. Let $P =_{df} x := 0\ ;\ \#1\ ;\ x := 1\ ;\ @(\uparrow x)$. The instantaneous actions $x := 0$ and $x := 1$ are both due to process P itself. Therefore, the sequence for indexing their contribution in P is $\langle\rangle$. □

Example 3.3. Let $P = I \parallel J,\ I = E \parallel F,\ J = G \parallel H,$
$$E = A \parallel B,\ H = C \parallel D.$$
where, the outside structure of processes A, B, F, G, C and D is not the parallel composition. Below is the graph that illustrates the structure of process P.

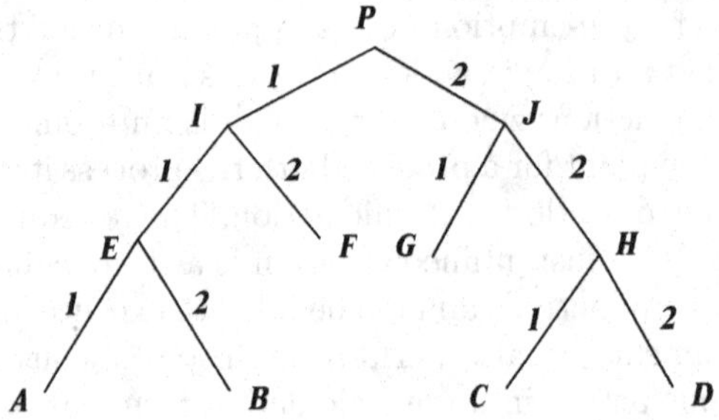

We assign a label for each edge. If it is the left edge of a process, the label is 1, otherwise the label is 2. Now we consider the sequence that can index the instantaneous action of parallel process P. If P's instantaneous action is due to process A, then the sequence that indexes the exact component of P's contribution is the sequence $\langle 1\rangle\langle 1\rangle\langle 1\rangle$[1]. If P's instantaneous action is due to process B, then the sequence that indexes the exact component of P's contribution is the sequence $\langle 1\rangle\langle 1\rangle\langle 2\rangle$. Similarly, if P's instantaneous action is due to process F, then the sequence that indexes the exact component of P's contribution is the sequence $\langle 2\rangle\langle 2\rangle\langle 2\rangle$. □

Now we introduce the concept of location status for a program, which is one of the following three forms:

(1) *index*, which can be $\langle\rangle$ or a non-empty thread sequence. It indicates an instantaneous action is due to which exact component of a parallel process.

(2) 0, which indicates the termination of an atomic action.

(3) *null*, which indicates a process is at a state where the process itself and its environment can both have a chance to perform its instantaneous action.

For example, in the above example (i.e., Example 3.3), let $A = x := 1\ ;\ x := x + 1\ ;\ x := x + 2$. If $x := 1$ is scheduled and completes its execution, the location status for the remaining process of P is $\langle 1\rangle\langle 1\rangle\langle 1\rangle$. This means that it will continue to execute the two subsequent statements $x := x+1$ and $x := x+2$.

The introduction of guarded choice is to support the parallel expansion laws. Guarded choice can be formalized with location status (i.e., *tag*), as defined below.

[1] $\langle 1\rangle\langle 1\rangle\langle 1\rangle$ stands for $\langle 1, 1, 1\rangle$.

Definition 3.3.
(1) h (P, tag) is a guarded component if it can be one of the forms below. Here, b is a Boolean condition and *index* can be $\langle\rangle$ or a non-empty thread sequence.

$$b\&(x := e)\ (P,\ index),\quad b\&(x := e)\ (P,\ 0),\quad @(g)\ (P,\ null),\quad \#1\ (P,\ null)$$

(2) $[\![\{h_1\ (P_1,\ tag_1),\ \ldots,\ h_n\ (P_n,\ tag_n)\}$ is a guarded choice if every element $h_i\ (P_i,\ tag_i)$ is a guarded component. □

For guarded component "h (P, tag)", if h is executed (or fired), the subsequent process is P and it is at the location status *tag*. Programs can be represented in the form of a guarded choice. For this aim, the guarded choice can only have five types:

(1) $[\!]_{i\in I}\{b_i\&(x_i := e_i)\ (P_i,\ tag_i)\}$
(2) $[\!]_{i\in I}\{@(\eta_i)\ (P_i,\ null)\}$
(3) $[\!]\{\#1\ (P,\ null)\}$
(4) $[\!]_{i\in I}\{b_i\&(x_i := e_i)\ (P_i,\ tag_i)\}\ [\!]\ [\!]_{j\in J}\{@(\eta_j)\ (Q_j,\ null)\}$
(5) $[\!]_{i\in I}\{@(\eta_i)\ (P_i,\ null)\}\ [\!]\ \{\#1\ (Q,\ null)\}$

The first type of guarded choice is composed of a set of assignment components, where the second type of guarded choice is only composed of a set of event guard components. The third type is composed of one time-delay component. The fourth type of guarded choice is composed of a set of assignment components and a set of event guard components. The fifth type of guarded choice is composed of a set of event guard components and a time delay component.

When mechanizing in Maude, we implement $b\&(x := e)\ (P,\ index)$ and $b\&(x := e)\ (P,\ 0)$ as "`GComponent1`", Similarly, $@(g)\ (P,\ null)$ and $\#1\ (P,\ null)$ are implemented as "`GComponent2`" and "`GComponent3`" respectively. All the guarded components are expressed as type "`GComponent`". Below is the detailed definition of guarded components in Maude.

```
fmod GUARDED-COMPONENT is pr VERILOG-PROGRAM .
    pr CONFIG .

    sorts GComponent1 GComponent2 GComponent3 GComponent .
    subsort GComponent1 GComponent2 GComponent3 < GComponent .

    sorts AssignmentGuard GuardPostfix GuardPostfix1 GuardPostfix2
          GuardPostfix3 .
    subsort GuardPostfix1 GuardPostfix2 GuardPostfix3 < GuardPostfix .

    op _&(_) : BoolExp Assignment -> AssignmentGuard [ctor] .
    op `(_,_`) : Program Index -> GuardPostfix1 [ctor] .
    op `(_,_`) : Program EndPoint -> GuardPostfix2 [ctor] .
    op `(_,_`) : Program Null -> GuardPostfix3 [ctor] .

    op __ : AssignmentGuard GuardPostfix1 -> GComponent1 [ctor] .
    op __ : AssignmentGuard GuardPostfix2 -> GComponent1 [ctor] .
    op __ : EventGuard GuardPostfix3 -> GComponent2 [ctor] .
    op __ : TimeControl GuardPostfix3 -> GComponent3 [ctor] .
endfm
```

`GComponents` are the key components of guarded choices. Based on the three `GComponents`, we can define the guarded choices, which we call `HealthyGC`.

```
subsort HGCType1 HGCType2 HGCType3 HGCType4 HGCType5 < HealthyGC .
op {_} : GComponent1 -> HGCType1 [ctor] .
op {_} : GComponent2 -> HGCType2 [ctor] .
op {_} : GComponent3 -> HGCType3 [ctor] .
op _[]_ : HGCType1 HGCType1 -> HGCType1 [ctor] .
op _[]_ : HGCType2 HGCType2 -> HGCType2 [ctor] .
op _[]_ : HGCType1 HGCType2 -> HGCType4 [ctor] .
op _[]_ : HGCType2 HGCType3 -> HGCType5 [ctor] .
```

In the above definitions, `HealthyGC` is defined as five subsorts, which are declared as sorts `HGCType1`, $\cdots$, `HGCType5`, representing the five types of guarded choices respectively. `HGCType1` and `HGCType2` are composed of `GComponent1` and `GComponent2` respectively, separated by `[]`. `HGCType3` is composed of a single `GComponent3`. `HGCType4` is concatenated by `HGCType1` and `HGCType2`, and `HGCType5` is concatenated by `HGCType2` and `HGCType3`.

3.3 Generating Algebraic Laws

Now we study the expansion laws for parallel composition, which is useful in deriving operational semantics from algebraic semantics. Based on the mechanism of parallel composition for Verilog, we summarize that there are five typical parallel expansion forms, described as *comp*1, *comp*2, $\cdots$, and *comp*5, shown below. The whole set of parallel expansion laws is reflected in the definition of head normal form for parallel composition in the next section. We use the notation $P =_{tag} Q$ to stand for $(P, tag) = (Q, tag)$, indicating that process P and Q are equivalent at location status tag. The notation (P, tag) stands for the behaviour of program P at location status tag.

First we consider the case that one parallel component is in the form of assignment guarded choice. In this case, for a parallel process, no matter which form another parallel component is in, any assignment can be scheduled. The location status of the remaining process after the scheduled assignment should be re-calculated shown in the "**par1**" function[2]. This case can be expressed in "*comp*1", which is defined recursively.

For example, assume $P =_{null} \|_{i\in I}\{b_i\&(x_i := e_i)\ (P_i,\, tag_i)\}$ and

Q be any process.

Then, $\|_{i\in I}\{b_i\&(x_i := e_i)\ \mathbf{par1}(P_i, Q, 1, tag_i))\}$ is one part of the parallel expansion of $P \| Q$ due to the initial assignments of P.

Now we consider the case that one parallel component is in the form of event-guarded choice. For a parallel process, we assume that another parallel component does not have event-guard initially. For this case, if an event guard is fired, the remaining process of the parallel process is the parallel composition of the

---

[2] $$\mathbf{par1}(P, Q, i, tag) =_{df} \begin{cases} (\varepsilon, 0) & \text{if } P=\varepsilon \text{ and } Q=\varepsilon \\ (\varepsilon \| Q, 0) & \text{if } P=\varepsilon \text{ and } Q\neq\varepsilon \text{ and } i=1 \\ (P \| \varepsilon, 0) & \text{if } P\neq\varepsilon \text{ and } Q=\varepsilon \text{ and } i=2 \\ (P \| Q, 0) & \text{if } P\neq\varepsilon \text{ and } tag=0 \text{ and } i=1 \\ (P \| Q, 0) & \text{if } Q\neq\varepsilon \text{ and } tag=0 \text{ and } i=2 \\ (P \| Q, \langle 1\rangle^\frown tag) & \text{if } P\neq\varepsilon \text{ and } tag\neq 0 \text{ and } i=1 \\ (P \| Q, \langle 2\rangle^\frown tag) & \text{if } Q\neq\varepsilon \text{ and } tag\neq 0 \text{ and } i=2 \end{cases}$$

remaining process of the first component and the second parallel component. This case can be expressed using "*comp*2". Meanwhile, *comp*2 can also be applied to the case that the first parallel component is in the form of time delay component.

For example, assume $Q =_{null} \|_{j\in J}\{@(\eta_j)\ (Q_j,\ null)\}$ and
P does not have event-guard initially.

Then, $\|_{j\in J}\{@(\eta_j)\ \mathbf{par}(P, Q_j)\}$[3] is one part of the parallel expansion of $P \parallel Q$ due to the initial event guard firing of Q.

Now we consider the case that both of the two parallel components are in the form of event-guarded choice. There are several types of the triggered cases. If one guard from one parallel part is triggered and all the guards from another parallel part cannot be triggered, the behaviour after the triggered case is the parallel composition of the subsequent process of one parallel part after the triggered guard with another parallel part. This can be defined in "*comp*3" and "*comp*4" recursively. On the other hand, if two guards from different parallel parts are triggered simultaneously, the behaviour after this type of triggered case is the parallel composition of the subsequent processes, after two triggered guards from each parallel part. This can be defined in "*comp*5" recursively.

For example, Assume $P =_{null} \|_{i\in I}\{@(\eta_i)\ (P_i,\ null)\}$ and
$Q =_{null} \|_{j\in J}\{@(\xi_j)\ (Q_j,\ null)\}$

Then

$$\|_{i\in I}\{@(\eta_i\ and\ \neg\xi)\ \mathbf{par}(P_i, Q)\} \tag{1}$$

$$\text{and}\quad \|_{j\in J}\{@(\xi_j\ and\ \neg\eta)\ \mathbf{par}(P, Q_j)\} \tag{2}$$

$$\text{and}\quad \|_{i\in I\wedge j\in J}\{@(\eta_i\ and\ \xi_j)\ \mathbf{par}(P_i, Q_j)\} \tag{3}$$

are the three firing cases for $P \parallel Q$. Here $\eta = or_{i\in I}\{\eta_i\}$ and $\xi = or_{j\in J}\{\xi_i\}$. *comp*3, *comp*4 and *comp*5 stand for the above three firing cases (1), (2) and (3) respectively.

Below is the detailed description of *comp*1, *comp*2, $\cdots$, and *comp*5 in Maude.

```
op comp1(_,_,_) : HGCType1 Program Index -> HGCType1 .
eq comp1({b &(x := e)(P1,tag1)},Q,<1>) = {b &(x := e)par1(P1,Q,<1>,tag1)} .
eq comp1({b &(x := e)(Q1,tag1)},P,<2>) = {b &(x := e)par1(P,Q1,<2>,tag1)} .
eq comp1({h1 Post1} [] hgc',P,i) = comp1({h1 Post1},P,i) []
                                   comp1(hgc',P,i) .
op comp2(_,_,_) : HealthyGC Program Index -> HealthyGC .
eq comp2({@(g)(P1,tag1)},Q,<1>) = {@(g)(par(P1,Q),tag1)} .
eq comp2({@(g)(Q1,tag1)},P,<2>) = {@(g)(par(P,Q1),tag1)} .
eq comp2({# 1(P1,tag1)},Q,<1>) = {# 1(par(P1,Q),tag1)} .
eq comp2({# 1(Q1,tag1)},P,<2>) = {# 1(par(P,Q1),tag1)} .
eq comp2({h1 Post1} [] hgc',P,i) = comp2({h1 Post1},P,i) []
                                   comp2(hgc',P,i) .
```

[3] $\mathbf{par}(P, Q) =_{df} \begin{cases} (\varepsilon,\ null) & \text{if} P = \varepsilon \text{ and } Q = \varepsilon \\ (P \parallel Q,\ null) & \text{otherwise} \end{cases}$

```
op comp3(_,_,_) : HGCType2 HGCType2 Program -> HGCType2 .
eq comp3({@(g1)(P1,null)}, hgct2, Q) = {@(g1 and ~ guard(hgct2))
                                       (par(P1,Q),null)} .
eq comp3({@(g1)(P1,null)} [] hgct2', hgct2, Q) =
            comp3({@(g1)(P1,null)},hgct2,Q) [] comp3(hgct2',hgct2,Q) .
op comp4(_,_,_) : HGCType2 HGCType2 Program -> HGCType2 .
eq comp4(hgct2, {@(g1)(Q1,null)}, P) = {@(g1 and ~ guard(hgct2))
                                       (par(P,Q1),null)} .
eq comp4(hgct2, {@(g1)(Q1,null)} [] hgct2', P) =
            comp4(hgct2,{@(g1)(Q1,null)},P) [] comp4(hgct2,hgct2',P) .
op comp5(_,_) : HGCType2 HGCType2 -> HGCType2 .
eq comp5({@(g1)(P1,null)},{@(g2)(Q1,null)}) = {@(g1 and g2)
                                             (par(P1,Q1),null)} .
eq comp5({@(g1)(P1,null)},{@(g2)(Q1,null)} [] hgct2) =
comp5({@(g1)(P1,null)},{@(g2)(Q1,null)})[]comp5({@(g1)(P1,null)},hgct2) .
eq comp5({@(g1)(P1,null)} [] hgct2,hgct2') =
               comp5({@(g1)(P1,null)},hgct2')[]comp5(hgct2,hgct2') .
```

All these five definitions are used to compute the components of parallel expansions of two processes. In order to compute the remaining process after the corresponding guard of the parallel expansion, the process not being scheduled will be added as a parameter to the computation.

4 Generating Head Normal Form

In order to support the derivation of operational semantics from algebraic semantics, we introduce the concept of head normal form. For program P, if its location status is tag, we use the notation $HF(P, tag)$ to stand for the head normal form of process P at the location status tag.

The head normal form of $HF(P, tag)$ is to make one step forward expansion for program P at the location status tag. For parallel program P, the parallel expansion laws can help to calculate the head normal form $HF(P, tag)$. As the operational semantics is also to make one step forward transition, the head normal form can support to derive the operational semantics.

4.1 Sequential Constructs

For sequential constructs, its initial location status can be $null$, $\langle\rangle$ and 0. Below are the definitions of the head normal form of sequential constructs at the location status tag.

```
eq    HF(x := e,tag) = ({t &(x := e)(nil,<>)},tag) .
eq    HF(Skip,tag) = ({t &(Skip)(nil,<>)},tag) .
eq    HF(@(x := e),tag) = ({t &(x := e)(nil,0)},tag) .
eq    HF(@(g),tag) = ({@(g)(nil,null)},tag) .
eq    HF(# 1,tag) = ({# 1(nil,null)},tag) .
eq    HF(# n,tag) = ({# 1(# (n - 1),null)},tag) .
ceq   HF(P ; Q,tag) = (seq(T,Q),tag) if (T,tag) := HF(P,tag) .
ceq   HF(P ; Q,tag) = (seq(T,Q),tag) if (T,tag) := HF(P,tag) .
ceq   HF(if b then P else Q,tag) = ({b &(Skip)(P,<>)} [] {~ b &(Skip)(Q,<>},tag) .
ceq   HF(while b do P,tag) = ({b &(Skip)(P ; while b do P,<>)} []
                                 {~ b &(Skip)(nil,<>)},tag) .
```

The first line defines the head normal form of $x := e$. Here "t" stands for *true* and "*nil*" stands for the empty process ε. After its execution, the location status is $\langle\rangle$. On the other hand, the third line defines the head normal form of assignment guard $@(x := e)$. After its execution, the location status is 0, indicating the completion of an atomic action.

4.2 Parallel Composition

For parallel process $P \parallel Q$, its location status can be *null*, 0 and *seq*. Firstly we consider the head normal form of $P \parallel Q$ at the location status *null*.

There are five types of guarded choice. We first consider the case that two parallel components of a parallel process are of the first three types. Their head normal forms are defined based on *comp*1, *comp*2, $\cdots$, *comp*5.

```
     ceq    HF(P || Q,null) = (comp1(hgct11,Q,<1>) [] comp1(hgct12,P,<2>) , null)
            if (hgct11,null) := HF(P,null) /\ (hgct12,null) := HF(Q,null) .
     ceq    HF(P || Q,null) = (comp1(hgct1,Q,<1>) [] comp2(hgct2,P,<2>) , null)
            if (hgct1,null) := HF(P,null) /\ (hgct2,null) := HF(Q,null) .
     ceq    HF(P || Q,null) = (comp1(hgct1,Q,<1>) , null)
            if (hgct1,null) := HF(P,null) /\ (hgct3,null) := HF(Q,null) .
     ceq    HF(P || Q,null) = (comp3(hgct21,hgct22,Q) [] comp4(hgct21,hgct22,P) []
                               comp5(hgct21,hgct22), null)
            if (hgct21,null) := HF(P,null) /\ (hgct22,null) := HF(Q,null) .
     ceq    HF(P || Q,null) = (comp2(hgct2,Q,<1>) [] comp2(hgct3,P,<2>), null)
            if (hgct2,null) := HF(P,null) /\ (hgct3,null) := HF(Q,null) .
     ceq    HF(P || Q,null) = ({# 1(par(R1,R2),null)}, null)
            if ({# 1(R1,null)},null) := HF(P,null) /\ ({# 1(R2,null)},null) :=
HF(Q,null) .
```

In the above definitions, we use the first case to explain our definition. The head normal forms of P and Q at the location status *null* are expressed as `hgct11` and `hgct12` respectively, and they are both of the first type of guarded choice. Hence, "`comp1(hgct11,Q,<1>)[]comp1(hgct12,P,<2>)`" is the head normal form of $P \parallel Q$ at the location status *null*, indicating that the assignments in P and Q can both be scheduled first and the location status after the execution of the corresponding assignment is calculated.

If a process is in the form of the fourth type of guarded choice (or the fifth type of guarded choice), it can be composed in parallel with any process (i.e., in the form of any type of guarded choice). The head normal form of the corresponding parallel process at location status *null* can be defined similarly. Below is the case that both of the parallel components are of the fourth type of guarded choice.

```
     ceq    HF(P || Q,null) = (comp1(hgct11,Q,<1>) [] comp1(hgct12,P,<2>) []
                               comp3(hgct21,hgct22,Q) [] comp4(hgct21,hgct22,P) []
                               comp5(hgct21,hgct22),null)
            if (hgct11[]hgct21,null) := HF(P,null) /\ (hgct12[]hgct22,null) :=
HF(Q,null) .
```

The above analysis considered the generating of head normal form for a parallel process at the location status *null*. Now we consider other cases for the location status of a parallel process. The first four **ceq**s below explore the case that one parallel part is at the state of the execution of an instantaneous action.

```
ceq   HF(P || Q,<1> ^ index) = (comp1({b &(x := e)(P1,index)},Q,<1>), <1> ^ index)
      if ({b &(x := e)(P1,index)},index) := HF(P,index) .

ceq   HF(Q || P,<2> ^ index) = (comp1({b &(x := e)(P1,index)},Q,<2>), <2> ^ index)
      if ({b &(x := e)(P1,index)},index) := HF(P,index) .

ceq   HF(P || Q,<1> ^ index) = (comp1({b &(x := e)(P1,0)},Q,<1>), <1> ^ index)
      if ({b &(x := e)(P1,0)},index) := HF(P,index) .

ceq   HF(Q || P,<2> ^ index) = (comp1({b &(x := e)(P1,0)},Q,<2>), <2> ^ index)
      if ({b &(x := e)(P1,0)},index) := HF(P,index) .

ceq   HF(P || Q,index) = (T,index) if (T,null) := HF(P || Q,null) .

ceq   HF(P || Q,0) = (T,0) if (T,null) := HF(P || Q,null) .
```

In the above definitions, the first and second case models the situation that a process continues to execute the next assignment in an atomic action. For parallel process $P \parallel Q$, the first case models the execution of next assignment which is contributed by process P, whereas the second case models the execution of next assignment which is due to Q. Now we explain the first case further. For process P at location status `index`, after the execution of the next assignment, the location status is still `index`. Then, for parallel process, it will execute the same next assignment contributed by P and the location status is expressed as "`<1>^index`".

Example 4.1. Let $P = ((x := x{+}1\ ;\ @(\uparrow y)) \parallel y := y{+}1) \parallel (\#1\ ;\ y := y{+}1)$. Now we consider the head normal form of process P at the location state *null*.

For process P, two assignments $x := x+1$ and $y := y+1$ in $(x := x+1\ ;\ @(\uparrow y)) \parallel y := y+1$ can have chances to be scheduled. Therefore, if $x := x+1$ is scheduled, the remaining process is $(@(\uparrow y) \parallel y := y+1) \parallel (\#1\ ;\ y := y+1)$ and the corresponding location status is $\langle 1\rangle\langle 1\rangle$.

On the other hand, for process P, if $y := y+1$ in $(x := x+1\ ;\ @(\uparrow y)) \parallel y := y+1$ is scheduled, the remaining process is $(x := x+1\ ;\ @(\uparrow y)) \parallel (\#1\ ;\ y := y{+}1)$. As this assignment is the last statement of parallel composition $(x := x+1\ ;\ @(\uparrow y)) \parallel y := y+1$, the location status is 0 after the execution of this assignment.

Using the command `red(uce)` provided by Maude, we can compute the head normal form of the example program,

`reduce in HEAD-NORM-FORM :`

$$(\quad \{t\ \&\ (x := x+1)\ ((@(\uparrow y) \parallel y := y+1) \parallel (\#1\ ;\ y := y+1)\ ,\ \langle 1\rangle\langle 1\rangle)\}$$
$$[\!]\ \{t\ \&\ (y := y+1)\ ((x := x+1\ ;\ @(\uparrow y)) \parallel (\#1\ ;\ y := y+1)\ ,\ 0)\}$$
$$,\ null\ )$$

5 Generating Operational Semantics from Algebraic Semantics

5.1 Transition Types

The transitions for Verilog are of the form $C \xrightarrow{\beta} C'$, where C and C' are configurations describing the states of an executing mechanism before and after a step respectively. Here we use β to represent the transition type. There are three types of configurations:

$$\langle P, \sigma, \emptyset \rangle \qquad \langle P, \sigma, \sigma', 1, seq \rangle \qquad \langle P, \sigma, \sigma', 0 \rangle$$

where:

(1) The first component P is a program text representing the program that remains to be executed.

(2) The second component σ in $\langle P, \sigma, \emptyset\rangle$ stands for the initial state, which can be regarded as the initial state of the atomic action that appears at the beginning of P. The second component σ in other configurations stands for the initial state of an atomic action that is currently being executed.

(3) The third component σ' ($\sigma' \neq \emptyset$) models the accumulation of the contribution of instantaneous actions in an atomic action. If the third component is $\emptyset$, it means the previous atomic action ends and the new atomic action has not been scheduled.

(4) If the third component is not empty, a control flag j should be supplied in the configuration as the fourth element. "$j = 0$" indicates that the current atomic action ends, where "$j = 1$" indicates that current atomic action is still executing.

(5) In order to model the scheduling policy for parallel processes, a thread sequence seq is supplied in the configuration if the third element is not empty (for explanations, see section 3.2), which is used to index the currently active sub-process in a nested parallel composition. Here, seq can be $\langle\rangle$ or a non-empty thread sequence.

The transition rules for Verilog programs can be grouped into the following three types: (1) Instantaneous transition $C \longrightarrow C'$; (2) Event transition $C \overset{\langle\sigma,\sigma'\rangle}{\longrightarrow} C'$; (3) Time advance transition $C \overset{1}{\longrightarrow} C'$. Below are the detailed descriptions:

1. Instantaneous transition

   T$_1$ A process can perform its first instantaneous action of an atomic action.
   $$\langle P, \sigma, \emptyset \rangle \longrightarrow \langle P', \sigma, \sigma', 1, seq \rangle$$
   T$_2$ A process can continue its following instantaneous action in an atomic action.
   $$\langle P, \sigma, \sigma', 1, seq \rangle \longrightarrow \langle P', \sigma, \sigma'', 1, seq \rangle$$
   T$_3$ A process completes an instantaneous section.
   $$\langle P, \sigma, \sigma', 1, seq \rangle \longrightarrow \langle P, \sigma, \sigma', 0 \rangle$$
   T$_4$ A process executes an assignment guard.
   $$\langle P, \sigma, \emptyset \rangle \longrightarrow \langle P', \sigma, \sigma', 0 \rangle$$

2. Event transition

   T$_5$ (1) A transition can be fired by the atomic action that has just completed. $\langle P, \sigma, \sigma', 0 \rangle \overset{\langle\sigma,\sigma'\rangle}{\longrightarrow} \langle P', \sigma', \emptyset \rangle$

   (2) A transition can be fired by the action of its environment.
   $$\langle P, \sigma, \emptyset \rangle \overset{\langle\sigma,\sigma'\rangle}{\longrightarrow} \langle P', \sigma', \emptyset \rangle$$

3. Time advance transition

   T$_6$ A process that cannot do anything else will allow time to advance. Time advances in unit steps.
   $$\langle P, \sigma, \emptyset \rangle \overset{1}{\longrightarrow} \langle P', \sigma, \emptyset \rangle$$

The configuration can be implemented in Maude as below.

```
fmod CONFIG is pr VERILOG-PROGRAM .
    pr ENVIRONMENT .
    ......
    op # : -> Init [ctor] .
    op 1 : -> Flag [ctor] .
    op 0 : -> EndPoint [ctor] .
    op <> : -> Index [ctor] .
    op <1> : -> Index [ctor] .
    op <2> : -> Index [ctor] .
    op _^_ : Index Index-> Index [ctor assoc id: <>] .

    op <_,_,_> : Program Env Init -> Config [ctor] .
    op <_,_,_,_,_> : Program Env Env Flag Index -> Config [ctor] .
    op <_,_,_,_> : Program Env Env EndPoint -> Config [ctor] .
endfm
```

The definition of configurations in Maude is based on the three types of configurations. The first type contains three components and ends with a # which is the only element of sort `Init` (i.e., representing $\emptyset$). And the second type contains five components among which the fourth is the `Flag` represented by `1` and the fifth is a `Index`. The third type contains four components and the fourth is the `EndPoint` represented by `0`.

5.2 Deriving Operational Semantics from Algebraic Semantics

The main purpose of this section is to derive the transition system for Verilog from its algebraic laws. This approach allows the operational semantics to be derived as theorems, rather than being presented as postulates or definitions.

Firstly we give the derivation strategy, which is based on the head normal of each program. For every program, its location status can be *null*, $\langle\rangle$ or *seq*.

Definition 5.1 (Derivation Strategy).

(1.a) If $HF(P, null) = (\ \|_{i\in I}\{b_i\&(x_i := e_i)\ (P_i, tag_i)\},\ \ null\ )$,
then P can perform transitions at states $\langle P, \sigma, \emptyset\rangle$ and $\langle P, \sigma, \sigma', 0\rangle$.

```
crl [1.a1] : . < P , env , # > => < Pi , env , env <- (x , e) , 1 , tag >
        if (hgct1,null) := HF(P,null) /\ (hgc [] {b &(x := e)(Pi,tag)} [] hgc', null)
        := (hgct1,null) /\ b[env] /\ tag =/= 0 .

crl [1.a1'] : . < P , env , # > => < Pi , env , env , 1 , tag >
        if (hgct1,null) := HF(P,null) /\ (hgc [] {b &(Skip)(Pi,tag)} [] hgc', null)
        := (hgct1,null) /\ b[env] /\ tag =/= 0 .

crl [1.a2] : . < P , env , # > => < Pi , env , env <- (x , e) , 0 >
        if (hgct1,null) := HF(P,null) /\ (hgc [] {b &(x := e)(Pi,tag)} [] hgc', null)
        := (hgct1,null) /\ b[env] /\ tag == 0 .

crl [1.a3] : . < P , env , env' , 0 > => < P , env' , # >
        if (hgct1,null) := HF(P,null) .
```

(1.b) If $HF(P, null) = (\ \|_{i\in I}\{@(\eta_i)\ (P_i, null)\},\ \ null\ )$,
then P can perform transitions at states $\langle P, \sigma, \emptyset\rangle$ and $\langle P, \sigma, \sigma', 0\rangle$.

```
crl [1.b1] : . < P , env , env' , 0 > => < P , env' , # >
        if (hgct2,null) := HF(P,null) /\ not fire(guard(hgct2))(env,env') .

crl [1.b2] : . < P , env , env' , 0 > => < Pi , env' , # >
        if (hgct2,null) := HF(P,null) /\ (hgc [] {@(g)(Pi,null)} [] hgc' , null) :=
        (hgct2,null) /\ fire(g)(env,env') .

crl [1.b3] : . < P , env , # > => < P , env , # >
        if (hgct2,null) := HF(P,null) .
```

(1.c) If $HF(P, null)\ =\ (\ \|\{\#1\ (R, null)\},\ \ null)$,
then P can perform transitions at states $\langle P, \sigma, \emptyset\rangle$ and $\langle P, \sigma, \sigma', 0\rangle$.

```
crl [1.c1] : < P , env , env' , 0 > => < P , env' , # >
      ({# 1(R,null)} , null) := HF(P,null) .

crl [1.c2] : < P , env , # > => < R , env , # >
      ({# 1(R,null)} , null) := HF(P,null) .
```

(1.d) If $HF(P, null) = (\|_{i\in I}\{b_i\&(x_i := e_i)\ (P_i,\ tag_i)\} \parallel \|_{j\in J}\{@(\eta_j)\ (R_j, null)\},$ $null\ ),$
then P can perform transitions at states $\langle P, \sigma, \emptyset\rangle$ and $\langle P, \sigma, \sigma', 0\rangle$.

```
crl [1.d1] : . < P , env , # > => < Pi , env , env <- (x , e) , 1 , tag >
      if (hgct1 [] hgct2,null):=HF(P,null) /\ (hgc [] {b &(x := e)(Pi,tag)} [] hgc',
      null):= (hgct1,null) /\ b[env] /\ tag =/= 0 .
crl [1.d1'] : . < P , env , # > => < Pi , env , env , 1 , tag >
      if (hgct1 [] hgct2,null) := HF(P,null) /\ (hgc [] {b &(Skip)(Pi,tag)} [] hgc',
      null) := (hgct1,null) /\ b[env] /\ tag =/= 0 .
crl [1.d2] : . < P , env , # > => < Pi , env , env <- (x , e) , 0 >
      if (hgct1 [] hgct2,null) := HF(P,null) /\ (hgc [] {b &(x := e)(Pi,tag)} []hgc',
      null) := (hgct1,null) /\ b[env] /\ tag == 0 .
crl [1.d3] : . < P , env , env' , 0 > => < P , env' , # >
      if (hgct1 [] hgct2,null) := HF(P,null) /\ not fire(guard(hgct2))(env,env') .
crl [1.d4] : . < P , env , env' , 0 > => < R , env' , # >
      if (hgct1 [] hgct2,null) := HF(P,null) /\ (hgc [] {@(g)(R,null)} [] hgc' , null)
      := (hgct2,null) /\ fire(g)(env,env') .
```

(1.e) If $HF(P, null) = (\|_{i\in I}\{@(\eta_i)\ (P_i, null)\} \parallel \{\#1\ (R, null)\},\ null\ ),$
then P can perform transitions at states $\langle P, \sigma, \emptyset\rangle$ and $\langle P, \sigma, \sigma', 0\rangle$.

```
crl [1.e1] : . < P , env , env' , 0 > => < P , env' , # >
   if (hgct2 [] {# 1(R,null)},null) := HF(P,null) /\ not fire(guard(hgct2))(env,env') .
crl [1.e2] : . < P , env , env' ,0 > => < R , env' , # >
   if (hgct2 [] {# 1(R,null)},null) := HF(P,null) /\ (hgc [] {@(g)(R,null)} [] hgc'
   , null) := (hgct2,null) /\ fire(g)(env,env') .

crl [1.e3] : . < P , env , # > => < R , env' , # >
   if (hgct2 [] {# 1(R,null)},null) := HF(P,null) .
```

(2.a) If $HF(P, seq) = (\|_{i\in I}\{b\&(x_i := e_i)\ (P_i,\ seq)\},\ \ seq\ ),$
then P can perform transitions at state $\langle P, \sigma, \sigma', 1, seq\rangle$.

```
crl [2.a]:. < P , env , env' , 1 , index > => < Pi , env , env <- (x , e) , 1 , index >
      if (hgct1,index) := HF(P,index) /\ (hgc [] {b &(x := e)(Pi,index)} [] hgc',
      index) := (hgct1,index) /\ b[env] .
crl [2.a'] : . < P , env , env' , 1 , index > => < Pi , env , env' , 1 , index >
      if (hgct1,index) := HF(P,index) /\ (hgc [] {b &(Skip)(Pi,index)} [] hgc',
      index) := (hgct1,index) /\ b[env] .
```

(2.b) If $HF(P, seq) = (\|_{i\in I}\{b_i\&(x_i := e_i)\ (P_i,\ 0)\},\ \ seq\ ),$
then P can perform transitions at state $\langle P, \sigma, \sigma', 1, seq\rangle$.

```
crl [2.b] : . < P , env , env' , 1 , index > => < Pi , env , env <- (x , e) , 0 >
      if (hgct1,index) := HF(P,index) /\ (hgc [] {b &(x := e)(Pi,0)} [] hgc',
      index) := (hgct1,index) /\ b[env] .
crl [2.b'] : . < P , env , env' , 1 , index > => < Pi , env , env' , 0>
      if (hgct1,index) := HF(P,index) /\ (hgc [] {b &(Skip)(Pi,0)} [] hgc',
      index) := (hgct1,index) /\ b[env] .
crl [2.b"] : . < P , env , env' , 1 , index > => < P , env , env' , 0 >
      if (hgct1 [] hgct2,index) := HF(P,index) .
crl [2.b"'] : . < P , env , env' , 1 , index > => < P , env , env' , 0 >
      if (hgct2 [] {# 1(R,null)},index) := HF(P,index) .
```

(3.a) If $HF(P, \langle\rangle) = (\|_{i\in I}\{g_i\ (P_i,\ tag_i)\},\ \ \langle\rangle\ )$ and $\forall i \in I \bullet tag_i \neq \langle\rangle,$
then P can perform transitions at state $\langle P, \sigma, \sigma', 1, \langle\rangle\rangle$.

```
crl [3.a] : . < P , env , env' , 1 , <> > => < P , env , env' , 0 >
      if (hgc , <>) := HF(P , <>) /\ tagnotempty(hgc) .
```

For the above derivation strategy, items ((1.a)–(1.e)) explore the situation that a program is at the location status *null*. The corresponding derivation strategy can be defined based on the five types of guarded choice of the head normal form of a program. If the head normal form of a program is expressed as the first type of guarded choice, the program can perform the first instantaneous action of an atomic action provided that the location status of the subsequent process is not 0. On the other hand, if the location status of the subsequent process is 0, this means that the program can perform an assignment guard transition. Meanwhile, the program can also perform a transition of event transition type. This can be expressed in item (1.a). When implementing in Maude, `hgct1` and `hgct2` stand for the first and second type of guarded choice.

Now we use rule [1.a1] as an example to make further explanation. From the conditions, we know that the head normal form of P at the location status *null* is `hgct1` and `hgct1` has a component `b&(x := e)(Pi,tag)`. In this case, process P can perform a transition reflecting the execution of that component (i.e., the assignment guarded component). The notation "`env<-(x,e)`" stands for a new state which is the same as `env` except assigning value `e` to `x`.

There are two types of event transitions. When designing the operational semantics, we take the understanding that, if a process has an event transition of the first type, it can also have an event transition of the second type, and vice-versa. When mechanizing the derivation of operational semantics, we take the understanding of regarding a system as closed. Therefore, the second type of event transition is not listed here.

Item (1.b) models the case that the head normal form of a program is expressed as the second type of guarded choice (i.e., event guarded choice). For this case, the program can perform an event transition, including the event transition that one of the guards is fired (i.e., [1.b2]), or the event transition that none of the guards are satisfied (i.e., [1.b1]). The program can also have time delay transition (i.e., [1.b3]), expressed as "`<P,env,#> => <P,env,#>`" in Maude. The notation "`fire(g)(env,env')`" in [1.b2] means that the change from state `env` to `evnv'` can fire the event guard `g`. The notation "`not fire(guard(hgct2))(env,env')`" in [1.b1] means that the state change from state `env` to`evnv'` cannot fire any guards in `hgct2` (i.e., the event guarded choice part of P).

For item (1.c), it models the case that a program is expressed as the time delay guarded choice. For this case, the program can perform time delay transition. It can also have event transition.

For item (1.d), it models the case that the head normal form of a program is expressed as the fourth type of guarded choice, i.e., the compound of the first and second type of guarded choice. For this case, the program can perform instantaneous transition (i.e., [1.d1], [1.d1'] and [1.d2]). It can also have event transition (i.e., [1.d3] and [1.d4]). As the behavior of assignment is instantaneous, the program cannot perform time delay transition. Transition [1.d1] (and [1.d1']) models the case that the process executes an assignment, whereas transition [1.d2] models the case that the process executes as assignment guard. [1.d3] models the event transition that all the event guards cannot be fired, whereas [1.d4] models the event transition that one guard is fired among all event guards.

Item (1.e) models the case that the head normal form of a program is expressed as the compound of the second and third type of guarded choice. At this case, the program can perform event transition based on firing condition of all guards. The program can also have time delay transition.

Items (2.a) and (2.b) model the situation that a process has already performed a sequence of instantaneous actions for an atomic action. Item (2.a) models the case that the process continues to execute the next instantaneous action for the atomic action. Therefore, it can perform the second type of instantaneous action, leaving the location status before and after the transition unchanged.

Now we consider a single threaded process (denoted by location status $\langle\rangle$), which performs a sequence of instantaneous actions and reaches at the point that the remaining process is guard, time delay or parallel process. In this case, for the head normal form of the remaining process, the subsequent process after each head cannot be $\langle\rangle$. For this case, the original process will perform the third type of instantaneous transitions, i.e., completing an atomic action. This case is illustrated in item (3.a).

Example 5.2. We take program P in Example 4.1 to illustrate the effectiveness of our derivation strategy. Assume that the initial values of x, y are both 0. The head normal form of program P was discussed in Example 4.1. We use the command "**`search`**" to get its transitions in Maude as following. But the display of the result of "**`search`**" is in a breadth-first style which is not very straightforward to see. We then use the "**`show path`** (state number)" command to show one of the path below. In order to display the result neatly, we also omit the rules used by the corresponding transition.

$$
\begin{array}{l}
< \ ((x := x + 1 \ ; \ @(\uparrow y)) \ \| \ y := y + 1) \ \| \ (\#1 \ ; \ y := y + 1) \ , \ \mathit{empty} \ , \# \ > \\
< \ (x := x + 1 \ ; \ @(\uparrow y)) \ \| \ (\#1 \ ; \ y := y + 1) \ , \ \mathit{empty} \ , \ (y, 1) \ , 0 \ > \\
< \ (x := x + 1 \ ; \ @(\uparrow y)) \ \| \ (\#1 \ ; \ y := y + 1) \ , \ (y, 1) \ , \ \# \ > \\
< \ @(\uparrow y) \ \| \ (\#1 \ ; \ y := y + 1) \ , \ (y, 1) \ , \ (y, 1)|(x, 1) \ , \ \langle 1 \rangle \ > \\
< \ @(\uparrow y) \ \| \ (\#1 \ ; \ y := y + 1) \ , \ (y, 1) \ , \ (y, 1)|(x, 1) \ , \ 0 \ > \\
< \ @(\uparrow y) \ \| \ (\#1 \ ; \ y := y + 1) \ , \ (x, 1)|(y, 1) \ , \ \# \ > \\
< \ @(\uparrow y) \ \| \ y := y + 1 \ , \ (x, 1)|(y, 1) \ , \ \# \ > \\
< \ @(\uparrow y) \ , \ (x, 1)|(y, 1) \ , \ (x, 1)|(y, 2) \ , \ 0 \ > \\
< \ \mathit{nil} \ , \ (x, 1)|(y, 2) \ , \ \# \ >
\end{array}
$$

The above is one execution sequence leading program P to the terminating state and the final state of variables is "$x = 1 \wedge y = 2$". For program P, there are two execution sequences leading program P to the terminating state. For another execution sequence, the final variable state is also "$x = 1 \wedge y = 2$". □

5.3 Mechanizing Operational Semantics

In the last subsection we provided the strategy for deriving the operational semantics from algebraic semantics. Our approach is via the concept of head normal form. Based on the derivation strategy, we can derive the full set of operational semantics for Verilog as theorems by strict proof. Now we consider the practical aspect of the derived operational semantics. We apply Maude in mechanizing the derived operational semantics. We select assignment, event guard and parallel composition here for illustrating the mechanization.

As the execution of $x := e$ is instantaneous, if $x := e$ is the first statement of an atomic action, it can be scheduled at once or the environment is allowed to perform some atomic actions. If $x := e$ is not the first action of an atomic action, it should be scheduled to execute at once without interruption by the environment. Time cannot advance for assignment. When animating the operational semantics, we do not know the environment's behaviour. Therefore, we take the understanding of regarding a system as closed. Although the second type of event transition can be derived, we regard it as not executable (see below for $x := e$ and $@(g)$). We use the keyword "[nonexec]" to show this.

```
rl : . < x := e , env , # > => < nil , env , env <- (x , e) , 1 , <> > .
rl : . < x := e , env , env' , 1 , <> > => < nil , env , env <- (x , e) , 1 , <> > .
rl : . < x := e , env , env' , 0 > => < x := e , env' , # > .
rl : . < x := e , env , # > => < x := e , env' , # > [nonexec] .
```

The guard $@(g)$ can be immediately fired after it is scheduled to execute; it is actually triggered by the execution of its previous action that has just completed. Another case is that the guard waits to be fired by its environment. Time can also advance before the guard becomes enabled.

```
rl : . < @(g) , env , env' , 1 , <> > => < @(g) , env , env' , 0 > .
rl : . < @(g) , env , env' , 0 > => < nil , env' , # > if fire(g)(env , env') .
rl : . < @(g) , env , env' , 0 > => < @(g) , env' , # > if not fire(g)(env , env') .
rl : . < @(g) , env , # > => < nil , env' , # > if fire(g)(env , env') [nonexec] .
rl : . < @(g) , env , # > => < @(g) , env' , # > if not fire(g)(env , env') [nonexec] .
rl : . < @(g) , env , # > => < @(g) , env , # > .
```

Now we consider the mechanizing of the derived operational semantics for parallel composition. If one of the two parallel parts of a Verilog program can perform the first instantaneous action of an atomic action, then the whole process can also make this transition.[4]

```
crl : . < P || Q , env , # > => < par(nil,Q) , env , env' , 0 >
  if . < P , env , # > => < nil , env , env' , 1 , seq > .
crl : . < Q || P , env , # > => < par(Q,nil) , env , env' , 0 >
  if . < P , env , # > => < nil , env , env' , 1 , seq > .
crl : . < P || Q , env , # > => < par(P',Q) , env , env' , 1 , <1> ^ seq >
  if . < P , env , # > => < P' , env , env' , 1 , seq > /\ P' =/= nil .
crl : . < Q || P , env , # > => < par(Q,P') , env , env' , 1 , <2> ^ seq >
  if . < P , env , # > => < P' , env , env' , 1 , seq > /\ P' =/= nil .
```

If one of the two parallel parts of a Verilog program continues to perform the instantaneous action of an atomic action, then the whole process can also make this transition.

```
crl : . < P || Q , env , env' , 1 , <1> ^ seq > => < par(P',Q) , env , env'',<1> ^ seq >
  if . < P , env , env' , 1 , seq > => < P' , env , env'' , 1 , seq > /\ P' =/= nil .
crl : . < Q || P , env , env' , 1 , <2> ^ seq > => < par(Q,P') , env , env'',<2> ^ seq >
  if . < P , env , env' , 1 , seq > => < P' , env , env'' , 1 , seq > /\ P' =/= nil .
```

[4] For this case, we can also have the situation that P or Q may be the empty process. In the consideration for other cases below, for $P \parallel Q$, P or Q maybe also be the empty process. We omit the transition rules which are similar to the normal situation.

If one of the two parallel parts of a Verilog program exits from an atomic action, then the whole process can also exit from the atomic action. A parallel process can also exit from its prior instantaneous section.

```
crl : . < P || Q , env , env' , 1 , <1> ^ seq > => < par(P',Q) , env , env' , 0 >
    if . < P , env , env' , 1 , seq > => < P' , env , env' , 0 > .
crl : . < Q || P , env , env' , 1 , <2> ^ seq > => < par(Q,P') , env , env' , 0 >
    if . < P , env , env' , 1 , seq > => < P' , env , env' , 0 > .
crl : . < P || Q , env , env' , 1 , <> > => < P || Q , env , env' , 0 > .
```

If one of the two parallel parts of a Verilog program executes an atomic assignment, then the whole process can also execute the atomic assignment.

```
crl : . < P || Q , env , # > => < par(P',Q) , env , env' , 0 >
    if . < P , env , # > => < P' , env , env' , 0 > .
crl : . < Q || P , env , # > => < par(Q,P') , env , env' , 0 >
    if . < P , env , # > => < P' , env , env' , 0 > .
```

$P \parallel Q$ can perform a triggered action caused by its predecessor or one of its components. $P \parallel Q$ allows the environment to perform an atomic action. $P \parallel Q$ allows time advance **iff** both components do so.

```
crl : . < P || Q , env , env' , 0 > => < par(P',Q') , env' , # >
    if . < P , env , env' , 0 > => < P' , env' , # > /\
       . < Q , env , env' , 0 > => < Q' , env' , # > .
crl : . < P || Q , env , # > => < par(P',Q') , env' , # >
    if . < P , env , # > => < P' , env' , # > /\ . < Q , env , # > => < Q' , env' , # > .
crl : . < P || Q , env , # > => < par(P',Q') , env , # >
    if . < P , env , # > => < P' , env , # > /\ . < Q , env , # > => < Q' , env , # > .
```

Example 5.3. Let P be the program described in Example 4.1 and Example 5.2. In Example 5.2, we have already considered the execution sequence of program P using the derivation strategy via algebraic semantics. Now we consider its execution based on the transition rules (i.e., the operational semantics in this section).

There are also two execution sequences leading program P to the terminating state. The first sequence is the same as the one described as Example 5.2 and the final state of program variables is also "$x = 1 \wedge y = 2$".

For the second execution sequence, the final state of program variables is also "$x = 1 \wedge y = 2$" and its detailed transition is as below. This execution sequence is the same as the second sequence in Example 5.2 leading program P to the terminating state (although we didn't list it).

$$\begin{array}{l}
< \ ((x := x+1 \ ; \ @(\uparrow y)) \ \parallel \ y := y+1) \ \parallel \ (\#1 \ ; \ y := y+1) \ , \ \mathit{empty} \ , \# \ > \\
< \ ((@(\uparrow y) \ \parallel \ y := y+1) \ \parallel \ (\#1 \ ; \ y := y+1) \ , \ \mathit{empty} \ , \ (x,1) \ , \ \langle 1 \rangle \ > \\
< \ ((@(\uparrow y) \ \parallel \ y := y+1) \ \parallel \ (\#1 \ ; \ y := y+1) \ , \ \mathit{empty} \ , \ (x,1) \ , \ 0 \ > \\
< \ (@(\uparrow y) \ \parallel \ y := y+1) \ \parallel \ (\#1 \ ; \ y := y+1) \ , \ (x,1) \ , \ \# \ > \\
< \ @(\uparrow y) \ \parallel \ (\#1 \ ; \ y := y+1) \ , \ (x,1) \ , \ (x,1)|(y,1), \ 0 \ > \\
< \ \#1 \ ; \ y := y+1 \ , \ (x,1)|(y,1), \ \# \ > \\
< \ y := y+1 \ , \ (x,1)|(y,1), \ \# \ > \\
< \ \mathit{nil} \ , \ (x,1)|(y,2), \ 1 \ , \ \langle\rangle \ >
\end{array}$$

The mechanical approach indicates that the transition system from the derived operational semantics is the same as the one from the derivation strategy. □

6 Conclusion and Future Work

This paper has presented how an algebraic semantics links with the operational semantics for Verilog, starting from the algebraic semantics. Our approach is to derive the operational semantics from the algebraic semantics. The mechanical method is applied in linking the two semantics. We used the equational and rewriting logic system Maude to support the mechanical implementation.

We have given the algebraic laws. Our approach is new, where a process is expressed as the guarded choice of a set of guarded components with location status. This guarded choice gives us a way to express how a process can be sequentialized, which also reflects the scheduling policy. In order to support the derivation, we introduced the concept of head normal form for every program at a location status. We have studied the derivation of the operational semantics for Verilog from its algebraic semantics. We have given the definition of the derivation strategy. Then a transition system (i.e., operational semantics) for Verilog can be derived via the derivation strategy. The algebraic laws, head normal form, derivation strategy and derived transition system are all implemented in the Maude system. The results mechanized indicate that the transition system of the derived operational semantics is the same as the one based on the derivation strategy.

Semantic linking is the challenging research [7]. For the future, we are continuing to explore further linking theories for Verilog semantics [8]. In particular the mechanical approach to the derivation of denotational semantics from algebraic semantics is also very challenging.

Acknowledgement. This work is supported by National Basic Research Program of China (No. 2011CB302904), National High Technology Research and Development Program of China (No. 2011AA010101 and No. 2012AA011205), National Natural Science Foundation of China (No. 61061130541 and No. 61021004), and Shanghai Leading Academic Discipline Project (No. B412).

References

1. Clavel, M., Durán, F., Eker, S., Lincoln, P., Martí-Oliet, N., Meseguer, J., Talcott, C.: The Maude 2.0 System. In: Nieuwenhuis, R. (ed.) RTA 2003. LNCS, vol. 2706, pp. 76–87. Springer, Heidelberg (2003)
2. Clavel, M., Durán, F.F., Eker, S., Lincoln, P., Martí-Oliet, N., Meseguer, J., Talcott, C.: Maude Manual (Version 2.6) (January 2011)
3. Gordon, M.J.C.: The semantic challenge of Verilog HDL. In: Proc. Tenth Annual IEEE Symposium on Logic in Computer Science, pp. 136–145. IEEE Computer Society Press (June 1995)
4. Gordon, M.J.C.: Relating event and trace semantics of hardware description languages. The Computer Journal 45(1), 27–36 (2002)
5. He, J., Xu, Q.: An operational semantics of a simulator algorithm. Technical Report 204, UNU/IIST, P.O. Box 3058, Macau SAR, China (2000)

6. He, J., Zhu, H.: Formalising Verilog. In: Proc. ICECS 2000: IEEE International Conference on Electronics, Circuits and Systems, pp. 412–415. IEEE Computer Society Press (December 2000)
7. Hoare, C.A.R.: Algebra of concurrent programming. In: Meeting 52 of WG 2.3 (2011)
8. Hoare, C.A.R., He, J.: Unifying Theories of Programming. Prentice Hall International Series in Computer Science (1998)
9. IEEE. IEEE Standard Hardware Description Language based on the Verilog Hardware Description Language, IEEE Standard 1364-1995. IEEE (1995)
10. IEEE. IEEE Standard Hardware Description Language based on the Verilog Hardware Description Language, IEEE Standard 1364-2001. IEEE (2001)
11. Li, Y., He, J.: Formalising Verilog: Operational semantics and bisimulation. Technical Report 217, UNU/IIST, P.O. Box 3058, Macau SAR, China (November 2000)
12. Martí-Oliet, N., Meseguer, J.: Rewriting logic as a logical and semantic framework. Electronic Notes in Theoretical Computer Science 4, 190–225 (1996)
13. Martí-Oliet, N., Meseguer, J.: Rewriting logic: Roadmap and bibliography. Theoretical Computer Science 285(2), 121–154 (2002)
14. Meseguer, J.: Twenty years of rewriting logic. Journal of Logic and Algebraic Programming (to appear)
15. Milner, R.: Communication and Concurrency. Prentice Hall International Series in Computer Science (1990)
16. Milner, R.: Communication and Mobile System: π-calculus. Cambridge University Press (1999)
17. Nissanke, N.: Realtime Systems. Prentice Hall International Series in Computer Science (1997)
18. Verdejo, A., Martí-Oliet, N.: Implementing ccs in maude 2. Electronic Notes in Theoretical Computer Science 71, 282–300 (2002)
19. Zhou, C., Hoare, C.A.R., Ravn, A.P.: A calculus of durations. Information Processing Letters 40(5), 269–276 (1991)
20. Zhu, H., Bowen, J.P., He, J.: Deriving operational semantics from denotational semantics for Verilog. In: Proc. APSEC 2001: 8th Asia-Pacific Software Engineering Conference, pp. 177–184. IEEE Computer Society Press (December 2001)
21. Zhu, H., Bowen, J.P., He, J.: From Operational Semantics to Denotational Semantics for Verilog. In: Margaria, T., Melham, T.F. (eds.) CHARME 2001. LNCS, vol. 2144, pp. 449–464. Springer, Heidelberg (2001)
22. Zhu, H., He, J.: A semantics of Verilog using Duration Calculus. In: Proc. International Conference on Software: Theory and Practice, pp. 421–432 (August 2000)
23. Zhu, H., He, J., Bowen, J.P.: From algebraic semantics to denotational semantics for verilog. Innovations in Systems and Software Engineering: A NASA Journal 4(4), 341–360 (2008)

Unifying Operational Semantics with Algebraic Semantics for Instantaneous Reactions

Chengcheng Wu[1], Yongxin Zhao[2], and Huibiao Zhu[1]

[1] Shanghai Key Laboratory of Trustworthy Computing
Software Engineering Institute, East China Normal University
{ccwu,hbzhu}@sei.ecnu.edu.cn
[2] School of Computing, National University of Singapore, Singapore
zhaoyx@comp.nus.edu.sg

Abstract. The signal calculus for event-based synchronous languages is developed for the specification and programming of embedded systems. This paper first explores a structural operational semantics for conceptually instantaneous reactions of the signal calculus, which exhibits how the effectiveness of such reactions is produced. Further, we investigate the unifying theory of operational semantics and algebraic semantics for instantaneous reactions. On one hand, all the algebraic laws characterizing the primitives and the combinators can be established in terms of the suggested structural operational semantics which claims the soundness of the algebraic semantics. On the other hand, reactions which are equivalent from the operational perspective can be reduced to the same normal form and this demonstrates the relative completeness of algebraic semantics with respect to the operational semantics.

1 Introduction

Real-time systems (RTS) are widely used in many areas including household electrical appliances, laboratory paraphernalia, Cyber Physical System, etc. All these systems have independent computing ability and can react to the environment through sensors and actuators. In essence, not only the correctness of such systems depends on the logical computing, but also the computing result should be taken at the right time. And this makes a great difference to traditional software systems. RTS have a more rigid time restriction and need to have some ability to predict the behaviors of the system while the scheduling algorithm is quite complex. Meanwhile, high security is eagerly expected while the interaction with the environment is complex and unpredictable. All of these lead to great challenges in modeling, designing, analyzing and verifying RTS.

The research on RTS has lasted for a long time. There have been a lot of modeling methods, calculus and reactive programs proposed to model, design, analyze and verify RTS. Modeling methods like Finite Automata [14] are popular in modeling traditional software system. In order to model RTS, Timed Automata [8,9] extends Büchi automata with clocks. And it's supported by many tools like UPPAAL [10] and Kronos [18]. ATP [15], Timed CSP [16,17] and HCSP [13] are

B. Wolff, M.-C. Gaudel, A. Feliachi (Eds.): UTP 2012, LNCS 7681, pp. 186–203, 2013.

widely used in the modeling of RTS as they use the method of process algebra. There are tool supports for timed process algebra as well, like PAT for Stateful Timed CSP. Esterel [2,3,5,6,11,12] is a synchronous language with many great processing methods which is very suitable for specifying and programming RTS [2,4,7].

Inspired by the Esterel language, we propose a signal calculus for event-based synchronous languages. Our calculus adopts the so-called synchronous hypothesis, i.e., instantaneous reaction to signals and immediate propagation of signals in each time-instant. In [1], the algebraic semantics of the instantaneous signal calculus (I-calculus) has been completely explored. A set of algebraic axioms is provided to characterize the properties of the primitives and the combinators. Further, the corresponding algebraic normal form is provided and every instantaneous reaction, however deeply structured, can be reduced into the normal form by a series of algebraic manipulations. Consequently, that two syntactically different but semantically equivalent instantaneous reactions can be proved from the equation of their algebraic presentations.

In this paper, we investigate the semantics for instantaneous reactions from an operational perspective. A structural operational semantics for instantaneous signal calculus is explored, which exhibits the effect of how reactions react to the environment. Further, we investigate the unifying theory of operational semantics and algebraic semantics for instantaneous reactions. On one hand, all the algebraic laws concerning the distinct features for instantaneous reactions can be established in terms of the suggested structural operational semantics, i.e., if the equality of two differently written instantaneous reactions is algebraically provable, the two reactions are also equivalent with respect to the operational semantics. Obviously, this claims the soundness of algebraic semantics. On the other hand, reactions which are equivalent from the operational perspective can be reduced to the same normal form and this demonstrates the relative completeness of algebraic semantics with respect to the operational semantics.

The remainder of this paper is organized in five sections. In section 2, we give a brief introduction to signals, event guards and I-Calculus which is the basis of our work. Then we propose our operational semantics in section 3. In section 4, we list the algebraic laws of I-Calculus and prove the soundness of algebraic laws based on the concept of program equivalence via operational semantics. And then in section 5, we prove the relative completeness of algebraic laws, by proving that the reactions which are equivalent in our operational semantics has the same normal form. Section 6 concludes the paper and presents some future work.

2 Instantaneous Reactions: I-Calculus

2.1 Event Guards

First we introduce broadcast signals and event guards. Signal is the basic communication and synchronization methods for different agents, systems and environments. In this paper, signals we are going to analyze have three status including *presence*$(+)$, *absence*$(-)$ and *unknown*(0). The order of the status is defined as $+ \geq 0$ and $- \geq 0$. And we use B to represent the status set $\{+, -, 0\}$. Generally, we use lowercase letters like s, t, m to represent signals. Letter S is usually used as the finite set of all signal names in our paper. We use the tuples like $(s, +)$, $(s, -)$, $(s, 0)$ to represent the *presence*, *absense* and *unknown* status of signal s.

Event is used to describe the status of signals we are observing. The change of events indicates the changes of the system and environment. An event is defined as a total function from the signal name set S to the status set B, i.e., $e : S \rightarrow B$. Generally, we use $\mathbb{E}$ to represent the set of all events. We use $(s, +) \in e$ or $e(s) = +$ to represent the existence of s in event e. The function $sig(e)$ defines the observation set consisting the names of all the signals included in the event e, e.g., $sig(e) = \{s, t\}$. The status of any signal in one event is unique. Then we give the definition of compatible events. Generally, when both $(s, +)$ and $(s, -)$ are not in an event, we mean that the state of s are unknown in the event or we can say $e(s) = 0$ though we have not explicitly written that $(s, 0) \in e$.

Definition 1 (Compatible). *Event e_1 and e_2 are compatible on the signal name set S if they agree with the status of all signals, i.e., $\forall s \in S \bullet e_1(s) = e_2(s) \vee (s, 0) \in e_1 \vee (s, 0) \in e_2$. We denote it by* $\mathsf{compatible}(e_1, e_2)$.

The pre-order of events is defined. We say event e_1 is better than event e_2 if $\forall s \in S \bullet e_1(s) \geq e_2(s)$. We denote this by $e_1 \geq e_2$. Then we can introduce the definition of event guards which is of the following form:

$$g ::= \epsilon \mid \emptyset \mid s^+ \mid s^- \mid g \cdot g \mid g + g \mid \overline{g}$$

An event guard can be regarded as a set of events that could trigger the guard. And $\overline{g}$ defines the set of all events that will not trigger guard g. The detailed meaning of these event guards is given in Table 1.

Table 1. The Meaning of Event Guards

$$[\![\epsilon]\!] =_{df} \mathbb{E} \quad [\![\emptyset]\!] =_{df} \emptyset \quad [\![s^+]\!] =_{df} \{e \mid (s, +) \in e \wedge e \in \mathbb{E}\}$$
$$[\![s^-]\!] =_{df} \{e \mid (s, -) \in e \wedge e \in \mathbb{E}\} \quad [\![g_1 + g_2]\!] =_{df} [\![g_1]\!] \cup [\![g_2]\!]$$
$$[\![g_1 \cdot g_2]\!] =_{df} \{e \mid e \in [\![g_1]\!] \wedge e \in [\![g_2]\!]\}$$
$$[\![\overline{g}]\!] =_{df} \{e \mid \forall f \in [\![g]\!] \bullet \neg \mathsf{compatible}(e, f)\}$$

After introducing the definition of event guards, we can define the triggering of an event guard by an event. If an event e can give rise to an event guard g, the event should be in the semantics set of the event guard, $e \in [\![g]\!]$.

Then we can define the order of guards depending on the event set of the guard. In this order, stronger guards are more difficult to be triggered.

Definition 2. *Given guards g_1 and g_2, we say guard g_1 is better than guard g_2 semantically if $[\![g_1]\!] \subseteq [\![g_2]\!]$. We denote this by $g_1 \geq g_2$.*

2.2 I-Calculus

Instantaneous reactions are used for modeling and programming the event-based synchronous languages. In this paper we only discuss conceptually instantaneous reactions like zero time reactions. The syntax of I-calculus is given as below:

$$I ::= !s \mid \Pi \mid \bot \mid g\&I \mid I\backslash s \mid I \parallel I$$

where $!s$ is an atomic action emitting signal s. Π is a skip reaction without doing anything. $\bot$ is a bad reaction which can only be generated by some conflict conditions. Generally, we do not allow a program contain $\bot$ directly because it is meaningless. That is to say $\bot$ is only used to represent the bad cases we are trying to avoid. And g is an event guard with the sense that in the component $g\&I$, I will only be executed when g is triggered. The function $ems(I)$ is defined to represent the set of signals which will be possibly emitted by I.

The meaning of the reactions is straightforward. The status of all signals can be sensed by all agents. $!s$ is an atomic action emitting a signal; Π is a skip reaction without doing anything and generally used to denote the termination status; $\bot$ indicates the reaction has caused conflict of some signal's status and generally used to denote the chaotic state; in reaction $g\&I$, if the guard g is triggered, the reaction will react like I, but if $\overline{g}$ is triggered, it will perform like Π, otherwise it will wait for the stable event of g. As an canceling reaction, $I\backslash s$ separates the actions on s between I and the outside event. $I_1 \parallel I_2$ represents the parallel reactions of I_1 and I_2. As mentioned before, all reactions in parallel interact with each other by the shared event.

Example 1. Let $I = s_2^+\&!s_1 \parallel (s_1^+ \cdot s_2^+)\&!s_3 \parallel s_1^-\&\bot$

Given an input event $e = \{s_2, +\}$, the guard s_2^+ will be triggered, and then s_1 will be emitted; immediately, the guard $s_1^+ \cdot s_2^+$ can be triggered; thus s_3 will be emitted. So, reaction I will react to the input event e by generating signal s_1 and s_3. But if $e = \{(s_1, -)\}$ is given as the input event, I will fall into chaos.

3 Operational Semantics

Operational semantics is used to define the meaning of computer programs. It can be expressed as a set of possible transitions which simulate the execution of programs. The transitions for I-Calculus are written in a special notation of structural operational semantics

$$C \longrightarrow C'$$

where C and C' are the two configurations describing the states of an executing mechanism before and after a step respectively. The formal definition of the configuration is as following. The structure of a configuration is written as $\langle I, e\rangle$ where I is a reaction and e is a special event recording the signal status for I.

Definition 3 (Configuration). *A configuration is an element of the cartesian product of the set of all reactions and the set of all events. Generally, we use* $\mathbb{I}$ *to represent the set of all reactions and use* E *to represent the set of all events. Then we get the definition of a configuration* C *as:*

$$C \in \mathbb{I} \times E.$$

Additionally, the chaos state $\langle \perp, e \rangle$ is also a configuration which is the worst situation of an execution for a reaction. And in this chaos state $\perp$ represents the chaos reaction. Before we define the transition rules, we give a set of definitions for our transition system.

Definition 4 ($\longrightarrow_*$). *The transition symbol* $\longrightarrow_*$ *in* $\langle I, e \rangle \longrightarrow_* \langle I', e' \rangle$ *means that the left configuration* $\langle I, e \rangle$ *turn into* $\langle I', e' \rangle$ *after zero or more transition steps within the transition rules in our operational semantics.*

As a property of transition, we have $e' \geq e$ for all transitions like $\langle I, e \rangle \longrightarrow_* \langle I', e' \rangle$.

Definition 5 (Stable Configuration). *A configuration* $\langle I, e \rangle$ *is stable in the status of signal* s *if for all* $e' \geq e$

$$\langle I, e' \rangle \longrightarrow_* \langle I', e'' \rangle \implies e(s) = e'(s) = e''(s).$$

In this case the configuration is denoted by $\langle I, e \rangle^s_{stable}$*. And if* $\langle I, e \rangle$ *is stable at the status of all signals, we denote it by* $\langle I, e \rangle_{stable}$*. Especially,* $\langle \Pi, e \rangle$ *is a stable state as well as a terminated state denoted by* $\langle \Pi, e \rangle_{term}$*. And* $\langle \perp, e \rangle$ *is not stable at any signals, so we denote it by* $\langle \perp, e \rangle_{chaos}$*.*

In the following subsections, we provide the operational semantics for our I-Calculus.

3.1 Primitives

(a) We can describe the configurations expressing the normal terminated state and chaos state as below:

$$\langle \Pi, e \rangle_{term}, \quad \langle \perp, e \rangle_{chaos}$$

The skip reaction just transforms a reaction into the terminated state which is regarded as the end of the execution for the reaction with the input event e. The chaos state indicates that the reaction has fallen into chaos which is the worst situation. Normally, a configuration needs a judgement step to determine its state. But for simplification, we sometimes bypass this step and mark the state of the configuration immediately in our transition systems.

(b) A process does an atomic action, emitting a signal:

$$\langle !s, e \rangle \longrightarrow \langle \perp, e \rangle, \text{ where } (s, -) \in e.$$
$$\langle !s, e \rangle \longrightarrow \langle \Pi, e' \rangle, \text{ where } (s, -) \notin e \text{ and } e' = e \oplus (s, +).$$

Emitting a signal is an atomic action of a reaction. The emitting of signal s will add $(s,+)$ to the given event e. We use $e \oplus (s,+)$ to represent $e \bigcup \{(s,+)\}$ for simplification. And this result event shows the way how the agent reacts to the environment. But if $(s,-)$ has already been in the given input event, the emitting action will lead to a conflict in the status of the signal. So we describe this situation as chaos.

3.2 Guarded Reactions

For a configuration $\langle g\&I, e\rangle$, we have the guarded transition as below:

$$\langle g\&I, e\rangle \longrightarrow \langle I,\ e\rangle,\ \text{if}\ e \in [\![g]\!]$$

$$\langle g\&I, e\rangle \longrightarrow \langle \Pi, e\rangle,\ \text{if}\ e \in [\![\overline{g}]\!]$$

where $e \in [\![g]\!]$ means that the input event e can satisfy the guard g. If the guard g is satisfied, the reaction after g would be executed. But if the opposite side of the guard g marked as $\overline{g}$ is satisfied by e, the g will never be satisfied by e. In this case, all the programs guarded by g will be skipped.

3.3 Parallel Reactions

The configuration of a parallel reaction is of the form

$$\langle I_1 || I_2, e\rangle$$

where I_1 and I_2 are two reactions with e as their common event.

(a) First of all, we introduce the following basic situations for parallel reactions:

$$\frac{\langle I_1, e\rangle_{term}}{\langle I_1 || I_2, e\rangle \longrightarrow \langle I_2, e\rangle}$$

$$\frac{\langle I_2, e\rangle_{term}}{\langle I_1 || I_2, e\rangle \longrightarrow \langle I_1, e\rangle}$$

$$\frac{\langle I_1, e\rangle_{chaos}}{\langle I_1 || I_2, e\rangle \longrightarrow \langle \bot, e\rangle_{chaos}}$$

$$\frac{\langle I_2, e\rangle_{chaos}}{\langle I_1 || I_2, e\rangle \longrightarrow \langle \bot, e\rangle_{chaos}}$$

These transition rules indicate that the operator $||$ has Π and $\bot$ as its zero and unit respectively.

(b) Then we describe the following transition rules for the parallel reactions in the two cases:

$$\frac{\langle I_1, e\rangle \longrightarrow \langle I_1', e'\rangle}{\langle I_1 || I_2, e\rangle \longrightarrow \langle I_1' || I_2, e'\rangle}$$

$$\frac{\langle I_2, e\rangle \longrightarrow \langle I_2', e'\rangle}{\langle I_1 || I_2, e\rangle \longrightarrow \langle I_1 || I_2', e'\rangle}$$

When two reactions are paralleled with a common event e, the parallel reaction will perform the component which could react to e. These two transition rules show the commutative property of the parallel operator and how two programs communicate with each other by sharing the common input event e and the output event e'. The following example shows how two components perform when both can be transited. Also this example shows that the transition order of the parallel components is irrelevant.

Example 2. $I = k^+\&!s \mid\mid !t\ I$ can react to the input event $e = \{(k, +)\}$ in two possible ways with the same output event.

$$\begin{aligned}
\langle k^+\&!s \mid\mid !t, e\rangle &\longrightarrow \langle !s \mid\mid !t, e_1\rangle, & e_1 &= \{(k+)\}\\
&\longrightarrow \langle \Pi \mid\mid !t, e_1\rangle, & e_1 &= \{(k+), (s, +)\}\\
&\longrightarrow \langle !t, e_1\rangle, & e_1 &= \{(k, +), (s, +)\}\\
&\longrightarrow \langle \Pi, e_1'\rangle_{term}, & e_1' &= \{(k, +), (s, +), (t, +)\}\\
\langle k^+\&!s \mid\mid !t, e\rangle &\longrightarrow \langle k^+\&!s \mid\mid \Pi, e_2\rangle, & e_2 &= \{(k, +), (t, +)\}\\
&\longrightarrow \langle k^+\&!s, e_2\rangle, & e_2 &= \{(k, +), (t, +)\}\\
&\longrightarrow \langle !s, e_2\rangle, & e_2 &= \{(k, +), (t, +)\}\\
&\longrightarrow \langle \Pi, e_2'\rangle_{term}, & e_2' &= \{(k, +), (s, +), (t, +)\}
\end{aligned}$$

3.4 Concealment

The configuration containing canceling operation is

$$\langle I \backslash s, e\rangle$$

in which s is a local signal to I. For all configurations like this, we can make the assumption that $s \notin sig(e)$ because we can rename s as t ($t \notin sig(e)$) in I if $s \in sig(e)$.

Then we have the transition rules for concealment:

$$\frac{\langle I, e\rangle \longrightarrow \langle \bot, e\rangle_{chaos}}{\langle I\backslash s, e\rangle \longrightarrow \langle \bot, e\rangle_{chaos}},$$

$$\frac{\langle I, e\rangle \longrightarrow \langle I', e'\rangle^s_{stable}}{\langle I\backslash s, e\rangle \longrightarrow \langle I[\bot/s^-, \epsilon/s^+, \Pi/!s], e\rangle}, \textit{ when } (s, +) \in e'$$

$$\frac{\langle I, e\rangle \longrightarrow \langle I', e'\rangle^s_{stable}}{\langle I\backslash s, e\rangle \longrightarrow \langle I[\bot/s^+, \epsilon/s^-], e'\rangle}, \textit{ when } (s, +) \notin e'$$

$$\frac{\langle I, e\rangle \longrightarrow \langle I', e'\rangle}{\langle I\backslash s, e\rangle \longrightarrow \langle I'\backslash s, e'\rangle}, \textit{ when } (s, +) \notin e'.$$

The first rule shows that the concealment operation on a chaos reaction will not change the chaos state. The second transition rule describes the action of emitting a local signal by the inner reaction. The emitting affects the inner components via replacing all s^+ in guard components and s^- by ϵ and $\bot$ respectively. Also, as the signal has been emitted, all the emitting action can be ignored via replacing $!s$ by Π. And we denote these replacements in I by $I[\bot/s^-, \epsilon/s^+, \Pi/!s]$. The third transition rule defines the opposite situation when the action of emitting the local signal does not exist. As the configuration $\langle I', e'\rangle^s_{stable}$ is stable at signal s and $(s, +)$ is not in e' currently, and s is a local signal whose status cannot be provided by the outside, in this situation we assign the absence value to the signal s. In order to be invisible to the outside, we make the replacement which replaces s^+ and s^- by $\bot$ and ϵ respectively. These replacements are denoted by $I[\bot/s^+, \epsilon/s^-]$.

These transition rules indicate that when the status of a local signal is determined, the label will be abandoned, the instances of the signal will be replaced by basic symbols like $\bot$, ϵ, Π. The last rule indicates that when we are not sure whether the result configuration is stable at the local signal, we should keep the concealment operator until we get a stable configuration. Here we give some examples to explain the rules for concealment.

Example 3. We give the following reactions to show how the concealment operator works.

$$\begin{aligned} I_1 &= (t^+\&!s \parallel s^+\&!k)\backslash s \\ I_2 &= (k^+\&!s)\backslash k \parallel t^+\&!k \\ I_3 &= (t^-\&!s \parallel s^+\&!k)\backslash t \\ I_4 &= (t^+\&!s \parallel s^+\&!k)\backslash t \end{aligned}$$

When the input event is $e = \{(t, +)\}$, the transition can be as following.

$$\begin{aligned}
\langle I_1, e\rangle &\longrightarrow \langle (!s \parallel s^+\&!k)\backslash s,\ \{(t,+)\}\rangle \\
&\longrightarrow \langle !k,\ \{(t,+)\}\rangle \\
&\longrightarrow \langle \Pi,\ \{(k,+),(t,+)\}\rangle_{term} \\
\langle I_2,\ e\rangle &\longrightarrow \langle (k^+\&!s)\backslash k \parallel !k,\ \{(t,+)\}\rangle \\
&\longrightarrow \langle (k^+\&!s)\backslash k,\ \{(k,+),(t,+)\}\rangle \\
&\quad \textit{as } k \notin ems(k^+\&!s), \textit{we have } \forall e_0 \bullet \langle k^+\&!s\rangle^k_{stable}, \textit{ then we have} \\
&\longrightarrow \langle \Pi,\ \{(k,+),(t,+)\}\rangle_{term} \\
\langle I_3,\ e\rangle &\longrightarrow \langle !s \parallel s^+\&!k,\ \{(t,+)\}\rangle \\
&\longrightarrow \langle \Pi \parallel s^+\&!k,\ \{(s,+),(t,+)\}\rangle \\
&\longrightarrow \langle s^+\&!k,\ \{(s,+),(t,+)\}\rangle \\
&\longrightarrow \langle !k,\ \{(s,+),(t,+)\}\rangle \\
&\longrightarrow \langle \Pi,\ \{(k,+),(s,+),(t,+)\}\rangle_{term} \\
\langle I_4,\ e\rangle &\longrightarrow \langle \Pi \parallel s^+\&!k,\ \{(t,+)\}\rangle \\
&\longrightarrow \langle s^+\&!k,\ \{(t,+)\}\rangle
\end{aligned}$$

4 Algebraic Laws and Its Soundness

In this section, we study the algebraic laws for I-calculus. Firstly, we give the concept of the equivalence of two reactions via operational semantics. The correctness of our algebraic laws is based on the equivalence of their reactions.

Definition 6. *The equivalence of two reactions is denoted by $I_1 =_O I_2$. The equivalence means that for any e we have*

$$\langle I_1, e\rangle \longrightarrow_* \langle \Pi, e'\rangle_{term} \iff \langle I_2, e\rangle \longrightarrow_* \langle \Pi, e'\rangle_{term},$$

$$or\ \langle I_1, e\rangle \longrightarrow_* \langle \bot, e_1\rangle_{chaos} \iff \langle I_2, e\rangle \longrightarrow_* \langle \bot, e_2\rangle_{chaos}$$

From the definition above, we know that when we say two reactions are equal, we mean that they have the same termination condition and the same chaos condition. Obviously we can obtain the laws which reflect the reflexivity, commutativity and transitivety of the equivalence of reactions.

Equiv-1 $I =_O I$ *(reflexivity)*
Equiv-2 $I_1 =_O I_2 \iff I_2 =_O I_1$ *(commutativity)*
Equiv-3 $\exists I_2 \bullet I_1 =_O I_2 \wedge I_2 =_O I_3 \iff I_1 =_O I_3$ *(transitivity)*

The algebraic laws of I-calculus can be classified into several groups. And among which, the correctness of the laws for parallel, primitives, concealment and dependence are palpable. So, in the following paragraphs we list all the laws and give proof for some representative laws. The proofs for some other laws are provided in the appendix.

The following laws show that the parallel operator is commutative, associative and idempotent. And Π and $\bot$ are the unit reaction and the zero reaction for parallel respectively.

Par-1 $I_1 \parallel I_2 =_O I_2 \parallel I_1$
Par-2 $(I_1 \parallel I_2) \parallel I_3 =_O I_1 \parallel (I_2 \parallel I_3)$
Par-3 $I \parallel I =_O I$
Par-4 $\bot \parallel I =_O \bot$
Par-5 $\Pi \parallel I =_O I$

The following laws for guards are established in our operational semantics.

Guard-1 $g_1\&(g_2\&I) =_O (g_1 \cdot g_2)\&I$
Guard-2 $g_1\&I \parallel g_2\&I =_O (g_1 + g_2)\&I$
Guard-3 $g\&(I_1 \parallel I_2) =_O g\&I_1 \parallel g\&I_2$
Guard-4 $\emptyset\&I =_O \Pi$
Guard-5 $\epsilon\&I =_O I$
Guard-6 $g\&\Pi =_O \Pi$

The laws for guards are very important in algebraic semantics. We give the proof for law guard-1 and the other proofs are provided in the appendix.

Guard-1 $g_1\&(g_2\&I) =_O (g_1 \cdot g_2)\&I$

Proof. First of all, we can prove that the chaos conditions for both reactions are the same, i.e., $e \in [\![g_1]\!] \wedge e \in [\![g_2]\!] \wedge \exists s \in ems(I) \bullet (s, -) \in e$ where e is the input event. Then we can give the proof regardless of chaos.

1. For any e, if we have the transition

$$\langle g_1\&(g_2\&I), e\rangle \longrightarrow_* \langle \Pi, e'\rangle_{term}$$

if all guards for I can be fired, we can find an intermediate state $\langle I, e\rangle$ that

$$\langle g_1\&(g_2\&I), e\rangle \longrightarrow_* \langle I, e\rangle \longrightarrow_* \langle \Pi, e'\rangle_{term},$$

where $e \in [\![g_1]\!]$ and $e \in [\![g_2]\!]$ from which we have $e \in [\![g_1 \cdot g_2]\!]$. So for the second reaction, we have

$$\langle (g_1 \cdot g_2)\&I, e\rangle \longrightarrow_* \langle I, e\rangle \text{ and } \langle I, e\rangle \longrightarrow_* \langle \Pi, e'\rangle_{term}.$$

if the negation of the guards for I can be fired, we can find that $e = e'$ and either $e \in [\![\overline{g_1}]\!]$ or $e \in [\![\overline{g_2}]\!]$ which implies that $e \in [\![\overline{g_1 \cdot g_2}]\!]$, then we have

$$\langle (g_1 \cdot g_2)\&I, e\rangle \longrightarrow \langle \phi\&I, e\rangle \longrightarrow \langle \Pi, e\rangle_{term}$$

Then we have proved that for any e,

$$\langle g_1\&(g_2\&I), e\rangle \longrightarrow_* \langle \epsilon, e'\rangle_{term} \Longrightarrow \langle (g_1 \cdot g_2)\&I, e\rangle \longrightarrow_* \langle \Pi, e'\rangle_{term}.$$

2. For any e, if we have the transition

$$\langle (g_1 \cdot g_2)\&I, e\rangle \longrightarrow_* \langle \Pi, e'\rangle_{term},$$

if all guards for I can be fired, we can find an intermediate state $\langle I, e\rangle$ that

$$\langle (g_1 \cdot g_2)\&I, e\rangle \longrightarrow_* \langle I, e\rangle \longrightarrow_* \langle \Pi, e'\rangle_{term}$$

where $e \in [\![g_1 \cdot g_2]\!]$ from which we have $e \in [\![g_1]\!]$ and $e \in [\![g_2]\!]$. So for the first reaction, we have

$$\langle g_1\&(g_2\&I), e\rangle \longrightarrow_* \langle I, e\rangle \text{ and } \langle I, e\rangle \longrightarrow_* \langle \Pi, e'\rangle_{term}.$$

if the negation of the guards for I can be fired, we can find that $e = e'$ and $e \in [\![\overline{g_1 \cdot g_2}]\!]$ which implies that either $e \in [\![\overline{g_1}]\!]$ or $e \in [\![\overline{g_2}]\!]$, then we have

$$\langle g_1\&(g_2\&I), e\rangle \longrightarrow \langle \phi\&(g_2\&I), e\rangle \longrightarrow \langle \Pi, e\rangle_{term}, \text{ or}$$

$$\langle g_1\&(g_2\&I), e\rangle \longrightarrow \langle g_1\&(\phi\&I), e\rangle \longrightarrow \langle g_1\&\Pi, e\rangle \longrightarrow_* \langle \Pi, e\rangle_{term}.$$

Then we have proved that for any e,

$$\langle (g_1 \cdot g_2)\&I, e\rangle \longrightarrow_* \langle \Pi, e'\rangle_{term} \Longrightarrow \langle g_1\&(g_2\&I), e\rangle \longrightarrow_* \langle \Pi, e'\rangle_{term}.$$

□

Now we study the algebraic laws for the concealment operator.

Conc-1 $(I\backslash s)\backslash t =_O (I\backslash t)\backslash s$

Conc-2 $(I_1 \parallel I_2)\backslash s =_O (I_1\backslash s) \parallel I_2$, provided that $s \notin I_2$

Conc-3 $(g\&I)\backslash s =_O g\&(I\backslash s)$, provided that $s \notin g$

Conc-4 $(g\&!s \parallel I)\backslash s =_O I[g/s^+, \overline{g}/s^-]$, provided that $s \notin g \wedge s \notin ems(I)$

We now list some laws for primitive commands. The reaction $s^-\&!s$ behaves like $\bot$ when s^- is triggered because it will violate the status of signal s. And the reaction $s^+\&!s$ behaves like Π because the emission of s will not change the status of s.

Prim-1 $s^-\&!s =_O s^-\&\bot$

Prim-2 $s^+\&!s =_O s^+\&\Pi$

The dependency law below shows how to expose the internal dependency explicitly in algebraic semantics. The proof can be found in the appendix.

Depend-axiom $g\&!s \parallel s^+\&I \quad =_O g\&!s \parallel (s^+ + g)\&I$

After all laws have been established in our framework of operational semantics, we can claim the soundness of algebraic semantics.

Theorem 1 (Soundness). *If two reactions are algebraically equivalent, they are also equivalent with the respect to the operational semantics.*

$$I_1 = I_2 \Longrightarrow I_1 =_O I_2$$

5 The Relative Completeness of Algebraic Semantics

In section 4, we have proved that the algebraic laws are established in the framework of our operational semantics. And in this section, we come to prove that reactions which are equivalent from the operational perspective should be algebraically equivalent. And thus we can prove the relative completeness of algebraic semantics with respect to the operational semantics.

In [1], the normal form for I-calculus has been proposed. From the algebraic aspect, the normal form provides a way to investigate the equivalence of two reactions. The equivalence of two reactions depends on the equivalence of their normal forms which can be reduced by the algebraic laws. In the normal form, all parallel sub-reactions can react to the environment signals simultaneously because they are all free of dependency.

Definition 7 (Normal Form). *The reaction $\parallel_{m\in M} g_m\&!s_m \parallel h\&\bot$ is a normal form for I-calculus if it satisfies the two conditions below, where the index set M is finite and all signals $s_i (i \in M)$ are different.*

1. $\forall m, n \in M, g \bullet (g \cdot s_n^+ \geq g_m \Rightarrow g \cdot g_n \geq g_m) \wedge (g \cdot s_n^+ \geq h \Rightarrow g \cdot g_n \geq h)$.
2. $\forall m \in M, g_m \cdot s_m^- \geq h \geq g_m$.

Example 4. Here we give an example of normal form.

$$NF = (s_1^- + s_2^+ + s_3^+)\&!s_1 \parallel (s_1^- + s_2^+ \cdot s_3^-)\&!s_2$$
$$\parallel (s_1^- + s_2^+)\&!s_3 \parallel (s_1^- + s_2^+ \cdot s_3^-)\&\bot$$

Obviously, two reactions in normal form are behaviorally equivalent if they have the same algebraic norm form. The following definition captures the intuition.

Definition 8. *$NF_1 = NF_2$ iff $h \equiv h'$ and $\forall i \in M \bullet g_i \equiv g_i'$, where $NF_1 = \parallel_{m \in M} g_m\&!s_m \parallel h\&\bot$ and $NF_2 = \parallel_{m \in M} g_m'\&!s_m \parallel h'\&\bot$ are normal forms.*

Theorem 2. *All instantaneous reactions can be reduced into normal forms.*

Theorem 2 indicates that every instantaneous reaction, however deeply structured, can be reduced into the normal form by a series of algebraic manipulation. The proof can be found in [1]. We can get a corollary from this theorem.

Corollary 1. *$I_1 = I_2$ iff $NF_1 = NF_2$, where NF_1 and NF_2 are the normal forms of reaction I_1 and I_2 respectively.*

Lemma 1. *$I_1 =_O I_2 \Longrightarrow NF_1 = NF_2$ where NF_1 and NF_2 are the normal form of reaction I_1 and I_2 respectively.*

Proof. We can make the assumption

$$NF_1 = \parallel_{m \in M} g_m\&!s_m \parallel h\&\bot$$

$$NF_2 = \parallel_{m \in M} g_m'\&!s_m \parallel h'\&\bot$$

Obviously we obtain that $NF_1 =_O I_1 =_O I_2 =_O NF_2$. When we have $NF_1 =_O NF_2$, we can get $h = h'$ which means that the chaos condition for NF_1 and NF_2 is the same. Then if we want to prove $NF_1 = NF_2$, we need to prove $\forall m \in M \bullet g_m \equiv g_m'$.

If we make the hypothesis that $\exists m \in M \bullet g_m \not\equiv g_m'$, there should be an event e that

$$e \in [\![g_m]\!] \wedge e \notin [\![g_m']\!] \vee e \in [\![g_m']\!] \wedge e \notin [\![g_m]\!]$$

We assume that there exists an input event e satisfying $e \in [\![g_m]\!] \wedge e \notin [\![g_m']\!]$. As $NF_1 =_O NF_2$, they will react to e with a same output event e'. We can obtain that $e \neq \bot$ or else we have $e \in [\![h']\!] \subseteq [\![g_m']\!]$. Also we have $(s_m, +) \in e'$ as we know that $e \in [\![g_m]\!]$. But we also assumed that $e \notin [\![g_m']\!]$ and have just deduced that $e \in [\![g_m']\!]$ which leads to a contradiction. So the assumption is incorrect, that is to say there is no event e satisfying $e \in [\![g_m]\!] \wedge e \notin [\![g_m']\!]$

Similarly, we can prove that there is no event e satisfying $e \in [\![g_m']\!] \wedge e \notin [\![g_m]\!]$. So the hypothesis is invalid and we have $\forall m \in M \bullet g_m \equiv g_m'$ Then we have $NF_1 = NF_2$. □

Based on the discuss above, we have proved lemma 1, $I_1 =_O I_2 \Longrightarrow NF_1 = NF_2$ and then we can obtain the relative completeness of algebraic semantics.

Theorem 3 (Relative Completeness). *If two reactions are equivalent from the operational perspective, they are also algebraically equivalent.*

$$I_1 =_O I_2 \Longrightarrow I_1 = I_2$$

Finally, by proving theorem 2 and theorem 3, we have established the linking theory of our operational semantics and the algebraic semantics.

Theorem 4. *Two reactions are equivalent from the operational perspective if and only if they are algebraically equivalent.*

$$I_1 =_O I_2 \Longleftrightarrow I_1 = I_2$$

The following example shows how two equal reactions react to the given event.

Example 5. Here are two different reactions.

$$\begin{aligned} I_1 &= (s_1^- \&!t \mid\mid t^+ \&!s_2)\backslash t \mid\mid s_2^+ \&!s_3 \mid\mid s_3^+ \&!s_1 \\ I_2 &= (s_1^- + s_2^+ + s_3^+)\&!s_1 \mid\mid (s_1^- + s_2^+ \cdot s_3^-)\&!s_2 \\ &\quad \mid\mid (s_1^- + s_2^+)\&!s_3 \mid\mid (s_1^- + s_2^+ \cdot s_3^-)\&\bot \end{aligned}$$

From the definition of normal form, we obtain that I_2 is a normal form. And from the algebraic laws, we can reduce the first reaction I_1 to I_2.

$$\begin{aligned} I_1 &= (s_1^- \&!t \mid\mid t^+ \&!s_2)\backslash t \mid\mid s_2^+ \&!s_3 \mid\mid s_3^+ \&!s_1 && \{depend-axiom\} \\ &= (s_1^- \&!t \mid\mid (s_1^- + t^+)\&!s_2)\backslash t \mid\mid s_2^+ \&!s_3 \mid\mid s_3^+ \&!s_1 && \{conc-4\} \\ &= s_1^- \&!s_2 \mid\mid s_2^+ \&!s_3 \mid\mid s_3^+ \&!s_1 && \{depend-1\} \\ &= s_1^- \&!s_2 \mid\mid (s_1^- + s_2^+)\&!s_3 \mid\mid s_3^+ \&!s_1 && \{depend-2\} \\ &= (s_1^-)\&!s_2 \mid\mid (s_1^- + s_2^+)\&!s_3 \mid\mid (s_1^- + s_2^+ + s_3^+)\&!s_1 && \{guard-2,3,4\} \\ &= (s_1^-)\&!s_2 \mid\mid (s_1^- + s_2^+)\&!s_3 \mid\mid (s_1^- + s_2^+ + s_3^+)\&!s_1 \\ &\quad \mid\mid (s_1^- + s_2^+ \cdot s_3^-)\&\bot && \{guard-2\} \\ &= (s_1^- + s_2^+ + s_3^+)\&!s_1 \mid\mid (s_1^- + s_2^+ \cdot s_3^-)\&!s_2 \\ &\quad \mid\mid (s_1^- + s_2^+)\&!s_3 \mid\mid (s_1^- + s_2^+ \cdot s_3^-)\&\bot \\ &= I_2 \end{aligned}$$

From these reducing steps we obtain that I_1 and I_2 are equal algebraically, $I_1 = I_2$. Then we give the transitions of these two reactions with the same input e to show that they are also equal in our operational semantics.

When the input e consists $(s_2, +)$ *and* $(s_3, -)$ or just consists $(s_1, -)$, both reactions will be terminated in chaos. We give the example transitions with the input event $e = \{(s_1, -)\}$.

$$\begin{aligned}
\langle I_2, e\rangle &\longrightarrow \langle \bot, e\rangle_{term}\\
\langle I_1, e\rangle &\longrightarrow \langle (!t \parallel t^+\&!s_2)\backslash t \parallel s_2^+\&!s_3 \parallel s_3^+\&!s_1, \{(s_1,-)\}\rangle\\
&\longrightarrow \langle !s_2 \parallel s_2^+\&!s_3 \parallel s_3^+\&!s_1, \{(s_1,-)\}\rangle\\
&\longrightarrow \langle s_2^+\&!s_3 \parallel s_3^+\&!s_1, \{(s_1,-),(s_2,+)\}\rangle\\
&\longrightarrow \langle !s_3 \parallel s_3^+\&!s_1, \{(s_1,-),(s_2,+)\}\rangle\\
&\longrightarrow \langle s_3^+\&!s_1, \{(s_1,-),(s_2,+),(s_3,+)\}\rangle\\
&\longrightarrow \langle !s_1, \{(s_1,-),(s_2,+),(s_3,+)\}\rangle\\
&\longrightarrow \langle \bot, e\rangle_{term}
\end{aligned}$$

When the input e consists $(s_2, +)$ and does not consist$(s_1, -)$, $(s_2, -)$ and $(s_3, -)$, both reactions will be terminated in $\langle \Pi, \{(s_1,+),(s_2,+),(s_3,+)\}\rangle_{term}$. We give the example transitions when $e = \{(s_2, +)\}$.

$$\begin{aligned}
\langle I_2, e\rangle &\to \langle !s_1 \parallel (s_1^- + s_2^+ \cdot s_3^-)\&!s_2 \parallel !s_3 \parallel (s_1^- + s_2^+ \cdot s_3^-)\&\bot, \{(s_2,+)\}\rangle\\
&\to \langle (s_1^- + s_2^+ \cdot s_3^-)\&!s_2 \| !s_3 \| (s_1^- + s_2^+ \cdot s_3^-)\&\bot, \{(s_1,+),(s_2,+)\}\rangle\\
&\to \langle (s_1^- + s_2^+ \cdot s_3^-)\&!s_2 \| (s_1^- + s_2^+ \cdot s_3^-)\&\bot, \{(s_1,+),(s_2,+),(s_3,+)\}\rangle\\
&\to \langle \Pi, \{(s_1,+),(s_2,+),(s_3,+)\}\rangle_{term}\\
\langle I_1, e\rangle &\longrightarrow \langle (s_1^-\&!t \parallel t^+\&!s_2)\backslash t \parallel !s_3 \parallel s_3^+\&!s_1, \{(s_2,+)\}\rangle\\
&\longrightarrow \langle (s_1^-\&!t \parallel t^+\&!s_2)\backslash t \parallel s_3^+\&!s_1, \{(s_2,+),(s_3,+)\}\rangle\\
&\longrightarrow \langle (s_1^-\&!t \parallel t^+\&!s_2)\backslash t \parallel !s_1, \{(s_2,+),(s_3,+)\}\rangle\\
&\longrightarrow \langle (s_1^-\&!t \parallel t^+\&!s_2)\backslash t, \{(s_1,-),(s_2,+),(s_3,+)\}\rangle\\
&\longrightarrow \langle (t^+\&!s_2)\backslash t, \{(s_1,-),(s_2,+),(s_3,+)\}\rangle\\
&\longrightarrow \langle (\Pi)\backslash t, \{(s_1,-),(s_2,+),(s_3,+)\}\rangle\\
&\longrightarrow \langle \Pi, \{(s_1,-),(s_2,+),(s_3,+)\}\rangle_{term}.
\end{aligned}$$

From the above two parts of transitions, we find that I_1 and I_2 are also equivalent with respect to the operational semantics, $I_1 =_O I_2$.

6 Conclusion

In this paper, we have investigated the semantics for instantaneous reactions from an operational perspective. We have explored a structural operational semantics for instantaneous signal calculus, which exhibits the effect of how reactions react to the environment. Further, we have investigated the linking theory of operational semantics and algebraic semantics for instantaneous reactions. On one hand, all the algebraic laws concerning the distinct features for instantaneous reactions can be established in terms of the suggested structural operational semantics, i.e., if the equality of two differently written instantaneous reactions is algebraically provable, the two reactions are also equivalent with respect to the operational semantics. Thus we have claimed the soundness of algebraic semantics in [1]. On the other hand, reactions which are equivalent from the operational perspective can be reduced to the same normal form and thus we have demonstrated the relative completeness of algebraic semantics with respect to the operational semantics.

In the future, we will take sequential reaction and time-delayed reactions into our consideration to complete the operational semantics for the instantaneous calculus. We are also trying to use the Rewriting system Maude [19,20] to link the operational semantics for Instantaneous Calculus.

Acknowledgement. This work is supported by National Basic Research Program of China (No. 2011CB302904), National High Technology Research and Development Program of China (No. 2011AA010101 and No. 2012AA011205), National Natural Science Foundation of China (No. 61061130541 and No. 61021004), and Shanghai Leading Academic Discipline Project (No. B412).

References

1. Zhao, Y., Jifeng, H.: Towards a Signal Calculus for Event-Based Synchronous Languages. In: Qin, S., Qiu, Z. (eds.) ICFEM 2011. LNCS, vol. 6991, pp. 1–13. Springer, Heidelberg (2011)
2. Berry, G., Gonthier, G.: The Esterel synchronous programming language: Design, semantics, implementation. Science of Computer Programming (SCP) 19(2), 87–152 (1992)
3. Berry, G.: The Constructive Semantics of Pure Esterel, Draft version (1999), `ftp://ftp-sop.inria.fr/meije/esterel/papers/constructiveness3.ps.gz`
4. Tini, S.: Structural Operational Semantics for Synchronous Languages. PhD thesis, Dipartimento di Informaticá, Universita degli Studi di Pisa, Pisa, Italy (2000)
5. Potop-Butucaru, D., Edwards, S.A., Berry, G.: Compiling Esterel, pp. I–XXI, 1–335. Springer (2007)
6. Shyamasundar, R.K., Ramesh, S.: Real Time Programming: Languages, Specification and Verifcations. World Scientific Publishing (2009)
7. Mousavi, M.: Causality in the Semantics of Esterel: Revisited. Electronic Proceedings in Theoretical Computer Science 18, 32–45 (2010)
8. Alur, R., Dill, D.L.: Automata for Modeling Real-time Systems. In: Paterson, M. (ed.) ICALP 1990. LNCS, vol. 443, pp. 322–335. Springer, Heidelberg (1990)
9. Alur, R., Dill, D.L.: A theory of timed automata. Theoretical Computer Science 126(2), 183–235 (1994)
10. Behrmann, G., David, A., Larson, K.G.: A tutorial on UPPAAL. In: International School on Formal Methods for the Design of Computer, Communication, and Software Systems (2004)
11. Berry, G.: The foundations of Esterel. In: Proof, Language, and Interaction, Essays in Honour of Robin Milner, pp. 425–454. The MIT Press (2000)
12. Boussinot, F.: Reactive C: An extension of C to program reactive systems. Software Practice Experience 21(4), 401–428 (1991)

13. He, J.: From CSP to hybrid systems. In: Roscure, A.W. (ed.) A Classical Mind, Essays in Honour of C.A.R. Hoare, pp. 171–189. Prentice-Hall International (1994)
14. Hopcroft, J.E., Ullman, J.D.: Introduction to Automata Theory, Languages and Compution. Addison-Wesley (1979)
15. Nicollin, X., Sifakis, J.: The algebra of timed processes, ATP: Theory and application. Inf. Comput. 114(1), 131–178 (1994)
16. Reed, G.M., Roscoe, A.W.: A Timed Model for Communicating Sequential Processes. In: Kott, L. (ed.) ICALP 1986. LNCS, vol. 226, pp. 314–323. Springer, Heidelberg (1986)
17. Reed, G.M., Roscoe, A.W.: The timed failures-stablity model for CSP. Theor. Comput. Sci. 211(1-2), 85–127 (1999)
18. Yovine, S.: Kronos: A verification tool for real-time systems. STTT 1(1-2), 123–133 (1997)
19. Clavel, M., Durán, F., Eker, S., Lincoln, P., Martí-Oliet, N., Meseguer, J., Talcott, C.: The Maude 2.0 System. In: Nieuwenhuis, R. (ed.) RTA 2003. LNCS, vol. 2706, pp. 76–87. Springer, Heidelberg (2003)
20. Clavel, M., Durán, F.F., Eker, S., Lincoln, P., Martí-Oliet, N., Meseguer, J., Talcott, C.: Maude Manual (Version 2.6) (January 2011)

Appendix

Firstly, we give the following lemma and its proof before we come to prove other laws.

Lemma 2. $g\&I \parallel I =_O I$

Proof. Obviously, the chaos conditions for both program are the same, i.e., $(s,-) \in e \ \wedge \ s \in ems(I)$ where e is the input event. Then, we consider the normal termination situations.

1. For all input event e, if we have

$$\langle I, e\rangle \longrightarrow_* \langle \Pi, e'\rangle_{term}$$

then we can have

$$\langle g\&I \parallel I, e\rangle \longrightarrow_* \langle g\&I \parallel \Pi, e'\rangle_{stable} \longrightarrow \langle \Pi, e'\rangle_{term}$$

2. For all input event e, if we have

$$\langle g\&I \parallel I, e\rangle \longrightarrow_* \langle \Pi, e'\rangle_{term}$$

then we can find an intermediate configuration $\langle g\&I \parallel \Pi, e'\rangle_{stable}$ that,

$$\langle g\&I \parallel I, e\rangle \longrightarrow_* \langle g\&I \parallel \Pi, e'\rangle_{stable} \longrightarrow \langle \Pi, e'\rangle_{term}$$

Therefore, we can get

$$\langle I, e\rangle \longrightarrow_* \langle \Pi, e'\rangle_{term}$$

□

Based on the aboves, we have proved that Lemma 2 is true. Now we come to prove the law of Guard-2.

Guard-2. $g_1\&I \parallel g_2\&I =_O (g_1 + g_2)\&I$

Proof. It's easy to find that the chaos conditions are the same. So we mainly focus on the proof regardless of chaos.

For any e, if we have the transition

$$\langle (g_1 + g_2)\&I, e\rangle \longrightarrow_* \langle \Pi, e'\rangle_{term},$$

if the guard for I can be fired, we can have $e \in [\![g_1 + g_2]\!]$. And we can give an intermediate configuration $\langle I, e\rangle$ that

$$\langle (g_1 + g_2)\&I, e\rangle \longrightarrow_* \langle I, e\rangle \longrightarrow_* \langle \Pi, e'\rangle_{term}$$

For simplification, we assume that $e \in [\![g_2]\!]$. Then we have the transition

$$\langle g_1\&I \parallel g_2\&I, e\rangle \longrightarrow \langle\ g_1\&I \parallel I, e\rangle \longrightarrow \langle I, e\rangle \longrightarrow_* \langle \Pi, e'\rangle_{term}$$

if the negation of the guard for I can be fired, we can have $e = e'$ and $e \in [\![\ \overline{g_1 + g_2}\ ]\!]$ which implies that $e \in [\![\overline{g_1}]\!]$ and $e \in [\![\overline{g_2}]\!]$, then we have

$$\langle g_1\&I \parallel g_2\&I, e\rangle \longrightarrow_* \langle\ \phi\&I \parallel \phi\&I, e\rangle \longrightarrow_* \langle \Pi \parallel \Pi, e\rangle \longrightarrow \langle \Pi, e\rangle_{term}$$

For the other side, the proof is just similar. Therefore, we have proved that guard-3 is true in our operational semantics. □

Guard-3. $g\&(I_1 \parallel I_2) =_O g\&I_1 \parallel g\&I_2$

Proof. Similar to the proof of Guard-2, the chaos conditions for each program are the same which can be expressed as $e \in [\![g]\!] \wedge (s, -) \in e \wedge \exists s \bullet (s \in ems(I_1) \vee s \in ems(I_2))$ with a given event e. Then we prove the equivalence of the normal termination conditions.

1. For any e we have the implementation

   $$\langle g\&(I_1 \parallel I_2), e\rangle \longrightarrow_* \langle \Pi, e\rangle \Longrightarrow e \in [\![g]\!].$$

   Hence, if the guard of $I_1 \parallel I_2$ can be fired we can find an intermediate state $\langle I_1 \parallel I_2, e\rangle$ of the transition.

   $$\langle g\&I_1 \parallel g\&I_2\rangle \longrightarrow_* \langle I_1 \parallel I_2, e\rangle \longrightarrow_* \langle \Pi, e'\rangle$$

   Therefore, we get the transition

   $$\langle g\&I_1 \| g\&I_2\rangle \longrightarrow_* \langle \Pi, e'\rangle.$$

   if the negation of the guard for $I_1 \| I_2$ can be fired, we can have $e = e'$ and $e \in [\![\overline{g}]\!]$, then we have

   $$\langle g\&I_1 \parallel g\&I_2\rangle \longrightarrow_* \langle \Pi \parallel \Pi, e\rangle \longrightarrow_* \langle \Pi, e\rangle$$

2. For any e we have the implementation

$$\langle g\&I_1 \parallel g\&I_2, e\rangle \longrightarrow_* \langle \Pi, e\rangle \Longrightarrow e \in [\![g]\!].$$

Hence, if the guards for I_1 and I_2 can be fired, we can find an intermediate state $\langle I_1 \parallel I_2, e\rangle$ of the transition.

$$\langle g\&(I_1 \parallel I_2), e\rangle \longrightarrow_* \langle I_1 \parallel I_2, e\rangle \longrightarrow_* \langle \Pi, e'\rangle$$

if the negation of the guards for I_1 and I_2 can be fired, we can find $e = e'$ and $e \in [\![\overline{g}]\!]$, then we have

$$\langle g\&(I_1 \parallel I_2), e\rangle \longrightarrow \langle \phi\&(I_1 \parallel I_2), e\rangle \longrightarrow \langle \Pi, e\rangle$$

Therefore, we get the transition

$$\langle g\&(I_1 \parallel I_2), e\rangle \longrightarrow_* \langle \Pi, e'\rangle.$$

Finally we have proved that guard-3 is correct in our operational semantics. □

For other guard related laws like guard-4 ($\emptyset\&I = \Pi$), guard-5 ($\epsilon\&I = I$) and guard-6 ($g\&\Pi = \Pi$), their proofs are similar.

Depend-Axiom. $g\&!s \parallel s^+\&I \;=_O\; g\&!s \parallel (s^+ + g)\&I$

Proof. Obviously, the chaos condition events for both reactions are the same, i.e., $e \in [\![g]\!] \wedge (s,-) \in e$ or $((s,+) \in e \;\vee\; e \in [\![g]\!]) \;\wedge\; \exists t \in ems(I) \bullet (t,-) \in e$. Therefore, we mainly focus on the proof based on the termination conditions. Also, if the negation of the guard for $!s$ can be fired, we can easily find that

$$g\&!s \parallel s^+\&I \;=_O s^+\&I =_O (s^+ + g)\&I =_O\; g\&!s \parallel (s^+ + g)\&I$$

then we come to consider the situation when the guard for $!s$ can be fired.

1. For any e, we have the implementation

$$\langle g\&!s \parallel s^+\&I, e\rangle \longrightarrow \langle \Pi, e'\rangle_{term} \Longrightarrow e \in [\![g]\!] \vee (s,+) \in e$$

   Then we can have $e \in [\![s^+ + g]\!]$ and then get the transition

$$\langle g\&!s \parallel (s^+ + g)\&I, e\rangle \longrightarrow \langle \Pi, e'\rangle$$

2. For any e, we have the implementation

$$\langle g\&!s \parallel (s^+ + g)\&I, e\rangle \longrightarrow \langle \Pi, e'\rangle_{term} \Longrightarrow e \in [\![s^+ + g]\!]$$

   Then we can have $e \in [\![g]\!] \vee (s,+) \in e$ and then get the transition

$$\langle g\&!s \parallel s^+\&I, e\rangle \longrightarrow \langle \Pi, e'\rangle$$

Based on the above parts, we have proved that the law of depend-axiom is true in our operational semantics. □

Higher-Order UTP for a Theory of Methods

Frank Zeyda and Ana Cavalcanti

University of York, Deramore Lane, York, YO10 5GH, UK
{frank.zeyda,ana.cavalcanti}@york.ac.uk

Abstract. Higher-order programming admits the view of programs as values and has been shown useful to give a semantics to object-oriented languages. In building a UTP theory for object-orientation, one faces four major challenges: consistency of the program model, redefinition of methods in subclasses, recursion and mutual recursion, and simplicity. In this paper, we discuss how the UTP treatment of higher-order programs impacts on these issues and propose solutions to emerging problems. Our solutions give rise to a novel UTP theory of methods.

Keywords: object-orientation, semantics, recursion, consistency.

1 Introduction

Higher-order programming is a paradigm that admits programs as values. Using the notation $\{\!|p|\!\}$ for the program value p, $\mathbf{var}\, m \bullet m := \{\!|x := x + 1|\!\}\ ;\ \mathbf{call}\, m$, for instance, is equivalent to the program $x := x + 1$. Thus, the local variable m holds a program value whereas x is an integer variable. Generally, we have that $\mathbf{call}\, \{\!|p|\!\}$ is equivalent to p, hence $\mathbf{call}\, \_$ can be regarded as the inverse of $\{\!|\_|\!\}$.

Higher-order programming has many useful applications and is prevalent in guise in many modern programming languages. An extensive semantic account based on predicate transformers is given in [9,10]. Our motivation is to reason about object-oriented programs: we take method definitions as assignments to program-valued variables that can be updated by method redefinitions.

There are a number of challenges in defining a comprehensive semantics of an object-oriented language and reasoning about object-oriented programs. Many of these have been addressed, for example, in [8,1,6,14]. Our objective in this paper is, however, not to present a comprehensive model for object-orientation but complement existing and on-going research efforts by presenting practical solutions to issues arising from the modelling and redefinition of class methods.

In [7], Hoare and He examine the integration of higher-order predicates into the Unifying Theories of Programming (UTP) framework. This includes the treatment of programs as values as well as procedures with parameters. A program value is said "to range over predicates, or rather some subset of predicates (or programs)". The word 'program' is used in the UTP sense here, thus referring to a predicate that is constructed from a syntactic (program) expression.

To build on such a theory to reason about (object-oriented) programs, we face four major challenges. The first is a consistent account of the notion of program value. Program values are used to specify the behaviour of methods.

B. Wolff, M.-C. Gaudel, A. Feliachi (Eds.): UTP 2012, LNCS 7681, pp. 204–223, 2013.

As mentioned above, we do not handle a complete object-oriented theory; our focus is on methods. Nonetheless, due to the modular nature of the UTP, our work can be combined with existing UTP theories that address complementary features such as modelling of classes and inheritance, as well as object references.

To reason about higher-order programs written in a particular language, we require a method by which program values can be constructed. This usually induces a particular model for program values in terms of predicates and begs the question if there are constraints that such a model has to satisfy.

For instance, does the model have to be an encoding of some form of syntax or can we equate program values directly with predicates of a suitable UTP theory? The latter would be tempting as it is in harmony with the philosophy of the UTP, which is agnostic to syntactic issues and focuses on the semantic properties of objects. However, there are potential pitfalls. To illustrate this, we assume that program values are higher-order predicates themselves. The $\{\!|\_|\!\}$ operator then becomes a type constructor that turns a higher-order predicate into a (program) value. Because the set of predicates with a single variable whose value ranges over some type is equipotent to the subsets of such values, the domain of the $\{\!|\_|\!\}$ function would have a higher cardinality than its range. Therefore, its use as a type constructor is unsound (it fails to be injective). This is a well known issue in recursive data type definitions, and is, for example, illustrated in [15]. We can remedy the situation by confining ourselves to finitely expressible predicates. For an arbitrary UTP theory, however, we usually do not assume that all elements of the underlying predicate lattice are finitely expressible; this would already amount to narrowing the discourse to more specific families of theories.

The above hence shows that we cannot admit just any predicate as a program value. The account in [7] does in fact restrict the admissible higher-order predicates indirectly by constraining the type of higher-order variables. This effectively excludes recursions like $p := \{\!|x := x + 1 \; ; \; \mathbf{call}\, p|\!\}$.

A second challenge that we face is method redefinition. In a view of methods as program variables, a method redefinition is an update to an existing program value. In the UTP theory of object-orientation presented in [14], for instance, this is handled by relying on the fact that program values are syntactic elements of a particular form that reflects the hierarchy of classes where the method is (re)defined. This is a simple elegant solution that enables the use of the copy rule to give semantics to method calls. On the other hand, it ties the theory to a specific syntax of programs, which is against the UTP philosophy.

Recursion, and, in particular, the extensive use of mutual recursion in object-oriented programs impose a third challenge. As already explained, the theory in [7] does not permit the use of a program variable itself in its value. This means that recursion has to be treated in the context defined by the particular notion of programs. In [14], this is achieved by taking fixed points in the UTP theory that is used to give semantics to the syntactic elements taken as program values. To treat mutual recursion, it is therefore necessary to give semantics to all method definitions (and their redefinitions) together. This is illustrated by the following example, where we have two program variables m_1 and m_2 that represent methods that mutually call each other (they calculate $\mid x - y \mid$). Prior to encoding the methods as a predicate, the recursions have to be eliminated.

$$m_1, m_2 := \{\!\!\{ \mu X, Y \bullet \left\langle \begin{array}{l} (x := x - 1 \,;\; Y) \lhd x > 0 \rhd \mathbf{II}, \\ (y := y - 1 \,;\; X) \lhd y > 0 \rhd \mathbf{II} \end{array} \right\rangle \}\!\!\}$$

As shown, this gives rise to fixed-point constructions in the program values. Another issue arises if m_1 is redefined later on. Such a redefinition does not merely affect the value of m_1, but also m_2 as the fixed point needs to be calculated afresh. Though this approach is feasible, it forfeits compositionality.

A final challenge is simplicity. Higher-order programs are just one of the many aspects of an object-oriented program. We strive for simplicity, although this can be fully appreciated only once we combine our theory with other UTP theories (to cater to concurrency, time, sharing, and so on).

Our contribution in this paper is to examine solutions to all these challenges to provide a UTP theory that can be used in the context of a theory of object-orientation like that in [14]. We first illustrate the construction of a sound semantic model for higher-order predicates. Importantly, our program model does not encode programs as syntax, but directly in terms of their semantics as predicates. We show how, in spite of that, we can still cope with method redefinition by using a combination of syntax and semantics in the program model; this also turns out to be useful for the semantic encoding of procedures with parameters.

Finally, we provide a sound solution for the (mutual) recursion problem. This does not affect the underlying semantic model of higher-order predicates and hence does not compromise consistency.

The structure of the paper is as follows. In Section 2 we review the UTP in its higher-order version. Section 3 describes a consistent model of higher-order predicates that is based on predicates rather than a fixed syntax. In Section 4 we propose a UTP theory of methods that overcomes the restriction on the use of recursion in [7]. Section 5 includes some discussions and revisits the initial problem presented above, and in Section 6 we report on related and future work.

2 Preliminaries

In this section, we discuss specific features of higher-order UTP, assuming the reader is familiar with standard UTP. We also give some brief background on the theory of object-orientation in [14], which motivated the work in this paper.

2.1 Higher-Order UTP

The Unifying Theories of Programming [7] is a mathematical framework that provides means for defining the semantics of a variety of programming languages and modelling notations. The primal extension in higher-order UTP is the inclusion of procedure variables. Procedure variables are declared and used just like standard variables. For example, $\mathbf{var}\, p : proc_{\{x,x'\}} \,;\; p := \{\!\!\{ x := x + 1 \}\!\!\}$ introduces a (local) procedure variable p that holds predicates whose alphabet is $\{x, x'\}$, and assigns to it the program $x := x + 1$. Procedure values are directly identified with predicates of some theory of designs or programs. The purpose of $\{\!|\_|\!\}$ is merely "to distinguish what is to be stored from what is to be executed" as stated in [7]. Otherwise, the brackets have no semantic significance and are simply omitted in a procedure call.

Procedure variables can be written as executable statements in a predicate. For example, $\mathbf{var}\, p\ ;\ p := \{\!|x := x+1|\!\}\ ;\ p\ ;\ \mathbf{end}\, p$ is equivalent to $x := x + 1$. The type of p has been omitted in the declaration, but we note that all variables, whether they are standard variables or procedure variables, need to have a type. The notion of a procedure type is explained in more detail in the next section. For clarity, we hereafter make the invocation of a procedure variable explicit by writing $\mathbf{call}\, p$ rather than just p as in [7].

A fundamental law about procedure calls is recaptured below.

$$(p := \{\!|Q|\!\}\ ;\ \mathbf{call}\, p) \;=\; (p := \{\!|Q|\!\}\ ;\ Q)$$

It entitles us to replace the invocation of a procedure by its definition and can be regarded as a manifestation of the copy rule.

An intricacy in higher-order UTP arises from the desire that procedure assignment ought to be monotonic with respect to refinement. Formally,

$$P \sqsubseteq Q \Rightarrow (p := \{\!|P|\!\}) \sqsubseteq (p := \{\!|Q|\!\})$$

This cannot be true if assignment has its standard meaning of equating the primed variable with the assigned expression. This issue and a new definition of refinement were first discussed in [9]. Hence, in higher-order UTP, the meaning of assignment is modified. Here, the semantics of $p := \{\!|Q|\!\}$ is a non-determinism that constrains the value of p' to be any refinement of Q.

$$p := \{\!|Q|\!\} \;\widehat{=}\; (\mathbf{true} \vdash (Q \sqsubseteq p')) \wedge (v \sqsubseteq v')$$

where $\alpha(p := \{\!|Q|\!\}) = \{p, p', v, v'\}$. The new definition implies that we require a notion of refinement of values. For standard values, this is just a flat order, and for program values it is the underlying refinement order on predicates.

Procedures with parameters are supported through functions that map values or variables to (higher-order) predicates. This is essentially the approach that is described in [2]. Permitted are both value and result parameters, and their semantics is expressed in terms of a more general construct $\{\!|\,\lambda\, x : \mathit{var}(T) \bullet P|\!\}$ which corresponds to a procedure that takes a variable of type T as a parameter.

In [7] further aspects of the theory are discussed related to functions and declarative programming. They are not relevant for the material in this paper though. In terms of terminology, we shall use the word 'program' from here on in preference of 'procedure' and reserve the later for programs with parameters. We next give a brief summary of Santos' theory of object-orientation.

2.2 A Theory of Object-Orientation

The theory in [14] builds on an integration of the theory of UTP designs and higher-order programs. The theory introduces observational variables that determine declared classes, their attributes, as well as the subclass order. Methods are encoded via higher-order program variables, and only one variable is used for all redefinitions (overridings) of a method in subclasses.

The theory supports declarations of classes, attributes and methods, and hence entails the possibility to reason about class and method definitions, as well as particular object-oriented programs. Dynamic binding is supported by imposing a certain syntactic structure on method definitions that resolves method binding as part of the method invocation. Namely each value of a method variable has a fixed syntactic structure illustrated below.

$$(p_1 \lhd \mathit{self}\ \mathbf{is}\ C_1 \rhd (p_2 \lhd \mathit{self}\ \mathbf{is}\ C_2 \rhd (\ldots (p_n \lhd \mathit{self}\ \mathbf{is}\ C_n \rhd \bot_{oo}) \ldots)))$$

Above, *self* is an auxiliary variable that determines the target of a method invocation. The p_i are basically specifications of the same method, albeit defined in different subclasses C_1, C_2, ..., C_n. The cascade of tests is used to resolve dynamic binding when the method is called on an object, with tests against more concrete types being carried out before tests against more abstract types.

Method redefinition in a class C has to inject a new test $(p \lhd \mathit{self}\ \mathbf{is}\ C \rhd ...)$ at the right place into this cascade, depending on where C fits into the subclass hierarchy. Redefinition of methods is therefore a syntactic transformation of the top-level cascade of tests; this is made possible in [14] by the fact that programs are uniformly treated as syntax.

3 A Program Model

Our first challenge is to provide a consistent account of a program model. As already explained, our goal is an account that does not assume a fixed syntax for program values but identifies them directly with the predicates of a UTP theory. This enables us to consider a generic theory of object-orientation, independent of the syntax in which we write, for instance, the body of a method.

On the other hand, to take advantage of the approach in [14] to method redefinition and dynamic binding, we do not exclude syntax entirely. In Section 3.1, we first prove soundness of treating program values directly as predicates of an arbitrary UTP theory. This is a useful insight for any work that uses higher-order UTP. Our motivation, as hinted above, is to eradicate any constraints on the underlying theory in which we express the computational effect of methods when instantiating a generic theory of object-orientation. We then extend this argument (Section 3.2) by making a case for the safe combination of syntax and semantics to support method redefinition as in [14]. This provides us with full flexibility on the one hand to remain in the realm of semantics but escape into syntax where this is beneficial to the model and operator definitions.

3.1 Consistency of Higher-Order Programs

As already pointed out, in a sound program model, program values cannot range over arbitrary predicates. The treatment in [7] rules this out by restrictions on alphabets that effectively prohibit recursion. More precisely, this is done by introducing a notion of variable type for higher-order predicates that does not admit circularity. The corresponding BNF-like encoding is reproduced below.

$$<\mathit{type}> ::= <\mathit{program\ type}> \mid <\mathit{base\ type}>$$
$$<\mathit{program\ type}> ::= \mathit{ProcType}(<\mathit{alphabet}>)$$
$$<\mathit{alphabet}> ::= \text{list of } (<\mathit{variable}> : <\mathit{type}>)$$
$$<\mathit{base\ type}> ::= \mathit{BaseType}(\mathit{int}) \mid \mathit{BaseType}(\mathit{bool}) \mid \ldots$$

The dots indicate that we might have further type constructors for base values, for instance, to create composite values like pairs or (finite) sets. As long as those constructors are sound and only recursive into $<\mathit{base\ type}>$, this is not an issue and does not invalidate any of the subsequent reasoning.

As briefly discussed in the introduction, with the restriction in [7] to predicates whose variable types are finite terms constructed by the above rules, recursion is effectively excluded. To illustrate this, we consider the invalid predicate

$$p := \{\!\!|\, x := x + 1\ ;\ \mathbf{call}\, p \,|\!\!\}$$

In this example, it is already clear though that to define the type of the variable p, we would need to refer to that type itself, and this circularity is not allowed. Mutual recursion gives rise to similar situations. We use $\{\!\!|\_|\!\!\}$ only informally here since we have not formally established its existence and semantics yet.

In the sequel we argue that the finitary nature of types is sufficient to ensure consistency. This is a result left implicit in [7]. The argument that we present clarifies important issues related to the treatment of higher-order programs. It can also be used as a basis for a formal treatment of the UTP theory of higher-order programs and its embedding in a theorem prover. Our argument is based on the inductive construction of a model. For this, we first define the notion of the rank of a type inductively over the type structure.

$$\mathit{rank}(\mathit{BaseType}(t)) = 0 \quad \text{and}$$
$$\mathit{rank}(\mathit{ProcType}(\text{list of } [v_1 : t_1, v_2 : t_2, \ldots])) = \mathit{max}\,\{\mathit{rank}(t_1), \mathit{rank}(t_2), \ldots\} + 1$$

Since types are finite by construction, the above recursion properly defines the rank of any given type. We define the rank of a variable to be the rank of its type. The rank of an alphabet is defined as the maximum rank of its variables, and the rank of a predicate is defined just as the rank of its alphabet.

Intuitively, the rank determines the maximal nesting level of program abstractions in a predicate. For instance, the predicates of rank 0 are just the standard predicates; predicates of rank 1 include program variables whose values are standard predicates; predicates of rank 2 moreover admit program values being rank 1 predicates, and so on. Thus, $x := 1$ is a rank 0 predicate, $m_1 := \{\!\!|\, x := 1 \,|\!\!\}$ is a rank 1 predicate, and $m_2 := \{\!\!|\, x := 1\ ;\ \mathbf{call}\, m_1 \,|\!\!\}$ is a rank 2 predicate.

The motivation for introducing a notion of rank is twofold: first we observe that it allows us to partition all higher-order predicates into an enumerable succession of higher-order predicate subsets since every valid predicate must have a finite rank. Secondly, we shall see that the concept of ranks is also central in a theory of methods, which we propose and discuss in Section 4.

We next give a constructive definition of a function $\mathit{pred}(n)$ that yields the predicates of a given rank; our motivation is to subsequently use it to construct the predicates of arbitrary ranks, and as mentioned in the last paragraph, these encompass all valid higher-order predicates. We name *StdPred* the standard (non-higher-order) predicates and define, again inductively,

$$\mathit{pred}(0) = \mathit{StdPred} \quad \text{and} \quad \mathit{pred}(n+1) = \mathit{lift}(\mathit{pred}(n), \mathit{pred}(n))$$

This definition rests on the existence of a lifting function $\mathit{lift}\,(ps, vs)$, which takes a set of predicates ps and lifts them into a set of predicates that introduce program variables that range over the values in vs, which are predicates themselves. By way of an example, we have that $\mathit{pred}(1) = \mathit{lift}(\mathit{StdPred}, \mathit{StdPred})$. These are the standard predicates augmented with variables whose values can range over standard predicates. We can convince ourselves that in general the application of $\mathit{lift}\,(ps, ps)$ admits predicates one rank higher than those in ps.

A precise constructive definition of *lift* can only be given with respect to a core semantic encoding of predicates, like the one in [12], which characterises them in terms of binding sets. Rather than defining *lift* for a specific model, we instead present an abstract axiomatic characterisation that relies on four operators, $\boxed{\alpha}\,p$, $m \boxed{=} v$, $\boxed{\sqcap}\,ps$ and $\boxed{\sqcup}\,ps$. The value of $\mathit{lift}(ps, vs)$ is equated with the smallest set of predicates hps that satisfies the following five properties.

A1 $ps \subseteq hps$

A2 $\forall\, m : \mathit{ProcType}(l) \bullet \forall\, v : vs \mid \mathit{SetOf}(l) = \boxed{\alpha}\,v \bullet m \boxed{=} v \in hps$

A3 $\forall\, ps \subseteq hps \bullet \boxed{\sqcap}\,ps \in hps$

A4 $\forall\, ps \subseteq hps \bullet \boxed{\sqcup}\,ps \in hps$

A5 $\boxed{\sqcap}$ and $\boxed{\sqcup}$ are the meet and join of a complete lattice $\boxed{\sqsubseteq}$

The axioms capture elemental correctness properties of the lifting that ensure completeness of the lifted model and that we retain the property of a complete lattice. The boxed operators have to be provided by the core predicate model. Here, $\boxed{\alpha}\,p$ determines the alphabet (set of variables) of a predicate p, $m \boxed{=} v$ constructs a simple equality between a variable m and a value v, and $\boxed{\sqcap}\,ps$ and $\boxed{\sqcup}\,ps$ are the greatest lower bound and least upper bound of a set of predicates with respect to an ordering that serves as refinement. The latter two operators are moreover used to define disjunction and conjunction of predicates in the lifted model. This is by virtue of $p_1 \boxed{\vee}\, p_2 = \boxed{\sqcap}\,\{p_1, p_2\}$ and $p_1 \boxed{\wedge}\, p_2 = \boxed{\sqcup}\,\{p_1, p_2\}$.

The first property **A1** establishes monotonicity, namely that each lift extends the previous predicate rank. From it we can prove, by induction over the rank, that $\forall\, n \leq m \bullet \mathit{pred}(n) \subseteq \mathit{pred}(m)$. The second property **A2** is a family of axioms for each alphabet given by the list l. The alphabet encoded by a list simply corresponds to the elements in the list, and we use the function *SetOf* to obtain the list elements as a set. **A2** introduces new predicates into the lifted model; they are just simple equalities over (new) program variables. We note that generally, the predicates in vs have a variety of types.

A3 and **A4** are closure properties that enable us to construct arbitrary predicates over the added program variables and values. We note that no closure axiom for negation is needed because $\boxed{\neg}\, m = v$, for instance, can be constructed by $\boxed{\sqcap}\, \{w \mid w \neq v \bullet m \boxed{=} w\}$, the disjunction of all predicates $m = w$ where $w \neq v$.

We can think of **A2** as providing the building blocks for constructing predicates over program variables of the successor rank. If we consider, for example, the lifting of rank 0 predicates, $m = \{\!|x := 1|\!\}$ and $m = \{\!|x := 2|\!\}$ are admitted by **A2** and $m = \{\!|x := 1|\!\} \lor m = \{\!|x := 2|\!\}$ is admitted by **A3**. In this way, the complete lattice of successor rank predicates is constructible. A refinement ordering $\boxed{\sqsubseteq}$ on predicates exists by **A5**. The top and bottom of the lattice are obtained by the meet and join over empty sets: $\boxed{\top} \mathrel{\widehat=} \boxed{\sqcap}\, \{\}$ and $\boxed{\bot} \mathrel{\widehat=} \boxed{\sqcup}\, \{\}$.

The question of the semantics of *lift* has now been pushed into the definition of $\boxed{\alpha}\, p$, $m \boxed{=} p$, $\boxed{\sqcap}\, ps$ and $\boxed{\sqcup}\, ps$ in a core predicate model. For their interpretation in that model, we require that the operators obey the algebraic laws that are presented in [7]. This validates the soundness of the operator definitions in the lifted predicate model. We next define the set *pred* as follows.

$$pred = \bigcup \{n \in \mathbb{N} \bullet pred(n)\}$$

It contains all predicates of any rank. We claim that if *StdPred* are the standard predicates, and the boxed operators are soundly defined, in the above sense, *pred* is also a model for precisely the higher-order predicates considered in [7]. The axioms **A1** to **A5** are sufficient to establish this. The purpose and motivation for the *lift* function now becomes clear as being primarily a utility for constructing the entire set of admissible higher-order predicates.

To conclude the consistency argument, we observe that $\{\!|\_|\!\}$ only has to be injective on the predicates that are well-formed, thus having non-circular types as introduced above. We trivially define it as follows.

$$\{\!|\_|\!\} =_{\mathrm{df}} (\lambda\, p : pred \bullet p) \quad \text{where} \quad \mathrm{dom}\, \{\!|\_|\!\} = pred$$

It is simply the identity on *pred*. Clearly, $\{\!|\_|\!\}$ is injective on *pred*, so it serves as a sound type constructor for program values. We have thus shown that it is safe to treat higher-order UTP predicates as semantics just like the standard ones, and in doing so also illustrated the layered construction of a predicate model. The cardinality of values from <*base type*> is moreover irrelevant. Namely, the carrier sets of base value types may be infinite, even uncountably so.

3.2 Syntax and Semantics in Program Values

We have now established the use of predicates directly as program values. On the other hand, in order to support the approach in [14] for redefinition of methods in subclasses, it turns out that part of the program value in fact has to be kept as syntax as explained in Section 2.2. Our treatment views them as predicates and, despite the discussed benefits, this invalidates the transformational approach. Our solution is to alter the iterative definition of $pred(n)$ as follows.

$$pred(n+1) = lift(pred(n), embed(pred(n)))$$

The only modification is the application of a function *embed* to the set of predicates that determines the values of programs at the next rank. This function realises the syntactic embedding of the semantic entities. The definition of *lift* remains fundamentally the same. The only implication is that the $\boxed{\alpha}$ function in **A2** now has to extract the alphabet of a predicate that is embedded in a segment of syntax. This is not a problem: we can define the extraction function inductively over the data type that encodes the syntactic structure.

In the above example, the syntax is specified by the following generic data type that represents a method in [14]. (We use the Z notation [16].)

$$\begin{array}{l} METH[PRED] ::= \\ \quad CondSytx \langle\!\langle METH \times CVALUE \times METH \rangle\!\rangle \mid BotSytx \mid Body \langle\!\langle PRED \rangle\!\rangle \end{array}$$

This is a Z definition of a new data type *METH*, which is generic (*PRED* is a type parameter). As usual, the bar is used to separate the definition of type-constructor functions and between $\langle\!\langle \ldots \rangle\!\rangle$ brackets, we specify the types of those functions. The type constructor *CondSytx* encodes the syntax $\underline{c}_1 \lhd \mathit{self}\ \mathbf{is}\ C \rhd \underline{c}_2$, where the underlined elements may themselves be pieces of syntax. *BotSytx* encodes the syntax of $\bot_{oo}$, the bottom element in the theory of [14]. The constructor *Body* is non-recursive and injects the semantics of a method body as a predicate, supplied by an element of the generic type *PRED*, into the syntactic domain defined by *METH*. Hence we have $embed(ps) = METH[ps]$.

We note that despite the presence of the *embed* function in the lifting, the result of the lifting is still a predicate set. On the other hand, the call operation has to be adjusted when identifying $METH[PRED]$ with program values. We require an additional layer of denotation in the definition of **call** m that turns a value from $METH[PRED]$ into a value of *PRED*. This can be achieved by interpreting the conditional and bottom with their usual definitions in the UTP. The denotation is inductively defined over $METH[PRED]$. It also serves as a basis for defining refinement on the syntactic program values.

Our conclusion in this section is that we have a certain leeway to mix syntax and semantics, as long as we can provide a way of embedding the semantics into the syntax and provide a denotation in terms of the embedded predicate model. Having established the soundness of a suitable program model for our purposes, in the next section we examine issues that emerge from method redefinition.

4 A Theory of Methods

In this section, we illustrate a fundamental challenge posed by method definition and redefinition in theories of object-orientation. This motivates us to propose a novel UTP theory of methods that overcomes the problem. It exploits the notion of programs as predicates, as established in the previous section, and is applicable and useful in any context where higher-order variables are used to record method behaviour. Importantly, it restores the simplicity of the treatment in [14] in the view of the issues raised and thereby paves the way for a compositional semantics.

In Section 4.1 we illustrate a fundamental problem with method redefinition in theories of object-orientation, and in Section 4.2 we present our solution. As mentioned, the primary motivation is to solve issues of compositionality when defining methods, but also to unify the treatment of method (re)definition.

4.1 Method Definition Revisited

As an example, we consider the following higher-order predicate.

$$S_1 \mathrel{\widehat{=}} m_1 := \{\!|x := x + 1|\!\} \,;\; m_2 := \{\!|x := x + 2 \,;\; \mathbf{call}\, m_1|\!\}$$

It captures the definition of two methods, recorded by the program variables m_1 and m_2. We observe that m_1 is a rank 1 variable whereas m_2 is a rank 2 variable. Hence, the predicate S_1 is a rank 2 predicate.

We first observe that, in general, to encode programs by way of method variables, we cannot restrict ourselves to predicates of a rank lower than 2. This begs the question whether rank 2 is enough to encode all possible object-oriented programs? Unfortunately, the answer is 'no'. For instance, assume we compose the predicate S_1 with the definition of another method m_3.

$$S_2 \mathrel{\widehat{=}} S_1 \,;\; m_3 := \{\!|x := x + 3 \,;\; \mathbf{call}\, m_2|\!\}$$

Clearly, the rank of variable m_3 has to be one greater than the one of variable m_2. This renders S_2 a rank 3 predicate. The issue is subtle because it depends on the careful accounting for types in program variables. This has important implications. In deciding the type of m_3, we need to have knowledge of the type of m_2 in S_1 — its name is not enough. This is because the alphabet of m_3 does not merely include standard variables for the inputs and outputs of the method, but also program variables for methods that are called by the method; and clearly, the type of m_3 depends on the type(s) of those variables too.

This means that in general, we cannot give a compositional account of method definition in cases where a method calls other methods, unless we make the type of the called method(s) a parameter of that definition. In that case, the definition of S_2 would not be a predicate but a function that, if applied to a type, yields a predicate, and further mechanisms would have to be put into place to instantiate this type parameter. This kind of treatment is not unsound, in particular with our result of admitting predicates of any rank, but it considerably complicates the theory of object-orientation and its application.

Method redefinition further complicates matters because it can result in the type of a method variable having to *change*. We consider the scenario where we introduce another method m_4 and then redefine m_1 to call it.

$$S_3 \mathrel{\widehat{=}} S_2 \,;\; m_4 := \{\!|x := x + 4|\!\} \,;\; m_1 := \{\!|\,\mathbf{call}\, m_4|\!\}$$

The variable m_1 above cannot possibly be the same m_1 as in the definition of S_1 because there its rank is 1 whereas here its rank has to be at least 2. We can envisage a solution in which we know in advance that m_1 would subsequently be redefined in terms of a program with a higher rank, and already use that higher rank in typing m_1 in S_1. Such knowledge, however, is doubtful in practice and certainly not available in a compositional treatment. In consequence, we have to redefine m_1 together with all previous method definitions that depend on its value. This gives rise to

$$S_{3b} \mathrel{\widehat=} \begin{pmatrix} m_1 := \{\!|\, \mathbf{call}\, m_4 |\!\}\ ;\ m_2 := \{\!| x := x + 2\ ;\ \mathbf{call}\, m_1 |\!\}; \\ m_3 := \{\!| x := x + 3\ ;\ \mathbf{call}\, m_2 |\!\}\ ;\ m_4 := \{\!| x := x + 4 |\!\} \end{pmatrix}$$

We thereby tame the impact of the type change of m_1 by adjusting the types and definitions of all method variables that directly or indirectly call m_1.

A similar problem arises even when redefinition does not involve a predicate of a higher rank. To illustrate this, instead of m_1 we redefine m_2 in S_2.

$$S_4 \mathrel{\widehat=} S_2\ ;\ m_4 := \{\!| x := x + 4 |\!\}\ ;\ m_2 := \{\!|\, \mathbf{call}\, m_4 |\!\}$$

The rank of the new program value of m_2 is the same as before, so this is not an issue. However, originally the variable m_4 was not in the alphabet of m_2. Introducing it during redefinition is again problematic since this changes the type of m_2, giving rise to exactly the same issues as illustrated before (since m_3 calls m_2). We could try and include all other method variables in the alphabet of any method variable we introduce. But then, what rank(s) should those other method variables have? This decision again imposes *a priori* restrictions on what calls between methods are permissible at a future point; this is not practical.

As a note, the finite nature of alphabets prohibits inclusion of all method variables, but we can get around this in practice by using a finite but large enough repository of method variables. Although this style of modelling is somewhat against the philosophy of the UTP, where alphabets are used in meaningful ways, it is difficult to avoid even in the solution we propose in the sequel.

Motivated by the above observations, we next present a treatment in which the rank of any method variable is not greater than 2. The rank of a predicate encoding an object-oriented program is thus not greater than 2 either.

4.2 A UTP Theory of Methods

We present our theory in the usual UTP style. The observational variables of the theory are program variables that represent methods. We only include program variables at rank 1 and rank 2 and call them method variables hereafter. The rationale for this is that all method definitions we introduce shall constrain rank 2 variables, while all calls within those definitions will be to rank 1 variables.

In the sequel we use overbars to highlight the rank of a method variable. Thus $\overline{m}$ is a rank 1 method variable and $\overline{\overline{m}}$ is a rank 2 method variable. No overbar indicates a standard program variable (rank 0). We note that the overbars are mere annotations that highlight the type of the variable.

To illustrate the main idea, below we encode the predicate S_1 presented earlier on in Section 4.1. We name it T, rather than S, to emphasise that this predicate belongs to the theory of methods we develop here.

$$T_1 \mathrel{\widehat=} \overline{\overline{m}}_1 := \{\!| x := x + 1 |\!\}\ ;\ \overline{\overline{m}}_2 := \{\!| x := x + 2\ ;\ \mathbf{call}\, \overline{m}_1 |\!\}$$

Close inspection reveals an important difference: the call is to $\overline{m}_1$ rather than to $\overline{\overline{m}}_1$ as it was the case in S_1. Method assignment is uniformly carried out to rank 2 variables, highlighted by two overbars in the assigned method variables $\overline{\overline{m}}_1$ and $\overline{\overline{m}}_2$. Although, in principle, the first assignment could be to a rank 1 variable, our approach puts uniformity above such *ad hoc* optimisations.

Next, we sequence T_1 with a predicate that introduces another method that calls m_2, as we did in S_2. This now yields

$$T_2 \mathrel{\widehat{=}} T_1 \,;\, \overline{\overline{m}}_3 := \{\!|x := x + 3 \,;\, \mathbf{call}\,\overline{m}_2|\!\}$$

Once again, the call is to $\overline{m}_2$ rather than $\overline{\overline{m}}_2$. This shows that the rank of method variables does not increase with subsequent definitions of methods, and neither does it increase upon method redefinition. However, $\overline{m}_x$ and $\overline{\overline{m}}_x$ are clearly different variables, and our theory hence has to create a link between them.

This is achieved by a single healthiness condition. It establishes a connection between rank 1 and rank 2 method variables of the same name. To formulate it, we require a way to refer to the name of a variable rather than its identity, which includes its type. To facilitate notation, we shall assume that $\overline{m}$ and $\overline{\overline{m}}$ have the same name, and moreover that a quantification $\forall \overline{m}\ \overline{\overline{m}} \bullet P[\overline{m}, \overline{\overline{m}}]$ is over variables that have rank 1 and rank 2 and the same name. In this way, we do not have to talk about names and types explicitly.

The healthiness condition **HM** is defined as follows.

$$\mathbf{HM}(P) \;=\; P \wedge (\forall \overline{m}\ \overline{\overline{m}} \mid \{\overline{m}, \overline{\overline{m}}\} \subseteq \alpha P \bullet [\mathbf{call}\,\overline{m} \Leftrightarrow \mathbf{call}\,\overline{\overline{m}}]_0)$$

It states that two method variables in P of the same name, but at different ranks, have to be consistent in terms of the constraints they impose on program variables ($[\_]_0$ is the closure operator over standard (program) variables).

We can think of **HM**, together with the constraints imposed on rank 2 method variables by a predicate of the theory, as defining a family of equations that constrain the value of rank 1 method variables and thereby yield an interpretation of methods purely in terms of standard predicates. This interpretation falls out when we quantify over the rank 2 method variables in a healthy predicate and observe the corresponding rank 1 method variables. It corresponds to an encoding of methods in terms of weakest fixed points of a recursive equation that uses recursive parameters instead of method variables. For instance, the predicate $(\exists \overline{\overline{m}}_1\ \overline{\overline{m}}_2 \bullet T_1)$ is equivalent to the concurrent assignment

$$\overline{m}_1, \overline{m}_2 := \{\!| \mu X, Y \bullet \langle x := x + 1, (x := x + 2 \,;\, X)\rangle |\!\}$$

where **call** statements in T_1 have been eliminated by virtue of a multi-variable recursion over standard predicates. For two variables, this takes the general form $\mu X, Y \bullet \langle F(X, Y), G(X, Y)\rangle$. We note that above only G recurses (into X) whereas F depends on neither X nor Y. Such a transformation was already used in [14] to deal with (mutual) recursions. Our claim is that both interpretations are mathematically equivalent. To support this conjecture, we first quote Hoare and He in [7]: "The inclusion of high order variables does not increase the power of the language". Secondly, in the particular example, we can use fixed-point laws to show that X is equivalent to $x := x + 1$ and Y is equivalent to $x := x + 3$. A formal proof is presented at the end of the section that this is exactly the value of $\overline{m}_1$ and $\overline{m}_2$ in T_1. Proving the general case is still future work and requires a precise definition of how to transform one representation into the other.

We next present some essential properties and laws of our theory.

Closure of operators. The notion of a conjunctive healthiness condition is formulated in [5] and means that the healthiness condition can be expressed in the form $\mathbf{CH}(P) = P \wedge \gamma$ for some constant predicate γ. In our case, that predicate is not constant though, as it depends on the alphabet of P. In particular, we have $\mathbf{HM}(P) = P \wedge \gamma_{\mathrm{HM}}\,(\alpha P)$ where

$$\gamma_{\mathrm{HM}}\,(a) \;=\; (\forall \overline{m}\;\overline{\overline{m}} \mid \{\overline{m}, \overline{\overline{m}}\} \subseteq a \bullet [\mathbf{call}\,\overline{m} \Leftrightarrow \mathbf{call}\,\overline{\overline{m}}]_0)$$

Despite this, we can recover essential closure properties that hold for conjunctive healthiness conditions. They are, however, subject to additional caveats. To formulate them, we first require a notion of compatibility of alphabets.

Definition 1. *Two alphabets a_1 and a_2 are compatible if, and only if,*

$$\forall \overline{m}\;\overline{\overline{m}} \bullet (\overline{m} \in a_1 \wedge \overline{\overline{m}} \in a_2) \Leftrightarrow (\overline{\overline{m}} \in a_1 \wedge \overline{m} \in a_2)$$

Intuitively, compatibility implies that if alphabets share a method variable with the same name but at different ranks, each alphabet has to include both instances of that variable. By way of illustration, the alphabet pairs $(\{\overline{m}_1, \overline{\overline{m}}_1\}, \{\overline{m}_1, \overline{\overline{m}}_1\})$, $(\{\overline{m}_1, \overline{\overline{m}}_1\}, \{\overline{m}_2, \overline{\overline{m}}_2\})$ and $(\{\overline{m}_1\}, \{\overline{\overline{m}}_2\})$ are compatible but $(\{\overline{m}_1\}, \{\overline{\overline{m}}_1\})$ is not.

It is easy to show that compatibility is reflexive and symmetric, however, it is not transitive. The latter we illustrate by observing that $(\{\overline{m}_1\}, \{\overline{m}_2\})$ and $(\{\overline{m}_2\}, \{\overline{\overline{m}}_1\})$ are compatible alphabet pairs, but $(\{\overline{m}_1\}, \{\overline{\overline{m}}_1\})$ is not.

Compatibility of alphabets enjoys closure properties with respect to set operations like union, intersection and difference. The following law specifies them.

Law 1. *Let (a_1, a_2) and (a_1, a_3) be compatible alphabets. Then,*

$$(a_1, a_2 \cup a_3)\;,\;\; (a_1, a_2 \cap a_3) \;\; \textit{and} \;\; (a_1, a_2 \setminus a_3) \;\; \textit{are compatible alphabets.}$$

An important property of γ_{HM} is formulated by the following lemma.

Lemma 1. *Let a_1 and a_2 be compatible alphabets. Then we have*

$$\gamma_{\mathrm{HM}}(a_1 \cup a_2) = \gamma_{\mathrm{HM}}(a_1) \wedge \gamma_{\mathrm{HM}}(a_2)$$

The law is proved by splitting the universal quantification in γ_{HM} into a conjunction of two parts in which $\overline{m}$ and $\overline{\overline{m}}$ range over a_1 and a_2, respectively; this succeeds because of the compatibility property. A mechanised theory in Isabelle HOL that proofs the above law and lemma is available [17]. The lemma enables us to prove closure under conjunction of **HM**-healthy predicates.

Law 2. *Let P and Q be* **HM***-healthy predicates with compatible alphabets. Then,*

$$P \wedge Q \;\; \textit{is a } \mathbf{HM}\textit{-healthy predicate.}$$

Proof. We show that $P \wedge Q$ is a fixed point of **HM**.

$$
\begin{aligned}
& P \wedge Q \\
\equiv\ & \text{“}P \text{ and } Q \text{ are } \mathbf{HM}\text{-healthy”} \\
& \mathbf{HM}(P) \wedge \mathbf{HM}(Q) \\
\equiv\ & \text{“unfolding definition of } \mathbf{HM}\text{”} \\
& (P \wedge \gamma_{\mathrm{HM}}(\alpha\, P)) \wedge (Q \wedge \gamma_{\mathrm{HM}}(\alpha\, Q)) \\
\equiv\ & \text{“reordering conjuncts”} \\
& (P \wedge Q) \wedge (\gamma_{\mathrm{HM}}(\alpha\, P) \wedge \gamma_{\mathrm{HM}}(\alpha\, Q)) \\
\equiv\ & \text{“Lemma 1”} \\
& (P \wedge Q) \wedge \gamma_{\mathrm{HM}}((\alpha\, P) \cup (\alpha\, Q)) \\
\equiv\ & \text{“rewriting } (\alpha\, P) \cup (\alpha\, Q) \text{ into } \alpha\,(P \wedge Q)\text{”} \\
& (P \wedge Q) \wedge \gamma_{\mathrm{HM}}(\alpha\,(P \wedge Q)) \\
\equiv\ & \text{“folding definition of } \mathbf{HM}\text{”} \\
& \mathbf{HM}(P \wedge Q)
\end{aligned}
$$

Unfortunately, compatibility of alphabets is insufficient for closure under disjunction. There, we require the stronger proviso of the alphabets being equal.

Law 3. *Let P and Q be* **HM***-healthy predicates with equal alphabets. Then,*

$P \vee Q$ *is a* **HM***-healthy predicate.*

In general, if we restrict ourselves to predicates over the same alphabet, all theorems for conjunctive healthiness conditions proved in [5] continue to hold. This is because in that case, we can treat $\gamma_{\mathrm{HM}}(\alpha\, P)$ as a constant. We thus have closure under sequential composition, too, proved by factoring $\gamma_{\mathrm{HM}}(a)$ into orthogonal constraints on undashed and dashed variables: $\gamma_{\mathrm{HM}}(in\ a) \wedge \gamma_{\mathrm{HM}}(out\ a)$. Requiring equal alphabets may nevertheless be a strong caveat, for instance, in the presence of local variable blocks that incur alphabet changes. The motivation for alphabet compatibility can also be understood as an attempt to weaken the assumptions of closure laws in our theory. Exploiting it further in order to discover laws with weaker assumptions is on-going research.

Lastly, also following from [5], the set of **HM**-healthy predicates over a fixed alphabet is a complete lattice, as it is the image of a monotonic and idempotent healthiness function [7]. Further properties detailed in [5] consider the interaction with designs; they also transfer to our work. We next examine how we use the theory to reason about programs.

Application example. We first introduce a utility law that allows us to extract properties of specific method variables from an **HM**-healthy predicate. This law facilitates reasoning about methods and will also be used later on. To express it concisely, we extend the use of the α operator to apply to method variables also, where it yields the alphabet of the underlying procedure type.

Law 4. *Assume P is* **HM**-*healthy and we have* $\{\overline{m}_x, \overline{\overline{m}}_x\} \subseteq \alpha P$, $\alpha \overline{m}_x \subseteq \alpha P$, *and* $\alpha \overline{\overline{m}}_x \subseteq \alpha P$. *Then,* $P = P \wedge (\mathbf{call}\, \overline{m}_x \Leftrightarrow \mathbf{call}\, \overline{\overline{m}}_x)$.

Proof

$$
\begin{aligned}
P \equiv\ & \text{“}P \textit{ is } \mathbf{HM}\textit{-healthy”} \\
& \mathbf{HM}(P) \\
\equiv\ & \text{“\textit{unfolding definition of} } \mathbf{HM}\text{”} \\
& P \wedge (\forall \overline{m}\ \overline{\overline{m}} \mid \{\overline{m}, \overline{\overline{m}}\} \subseteq \alpha P \bullet [\mathbf{call}\, \overline{m} \Leftrightarrow \mathbf{call}\, \overline{\overline{m}}]_0) \\
\equiv\ & \text{“\textit{specialisation of quantification with} } \overline{m}_x \text{ \textit{and} } \overline{\overline{m}}_x\text{”} \\
& P \wedge \ldots \wedge [\mathbf{call}\, \overline{m}_x \Leftrightarrow \mathbf{call}\, \overline{\overline{m}}_x]_0 \\
\equiv\ & \text{“\textit{specialisation of quantification (universal closure)}”} \\
& P \wedge \ldots \wedge (\mathbf{call}\, \overline{m}_x \Leftrightarrow \mathbf{call}\, \overline{\overline{m}}_x) \\
\equiv\ & \text{“\textit{logic and folding definition of} } \mathbf{HM}\text{”} \\
& \mathbf{HM}(P) \wedge (\mathbf{call}\, \overline{m}_x \Leftrightarrow \mathbf{call}\, \overline{\overline{m}}_x) \\
\equiv\ & \text{“}P \textit{ is } \mathbf{HM}\textit{-healthy”} \\
& P \wedge (\mathbf{call}\, \overline{m}_x \Leftrightarrow \mathbf{call}\, \overline{\overline{m}}_x)
\end{aligned}
$$

Another useful law is a predicative version of the substitution rule.

Law 5. $P[Q_1] \wedge (Q_1 \Leftrightarrow Q_2) = P[Q_2] \wedge (Q_1 \Leftrightarrow Q_2)$ *where the notation* $P[Q]$ *expresses that the predicate* Q *occurs in another predicate* P.

Let us revisit S_1. We encode it in our theory as illustrated below.

$$T_1 \mathrel{\widehat{=}} \mathbf{HM}(\overline{\overline{m}}_1 := \{\!|x := x + 1|\!\}\ ;\ \overline{\overline{m}}_2 := \{\!|x := x + 2\ ;\ \mathbf{call}\, \overline{m}_1|\!\})$$

We note that the assignments above are relational assignments rather than generalised higher-order assignments. The simple technical reason for this is to take advantage of the one-point rule; it is not a limitation of our theory.

The transformation below exemplifies how we reason about T_1.

$$
\begin{aligned}
T_1 \equiv\ & \text{“unfolding definition of } \mathbf{HM}\text{, let } \gamma^*_{\mathrm{HM}} \mathrel{\widehat{=}} \gamma_{\mathrm{HM}}(\{\overline{m}_1, \overline{m}_2, \overline{\overline{m}}_1, \overline{\overline{m}}_2\})\text{”} \\
& (\overline{\overline{m}}_1 := \{\!|x := x + 1|\!\}\ ;\ \overline{\overline{m}}_2 := \{\!|x := x + 2\ ;\ \mathbf{call}\, \overline{m}_1|\!\}) \wedge \gamma^*_{\mathrm{HM}} \\
\equiv\ & \text{“unfolding sequential compositions and assignments, one-point rule”} \\
& (\overline{\overline{m}}'_1 = \{\!|x := x + 1|\!\} \wedge \overline{\overline{m}}'_2 = \{\!|x := x + 2\ ;\ \mathbf{call}\, \overline{m}'_1|\!\}) \wedge \gamma^*_{\mathrm{HM}} \\
\equiv\ & \text{“Law 4 with } (\overline{m}'_1, \overline{\overline{m}}'_1) \text{ and } (\overline{m}'_2, \overline{\overline{m}}'_2)\text{, predicate is } \mathbf{HM}\text{-healthy”} \\
& \left(\begin{array}{l}
\overline{\overline{m}}'_1 = \{\!|x := x + 1|\!\} \wedge \overline{\overline{m}}'_2 = \{\!|x := x + 2\ ;\ \mathbf{call}\, \overline{m}'_1|\!\} \wedge \\
(\mathbf{call}\, \overline{m}'_1 \Leftrightarrow \mathbf{call}\, \overline{\overline{m}}'_1) \wedge (\mathbf{call}\, \overline{m}'_2 \Leftrightarrow \mathbf{call}\, \overline{\overline{m}}'_2)
\end{array}\right) \wedge \gamma^*_{\mathrm{HM}} \\
\equiv\ & \text{“one-point rule using } \overline{\overline{m}}'_1 = \{\!|x := x + 1|\!\} \text{ and } \overline{\overline{m}}'_2 = \{\!|x := x + 2\ ;\ \mathbf{call}\, \overline{m}'_1|\!\}\text{”} \\
& \left(\begin{array}{l}
\overline{\overline{m}}'_1 = \{\!|x := x + 1|\!\} \wedge \overline{\overline{m}}'_2 = \{\!|x := x + 2\ ;\ \mathbf{call}\, \overline{m}'_1|\!\} \wedge \\
(\mathbf{call}\, \overline{m}'_1 \Leftrightarrow \mathbf{call}\, \{\!|x := x + 1|\!\}) \wedge \\
(\mathbf{call}\, \overline{m}'_2 \Leftrightarrow \mathbf{call}\, \{\!|x := x + 2\ ;\ \mathbf{call}\, \overline{m}'_1|\!\})
\end{array}\right) \wedge \gamma^*_{\mathrm{HM}}
\end{aligned}
$$

$$\equiv \text{“cancellation law: } \mathbf{call}\, \{\!|p|\!\} = p\text{”}$$

$$\begin{pmatrix} \overline{\overline{m}}_1' = \{\!|x := x+1|\!\} \wedge \overline{\overline{m}}_2' = \{\!|x := x+2\,;\ \mathbf{call}\,\overline{m}_1'|\!\} \wedge \\ (\mathbf{call}\,\overline{m}_1' \Leftrightarrow x := x+1) \wedge \\ (\mathbf{call}\,\overline{m}_2' \Leftrightarrow (x := x+2\,;\ \mathbf{call}\,\overline{m}_1')) \end{pmatrix} \wedge \gamma^*_{\mathrm{HM}}$$

$$\equiv \text{“Law 5 using } \mathbf{call}\,\overline{m}_1' \Leftrightarrow x := x+1\text{ ”}$$

$$\begin{pmatrix} \overline{\overline{m}}_1' = \{\!|x := x+1|\!\} \wedge \overline{\overline{m}}_2' = \{\!|x := x+2\,;\ \mathbf{call}\,\overline{m}_1'|\!\} \wedge \\ (\mathbf{call}\,\overline{m}_1' \Leftrightarrow x := x+1) \wedge \\ (\mathbf{call}\,\overline{m}_2' \Leftrightarrow (x := x+2\,;\ x := x+1)) \end{pmatrix} \wedge \gamma^*_{\mathrm{HM}}$$

$$\equiv \text{“simplification of sequence: } (x := x+2\,;\ x := x+1) = (x := x+3)\text{”}$$

$$\begin{pmatrix} \overline{\overline{m}}_1' = \{\!|x := x+1|\!\} \wedge \overline{\overline{m}}_2' = \{\!|x := x+2\,;\ \mathbf{call}\,\overline{m}_1'|\!\} \wedge \\ (\mathbf{call}\,\overline{m}_1' \Leftrightarrow x := x+1) \wedge \\ (\mathbf{call}\,\overline{m}_2' \Leftrightarrow x := x+3) \end{pmatrix} \wedge \gamma^*_{\mathrm{HM}}$$

The last step makes precise the effect of calling the methods $\overline{m}_1$ and $\overline{m}_2$. It agrees with our intuition and moreover shows the validity of the copy rule.

To summarise, in this section we have presented a novel theory of methods that deals with the issues raised when using higher-order UTP to model object-oriented software. For instance, it allows us to redefine $\overline{\overline{m}}_1$ in T_1 as follows.

$$T_2 \ \widehat{=}\ T_1\,;\ \mathbf{HM}(\overline{\overline{m}}_1 := \{\!|(x := x+1\,;\ \mathbf{call}\,\overline{m}_1) \lhd x < 10 \rhd \mathbf{II}|\!\})$$

where $\mathbf{II}$ has a suitable alphabet. This introduces a call into the method body. The types of $\overline{\overline{m}}_1$ is exactly as before, assuming that $\overline{\overline{m}}_1$ and $\overline{\overline{m}}_2$ *a priori* have $\overline{m}_1$ and $\overline{m}_2$ in their alphabets; this ceases to be a problem in our theory as it does not constrain calls. Thus compositionality of method (re)definition is restored.

5 Discussion

In this section we first discuss the treatment of procedures with parameters and secondly tackle the problem of (mutual) recursion in our theory of methods.

5.1 Procedures with Parameters

In our treatment so far, we have ignored the possibility of program values being procedures — that is having parameters. A standard approach to support procedures is to encode them as functions [2] whose domains correspond to the kind of objects being passed to the procedure (a variable or value) and whose range is the underlying semantic model of the procedure body. Higher-order UTP adopts a similar approach to realise parameter passing. For instance, we can define a procedure p_1 with a name parameter n as follows.

$$p_1 := \{\!|\,\lambda\, n : var(\mathbb{Z}) \bullet n := n + x|\!\}$$

It takes an integer variable as its argument and adds the value of x to it. It is a function from variables to predicates. This procedure is besides ‘polymorphic’ in the sense that the alphabet of the predicate that results from applying p_1 is determined by the argument. For instance, we have that the alphabet of the predicate resulting from the call $p_1(x)$ includes $\{x, x', y, y'\}$ whereas the call $p_1(z)$ gives rise to a predicate whose alphabet is $\{y, y', z, z'\}$.

The polymorphic nature of procedures is difficult to reconcile with the model construction in Section 3.1. This is because the notion of type that is used there and taken from [7] is not appropriate anymore, precisely because no *a priori* knowledge of the alphabet of a procedure's predicate is possible. Because of this, we confine ourselves to procedures that are non-polymorphic. They are the procedures that only admit value parameters. An example is given below.

$$p_2 := \{\!|\, \lambda\, v : val(\mathbb{Z}) \bullet x := x + v \,|\!\}$$

We note though that the absence of result parameters does not prohibit or constrain the use of object references (pointers) [3]. Java, for instance, only includes value parameters. To integrate these kinds of procedures into our higher-order program model, we can, in essence, use the same technique as in Section 3.2. This is by introducing additional syntax that corresponds to the declaration of formal procedure parameters. Once again, a data type is used for this purpose.

$$PROC[BODY] ::= ValArg \langle\!\langle TYPE \times PROC[BODY] \rangle\!\rangle \mid Body \langle\!\langle BODY \rangle\!\rangle$$

Above, *TYPE* encodes the type of a parameter; we assume this is *<base type>*. The recursion in *ValArg* enables us to support procedures with arbitrary numbers of parameters, as an object of a unified type *PROC*[*BODY*] where *BODY* provides the semantic model of the procedure body. We note that in the theory of object-orientation in [14], *BODY* is itself syntax, which is not a problem.

Importantly, a new definition of **call**, refinement and at least assignment (to support refinement of procedure values) have to be provided for *PROC*[*BODY*]. These definitions take advantage of a function *apply* that applies a procedure to a list of arguments; its signature is illustrated below.

$$apply : PROC[BODY] \to \mathrm{seq}(VALUE) \to BODY$$

The *apply* function has a simple inductive definition which we omit. Refinement is defined as a pointwise extension of $\sqsubseteq_{body}$, the refinement of objects of type *BODY*. It only considers argument sequences of the correct length and type, which is determined by an auxiliary function *valid*.

$$p_1 \sqsubseteq_{proc} p_2 = \forall\, args \mid valid(p_1, p_2, args) \bullet (apply\ p_1\ args) \sqsubseteq_{body} (apply\ p_2\ args)$$

The new call operation **pcall** is defined as $\mathbf{pcall}\, p(args) \mathrel{\widehat=} \mathbf{call}(apply\ p\ args)$ where **call** provides the semantics of calls on entities of type *BODY*, which we assume already exists. If needed, other operators can be provided via pointwise lifting too, using the same approach as in [2].

The above shows how we can integrate limited support for parametrised procedures into our model without compromising soundness. Its primary limitation is that it excludes result parameters. Result parameters are, it seems, needed in order to support methods with return values. This is an open issue that we are currently investigating and planning to report on in follow-up work.

5.2 Mutual Recursion

We return now to the problem in the introduction of encoding

$$S \mathrel{\widehat=} m_1, m_2 := \{\!\!|\, \mu\, X, Y \bullet \left\langle \begin{array}{l} (x := x - 1\,;\; Y) \lhd x > 0 \rhd \mathrm{I\!I}, \\ (y := y - 1\,;\; X) \lhd y > 0 \rhd \mathrm{I\!I} \end{array} \right\rangle |\!\!\}$$

In our theory of methods, this can now be written as

$$T_1 \mathrel{\widehat=} \mathbf{HM}(\overline{\overline{m}}_1 :=_A \{\!\!|(x := x - 1\,;\; \mathbf{call}\, \overline{m}_2) \lhd x > 0 \rhd \mathrm{I\!I}|\!\!\}) \quad \text{and}$$

$$T_2 \mathrel{\widehat=} \mathbf{HM}(\overline{\overline{m}}_2 :=_A \{\!\!|(y := y - 1\,;\; \mathbf{call}\, \overline{m}_1) \lhd y > 0 \rhd \mathrm{I\!I}|\!\!\}) \quad \text{and}$$

$$T \mathrel{\widehat=} T_1\,;\; T_2$$

where $A \mathrel{\widehat=} \{\overline{m}_1, \overline{m}_1', \overline{m}_2, \overline{m}_2', \overline{\overline{m}}_1, \overline{\overline{m}}_1', \overline{\overline{m}}_2, \overline{\overline{m}}_2'\}$ and

$$\alpha\, \overline{\overline{m}}_1 = \alpha\, \overline{\overline{m}}_1' = \alpha\, \overline{\overline{m}}_2 = \alpha\, \overline{\overline{m}}_2' = \{\overline{m}_1, \overline{m}_1', \overline{m}_2, \overline{m}_2'\}$$

We observe that T_1 introduces the method definition for m_1 and T_2 introduces the method definition for m_2. Neither of them relies on a fixed-point construction, and compositionality is illustrated by the combined definition T that composes the individual method definitions in sequence. For composability, the alphabets of the assignments have to be suitably extended with A.

Although this is not proved here, we claim that

$$S \Leftrightarrow (\exists\, \overline{\overline{m}}_1, \overline{\overline{m}}_1', \overline{\overline{m}}_2, \overline{\overline{m}}_2' \bullet T)$$

A proof of this conjecture requires special laws that permit one to move between formulations in terms of recursive calls to rank 1 method variables and fixed points; we are currently examining those laws. It seems that in order to reason about particular programs, the form in S may have practical advantages. However, to reason about features of object-orientation, the form in T is superior because there we profit from compositional method (re)definition.

Above we introduced an alphabet A that contains all method variables under consideration. In practice, it is necessary to fix such an alphabet since otherwise, we still run into the problems discussed in Section 4.1 regarding the types of method variables. We recapture that in the theory of methods, there is, however, no problem in fixing this alphabet as this *per se* does not restrict calls. The fixing of alphabets in general involves the provision of a predefined repository of method variables in which the rank 2 variables have all rank 1 variables in their alphabets; we believe that this is largely a technical (and tractable) issue.

Finally, it is even possible to redefine recursive methods individually. For instance, we may redefine $\overline{\overline{m}}_1$ in T as follows.

$$T\,;\; \mathbf{HM}(\overline{\overline{m}}_1 :=_A \{\!\!|\,\mathbf{call}\, \overline{m}_2|\!\!\})$$

Importantly, this redefinition implicitly also alters the behaviour of $\overline{\overline{m}}_2$, which now leaves x unaffected and sets y to 0. It appears that the theory of methods solves the problem of redefinition gracefully also in the context of (mutual) recursion. This may be at the cost of a possibly more complicated strategy for reasoning about the properties of methods, such as proving that the above specification implies that $[\mathbf{call}\, \overline{m}_2 \Leftrightarrow y := 0]$. We are currently investigating this.

6 Conclusion

We have examined the ramifications of higher-order UTP in theories of object-orientation and presented solutions to four major challenges: consistency of the program model, redefinition of methods in subclasses, the treatment of recursion and mutual recursion, and simplicity. We briefly comment on each of them.

Consistency is achieved by the inductive construction of a program model that caters for our needs to combine syntax and semantics, as well as procedures with parameters. We thereby proved a result that was left implicit in [7], namely that arbitrary theories can be used in place of the program model. The construction also provides guidance for mechanisation in a theorem prover. There are still open issues with regards to supporting result parameters; it seems that in order to do so, we have to elaborate the notion of variable type to reflect the signature of polymorphic procedures. This is on-going research work.

A number of issues that arise from method (re)definition have been discussed and we have presented a novel solution in terms of a UTP theory. The important contribution of the theory is to restore compositionality. Almost as a side effect, it also gracefully handles recursive definitions in a compositional manner. Notably, this is useful for the theory of object-orientation in [14], as it eliminates the need to rewrite recursive methods into multi-variable fixed-point terms.

Simplicity is achieved as our theory of methods provides a uniform treatment of types: method definitions are assignments to rank 2 variables while method calls are to rank 1 variables. The only complication that persists is that we have to introduce an *a priori* repository of method variables which determines the minimal alphabet of all rank 2 method variables (the set A in Section 5.2).

As related work, we first note Naumann's foundational work on the semantics of higher-order imperative programming [9,10]. It is based on predicate transformers and tackles features of object-oriented programs, such as inheritance and dynamic binding through the use of record subtyping. In [6], Jifeng et al. introduce rCOS, a UTP-based refinement calculus for object systems. It is based on a fixed syntax and defines the semantics of an object-oriented program by way of a denotation function; this seems to side-step the explicit use of procedure variables, although the treatment of recursion is not discussed.

Recent work by Chin et al. [4] proposes a modular verification technique for object-oriented programs based on separation logic. Their approach seems efficient and pragmatic, but is tied to a design-based view of method specifications. Our aim is to create a framework that can be integrated with arbitrary theories of programming. Lessons may be learned from [4] in terms of modular reasoning.

There are two main strands for future work. The first one is to formulate and prove more laws and properties of the theory of methods, and show how they are used in practice to reason about object-oriented programs. We expect there exist further interesting laws waiting for discovery, in particular in conjunction with fixed points and the theory of designs.

A second strand is the mechanisation of higher-order UTP as well as the theory in [14]. We already have preliminary but promising results on such a mechanisation in the Isabelle HOL prover [11]; it extends the semantic model of alphabetised predicates that was used in [13] and [18] to incorporate program values. A delicate open issue is that presently we rely on custom axioms for the type morphism $\{\!|\_|\!\}$ and its inverse; future work will aim to remove those axioms.

Acknowledgements. We thank the anonymous reviewers for their useful comments. This work was funded by the EPSRC grant EP/H017461/1.

References

1. Abadi, M., Cardelli, L.: A Theory of Objects. Springer (1996)
2. Back, R.-J., Preoteasa, V.: Reasoning About Recursive Procedures with Parameters. In: Proceedings of the 2003 ACM SIGPLAN Workshop on Mechanized Reasoning about Languages with Variable Binding. ACM (August 2003)
3. Cavalcanti, A., Wellings, A., Woodcock, J.: The Safety-Critical Java Memory Model: A Formal Account. In: Butler, M., Schulte, W. (eds.) FM 2011. LNCS, vol. 6664, pp. 246–261. Springer, Heidelberg (2011)
4. Chin, W.-N., David, C., Nguyen, H.H., Qin, S.: Enhancing Modular OO Verification with Separation Logic. ACM SIGPLAN Not 43(1), 87–99 (2008)
5. Harwood, W., Cavalcanti, A., Woodcock, J.: A Theory of Pointers for the UTP. In: Fitzgerald, J.S., Haxthausen, A.E., Yenigun, H. (eds.) ICTAC 2008. LNCS, vol. 5160, pp. 141–155. Springer, Heidelberg (2008)
6. He, J., Li, X., Liu, Z.: rCOS: A refinement calculus for object systems. Theoretical Computer Science 365(1-2), 109–142 (2006)
7. Hoare, C.A.R., He, J.: Unifying Theories of Programming. Prentice Hall Series in Computer Science. Prentice Hall (February 1998)
8. Kassios, I.T.: Decoupling in Object Orientation. In: Fitzgerald, J.S., Hayes, I.J., Tarlecki, A. (eds.) FM 2005. LNCS, vol. 3582, pp. 43–58. Springer, Heidelberg (2005)
9. Naumann, D.: Predicate Transformer Semantics of an Oberon-Like Language. In: Proceedings of the IFIP TC2/WG2.1/WG2.2/WG2.3 Working Conference on Programming Concepts, Methods and Calculi, PROCOMET 1994, pp. 467–487 (1994)
10. Naumann, D.: Predicate transformers and higher-order programs. Theoretical Computer Science 150(1), 111–159 (1995)
11. Nipkow, T., Paulson, L.C., Wenzel, M.T.: Isabelle/HOL. LNCS, vol. 2283. Springer, Heidelberg (2002)
12. Nuka, G., Woodcock, J.: Mechanising a Unifying Theory. In: Dunne, S., Stoddart, B. (eds.) UTP 2006. LNCS, vol. 4010, pp. 217–235. Springer, Heidelberg (2006)
13. Oliveira, M., Cavalcanti, A., Woodcock, J.: Unifying Theories in ProofPower-Z. In: Dunne, S., Stoddart, B. (eds.) UTP 2006. LNCS, vol. 4010, pp. 123–140. Springer, Heidelberg (2006)
14. Santos, T., Cavalcanti, A., Sampaio, A.: Object-Orientation in the UTP. In: Dunne, S., Stoddart, B. (eds.) UTP 2006. LNCS, vol. 4010, pp. 18–37. Springer, Heidelberg (2006)
15. Spivey, M.: The Consistency Theorem for Free Type Definitions in Z. Formal Aspects of Computing 8, 369–375 (1996)
16. Woodcock, J., Davies, J.: Using Z: Specification, Refinement and Proof. International Series in Computer Science. Prentice Hall (July 1996)
17. Zeyda, F.: A Theory of Methods: Validation of Laws. Technical report (July 2012), `http://www.cs.york.ac.uk/circus/hijac/publication.html`
18. Zeyda, F., Cavalcanti, A.: Mechanical reasoning about families of UTP theories. Science of Computer Programming 77(4), 444–479 (2012)

Denotational Semantics for a Probabilistic Timed Shared-Variable Language

Huibiao Zhu[1], Jeff W. Sanders[2], Jifeng He[1], and Shengchao Qin[3]

[1] Shanghai Key Laboratory of Trustworthy Computing
Software Engineering Institute, East China Normal University
3663 Zhongshan Road (North), Shanghai, China, 200062
{hbzhu,jifeng}@sei.ecnu.edu.cn
[2] African Institute for Mathematical Sciences
6-8 Melrose Road, Muizenberg 7945, South Africa
jsanders@aims.ac.za
[3] School of Computing, University of Teesside
Middlesbrough TS1 3BA, UK
s.qin@tees.ac.uk

Abstract. Complex software systems typically involve features like time, concurrency and probability, where probabilistic computations play an increasing role. It is challenging to formalize languages comprising all these features. We have proposed a language, which integrates probability with time and shared-variable concurrency (called *PTSC* [19]). We also explored its operational semantics, where a set of algebraic laws has been investigated via bisimulation.

In this paper we explore the denotational semantics for our probabilistic language. In order to deal with the above three features and the nondeterminism, we introduce a tree structure, called P-tree, to model concurrent probabilistic programs. The denotational semantics of each statement is formalized in the structure of P-tree. Based on the achieved semantics, a set of algebraic laws is explored; i.e., especially those parallel expansion laws. These laws can be proved via our achieved denotational semantics.

1 Introduction

As probabilistic computations play an increasing role in solving various problems [16], various proposals on probabilistic languages have been reported [1–3, 5, 8–10, 13–15]. Complex software systems typically involve important features like real-time [12], probability and shared-variable concurrency. The shared-variable mechanism is typically used for communications among components running in parallel, such as the Java programming language and the Verilog hardware description language. It proves to be challenging to formalize it [6, 17, 18]. Therefore, system designers would expect a formal model that incorporates all these features to be available for them to use.

In [19], we have integrated a formal language model, which equips with probability, time and shared-variable concurrency. Our model is meant to facilitate the specification of complex software systems. The probability feature is reflected by the probabilistic nondeterministic choice, probabilistic guarded choice and the probabilistic scheduling

B. Wolff, M.-C. Gaudel, A. Feliachi (Eds.): UTP 2012, LNCS 7681, pp. 224–247, 2013.

of actions from different concurrent components in a program. For this proposed language model, an operational semantics was formalized. On the top of the operational model, an abstract bisimulation relation was defined and several algebraic laws have been derived for program equivalence.

The *PTSC* model proposed in this paper has recently been used to specify a circuit in the register-transfer level [11]. The circuit takes two integers as the input and sums up them as the output, where the register containing one of the inputs may be faulty. Our algebraic laws proposed for the *PTSC* language have also been employed to verify that an implementation of the circuit with probabilistic behavior conforms to the probabilistic specification.

As advocated in Hoare and He's Unifying Theories of Programming (*UTP*) [7], three different styles of mathematical representations are normally used: operational, denotational, and algebraic ones. Denotational semantics provides mathematical meanings to programs. Compared with operational semantics, it is more abstract. As *PTSC* integrates probability, time and shared-variable in one single model, it is challenging to formalize its denotational semantics. This paper studies the denotational semantics for *PTSC*. In order to deal with the above three features, together with the feature of nondeterminism, we introduce the concept of P-Tree in our model. The P-tree structure can be considered as the extension of traditional trace structure. Based on the achieved denotational semantics and the exploration of the equivalence of P-trees, a set of algebraic laws is investigated.

For exploring the unifying of the semantics for *PTSC*, we have explored the link between operational semantics and algebraic semantics [20]. Our approach in [20] is to derive operational semantics from algebraic semantics for our proposed probabilistic language. Moreover, we have also explored the animation of the link between the two semantics. Our approach can be considered as the soundness and completeness exploration of operational semantics from algebraic viewpoint, both theoretically and practically.

The remainder of this paper is organized as follows. Section 2 introduces our probabilistic language with time and shared-variable concurrency (i.e., *PTSC*). Section 3 explores the denotational semantic model. In order to deal with the above three features, together with the feature of nondeterminism, we introduce a tree structure in our semantic model, called P-tree. Section 4 investigates the denotational semantics for each statement of *PTSC*. Our P-tree structure is successfully applied in the exploration. For the aim of explore program equivalence, we provide an equivalence relation for P-trees. Based on the achieved semantics and the equivalence of P-tree structure, a set of algebraic laws is explored in section 5. Section 6 concludes the paper.

2 The Language *PTSC*

The *PTSC* language integrates probability and time with shared-variable concurrency. It has been designed to express the scheduling of threads, incorporating with concurrency and nondeterminism as well as probability and time. It is thus well suited to *discrete event simulation* where those features are present. The *PTSC* language has the following syntactical elements:

$$P ::= \textbf{Skip} \mid x := e \mid \textbf{Chaos} \mid \textbf{if}\ b\ \textbf{then}\ P\ \textbf{else}\ P \mid \textbf{while}\ b\ \textbf{do}\ P$$
$$\mid @b\ P \mid \#n\ P \mid P\ ;\ P$$
$$\mid P \sqcap P \mid P \sqcap_p P \mid P \parallel P \mid P \parallel_p P$$

Note that:

(1) $x := e$ is the atomic assignment. **Skip** behaves the same as $x := x$. **Chaos** stands for the divergent process.

(2) Regarding $@b\ P$, when the Boolean condition b is satisfied, process P can have the chance to be scheduled. The program $@b\ P$ can wait the environment to fire the event if the Boolean condition b is not met currently. For $\#n\ P$, after n time units elapse, process P can be scheduled.

(3) Similar to a conventional programming language, **if** b **then** P **else** Q stands for the conditional, whereas **while** b **do** P stands for the iteration.

(4) The mechanism for parallel composition is a shared-variable interleaving model with probability feature. For probabilistic parallel composition $P \parallel_p Q$, if process P can perform an atomic action, $P \parallel_p Q$ has conditional probability p to do that atomic action. On the other hand, if process Q can perform an atomic action, $P \parallel_p Q$ has conditional probability $1-p$ to perform that action. On the other hand, $P \parallel Q$ stands for the general parallel composition.

(5) $\sqcap$ stands for the nondeterministic choice, whereas $\sqcap_p$ stands for the probabilistic nondeterministic choice. $P \sqcap_p Q$ indicates that the probability for $P \sqcap_p Q$ to behave as P is p, where the probability for $P \sqcap_p Q$ to behave as Q is $1-p$.

In order to facilitate algebraic reasoning, we enrich our language with a *guarded choice*. As our parallel composition has probability feature, the guarded choice also shares this feature. Guarded choice is classified into five types:

(1) $\|_{i\in I}\{[p_i]\ choice_{j\in J_i}(b_{ij}\&(x_{ij} := e_{ij})\ P_{ij})\}$

(2) $\|_{i\in I}\{@b_i\ P_i\}$

(3) $\|\{\#1\ R\}$

(4) $\|_{i\in I}\{[p_i]\ choice_{j\in J_i}(b_{ij}\&(x_{ij} := e_{ij})\ P_{ij})\}$
$\|\|_{k\in K}\{@b_k\ Q_k\}$

(5) $\|_{i\in I}\{@b_i\ P_i\}\|\{\#1\ R\}$

Regarding $\|_{i\in I}\{[p_i]\ choice_{j\in J_i}(b_{ij}\&(x_{ij} := e_{ij})\ P_{ij})\}$ in the guarded choice type (1) and (4), it should satisfy the following healthiness conditions:

(a) $\forall i \bullet (\bigvee_{j\in J_i} b_{ij} = true)$ and
$(\forall j_1, j_2 \bullet (j_1 \neq j_2) \Rightarrow ((b_{ij_1} \wedge b_{ij_2}) = false))$

(b) $\Sigma_{i\in I}\, p_i = 1$

The first type is composed of a set of assignment-guarded components. The condition (a) indicates that for any $i \in I$, the Boolean conditions b_{ij} from "$choice_{j\in J_i}(b_{ij}\&(x_{ij} := e_{ij})\ P_{ij})$" are complete and disjoint. Therefore, there will be exactly one component $b_{ij}\&(x_{ij} := e_{ij})\ P_{ij}$ selected among all $j \in J_i$. Furthermore, for any $i \in I$, the possibility for a component $(x_{ij} := e_{ij})\ P_{ij}$ (where b_{ij} is met) to be scheduled is p_i and it should satisfy the second healthiness condition.

The second type is composed of a set of event-guarded components. If one guard is satisfied, the subsequent behaviour for the whole process will be followed by its subsequent behaviour of the satisfied component. The firing of these guards is disjoint.

The third type is composed of one time delay component. Initially, it cannot do anything except letting time advance one unit.

The fourth type is the guarded choice composition of the first and second type of guarded choice. If there exists one b_k $(k \in K)$ being satisfied currently, then the event $@\, b_k$ is fired and the subsequent behaviour is Q_k. If there is no satisfied b_k, the behaviour of the fourth type of guarded choice is the same as that of the first type.

The fifth type is the compound of the second and third type of guarded choice. Currently, if there exists i $(i \in I)$ such that b_i is satisfied, then the subsequent behaviour of the whole guarded choice is P_i. On the other hand, if there is no i $(i \in I)$ such that b_i is satisfied currently, then the whole guarded choice cannot do anything initially except letting time advance one unit. The subsequent behaviour is the same as the behaviour of R.

As the first type of guarded choice does not have time advancing behavior, there is no type of guarded choice composing of the first and third type of guarded choice.

3 The Denotational Semantic Model for *PTSC*

In order to deal with shared-variable, probability and time in our model, we introduce the concept of snapshots for our denotational model.

A snapshot is expressed as a triple $(tag,\ p,\ \sigma)$, where:

(1) σ stands for the contributed state. These states are contributed by the program itself or the environment.
(2) tag can be 0, 0^-, 1 and $\surd$. If $tag = 0$, it indicates that the contribution of σ is due to the environment. If $tag = 1$, it indicates the contribution of σ is due to the process itself. On the other hand, if $tag = \surd$, it indicates that time advances one unit and the state σ is the same as the previous one. Flag 0^- is used to model the case that after the environment actions, the subsequent process will be assignment.
(3) For the second element, it is used to express the probability of the contributed state. If $tag = \surd$, it will be $\emptyset$, indicating that we do not need to consider the probability for time delay. On the other hand, if $tag = 0, 0^-, 1$, the second element p will be the probability of the contributing the state σ.

Based on the concept, we are now ready in defining the concept of P^--trees. The introduction of P^--tree can be used in formalizing the denotational semantics for *PTSC*.

Definition 3.1 (P^--tree)

(1) st is P^--tree, where st stands for the execution state. Here, st can be div, $wait$ or ter.
(2) $\{\!|(tag, p_i, \sigma_i) : U_i \mid i \in I \wedge \Sigma_{i \in I}\, p_i = 1|\!\}$ is P^--tree if each element in every U_i is P^--tree.
(3) $\{\!|(\surd, \emptyset, \sigma) : U\}|\!\}$ is P^--tree if each element in U is P^--tree.

Note that $st \in U_i(\text{or } U)$ **iff** $U_i = \{st\}$ (or $U = \{st\}$). □

Here, the notation "$\{\mid \mid\}$"stands for a bag. For a P^--tree, st can be used to model the corresponding leaf. It stands for the execution state of the corresponding execution path. During the execution, a program can be in divergent state (i.e., div), waiting state (i.e., $wait$) or terminating state (i.e., ter).

For $\{\mid (tag, p_i, \sigma_i) : U_i \mid i \in I \wedge \Sigma_{i \in I}\, p_i = 1 \mid\}$, the property "$\Sigma_{i \in I}\, p_i = 1$" indicates that the summation of all the probabilities for all the corresponding newly updated states is 1. Here, tag can be 0, 1. If $tag = 1$, it indicates that all the newly updated states with the corresponding probabilities are contributed by the program itself. On the other hand, if $tag = 0$, it indicates that all the newly updated states with the corresponding probabilities are contributed by the environment. Moreover, $tag = 0^-$ is used to model the case that after the environment's behavior, the subsequent behavior for the process is the assignment action.

For $\{\mid (\surd, \emptyset, \sigma) : U \mid\}$, the snapshot $(\surd, \emptyset, \sigma)$ here is used to model one unit delay behavior. The notation $\emptyset$ in snapshot $(\surd, \emptyset, \sigma)$ indicates that time delay does not concern probability, whereas $\surd$ stands for one unit time advancing and σ stands for the state after the time delay.

Further, for $(tag, \mu, \sigma) : U$ in a P^--tree, if $st \in U$, it indicates that it cannot contain more than one leaf point. For example, $\{ter, wait\}$ is not allowed. Next we use some examples to illustrate our P^--tree.

Example 3.2. Let $Q_1 =_{df} x := 1\ ;\ \#1\ ;\ x := x + 1 \sqcap_{0.4} x := x + 2$. We find that below is one P^--tree of program Q_1.

$$\{\mid (1, 1, \sigma_1) : \{T_0\} \mid\}$$

$$\begin{aligned} \text{where,}\quad T_0 &= \{\mid (\surd, \emptyset, \sigma_1) : \{T_1\} \mid\} \quad \text{and} \\ T_1 &= \{\mid (1, 0.4, \sigma_1) : \{T_{1,1}\},\ (1, 0.6, \sigma_1) : \{T_{1,2}\} \mid\} \quad \text{and} \\ T_{1,1} &= \{\mid (1, 1, \sigma_2) : \{ter\} \mid\},\ T_{1,2} = \{\mid (1, 1, \sigma_3) : \{ter\} \mid\} \end{aligned}$$

Here, $\sigma_1 = \{x \mapsto 1\}$, $\sigma_2 = \{x \mapsto 2\}$ and $\sigma_3 = \{x \mapsto 3\}$.

For snapshot $(1, 1, \sigma_1)$, it is used to model the contribution of $x := 1$. Snapshot $(\surd, \emptyset, \sigma_1)$ is used to model $\#1$. Tree T_1 models the behavior of $x := x + 1 \sqcap_{0.4} x := x := x + 2$, whereas tree $T_{1,1}$ and $T_{1,2}$ model the behaviour of $x := x+1$ and $x := x+2$ respectively.

Furthermore, let $Q_2 =_{df} x := 1\ ;\ \#1\ ;\ x := x+1 \sqcap x := x+2$, below is the P^--tree of program Q_2.

$$\{\mid (1, 1, \sigma_1) : \{T_2\} \mid\}$$

$$\begin{aligned} \text{where,}\quad T_2 &= \{\mid (\surd, \emptyset, \sigma_1) : \{T_{3,r} \mid 0 \le r \le 1\} \mid\} \text{ and} \\ T_{3,r} &= \{\mid (1, r, \sigma_1) : \{T_{1,1}\},\ (1, 1 - r, \sigma_1) : \{T_{1,2}\} \mid\} \end{aligned}$$

Here, $T_{1,1}$ and $T_{1,2}$ have been defined in the above for modelling $x := x + 1$ and $x := x+2$ respectively. $T_{3,r}$ is used to model the probabilistic choice $x := x+1 \sqcap_r x := x + 2$. Hence, $\{T_{3,r} \mid 0 \le r \le 1\}$ can model the behaviour of nondeterministic choice $x := x + 1 \sqcap x := x + 2$. □

Next we use an example to illustrate how a process's behaviour and its environment's behaviour cooperate.

Example 3.3. Let $Q_1 = x := 1 \sqcap_{0.4} x := 2$, $Q_2 = y := 1 \sqcap_{0.3} y := 2$, $Q = Q_1 \parallel Q_2$. Consider the P^--trees for process Q_1, Q_2 and Q respectively.

We consider the case that, for process Q, the assignment in Q_1 is scheduled first. In this case, below is one P^--tree for Q_1 at the initial state (tag, μ, σ_0).

$$\begin{aligned}(tag, \mu, \sigma_0) : \{ \{\!| \, & (1, 0.4, \sigma_0) : \{ \{\!|(1, 1, \sigma_1) : \{ter\}|\!\} \}, \\ & (1, 0.6, \sigma_0) : \{ \{\!|(1, 1, \sigma_2) : \{ter\}|\!\} \} \\ & |\!\} \}\end{aligned}$$

where, $\sigma_0 = \{x \mapsto 0,\ y \mapsto 0\}$, $\sigma_1 = \{x \mapsto 1,\ y \mapsto 0\}$, $\sigma_2 = \{x \mapsto 2,\ y \mapsto 0\}$.

As Q_1 is scheduled first, similarly, below is the corresponding P^--tree for Q_2 at the initial state (tag, μ, σ_0).

$$\begin{aligned}(tag, \mu, \sigma_0) : \{ \{\!| \, & (0^-, 0.4, \sigma_0) : \{ \{\!|(0^-, 1, \sigma_1) : \{T_2\}|\!\} \}, \\ & (0^-, 0.6, \sigma_0) : \{ \{\!|(0^-, 1, \sigma_1) : \{T_2'\}|\!\} \} \\ & |\!\} \}\end{aligned}$$

$$\begin{aligned}\text{where,}\quad T_2 &= \{\!| \, (1, 0.3, \sigma_1) : \{\{\!|(1, 1, \sigma_1') : \{ter\}|\!\}\}, \\ &\qquad (1, 0.7, \sigma_1) : \{\{\!|(1, 1, \sigma_1'') : \{ter\}|\!\}\} \, |\!\} \\ T_2' &= \{\!| \, (1, 0.3, \sigma_2) : \{\{\!|(1, 1, \sigma_2') : \{ter\}|\!\}\}, \\ &\qquad (1, 0.7, \sigma_2) : \{\{\!|(1, 1, \sigma_2'') : \{ter\}|\!\}\} \, |\!\}\end{aligned}$$

$$\begin{aligned}\text{where,}\quad & \sigma_1' = \{x \mapsto 1,\ y \mapsto 1\}, \quad \sigma_1'' = \{x \mapsto 1,\ y \mapsto 2\} \\ & \sigma_2' = \{x \mapsto 2,\ y \mapsto 1\}, \quad \sigma_2'' = \{x \mapsto 2,\ y \mapsto 2\}\end{aligned}$$

Hence, below is the corresponding P^--tree for process Q (i.e., parallel process $Q_1 \parallel Q_2$), which is the merge of the P^--tree of process Q_1 and the corresponding P^--tree of Q_2.

$$\begin{aligned}(tag, \mu, \sigma_0) : \{ \{\!| \, & (1, 0.4, \sigma_0) : \{ \{\!|(1, 1, \sigma_1) : \{T_2\}|\!\} \}, \\ & (1, 0.6, \sigma_0) : \{ \{\!|(1, 1, \sigma_2) : \{T_2'\}|\!\} \} \\ & |\!\} \}\end{aligned}$$

Similarly, we can also analyze the P^--tree of process Q for the case that the assignment in Q_2 is scheduled first. □

Definition 3.3 (P-tree)

$(tag, \mu, \sigma) : U$ is P-tree if each element in U is P^--tree. □

P-tree is composed of an initial snapshot and a set of P^--trees. The P-tree $(tag, \mu, \sigma) : U$ indicates that each P^--tree in U is initially at the state shown in snapshot (tag, μ, σ). Next we define the sequential composition for P^--trees and P-trees.

Definition 3.4 (Sequential Composition of P^--trees)

(1) $\quad ((tag_0, \mu_0, \sigma_0) : \{st\})\ ;\ \{(tag, \mu, \sigma) : V \mid (tag, \mu, \sigma) \in \Sigma\}$

$$=_{df} \begin{cases} (tag_0, \mu_0, \sigma_0) : V, & \text{if } st = ter \\ (tag_0, \mu_0, \sigma_0) : \{st\}, & \text{if } st = wait \lor st = div \end{cases}$$

If $U \neq \{st\}$, then

$$((tag_0, \mu_0, \sigma_0) : U) \,;\, \{\, (tag, \mu, \sigma) : V \mid (tag, \mu, \sigma) \in \Sigma \,\}$$
$$=_{df} (tag_0, \mu_0, \sigma_0) : \{\, T \,;\, \{\, (tag, \mu, \sigma) : V \mid (tag, \mu, \sigma) \in \Sigma \,\} \mid T \in U \,\}$$

(2) $$\{\!|(tag_i, \mu_i, \sigma_i) : U_i \mid i \in I|\!\} \,;\, \{(tag, \mu, \sigma) : V \mid (tag, \mu, \sigma) \in \Sigma\}$$
$$=_{df} \{\!|\, (tag_i, \mu_i, \sigma_i) : (U_i \,;\, \{(tag, \mu, \sigma) : V \mid (tag, \mu, \sigma) \in \Sigma\}) \mid i \in I \,|\!\}$$

(3) $$\{(tag, \mu, \sigma) : U \mid (tag, \mu, \sigma) \in \Sigma\} \,;\, \{(tag_1, \mu_1, \sigma_1) : V \mid (tag_1, \mu_1, \sigma_1) \in \Sigma\}$$
$$=_{df} \{\, ((tag, \mu, \sigma) : U) \,;\, \{(tag_1, \mu_1, \sigma_1) : V \mid (tag_1, \mu_1, \sigma_1) \in \Sigma\}) \mid (tag, \mu, \sigma) \in \Sigma \,\}$$

□

Here, the notation Σ stands for the set containing all the snapshots. The above definition deals with the sequential composition of P-trees or P^--trees. The first one considers the sequential composition of P-tree and a set of P-trees (at any different initial state). Its definition can be divided into two cases according to the case that the first P-tree is a leaf point or not. The leaf point can be the terminating state, waiting state or divergence state.

The second one considers the sequential composition of a P^--tree and a set of P-trees (at any different initial state). The third one considers the sequential composition of a set of P-trees with another set of P-trees. Both of the two sets of P-trees can be at any different initial state.

Example 3.5. Let $P =_{df} x := 0 \sqcap x := 1$ and $Q =_{df} y := 0 \sqcap_{0.5} y := 1$. Now we want to calculate $Prob(P; Q, x = y)$ and $Prob(Q; P, x = y)$. Assume the initial states of x and y are -1 respectively. Here the notation $Prob(W, c)$ stands for the probability that the final state of program W satisfies condition c.

First, we consider the P-tree for program $P; Q$, shown below.

$$\begin{aligned}(tag, \mu, \sigma) : \{\, \{\!|\, & (1, r, \sigma) : \{\{\!|(1, 1, \sigma_0) : \{T_1\}|\!\}\},\\ & (1, 1-r, \sigma) : \{\{\!|(1, 1, \sigma_1) : \{T_2\}|\!\}\}\\ & |\!\} \mid 0 \leq r \leq 1 \,\}\end{aligned}$$

$$\begin{aligned}\text{where, } T_1 &= \{\!|\ (1, 0.5, \sigma_0) : \{\{\!|(1, 1, \sigma_0') : \{ter\}|\!\}\},\\ &\qquad (1, 0.5, \sigma_0) : \{\{\!|(1, 1, \sigma_0'') : \{ter\}|\!\}\}\ |\!\}\\ T_2 &= \{\!|\ (1, 0.5, \sigma_1) : \{\{\!|(1, 1, \sigma_1') : \{ter\}|\!\}\},\\ &\qquad (1, 0.5, \sigma_1) : \{\{\!|(1, 1, \sigma_1'') : \{ter\}|\!\}\}\ |\!\}\end{aligned}$$

$$\sigma = \{x \mapsto -1,\ y \mapsto -1\},$$
$$\sigma_0 = \{x \mapsto 0,\ y \mapsto -1\},\quad \sigma_0' = \{x \mapsto 0,\ y \mapsto 0\},\quad \sigma_0'' = \{x \mapsto 0,\ y \mapsto 1\},$$
$$\sigma_1 = \{x \mapsto 1,\ y \mapsto -1\},\quad \sigma_1' = \{x \mapsto 1,\ y \mapsto 0\},\quad \sigma_1'' = \{x \mapsto 1,\ y \mapsto 1\},$$

Based on the P-tree for program $P; Q$, we can have:

$$\begin{aligned}& Prob(P \,;\, Q,\ x = y)\\ =\ & min\{r \times 1 \times 0.5 \times 1 + (1-r) \times 1 \times 0.5 \times 1 \mid 0 \leq r \leq 1\}\\ =\ & min\{0.5 \mid 0 \leq r \leq 1\}\ =\ 0.5\end{aligned}$$

Next we consider the P-tree for program $Q; P$, shown below.

$$(tag, \mu, \sigma) : \{ \ \{\!\!| (1, 0.5, \sigma) : \{ \ \{\!\!| (1, 1, \sigma_2) : \{T_{3,r} \mid 0 \leq r \leq 1\} \ |\!\!\} \ \}, \\ (1, 0.5, \sigma) : \{ \ \{\!\!| \ (1, 1, \sigma_3) : \{T_{4,r} \mid 0 \leq r \leq 1\} \ |\!\!\} \ \} \\ |\!\!\} \ \}$$

where,
$$T_{3,r} = \{\!\!| \ (1, r, \sigma_2) : \{\{\!\!|(1, 1, \sigma_2') : \{ter\}|\!\!\}\}, \\ (1, 1-r, \sigma_2) : \{\{\!\!|(1, 1, \sigma_2'') : \{ter\}|\!\!\}\} \ |\!\!\}$$
$$T_{4,r} = \{\!\!| \ (1, r, \sigma_3) : \{\{\!\!|(1, 1, \sigma_3') : \{ter\}|\!\!\}\}, \\ (1, 1-r, \sigma_3) : \{\{\!\!|(1, 1, \sigma_3'') : \{ter\}|\!\!\}\} \ |\!\!\}$$

$$\sigma_2 = \{x \mapsto -1, \ y \mapsto 0\}, \ \ \sigma_2' = \{x \mapsto 0, \ y \mapsto 0\}, \ \ \sigma_2'' = \{x \mapsto 1, \ y \mapsto 0\},$$
$$\sigma_3 = \{x \mapsto -1, \ y \mapsto 1\}, \ \ \sigma_3' = \{x \mapsto 0, \ y \mapsto 1\}, \ \ \sigma_3'' = \{x \mapsto 1, \ y \mapsto 1\},$$

Based on the P-tree for program $Q; P$, we can have:

$$Prob(Q \ ; \ P, \ x = y) \\ = 0.5 \times 1 \times min\{r \times 1 \mid 0 \leq r \leq 1\} + 0.5 \times 1 \times min\{r \times 1 \mid 0 \leq r \leq 1\} \\ = 0$$

□

In order to support to later formalization of each statement, we introduce the concept of $idle0(tag, b)$ P^--tree (tag can be 0 or 0^-, and b is a Boolean condition).

Definition 3.6 ($idle0(tag, b)$ P^--tree)

(1) st is $idle0(tag, b)$, where $st = wait$ or ter.

(2) $\{\!\!|(tag, p_i, \sigma_i) : S_i \mid i \in I|\!\!\}$ is $idle0(tag, b)$, if for any $i \in I$, $b(\sigma_i)$ and $\forall X \in S_i \bullet$ X is $idle0(tag, b)$.

where, $tag = 0$ or 0^-. □

For the snapshots in an $idle0(0, b)$ P^--tree, the flag parts are all 0. This indicates that all the newly added states (with probabilities) are contributed by the environment and Boolean condition b is satisfied for all these newly added states. Further, there are no $(\surd, \emptyset, \sigma)$ snapshots in an $idle0(0, b)$ P^--tree. This means that all actions reflected in an $idle0(0, b)$ P^--tree is instantaneous. Similarly, the concept of $idle0(0^-, b)$ P^--tree is defined in the above definition.

Now we can also define the concept of $idle(tag, b)$ P^--tree ($tag = 0$ or 0^-, and b is a Boolean condition). An $idle(tag, b)$ tree not only can contain instantaneous action, but also can contain time delay snapshots.

(1') st is $idle(tag, b)$, where $st = wait$ or ter.

(2') $\{\!\!|(tag, p_i, \sigma_i) : S_i \mid i \in I|\!\!\}$ is $idle(tag, b)$, if for any $i \in I$, $b_i(\sigma)$ and $\forall X \in S_i \bullet$ X is $idle(tag, b)$.

(3') $\{\!\!|(\surd, \emptyset, \sigma) : S|\!\!\}$ is $idle(tag, b)$, if $b(\sigma)$ and $\forall X \in S \bullet X$ is $idle(tag, b)$.

where, $tag = 0$ or 0^-. □

Based on the definitions of P-trees and P^--trees, the denotational semantics for process P can be formalized in the form below.

$$\{\, (tag, \mu, \sigma) : U \mid (tag, \mu, \sigma) \in \Sigma \,\}$$

Here, U contains a set of P^--trees and Σ stands for the set containing all snapshots.

4 Denotational Semantics for *PTSC* Statements

Based on the introduction of *P*-tree (and P^--tree), this section is to study the denotational semantics for *PTSC*, including sequential constructs, timed constructs, probabilistic choice, nondeterminism, guarded choice and parallel composition.

4.1 Sequential Constructs

Assignment. Assignment is considered as an atomic action. Before the assignment is scheduled, the environment may also have a chance to be scheduled to perform actions.

Firstly, we define function *append*(T, x, e), which appends the assignment of variable x with e to P^--tree T.

$$\begin{aligned} &append(\{\!|(tag_i, \mu_i, \sigma_i) : U_i \mid i \in I|\!\}, x, e) \\ =_{df}\ &\{\!|(tag_i, \mu_i, \sigma_i) : \{\, attach(\sigma_i, U_i, x, e) \,\} \mid i \in I|\!\} \end{aligned}$$

where,

$$\begin{aligned} &attach(\sigma, U, x, e) \\ =_{df}\ &(\, (1, 1, \sigma[e/x]) : \{ter\}) \lhd U = \{ter\} \rhd \\ &\qquad (\, U \lhd U = \{wait\} \vee U = \{div\} \rhd (\forall T \in U \bullet append(T, x, e))\,) \end{aligned}$$

Here, $attach(\sigma, U, x, e)$ means adding a new snapshot (the update of variable x with e) to the terminating leaf of all P^--trees in U. Its definition can be defined recursively. When a leaf is encountered, if it is a terminating leaf, the adding will be performed. On the other hand, when divergence leaf or waiting leaf is encountered, the adding will not be performed.

Similarly,

$$\begin{aligned} &append((tag, \mu, \sigma) : U, x, e) \\ =_{df}\ &(tag, \mu, \sigma) : \{\, attach(\sigma, T, x, e) \mid \forall T \in U \,\} \end{aligned}$$

Then, the semantics of $x := e$ can be described as the tree behaviour shown below. Formula $idle(0^-, true)$ here indicates that, before the assignment is scheduled, the environment can have chances to perform instantaneous actions. The symbol 0^- indicates that, after the environment's instantaneous actions, the process itself will perform assignment action.

$$\begin{aligned} &[\![x := e]\!] \\ =_{df}\ &\{\, append((tag, \mu, \sigma) : U,\ x,\ e) \mid (tag, \mu, \sigma) \in \Sigma\ \wedge \\ &\qquad\qquad \forall X \in U \bullet X \text{ is } idle0(0^-, true) \,\} \end{aligned}$$

Chaos. For Chaos statement, its denotational semantics can be defined as below:

$$[\![\textbf{Chaos}]\!] =_{df} \{\, (tag, \mu, \sigma) : \{div\} \mid (tag, \mu, \sigma) \in \Sigma \,\}$$

Sequential Composition. $(P \; ; \; Q)$ behaves like P before P terminates, and then behaves like Q afterwards.

$$[\![P \; ; \; Q]\!] =_{df} [\![P]\!] \; ; \; [\![Q]\!]$$

Conditional. The definition of conditional can be defined as below.

$$\begin{aligned} & [\![\mathbf{if}\ b\ \mathbf{then}\ P\ \mathbf{else}\ Q]\!] \\ =_{df} & \{ \ (tag, \mu, \sigma) : U \lhd b(\sigma) \rhd (tag, \mu, \sigma : V) \\ & \quad \mid (tag, \mu, \sigma) \in \Sigma \wedge (tag, \mu, \sigma) : U \in [\![P]\!] \\ & \quad \quad \wedge (tag, \mu, \sigma) : V \in [\![Q]\!] \ \} \end{aligned}$$

Iteration. In order to define the semantics of iteration, we define the partial order below.

$$\begin{aligned} & \{\!|(tag_i, \mu_i, \sigma_i) : U_i \mid i \in I|\!\} \sqsupseteq \{\!|(tag_j, \mu_j, \sigma_j) : V_j\} \mid j \in J|\!\} \\ =_{df} & \forall i \in I \bullet \exists j \in J \bullet (tag_i, \mu_i, \sigma_i) : U_i \in \{\!|(tag_i, \mu_i, \sigma_i) : U_i|\!\} \ \wedge \\ & \quad (tag_j, \mu_j, \sigma_j) : V_j \in \{\!|(tag_j, \mu_j, \sigma_j) : V_j|\!\} \ \wedge \\ & \quad (tag_i, \mu_i, \sigma_i) = (tag_j, \mu_j, \sigma_j) \ \wedge \\ & \quad \forall X \in U_i \bullet \exists Y \in V_j \bullet (X \sqsupseteq Y \wedge X \approx Y) \end{aligned}$$

where, the equivalence relation $\approx$ on trees will be defined in section 5.

Then we can use this order to give the order $\sqsupseteq$ for programs. Based on this, we can give the definition for iteration. The iteration construct is defined in the same way as its counterpart in conventional programming language.

$$[\![\mathbf{while}\ b\ \mathbf{do}\ P]\!] =_{df} \mu X \bullet [\![\mathbf{if}\ b\ \mathbf{then}\ (P; X)\ \mathbf{else}\ II]\!]$$

where:

(1) $[\![II]\!] =_{df} \{ \ (tag, \mu, \sigma) : \{ter\} \mid (tag, \mu, \sigma) \in \Sigma \ \}$
(2) The notation $\mu X \bullet F(X)$ denotes the weakest fixed point of the monotonic function F.

4.2 Timed Constructs

Time Delay. Firstly we consider the time delay statement. The definition is based on two $tick$ and $tick'$ functions.

$$\begin{aligned} & tick'((tag, \mu, \sigma) : \{st\}) \\ =_{df} & \begin{cases} (tag, \mu, \sigma) : \{st\} & \text{if } st = wait \text{ or } div \\ (tag, \mu, \sigma) : \{(\surd, \emptyset, \sigma) : \{ter\}\} & \text{if } st = ter \end{cases} \end{aligned}$$

and

$$tick'((tag, \mu, \sigma) : U) =_{df} (tag, \mu, \sigma) : \{tick(X) \mid X \in U\}$$

Then, a further function $tick$ can be defined as:

$$tick(\{\!|(tag_i, \mu_i, \sigma_i) : U_i \mid i \in I|\!\})$$

$$=_{df} \{\!\!|\ tick'((tag_i, \mu_i, \sigma_i) : U_i) \mid i \in I\ |\!\!\}$$

Based on the above definitions, we can have the semantics of #1 via the tree behaviour.

$$[\![\#1]\!] =_{df} \{\ (tag, \mu, \sigma) : \{tick(X) \mid X \text{ is } idle0(0, true)\} \mid (tag, \mu, \sigma) \in \Sigma\ \}$$

$$[\![\#n]\!] =_{df} [\![\#1]\!]\ ;\ [\![\#(n-1)]\!]$$

For #1, before time advancing, the environment may perform assignments with certain probabilities at the current time point. This behaviour can be expressed as an $idle0(0, true)$ tree. For the behaviour of $\#n$, it can be defined recursively.

Event Guard. Now we are ready to consider the event triggering behaviour. Firstly we define the concept of $trig(b, f)$ ($f = 0$ or 1) as below.

$$\{\!\!|\ (0, p_i, \sigma_i) : U_i \mid i \in I\ |\!\!\} \text{ is } trig(b, f),$$

if it satisfies the following conditions

$$\begin{pmatrix} \exists i \in I \bullet b(\sigma_i) \wedge \\ \forall i \in I \bullet b(\sigma_i) \Rightarrow U_i = \{ter\} \wedge \\ \forall i \in I \bullet \neg b(\sigma_i) \Rightarrow \forall X \in U_i \bullet X \text{ is } leaffired(b, f) \end{pmatrix}$$

For the concept of $leaffired(b, f)$ P^--tree ($f = 0$ or 1), it can be defined as below.

(1) $\{\!\!|\ (0, p_i, \sigma_i) : U_i \mid i \in I\ |\!\!\}$ is $leaffired(b, f)$ ($f = 0$ or 1) if it satisfies the following condition

$$\forall i \in I \bullet \begin{pmatrix} b(\sigma_i) \Rightarrow U_i = \{ter\} \wedge \\ \neg b(\sigma_i) \Rightarrow \forall X \in U_i \bullet X \text{ is } leaffired(b, f) \end{pmatrix}$$

(2) $\{\!\!|\ (\surd, \emptyset, \sigma) : U\ |\!\!\}$ is $leaffired(b, 1)$ if it satisfies the following condition

$$\begin{pmatrix} b(\sigma) \Rightarrow U = \{ter\} \wedge \\ \neg b(\sigma) \Rightarrow \forall X \in U \bullet X \text{ is } (leaffired(b, 0) \vee leaffired(b, 1)) \end{pmatrix}$$

For $@b$, there are two firing cases. The first case is that event $@b$ is fired at the initial state, which is denoted as formula $Immefired(b)$. The second case is that it waits for the environment to fire it. This case can be described using two formulae $Await(b, 1)$ and $Trig(b, 1)$. Formula $Await(b, 1)$ indicates that all the environment behaviour cannot fire $@b$. $Trig(b, 1)$ indicates that $@b$ is fired finally. Then the semantics of $@\,b$ can be defined as:

$$[\![@\,b]\!] =_{df} Immefired(b) \cup (Await(b, 1)\ ;\ Trig(b, 1))$$

where,

$$Immefired(b)$$
$$=_{df} \{\ (tag, \mu, \sigma) : \{ter\} \mid (tag, \mu, \sigma) \in \Sigma \wedge b(\sigma)\ \}$$

$$Await(b, f)$$
$$=_{df} \{\ (tag, \mu, \sigma) : U \mid (tag, \mu, \sigma) \in \Sigma \wedge \neg b(\sigma) \wedge \forall X \in U \bullet (f = 0 \wedge X \text{ is } idle0(0, \neg b) \vee f = 1 \wedge X \text{ is } idle(0, \neg b))\ \}$$

$$Trig(b, f)$$
$$=_{df} \{ (tag, \mu, \sigma) : U \mid (tag, \mu, \sigma) \in \Sigma \wedge \neg b(\sigma) \wedge \forall X \in U \bullet X \text{ is } trig(b, f) \}$$

Here, $f = 0,\ 1$.

4.3 Probabilistic Nondeterminism

Firstly we consider the definition for probabilistic nondeterminism $P \sqcap_r Q$.

$$[\![P \sqcap_r Q]\!]$$
$$=_{df} \{ (tag, \mu, \sigma) : U \mid (tag, \mu, \sigma) \in \Sigma \ \wedge \ \forall X \in U \ \bullet \ X \text{ is } idle0(0^-, true) \} ;$$
$$\{ (tag, \mu, \sigma) : \{T(r)\} \mid (tag, \mu, \sigma) \in \Sigma \}$$

where,

$$T(r) =_{df} \{\!| (1, r, \sigma) : U,\ (1, 1 - r, \sigma) : V |\!\}$$

and, $(tag, \mu, \sigma) : U \in [\![P]\!]$, $(tag, \mu, \sigma) : V \in [\![Q]\!]$

Moreover, we can give the definition for $P \sqcap Q$.

$$[\![P \sqcap Q]\!]$$
$$=_{df} \{ (tag, \mu, \sigma) : U \mid (tag, \mu, \sigma) \in \Sigma \ \wedge \ \forall X \in U \ \bullet \ X \text{ is } idle0(0^-, true) \} ;$$
$$\{ (tag, \mu, \sigma) : \{T(r) \mid 0 \leq r \leq 1\} \mid (tag, \mu, \sigma) \in \Sigma \}$$

4.4 Guarded Choice

As mentioned earlier, there are five types of guarded choice. Now we give the denotational semantics for these five types of guarded choice.

Assignment Guarded Choice. Firstly, we consider the assignment guarded choice, which is composed of a set of assignment guarded components.

Let $P = \ \|_{i \in I} \{[p_i]\ choice_{j \in J_i} (b_{ij} \& (x_{ij} := e_{ij})\ P_{ij})\}$

Then,

$$[\![P]\!]$$
$$=_{df} \{((tag, \mu, \sigma) : idle0(0^-, true)) \ ; \ ImmeAssi(\{P\}) \mid (tag, \mu, \sigma) \in \Sigma\}$$

where,

$$ImmeAssi(S) =_{df} \{(tag, \mu, \sigma) : \{T(P) \mid P \in S\} \mid (tag, \mu, \sigma) \in \Sigma\}$$
$$T(P) =_{df} \{\!| \forall j \in J_i \bullet \text{if } b_{ij} \text{ then } (1, p_i, \sigma_{ij}) : V_{ij}$$
$$\mid i \in I \wedge (1, p_i, \sigma_{ij}) : V_{ij} \in [\![P_{ij}]\!] |\!\}$$

The formula $idle0(0^-, true)$ here indicates that, before any assignment is scheduled, the environment will have chances to perform the instantaneous actions. The execution of assignment guarded components is expressed by formulae $ImmeAssi(\{P\})$ and $T(P)$.

Event Guarded Choice. Now we consider the denotational semantics for the second type of guarded choice, which is composed of a set of event guarded components.

Let $P = \|_{i\in I}\{@b_i\, P_i\}$.

Then,

$$\begin{aligned} & [\![P]\!] \\ =_{df}\; & Immefired(\|_{i\in I}\{@b_i\, P_i\}) \\ & \cup\ (Await(b,1)\ ;\ Trig(b,1)\ ;\ Imme(\|_{i\in I}\{@b_i\, P_i\})) \end{aligned}$$

where,

$$\begin{aligned} b &= \vee_{i\in I}\, b_i \\ & Immefired(\|_{i\in I}\{@b_i\, P_i\}) \\ =_{df}\; & \{(tag,\mu,\sigma) : U \mid (tag,\mu,\sigma)\in \Sigma \wedge \\ & \qquad \exists i \in I \bullet (b_i(\sigma) \wedge (tag,\mu,\sigma) : U \in [\![P_i]\!])\} \end{aligned}$$

Time Delay Guarded Choice. For the third type of guarded choice, it is composed of only one time delay component.

$$[\![\|\{\#1\ P\}]\!] =_{df} [\![\#1]\!]\ ;\ [\![P]\!]$$

Guarded Choice Composing of Assignment Guarded Choice and Event Guarded Choice. For the fourth type of guarded choice, it is composed of a set of assignment guarded components and a set of event guarded components.

Let $P = \|_{i\in I}\{[p_i]\ choice_{j\in J_i}(b_{ij}\&(x_{ij} := e_{ij})\, P_{ij})\}\|\|_{k\in K}\{@c_k\, Q_k\}$ and

$P1 = \|_{i\in I}\{[p_i]\ choice_{j\in J_i}(b_{ij}\&(x_{ij} := e_{ij})\, P_{ij})\}$.

Then,

$$\begin{aligned} & [\![P]\!] \\ =_{df}\; & Immefied(\|_{k\in K}\{@c_k\, Q_k\}) \\ & \cup\ (\ Await(c,0)\ ;\ ImmAssi(P1)\ ) \\ & \cup\ (\ Await(c,0)\ ;\ Trig(c,0)\ ;\ Imme(\|_{k\in K}\{@c_k\, Q_k\})\ ) \end{aligned}$$

where, $c = \vee_{k\in K}\, c_k$

As the fourth type of guarded choice contains assignment guarded components, the waiting period of waiting the event guards to be fired is at the current time point. The formulae $Await(c,0)$ and $Trig(c,0)$ are applied.

Guarded Choice Composing of Event Guarded Choice and Time Delay Guarded Choice. Now we consider the denotational semantics for the fifth type of guarded choice, which is composed of event guarded choice and time delay guarded choice.

Let $P = \|_{i\in I}\{@b_i\, P_i\}\|\{\#1\ R\}$.

Then,

$$\begin{aligned} &[\![P]\!] \\ =_{df}\ & Immefired(\|_{i\in I}\{@b_i\, P_i\}) \\ &\cup\ (\ Await(b,0)\ ;\ Trig(b,0)\ ;\ Imme(\|_{i\in I}\{@b_i\, P_i\})\ ) \\ &\ \ (\ Await(b,0)\ ;\ \mathbf{phase1}\ ;\ [\![R]\!]\ ) \end{aligned}$$

where, $b = \vee_{i\in I}\, b_i$

$$\mathbf{phase1} =_{df} \{\ (tag,\mu,\sigma) : \{\{\!|(\surd,\emptyset,\sigma) : \{ter\}|\!\}\} \mid (tag,\mu,\sigma)\in\Sigma\ \}$$

For the fifth type of guarded choice, the event guards can be fired immediately, or waiting for the environment to fire them. The waiting period should be at the current time point. If at the current time point, all the events are not fired, then time will advance one unit. This can be expressed by formula **phase1**.

Or Construct for Guarded Choice. In order to support the expansion laws of general parallel composition, we introduce the concept of the **or** Construct for Guarded Choice. Below are the two cases for the **or** Construct.

(1) Let $P = \|_{i\in I}\{[p_i]\ choice_{j\in J_i}(b_{ij}\&(x_{ij} := e_{ij})\, P_{ij})\}$ and
$Q = \|_{k\in K}\{[q_k]\ choice_{l\in L_k}(c_{kl}\&(y_{kl} := f_{kl})\, Q_{kl})\}$.

Then,

$$\begin{aligned} &[\![P \mathbf{\ or\ } Q]\!] \\ =_{df}\ & \{((tag,\mu,\sigma) : idle0(0^-, true))\ ;\ ImmeAssi(\{P,Q\}) \mid (tag,\mu,\sigma)\in\Sigma\} \end{aligned}$$

(2) Let

$$\begin{aligned} P &= \|_{i\in I}\{[p_i]\ choice_{j\in J_i}(b_{ij}\&(x_{ij} := e_{ij})\, P_{ij})\} \\ &\quad \|\|_{m\in M}\{@c_m\, R_m\} \\ P1 &= \|_{i\in I}\{[p_i]\ choice_{j\in J_i}(b_{ij}\&(x_{ij} := e_{ij})\, P_{ij})\} \\ Q &= \|_{k\in K}\{[q_k]\ choice_{l\in L_k}(b_{kl}\&(y_{kl} := f_{kl})\, Q_{kl})\} \\ &\quad \|\|_{m\in M}\{@c_m\, R_m\} \\ Q1 &= \|_{k\in K}\{[q_k]\ choice_{l\in L_k}(b_{kl}\&(y_{kl} := f_{kl})\, Q_{kl})\} \end{aligned}$$

Then,

$$\begin{aligned} &[\![P \mathbf{\ or\ } Q]\!] \\ =_{df}\ & Immefired(\|_{m\in M}\{@c_m\, R_m\}) \\ &\cup\ (\ Await(c,0)\ ;\ ImmAssi(\{P1,Q1\})\ ) \\ &\cup\ (\ Await(c,0)\ ;\ Trig(c,0)\ ;\ Imme(\|_{m\in M}\{@c_m\, R_m\})\ ) \end{aligned}$$

where, $c = \vee_{m\in M}\, c_m$

4.5 Probabilistic Parallel Composition

Now we consider the probabilistic parallel composition. In order to deal with the definition for probability parallel composition, we first define the probabilistic merge operator $\otimes_r$. This can be done by the case analysis.

Firstly we consider the case that P can perform probabilistic atomic actions initially. If Q can also perform probabilistic atomic actions initially, $P \otimes_r Q$ can also perform probabilistic atomic actions initially from both P and Q. And the probability of these assignments needs to be updated with the probability parameter r (or $1 - r$).

If Q can observe the environment's behaviour and its subsequent behaviour is assignment, we regard $P \otimes_r Q$ as undefined. This consideration is reflected in (1.b) and it can support the understanding of (1.a).

If Q can observe the environment's behaviour and its subsequent behaviour is not assignment, their merge $P \otimes_r Q$ can also perform these assignments from P without any change of the probabilities. This understanding supports the definition of event firing behaviour.

On the other hand, if Q can do time delay, their merge $P \otimes_r Q$ is undefined. This is because assignment is the instantaneous behavior and the two process cannot be compared.

Below are the detailed definition for the above four cases when P can perform probabilistic atomic actions initially.

(1) If $P = \{\!|(1, p_i, \sigma_i) : U_i \mid i \in I|\!\}$ and

(1.a) if $Q = \{\!|(1, q_k, \sigma_k) : V_k \mid k \in K|\!\}$, then

$$\begin{aligned} &P \otimes_r Q \\ &=_{df} \{\!|\ (1, r \times p_i, \sigma_i) : \{X \otimes_r Q \mid X \in U_i\}, \\ &\qquad (1, (1 - r) \times p_k, \sigma_k) : \{P \otimes_r Y \mid Y \in V_k\} \ \mid i \in I \wedge k \in K\ |\!\} \end{aligned}$$

(1.b) if $Q = \{\!|(0^-, q_k, \sigma_k) : V_k \mid k \in K|\!\}$, then $P \otimes_r Q =_{df} undefined$

(1.c) if $Q = \{\!|(0, q_k, \sigma_k) : V_k \mid k \in K|\!\}$, then there exists a permutation j_1, $j_2, \cdots, j_{|I|}$ of K such that $\forall i \in \bullet p_i = q_{j_i}$ and $\sigma_i = \sigma_{j_i}$, and there exists a bijection $f_i : U_i \to V_{j_i}$ such that $\forall X \in U_i \bullet X \otimes_r f_{j_i}(X)$ is well-defined

$$P \otimes_r Q =_{df} \{\!|(1, p_i, \sigma_i) : \{X \otimes_r f_{j_i}(X) \mid X \in U_i\} \mid i \in U|\!\}$$

(1.d) if $Q = \{\!|(\surd, \emptyset, \sigma) : V|\!\}$, then $P \otimes_r Q =_{df} undefined$

Secondly, we consider the case when P is in observing the environment's behaviour and its subsequent behaviour is probabilistic assignment. Item (2.a) is similar to (1.b). The analysis for (2.b) is also similar to (1.b). Furthermore, If Q is in observing the environment's behaviour and its subsequent behaviour is not probabilistic assignment, we regard their merge ($P \otimes_r Q$) is still in observing the environment's behaviour and its subsequent behaviour is still assignment action. On the other hand, item (2.d) considers the case that Q can let time advance. As P is currently in observing the environment's instantaneous action, we regard $P \otimes_r Q$ as undefined in this case.

(2) If $P = \{\!|(0^-, p_i, \sigma_i) : U_i\} \mid i \in I|\!\}$ and

(2.a) if $Q = \{\!|(1, q_k, \sigma_k) : V_k\} \mid k \in K|\!\}$, then $P \otimes_r Q =_{df} undefined$

(2.b) if $Q = \{\!|(0^-, q_k, \sigma_k) : V_k\}| \ k \in K|\!\}$, then $P \otimes_r Q =_{df} undefined$

(2.c) if $Q = \{\!|(0, q_k, \sigma_k) : V_k\}|\ k \in K|\!\}$, then there exists a permutation j_1, $j_2, \cdots, j_{|I|}$ of K such that $\forall i \in \bullet p_i = q_{j_i}$ and $\sigma_i = \sigma_{j_i}$, and there exists a bijection $f_i : U_i \to V_{j_i}$ such that $\forall X \in U_i \bullet X \otimes_r f_{j_i}(X)$ is well-defined

$$P \otimes_r Q =_{df} \{\!|(0^-, p_i, \sigma_i) : \{X \otimes_r f_{j_i}(X) \mid X \in U_i\} \mid i \in I|\!\}$$

(2.d) if $Q = \{\!|(\surd, \emptyset, \sigma) : V\}|\!\}$, then $P \otimes_r Q =_{df} undefined$

Thirdly, we consider the case that P is in observing the environment's behaviour and its subsequent behaviour is not probabilistic assignment. Item (3.a) and (3.b) are similar to (1.c) and (2.c) respectively. On the other hand, if Q is also in observing the environment's behaviour and its subsequent behaviour is not probabilistic assignment, their merge ($P \otimes_r Q$) belongs to the same execution type. The consideration for (3.d) is similar to (2.d).

(3) If $P = \{\!|(0, p_i, \sigma_i) : U_i \mid i \in I|\!\}$ and

(3.a) if $Q = \{\!|(1, p_k, \sigma_k) : V_k\} \mid k \in K|\!\}$, then $P \otimes_r Q$ is the same as (1.c)

(3.b) if $Q = \{\!|(0^-, p_k, \sigma_k) : V_k\} \mid k \in K|\!\}$, then $P \otimes_r Q$ is the same as (2.c)

(3.c) if $Q = \{\!|(0, p_k, \sigma_k) : V_k\} \mid k \in K|\!\}$, then there exists a permutation j_1, $j_2, \cdots, j_{|I|}$ of K such that $\forall i \in \bullet p_i = q_{j_i}$ and $\sigma_i = \sigma_{j_i}$, and there exists a bijection $f_i : U_i \to V_{j_i}$ such that $\forall X \in U_i \bullet X \otimes_r f_{j_i}(X)$ is well-defined

$$P \otimes_r Q =_{df} \{\!|(0, p_i, \sigma_i) : \{X \otimes_r f_{j_i}(X) \mid X \in U_i\} \mid i \in I|\!\}$$

(3.d) if $Q = \{\!|(\surd, \emptyset, \sigma) : V|\!\}$, then $P \otimes_r Q =_{df} undefined$

Lastly, we consider that the case that P can perform time delay initially. Item (4.a), (4.b) and (4.c) are all about performing or observing instantaneous actions initially. Hence, their merges ($P \otimes_r Q$) are considered as undefined. Item (4.d) indicates that Q can also let time advance. Therefore, their merge ($P \otimes_r Q$) can also do time advancing initially.

(4) If $P = \{\!|(\surd, \emptyset, \sigma) : U\}|\!\}$ and

(4.a) if $Q = \{\!|(1, p_k, \sigma_k) : V_k\} \mid k \in K|\!\}$, then $P \otimes_r Q =_{df} undefined$

(4.b) if $Q = \{\!|(0^-, p_k, \sigma_k) : V_k\} \mid k \in K|\!\}$, then $P \otimes_r Q =_{df} undefined$

(4.c) if $Q = \{\!|(0, p_k, \sigma_k) : V_k \mid k \in K|\!\}$, then $P \otimes_r Q =_{df} undefined$

(4.d) if $Q = \{\!|(\surd, \emptyset, \sigma) : V|\!\}$, then there exists a bijection $f : U \to V$ such that $\forall X \in U \bullet X \otimes_r f(X)$ is well-defined

$$P \otimes_r Q =_{df} \{\!|(\surd, \emptyset, \sigma) : \{X \otimes_r f(X) \mid X \in U\}|\!\}$$

Further, we also need the table below to complete the definition of $\otimes_r$.

$div \otimes_r div =_{df} div$	$div \otimes_r wait =_{df} div$	$div \otimes_r ter =_{df} div$
$wait \otimes_r div =_{df} div$	$wait \otimes_r wait =_{df} wait$	$wait \otimes_r ter =_{df} wait$
$ter \otimes_r div =_{df} div,$	$ter \otimes_r wait =_{df} wait$	$ter \otimes_r ter =_{df} ter$

We also need the following definition for further support. Here we assume that T is not empty (i.e., $T \neq st$).

$div \otimes_r T =_{df} div$	$T \otimes_r div =_{df} div$
$ter \otimes_r T =_{df} T$	$T \otimes_r ter =_{df} T$

Further, if $T \neq div$, then $wait \otimes_r T = wait$ and $T \otimes_r wait =_{df} wait$

Based on the definition of $\otimes_r$, now we can give the semantics for probabilistic parallel programs.

$$\begin{aligned} & [\![P \parallel_r Q]\!] \\ =_{df} & \{ (tag, \mu, \sigma) : \{X \otimes_r Y \mid X \in U \wedge Y \in V \wedge X \otimes_r Y \text{is well-defined}\} \\ & \mid (tag, \mu, \sigma) \in \Sigma \wedge (tag, \mu, \sigma) : U \in [\![P]\!] \wedge (tag, \mu, \sigma) : V \in [\![Q]\!] \} \end{aligned}$$

4.6 General Parallel Composition

Now we start to define the semantics for general parallel composition $\|$. We first give the definition for the merge operator $\otimes$, which is symmetric.

Firstly we consider the case that P can perform probabilistic atomic actions initially.

(1) If $P = \{\!|(1, p_i, \sigma_i) : U_i \mid i \in I|\!\}$ and

(1.a) if $Q = \{\!|(1, q_k, \sigma_k) : V_k\} \mid k \in K|\!\}$, then $P \otimes Q =_{df} undefined$

(1.b) if $Q = \{\!|(tag, q_k, \sigma_k) : V_k\} \mid k \in K|\!\}$ $(tag = 0^-$ or $0)$, then there exists a permutation $j_1, j_2, \cdots, j_{|I|}$ of K such that $\forall i \in \bullet p_i = q_{j_i}$ and $\sigma_i = \sigma_{j_i}$, and there exists a bijection $f_i : U_i \rightarrow V_{j_i}$ such that $\forall X \in U_i \bullet X \otimes f_{j_i}(X)$ is well-defined

$$P \otimes Q =_{df} \{\!|(1, p_i, \sigma_i) : \{X \otimes f_{j_i}(X) \mid X \in U_i\} \mid i \in I|\!\}$$

(1.d) if $Q = \{\!|(\surd, \emptyset, \sigma) : V|\!\}$, then $P \otimes Q =_{df} undefined$

Secondly, we consider the case that P is in the observing the environment's behaviour and its subsequent behaviour is the probabilistic assignment.

(2) If $P = \{\!|(0^-, p_i, \sigma_i) : U_i \mid I \in I|\!\}$ and

(2.b) if $Q = \{\!|(tag, q_k, \sigma_k) : V_k \mid k \in K|\!\}$ $(tag = 0^-$ or $0)$, then there exists a permutation $j_1, j_2, \cdots, j_{|I|}$ of K such that $\forall i \in \bullet p_i = q_{j_i}$ and $\sigma_i = \sigma_{j_i}$, and there exists a bijection $f_i : U_i \rightarrow V_{j_i}$ such that $\forall X \in U_i \bullet X \otimes f_{j_i}(X)$ is well-defined

$$P \otimes Q =_{df} \{\!|(0^-, p_i, \sigma_i) : \{X \otimes f_{J_i}(X) \mid X \in U_i\} \mid i \in I|\!\}$$

(2.d) if $Q = \{\!|(\surd, \emptyset, \sigma) : V|\!\}$, then $P \otimes Q =_{df} undefined$

Thirdly, we consider the case that P is in the observing the environment's behaviour and its subsequent behaviour is not the probabilistic assignment.

(3) If $P = \{\!|(0, p_i, \sigma_i) : U_i \mid i \in I|\!\}$ and

(3.c) if $Q = \{\!|(0, q_k, \sigma_k) : V_k \mid k \in K|\!\}$, then there exists a permutation j_1, j_2, $\cdots$, $j_{|I|}$ of K such that $\forall i \in \bullet p_i = q_{j_i}$ and $\sigma_i = \sigma_{j_i}$, and there exists a bijection $f_i : U_i \to V_{j_i}$ such that $\forall X \in U_i \bullet X \otimes f_{j_i}(X)$ is well-defined

$$P \otimes Q =_{df} \{\!|(0, p_i, \sigma_i) : \{X \otimes f_{j_i}(X) \mid X \in U_i\} \mid i \in I|\!\}$$

(3.d) if $Q = \{\!|(\surd, \emptyset, \sigma) : V|\!\}$, then $P \otimes Q =_{df} \mathit{undefined}$

Fourthly, we consider the case that P can perform time delay initially.

(4) If $P = \{\!|(\surd, \emptyset, \sigma) : U|\!\}$ and

(4.d) if $Q = \{\!|(\surd, \emptyset, \sigma) : V|\!\}$, then there exists a bijection $f : U \to V$ such that $\forall X \in U \bullet X \otimes f(X)$ is well-defined

$$P \otimes_r Q =_{df} \{\!|(\surd, \emptyset, \sigma) : \{X \otimes f(X) \mid X \in U\}|\!\}$$

For the definition of $st \otimes st'$ and $st \otimes T$ (st can be ter, $wait$ or div), they are similar to those in the definition of $\otimes_r$.

Based on the above defined merge operator $\otimes$, now we are ready to give the semantics for general parallel composition.

$$\begin{aligned}&[\![P \parallel Q]\!]\\ =_{df} &\{\ (tag, \mu, \sigma) : \{X \otimes Y \mid X \in U\ \wedge\ Y \in V\ \wedge\ X \otimes Y \text{is well-defined}\}\\ &\qquad \mid (tag, \mu, \sigma) \in \Sigma\ \wedge\ (tag, \mu, \sigma) : U \in [\![P]\!] \wedge (tag, \mu, \sigma) : V \in [\![Q]\!]\ \}\end{aligned}$$

5 Program Equivalence

In this section we are exploring some *flattening* relations between P-trees (or P^--trees). It will be used in giving the definitions for the concept of tree equivalence. Based on the concept of the equivalence of P-trees (or P^--trees), we can define the equivalence between *PTSC* programs.

Below we define a set of flattening relations R_i and R'_i ($i = 0, 1, 2, 3$). Based on these flattening relations, we define $R =_{df} Id \cup \bigcup_{i \in \{0,1,2,3\}} (R_i \cup R_i^{-1})$ and $R' =_{df} Id \cup \bigcup_{i \in \{0,1,2,3\}} (R'_i \cup R_i'^{-1})$.

For $\{\!|(tag, 1, \sigma) : U,\ (tag, 0, \sigma) : V\}|\!\}$, due to the 0 probability, the branch $(tag, 0, \sigma) : V$ can be eliminated. This means that the two P^--trees $\{\!|(tag, 1, \sigma) : U,\ (tag, 0, \sigma) : V\}|\!\}$ and $\{\!|(tag, 1, \sigma) : U|\!\}$ should be equivalent. Therefore, we give the definition of flattening relation R_0.

Definition 5.1 (*Flattening Relation* R_0)

(1) $\{\!|(tag, 1, \sigma) : U,\ (tag, 0, \sigma) : V\}|\!\}\ R_0\ \{\!|(tag, 1, \sigma) : W|\!\}$, where $U\,R\,W$[1].

(2) If $\forall X \in U \bullet \exists Y \in Y \bullet (X, Y) \in R_0$ and $\forall Y \in V \bullet \exists X \in U \bullet (X, Y) \in R_0$, then $(tag, \mu, \sigma) : U\ R'_0\ (tag, \mu, \sigma) : V$. □

[1] Let U and V be two sets of P^--trees and S be a relation between P^--trees. The notation $U\,S\,V$ means that $\forall X \in U \bullet \exists Y \in Y \bullet (X, Y) \in S$ and $\forall Y \in V \bullet \exists X \in U \bullet (X, Y) \in S$

For $\{\{\!|(1,1,\sigma):U|\!\}\}$ at the initial state (tag,μ,σ), the contributed snapshot $(1,1,\sigma)$ indicates that the process performs assignment-like action with probability 1 and the data state remains the unchanged. This means that the contributed new snapshot can be eliminated, indicating that $(tag,\mu,\sigma):\{\{\!|(1,1,\sigma):U|\!\}\}$ is the same as $(tag,\mu,\sigma):U$. We give the definition of flattening relation R_1 for aiming this.

Definition 5.2 (*Flattening Relation R_1*)

(1) $(tag,\mu,\sigma):\{\{\!|(1,1,\sigma):U|\!\}\}\ R_1'\ (tag,\mu,\sigma):V,$ where $U\,R\,V$.

(2) If $(tag_i,\mu_i,\sigma_i):U_i\ R_1'(tag_i,\mu_i,\sigma_i):V_i,\ \ i\in I$

then $\{\!|(tag_i,\mu_i,\sigma_i):U_i \mid i\in I\}|\!\}\ R_1\,\{\!|(tag_i,\mu_i,\sigma_i):V_i \mid i\in I\}|\!\}$ □

For P^--tree $\{\!|(1,r,\sigma):U,\ (1,1-r,\sigma):U|\!\}$ at the initial state (tag,μ,σ), we find that the two probabilistic branches of the P^--tree enter into the same process. The two data sates are the same as the σ, the sum of the two corresponding probabilities are 1, and the two subsequent behaviours are the same. Therefore, we can say the behaviour of the P^--tree $\{\!|(1,r,\sigma):U,\ (1,1-r,\sigma):U|\!\}$ at the initial state (tag,μ,σ) should be the same as the behaviour $(tag,\mu,\sigma):U$. Our definition for flattening relation R_2 is for achieving this kind of equivalence.

Definition 5.3 (*Flattening Relation R_2*)

(1) $(tag,\mu,\sigma):\{\ \{\!|(1,r,\sigma):U,\ (1,1-r,\sigma):U|\!\}\ \}\ R_2'\ (tag,\mu,\sigma):V,$
where $U\,R\,V$.

(2) $(tag,\mu,\sigma):\{\{\!|(1,r,\sigma):U,\ (1,1-r,\sigma):U|\!\}\mid r\in A\}\ R_2'\ (tag,\mu,\sigma):V,$
where $U\,R\,V$

(3) If $(tag_i,\mu_i,\sigma_i):U_i\ R_2'\ (tag_i,\mu_i,\sigma_i):V_i,\ \ i\in I$

then $\{\!|(tag_i,\mu_i,\sigma_i):U_i\}\mid i\in I|\!\}\ R_2\ \{\!|(tag_i,\mu_i,\sigma_i):V_i\mid i\in I\}|\!\}$ □

Definition 5.4 (*Flattening Relation R_3*)

(1) Define $P\ R_3'\ Q,$ where:

$P=(tag,\mu,\sigma):\{\{\!|(1,p,\sigma):U,(1,1-p,\sigma):\{\{\!|(1,q,\sigma):V,(1,1-q,\sigma):W|\!\}\}|\!\}\}$

$Q=(tag,\mu,\sigma):\{\{\!|(1,y,\sigma):\{\{\!|(1,x,\sigma):U',(1,1-x,\sigma):V'\}|\!\}\},(1,1-y,\sigma):W'\}|\!\}\}$

where, $U\,R\,U',\ \ V\,R\,V',\ \ W\,R\,W',$

and, $x=p/(p+q-p\times q),\ \ y=p+q-p\times q$

(2) If $(tag_i,\mu_i,\sigma_i):U_i\ R_3'\ (tag_i,\mu_i,\sigma_i):V_i,\ \ i\in I$

then $\{\!|(tag_i,\mu_i,\sigma_i):U_i\mid i\in I|\!\}\ R_3\ \{\!|(tag_i,\mu_i,\sigma_i):V_i\}\mid i\in I|\!\}$ □

In the above definition for flattening relation R_3, for P and Q, both of them have three execution branches (i.e., U, V and W). The three new data states for U, V and W (i.e., U', V' and W') are the same as the initial data state of P and Q. Further, the probabilities to reach to U (i.e., U') for P and Q are both p, whereas the probabilities to reach to V (i.e., V') for P and Q are both $(1-p)\times q$. And the probability to reach to W (i.e., W') for both P and Q are $(1-p)\times(1-q)$. This indicates that P and Q should have the same behaviour.

Based on the above definitions of flattening relations and R (and R'), we know that R (and R') is an equivalence relation. Let $\approx$ and $\approx'$ stand for the largest relations satisfying R and R' respectively.

Now we start to consider program equivalence. Its definition can be based on the equivalence $\approx$ and $\approx'$ (for P^{-}-trees and P-trees), shown below.

Definition 5.5 (Program Equivalence)

$$P \approx Q$$
$$=_{df} \forall (tag, \mu, \sigma) : U \in [\![P]\!], (tag, \mu, \sigma) : V \in [\![Q]\!] \bullet$$
$$(tag, \mu, \sigma) : U \approx' (tag, \mu, \sigma) : V \qquad \square$$

6 Algebraic Laws

In this section we explore the algebraic laws for *PTSC* programs based on the defined program equivalence. For assignment, conditional, iteration, nondeterministic choice and sequential composition, our language enjoys similar algebraic properties as those reported in [4, 7]. In what follows, we shall only focus on novel algebraic properties with respect to time, probabilistic nondeterministic choice and parallel composition.

6.1 Sequential Constructs

Two consecutive time delays can be combined into a single one, where the length of the delay is the sum of the original two lengths.

(delay-1) $\#n; \#m \ \approx \ \#(n+m)$

Probabilistic nondeterministic choice is idempotent.

(prob-1) $P \sqcap_p P \approx P$

However, it is not purely symmetric and associative. Its symmetry and associativity rely on the change of the associated probabilities:

(prob-2) $P \sqcap_{p_1} Q \approx Q \sqcap_{1-p_1} P$

(prob-3) $P \sqcap_p (Q \sqcap_q R) \ \approx \ (P \sqcap_x Q) \sqcap_y R$

where $x = p/(p+q-p \times q)$ and $y = p+q-p \times q$

6.2 Parallel Construct

Probabilistic parallel composition is also not purely symmetric and associative. Its symmetry and associativity rely on the change of the associated probabilities as well.

(par-1) $P \parallel_p Q \ \approx \ Q \parallel_{1-p} P$

(par-2) $P \parallel_p (Q \parallel_q R) \ \approx \ (P \parallel_x Q) \parallel_y R.$

where, $x = p/(p+q-p \times q)$ and $y = p+q-p \times q$

For general parallel composition, it is purely symmetric and associative.

(par-1') $P \parallel Q \approx Q \parallel P$

(par-2') $P \parallel (Q \parallel R) \approx (P \parallel Q) \parallel R$

In what follows we give a collection of parallel expansion laws, which enable us to expand a probabilistic parallel composition to a guarded choice construct. As mentioned earlier, there exist five types of guarded choice. To take into account a probabilistic parallel composition of two arbitrary guarded choices, we end up with fifteen different expansion laws. Similarly, for general parallel composition, we also have fifteen different expansion laws. We select some parallel expansion cases for both probabilistic and general parallel compositions.

Firstly, we consider the case that both of the two parallel components are with the form of assignment-guarded choice. The expansion law is shown is (par-3-1).

(par-3-1) Let

$$P = \|_{i\in I}\{[p_i]\ choice_{j\in J_i}(b_{ij}\&(x_{ij} := e_{ij})\ P_{ij})\} \text{ and}$$
$$Q = \|_{k\in K}\{[q_k]\ choice_{l\in L_k}(b_{kl}\&(x_{kl} := e_{kl})\ P_{kl})\}$$

Then

$$\begin{aligned} & P \parallel_r Q \\ \approx\ & \|_{i\in I}\{[r \times p_i]\ choice_{j\in J_i}(b_{ij}\&(x_{ij} := e_{ij})\ P_{ij} \parallel_r Q\} \\ & \|\|_{k\in K}\{[(1-r) \times q_k]\ choice_{l\in L_k}(b_{kl}\&(x_{kl} := e_{kl})\ P \parallel_r Q_{kl}\} \end{aligned}$$

and

$$\begin{aligned} & P \parallel Q \\ \approx\ & \|_{i\in I}\{[p_i]\ choice_{j\in J_i}(b_{ij}\&(x_{ij} := e_{ij})\ P_{ij} \parallel Q\} \\ \textbf{or}\ & \|_{k\in K}\{[q_k]\ choice_{l\in L_k}(b_{kl}\&(x_{kl} := e_{kl})\ P \parallel Q_{kl}\} \end{aligned}$$

Next we consider the case that one parallel component is with the form of assignment guarded choice and another component is with the form of event guarded choice. Law (par-3-2) below shows the expansion law for probabilistic and general parallel composition. The probability factor for the initial step expansion does not affect for the two parallel compositions.

(par-3-2) Let

$$P = \|_{i\in I}\{[p_i]\ choice_{j\in J_i}(b_{ij}\&(x_{ij} := e_{ij})\ P_{ij})\} \text{ and } Q = \|_{k\in K}\{@c_k\ Q_k\}$$

Then

$$\begin{aligned} & P \odot Q \\ \approx\ & \|_{i\in I}\{[p_i]\ choice_{j\in J_i}(b_{ij}\&(x_{ij} := e_{ij})\ P_{ij} \odot Q\} \\ & \|\|_{k\in K}\{@c_k\ P \odot Q_k\} \end{aligned}$$

where, $\odot \in \{\ \parallel_r,\ \parallel\ \}$.

Now we consider the case that one parallel component is with the form of assignment guarded choice and another component is with the form of time delay component. Only assignment guards can be scheduled initially. This case is expressed in law (par-3-3).

(par-3-3) Let

$$P = \|_{i\in I}\{[p_i]\ choice_{j\in J_i}(b_{ij}\&(x_{ij} := e_{ij})\ P_{ij})\} \text{ and } Q = \|\{\#1\ R\}$$

Then

$$P \odot Q$$
$$\approx \, \|_{i \in I}\{[p_i]\ choice_{j \in J_i}(b_{ij}\&(x_{ij} := e_{ij})\ P_{ij} \odot Q\}$$

where, $\odot \in \{\ \|_r,\ \|\ \}$.

If one parallel component is with the form of assignment guarded choice and another parallel component is with the form of the guarded choice composing of assignment guarded components and event guarded components. Law (par-3-4) shows the expansion for the probabilistic parallel composition and general parallel composition for this case.

(par-3-4) Let

$$P = \|_{i \in I}\{[p_i]\ choice_{j \in J_i}(b_{ij}\&(x_{ij} := e_{ij})\ P_{ij})\} \text{ and}$$
$$Q = \|_{k \in K}\{[q_k]\ choice_{l \in L_k}(b_{kl}\&(x_{kl} := e_{kl})\ Q_{kl})\}$$
$$\|\|_{m \in M}\{@c_m\ R_m\}$$

Then

$$P \|_r Q$$
$$\approx \, \|_{i \in I}\{[r \times p_i]\ choice_{j \in J_i}(b_{ij}\&(x_{ij} := e_{ij})\ P_{ij} \|_r Q)\}$$
$$\|\|_{k \in K}\{[(1-r) \times q_k]\ choice_{l \in L_k}(b_{kl}\&(x_{kl} := e_{kl})\ P \|_r Q_{kl}\}$$
$$\|\|_{m \in M}\{@c_k\ P \|_r R_m\}$$

$$P \| Q$$
$$\approx \, \|_{i \in I}\{[p_i]\ choice_{j \in J_i}(b_{ij}\&(x_{ij} := e_{ij})\ P_{ij} \| Q)\}$$
$$\|\|_{m \in M}\{@c_k\ P \| R_m\}$$

or

$$\|_{k \in K}\{[q_k]\ choice_{l \in L_k}(b_{kl}\&(x_{kl} := e_{kl})\ P \| Q_{kl}\}$$
$$\|\|_{m \in M}\{@c_k\ P \| R_m\}$$

Now we consider the case that both of the two parallel components are of the form of event guarded choice. For probabilistic parallel composition and general parallel composition, there are three event triggered cases. Also the probability factor does not have effects in the initial step expansion. This is illustrated in law (par-3-6).

(par-3-6) Let $P = \|_{i \in I}\{@b_i\ P_i\}$ and $Q = \|_{j \in J}\{@c_j\ Q_j\}$

Then

$$P \odot Q$$
$$\approx \, \|_{i \in I}\{@(b_i \wedge \neg c)\ P_i \odot Q\}\|\|_{j \in J}\{@(c_j \wedge \neg b)\ P \odot Q_j\}$$
$$\|\|_{i \in I \wedge j \in J}\{@(b_i \wedge c_j)\ P_i \odot Q_j\}$$

where, $\odot \in \{\ \|_r,\ \|\ \}$

$$b = \vee_{i \in I}\, b_i, \text{ and } c = \vee_{j \in J}\, c_j$$

We now move to the case that both of the two parallel components are of the form comprising assignment-guarded components and event-guarded components. Law (par-3-13) stands for the expansion for probabilistic parallel composition and general parallel composition.

(par-3-13) Let

$$P = \|_{i\in I}\{[p_i]\ choice_{j\in J_i}(b_{ij}\&(x_{ij} := e_{ij})\ P_{ij})\}[\!]\|_{k\in K}\{@b_k\ R_k\}$$

and $$Q = \|_{l\in L}\{[q_l]\ choice_{m\in M_l}(c_{lm}\&(x_{lm} := e_{lm})\ P_{lm})\}[\!]\|_{n\in N}\{@c_n\ T_n\}$$

Then

$$\begin{aligned}
&P \parallel_r Q\\
\approx\ &\|_{i\in I}\{[r\times p_i]\ choice_{j\in J_i}(b_{ij}\&(x_{ij} := e_{ij})\ P_{ij} \parallel_r Q)\}\\
&[\!]\|_{l\in L}\{[(1-r)\times q_l]\ choice_{m\in M_l}(c_{lm}\&(x_{lm} := e_{lm})\ P, \parallel_r Q_{lm})\}\\
&[\!]\|_{k\in K}\{@(b_k \wedge \neg c)\ R_k \parallel_r Q\}[\!]\|_{n\in N}\{@(c_n \wedge \neg b)\ R_k \parallel_r Q\}\\
&[\!]\|_{k\in K\wedge n\in N}\{@(b_k \wedge c_n)\ R_k \parallel_r Q_n\}
\end{aligned}$$

$$\begin{aligned}
&P \parallel Q\\
\approx\ &\|_{i\in I}\{[p_i]\ choice_{j\in J_i}(b_{ij}\&(x_{ij} := e_{ij})\ P_{ij} \parallel Q)\}\\
&[\!]\|_{k\in K}\{@(b_k \wedge \neg c)\ R_k \parallel Q\}[\!]\|_{n\in N}\{@(c_n \wedge \neg b)\ R_k \parallel Q\}\\
&[\!]\|_{k\in K\wedge n\in N}\{@(b_k \wedge c_n)\ R_k \parallel Q_n\}
\end{aligned}$$

or

$$\begin{aligned}
&\|_{l\in L}\{[q_l]\ choice_{m\in M_l}(c_{lm}\&(x_{lm} := e_{lm})\ P, \parallel Q_{lm})\}\\
&[\!]\|_{k\in K}\{@(b_k \wedge \neg c)\ R_k \parallel Q\}[\!]\|_{n\in N}\{@(c_n \wedge \neg b)\ R_k \parallel Q\}\\
&[\!]\|_{k\in K\wedge n\in N}\{@(b_k \wedge c_n)\ R_k \parallel Q_n\}
\end{aligned}$$

where, $b = \vee_{k\in K}\, b_k$ and $c = \vee_{n\in N}\, c_n$

7 Conclusion

Recently we have proposed the language *PTSC* [19], which integrates probability, time and shared-variable concurrency. In this paper, we studied the denotational semantics for *PTSC*. For dealing with the above three features, as well as the nondeterminism, we introduced the concept of P-tree in our denotational semantics. Based on the P-tree, we defined the denotational semantics for each *PTSC* statement. In order to deal with program equivalence based on the achieved denotational semantics, we defined a set of flattening relations. We have explored a set of algebraic laws for *PTSC*, especially a set of parallel expansion laws. The correctness of these laws is based on the concept of program equivalence.

For the future, we would like to link the denotational semantics with operational semantics and algebraic semantics respectively. Moreover, the deduction approach for *PTSC* is also challenging to work on.

Acknowledgement. This work is supported by National Basic Research Program of China (No. 2011CB302904), National High Technology Research and Development Program of China (No. 2011AA010101 and No. 2012AA011205), National Natural Science Foundation of China (No. 61061130541 and No. 61021004), and Shanghai Leading Academic Discipline Project (No. B412).

References

1. den Hartog, J.: Probabilistic Extensions of Semantic Models. PhD thesis, Vrije University, The Netherlands (2002)
2. den Hartog, J., de Vink, E.: Mixing up nondeteminism and probability: A premliminary report. Electronic Notes in Theoretical Computer Science 22 (1999)
3. den Hartog, J., de Vink, E., de Bakker, J.: Metric semantics and full abstractness for action refinement and probabilistic choice. Electronic Notes in Theoretical Computer Science 40 (2001)
4. He, J.: Provably Correct Systems: Modelling of Communication Languages and Design of Optimized Compilers. The McGraw-Hill International Series in Software Engineering (1994)
5. He, J., Seidel, K., McIver, A.: Probabilistic models for the guarded command language. Science of Computer Programming 28(2-3), 171–192 (1997)
6. He, J., Zhu, H.: Formalising Verilog. In: Proc. ICECS 2000: IEEE International Conference on Electronics, Circuits and Systems, pp. 412–415. IEEE Computer Society Press (December 2000)
7. Hoare, C.A.R., He, J.: Unifying Theories of Programming. Prentice Hall International Series in Computer Science (1998)
8. McIver, A., Morgan, C.: Partial correctness for probabilistic demonic programs. Theoretical Computer Science 266(1-2), 513–541 (2001)
9. McIver, A., Morgan, C.: Abstraction, Refinement and Proof of Probability Systems. Monographs in Computer Science. Springer (October 2004)
10. McIver, A., Morgan, C., Seidel, K.: Probabilistic predicate transformers. ACM Transactions on Programming Languages and Systems 18(3), 325–353 (1996)
11. Ndukwu, U., Sanders, J.W.: Reason about a distributed probabilistic system. Technical Report 401, UNU/IIST, P.O. Box 3058, Macau SAR, China (August. 2008)
12. Nissanke, N.: Realtime Systems. Prentice Hall International Series in Computer Science (1997)
13. Núñez, M.: Algebraic theory of probabilistic processes. The Journal of Logic and Algebraic Programming 56, 117–177 (2003)
14. Núñez, M., de Frutos-Escrig, D.: Testing semantics for probabilistic LOTOS. In: Proc FORTE 1995: IFIP TC6 Eighth International Conference on Formal Description Techniques, Montreal, Canada. IFIP Conference Proceedings, vol. 43, pp. 367–382. Chapman and Hall (1996)
15. Núñez, M., de Frutos-Escrig, D., Díaz, L.F.L.: Acceptance Trees for Probabilistic Processes. In: Lee, I., Smolka, S.A. (eds.) CONCUR 1995. LNCS, vol. 962, pp. 249–263. Springer, Heidelberg (1995)
16. Park, S., Pfenning, F., Thrun, S.: A probabilistic language based upon sampling functions. In: Proc. POPL 2005: 32nd ACM SIGPLAN-SIGACT Symposium on Principles of Programming Languages, pp. 171–182. ACM (January 2005)
17. Zhu, H.: Linking the Semantics of a Multithreaded Discrete Event Simulation Language. PhD thesis, London South Bank University (February 2005)
18. Zhu, H., He, J., Bowen, J.P.: From algebraic semantics to denotational semantics for verilog. Innovations in Systems and Software Engineering: A NASA Journal 4(4), 341–360 (2008)
19. Zhu, H., Qin, S., He, J., Bowen, J.P.: PTSC: probability, time and shared-variable concurrency. Innovations in Systems and Software Engineering: A NASA Journal 5(4), 271–284 (2009)
20. Zhu, H., Yang, F., He, J., Bowen, J.P., Sanders, J.W., Qin, S.: Linking operational semantics and algebraic semantics for a probabilistic timed shared-variable language. J. Log. Algebr. Program. 81(1), 2–25 (2012)

References

1. [illegible] (1971)
2. [illegible] probability: A [illegible] Computer Science 2 (2009)
3. [illegible] Science [illegible]
4. [illegible] Modelling [illegible] Communication [illegible] and [illegible]
5. [illegible] (2006) [illegible]
6. [illegible] 2005 [illegible] ICTP Computer [illegible]
7. [illegible] Prentice Hall [illegible]
8. [illegible] The method [illegible]
9. [illegible] Probability [illegible]
10. [illegible] 25 [illegible] (1996)
11. [illegible] Technical [illegible]
12. [illegible]
13. [illegible]
14. [illegible]
15. [illegible]
16. [illegible]
17. [illegible]
18. [illegible]
19. [illegible]
20. [illegible]

Author Index